Hussein of Jordan

By the same author

Charge to Glory
Scarlet Lancer
The Barren Rocks of Aden
From Sepoy to Subedar (ed.)
Bokhara Burnes
John Burgoyne of Saratoga
The Duke of Wellington's Regiment
The 16th/5th The Queen's Royal Lancers
Imperial Sunset
Glubb Pasha
'A Hell of a Licking': The Retreat from Burma 1941–2

Hussein of Jordan

Searching for a Just and Lasting Peace

James Lunt

William Morrow and Company, Inc.
New York

This book is dedicated by gracious permission to
His Majesty King Hussein bin Talal
of the Hashemite Kingdom of Jordan

CONTENTS

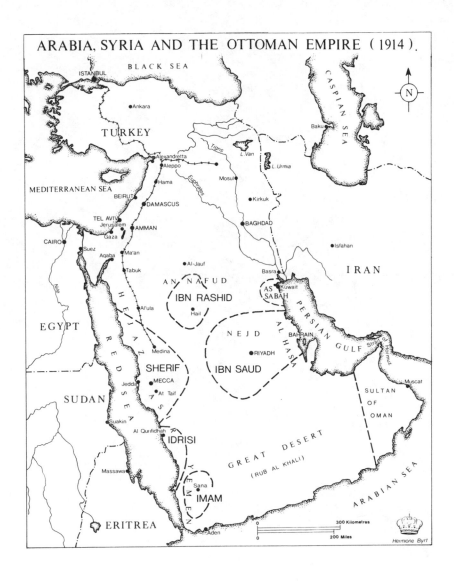

ARABIA, SYRIA AND THE OTTOMAN EMPIRE (1914).

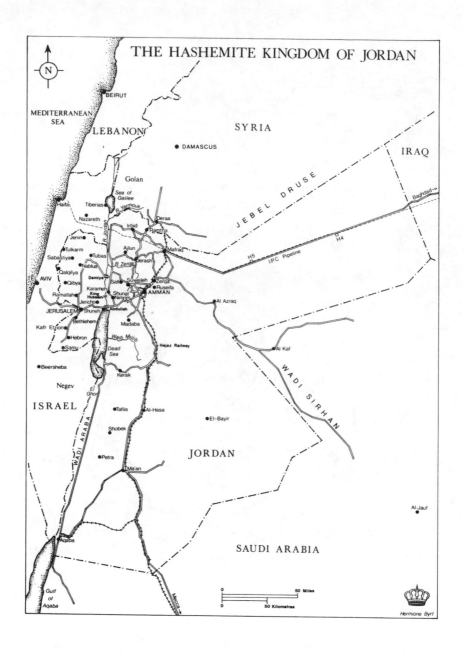

THE HASHEMITE KINGDOM OF JORDAN

N

MEDITERRANEAN
SEA

BEIRUT

LEBANON

SYRIA

IRAQ

DAMASCUS

Baghdad→

Golan

JEBEL DRUSE

Sea of
Galilee

Haifa   Tiberias

Nazareth

R. Yarmouk

Deraa

Irbid

Hamtha

H4

Jenin

Ailun

Mafraq

H5

IPC Pipeline

Tulkarm   Tubas

Sabastiya

Jerash

R. Zerqa

Qalqilya   Nablus   Damiya

Zerqa

TEL AVIV   Qibya   Salt   Suweileh

Ruseifa

Karameh   Shunat   AMMAN

Al Azraq

Ramallah   King   Nimrin

Hussein

Jericho

JERUSALEM   Shuneh   Abdullah

Bethlehem   Madaba

Kafr Etzion

WADI SIRHAN

Hebron   Wadi Mujib

Samu   Dead   Hejaz Railway

Sea   Al Kaf

Beersheba

Negev   Kerak

El
Ghor

ISRAEL   Tafila   Al-Hasa

El-Bayir

Shobek

Petra   JORDAN

Ma'an

Al-Jauf

Aqaba

SAUDI ARABIA

Gulf
of
Aqaba   0   50 Miles

0   50 Kilometres

WADI ARABA

Hermione Byrt

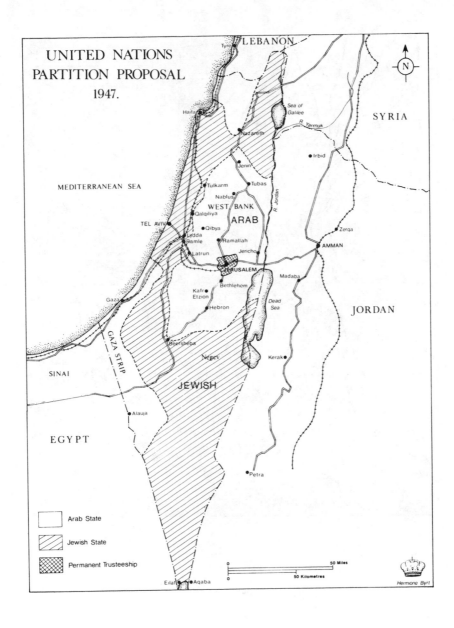

UNITED NATIONS
PARTITION PROPOSAL
1947.

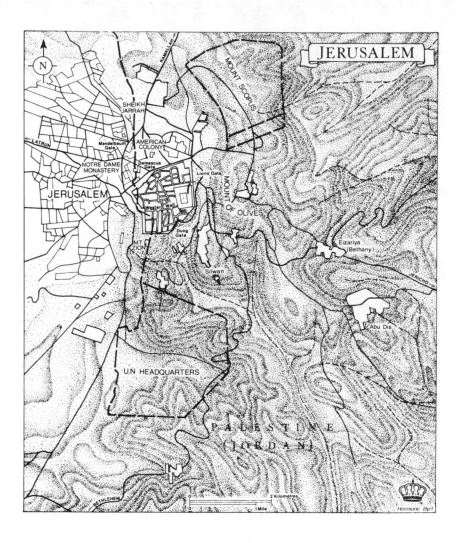

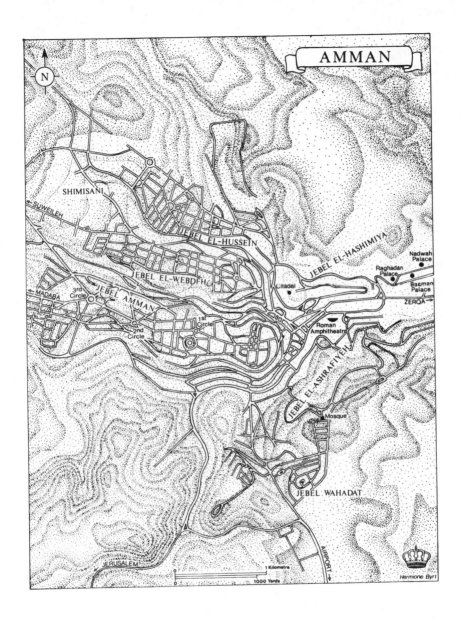

THE HASHEMITE FAMILY TREE
(in the male line)

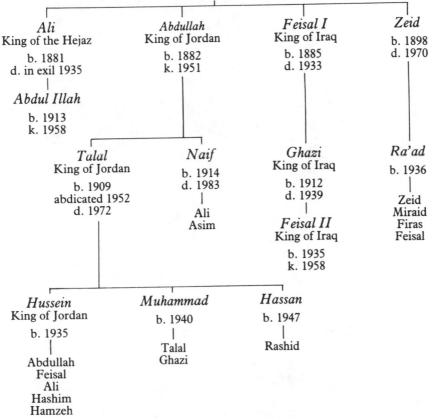

King Hussein bin Ali
of the Hejaz

b. 1853
d. in exile 1931

Ali	*Abdullah*	*Feisal I*	*Zeid*
King of the Hejaz	King of Jordan	King of Iraq	b. 1898
b. 1881	b. 1882	b. 1885	d. 1970
d. in exil 1935	k. 1951	d. 1933	

Abdul Illah

b. 1913
k. 1958

Talal	*Naif*	*Ghazi*	*Ra'ad*
King of Jordan	b. 1914	King of Iraq	b. 1936
b. 1909	d. 1983	b. 1912	
abdicated 1952		d. 1939	Zeid
d. 1972	Ali		Miraid
	Asim	*Feisal II*	Firas
		King of Iraq	Feisal
		b. 1935	
		k. 1958	

Hussein	*Muhammad*	*Hassan*
King of Jordan	b. 1940	b. 1947
b. 1935		
	Talal	Rashid
Abdullah	Ghazi	
Feisal		
Ali		
Hashim		
Hamzeh		

(a) King Hussein has married four times – to Princess Dina Abdel Hamid in 1955 whom he divorced in 1957, and by whom he had a daughter Alia; to Princess Muna (Toni Gardiner) in 1961 by whom he had two sons (Abdullah and Feisal) and two daughters (twins) (Zein and Aisha), and whom he divorced in 1972; to Alia Toukan in 1972 by whom he had a son (Ali) and a daughter (Haya), and who also adopted a daughter (Abir Muheisen). Queen Alia was killed in a helicopter accident on 9 February 1977. In 1978 he married Queen Noor (Lisa Hallaby) by whom he has had two sons (Hashim and Hamzeh) and two daughters (Iman and Raiyah).

(b) Prince Muhammad married Firial Irsheid by whom he had two sons (Talal and Ghazi) and whom he has since divorced. He later married Taghreed al-Majali, daughter of Hazza Majali, who was assassinated in 1960 when Prime Minister.

(c) Crown Prince Hassan is married to Princess Sarvath, daughter of the late Sir Muhammad Ikramullah Khan of Pakistan, by whom he has one son (Rashid) and three daughters (Rahmah, Sumyeih and Badeih).

AUTHOR'S FOREWORD

In this biography of one of the foremost Arab leaders of our times, and also a world statesman, I have done my best to remain objective, although I do not doubt that my admiration for the King will be evident. I make no apologies for this.

There are two kinds of biography, we have been told: 'The kind in which, like a novelist, the biographer persuades himself that he possesses the key to all that is essential about his central character and lays out his narrative accordingly; and the kind in which, in effect, he says to the reader: "Here is all that is known and that has been said about my subject. You must decide for yourself what kind of man he is." ' I have chosen the second course.

There can, however, be no understanding of King Hussein, nor of the decisions he has had to take at various critical times during his reign, without some knowledge of the principles by which he has been guided since first he ascended the throne thirty-five years ago. I have therefore thought it necessary to set down these principles at the beginning of this book, in the hope that it will explain to the reader those of the King's decisions that might otherwise seem to have been rash, or over-cautious, or even quixotic.

Firstly, there is his dedication to his Hashemite heritage. He was brought up to believe by his grandfather, King Abdullah, in the manifest destiny of the Hashemite family, as the standard bearers in the Great Arab Revolt which liberated the Arabs from the rule of the Ottoman Turks at the end of the First World War. Moreover, King Hussein's unbroken descent from the Prophet Muhammad, which makes him head of the noblest family in Islam, confers on him obligations which he has at all times endeavoured to honour, regardless of the dangers and the difficulties.

Secondly, there is his commitment to Arabism, or Arab unity. This was the inspiration that led his great-grandfather, Sharif Hussein bin Ali of Mecca, to take up arms against the Ottomans in the cause of Arab freedom. Although Arabs hold a variety of views on the form such unity should take, they believe strongly in the ideal. The King himself conceives of a broader nationalism, within which each Arab state will preserve its own integrity, until in the course of time it becomes possible for them to forge a more comprehensive union.

Thirdly, there is his commitment to Arab solidarity. The King believes that occasions will arise when the views of individual states must be set aside in the interests of the general whole. It was with this in mind that he agreed to break off relations with the Federal German Republic in 1965 at the request of President Nasser, although at the time the King was opposed to such a step.

Fourthly, there is his commitment to the cause of Palestine and the Palestinian people. In the King's view, his great-grandfather, Sharif Hussein, chose rather to abdicate than to agree to the 'alienation of Palestine from the rest of the Arab homeland'. King Hussein has never ceased to support the Palestinian people in their struggle to be free.

Fifthly, there is his commitment to oppose Communism in the Arab world. He believes the atheistic basis of Communism makes it incompatible with Islam. This has in turn resulted in his commitment to the West.

Finally, there is his commitment to the continued existence of Jordan under the Hashemite family. Jordan is particularly vulnerable to outside pressures. Its continued existence depends partly on its internal stability and partly on its relations with its Arab neighbours and with other countries as well. It is this commitment to survival that will always influence King Hussein's diplomacy, to the extent that it may sometimes seem to conflict with the principle of Arab solidarity. But, unless the state survives, everything else falls to the ground.

These, then, are the principles which have guided and which continue to guide the King in his difficult task. It will be for the reader to decide how successful he has been in abiding by them in the many difficult decisions he has had to take in the course of his reign so far.

It needs to be explained, I feel, that this is not an 'official' biography; I have not been commissioned either by the King or by the government of Jordan to write it. It has, however, been written with the King's agreement, and with the co-operation of many Jordanians, for which I am very grateful. The opinions and views expressed are, however, mine alone. They do not commit either the King or his advisers in any way whatsoever.

James Lunt
1 November 1988

INTRODUCTION

The House of Hashim

'Ismuhu Sharif, Shaksuhu Sharif, Nafsuhu Sharif' ('His name is noble, his character is noble, and he himself is noble').[1]

Hussein, third of the Hashemite House to rule over Jordan, was born in his father's house close to the Raghadan Palace in Amman, on 14 November 1935. It was an auspicious event for his father and mother, the Emir Talal and the Emira Zein, who had been married the previous November. Talal was the eldest son and heir to the Emir Abdullah, ruler of Transjordan, who drove proudly through the cheering crowds in Amman on his way to the Mosque to give thanks to God for the gift of a grandson. The Hashemite House was safe in Jordan; the succession had been made secure.

The Hashemite family is the noblest in Islam, owing to its direct descent from the Prophet Muhammad. They are of the Prophet's tribe, Al Quraish, and of His clan, Al Hashim. They are descended from the Prophet's daughter, Fatima, and her husband Ali, the line unbroken for nearly fourteen centuries. They belong to the Dawi 'Awn section of the Hashemite clan, and it was from the Dawi 'Awn and Dawi Zeid sections that the Prince of Mecca and Guardian of the Holy Places was chosen.

They are styled *Sharif*, the word meaning noble and signifying descent from the Prophet. The Arabic plural is *Ashraf*, and there are many who claim descent from the Prophet and who are styled *Sharif*; but only Hashemites of the Dawi 'Awn and Dawi Zeid sections could expect to be named Prince of Mecca. In 1908, when this story begins, the Sultan–Caliph in Istanbul named Sharif Hussein bin Ali of the Dawi 'Awn, then living in exile in the Ottoman capital, as Grand Sharif and Prince of Mecca. It was to be eight years later on 10 June, the 9th Sha'ban in the Muslim calendar, when Sharif Hussein fired the first shot to herald the Great Arab Revolt against the Ottoman Turks, under whose heel the Arabs had suffered for 400 years. Two years later, on 1 October 1918, the Arab army under Emir Feisal, third son of Sharif Hussein, entered Damascus, and Ottoman rule was ended.

The British had promised Sharif Hussein, in return for his rebellion, financial aid, advice and arms, the reward to be the eventual liberation of the Arab provinces from Ottoman rule, and their self-rule thereafter. One Arab army, composed partly of Arab regulars who had deserted from the Ottoman army and partly of bedouin tribesmen, was to fight on the desert flank of the British army, which was advancing from Egypt into Palestine; this Arab army was led by the Emir Feisal, among whose British advisers was Colonel T.E. Lawrence. Another Arab army, under the Emirs Ali and Abdullah, Sharif Hussein's eldest and second sons, captured Taif from the Turks and besieged them in Medina.

The British government, unfortunately, reneged on the promises made to Sharif Hussein. By a secret agreement with France, negotiated in 1916 by Sir Mark Sykes and M.F. Georges-Picot, the two principal Western allies were to divide Turkey's former Arab provinces between them until such time as their new masters judged they were fit to rule themselves. Sharif Hussein, who was understandably outraged by what he considered to be a betrayal, was to be left to rule the Hejaz, of which he was proclaimed King in 1917. The Sykes–Picot Agreement, as it came to be called, divided the former Ottoman province of Syria into three parts, the French receiving Syria and Lebanon, the British Palestine. The British also received Iraq, formerly known as Mesopotamia. This was ratified at a meeting held at San Remo in April 1920. The Arab states were to be mandates of the newly established League of Nations, an almost meaningless designation to the majority of the Arab inhabitants.

There was a further, and even more far-reaching, complication. In November 1917, A.J. Balfour, the then Foreign Secretary, speaking on behalf of the British government, announced support for 'the establishment in Palestine of a national home for the Jewish people'. The Arabs felt doubly betrayed since this could be done only at the expense of the Palestinian Arabs, who had been established in Palestine for more than fourteen centuries. Sharif Hussein made it plain that he could never agree to this, but his protests were studiously ignored. What is more, the Emir Feisal, who had already been elected King of Syria by the Syrian Assembly, was evicted by the French, who had come to claim the spoils of victory, and was forced into exile. In Iraq, where Feisal's elder brother Abdullah had been offered the crown, the wishes of the Iraqi representatives were similarly ignored by the British. The Arabs had been betrayed by those on whose good word they had relied. It has to be said that by no means every member of the British government and administration agreed with this policy. Neither the Foreign Secretary, Lord Curzon, nor the Chief of the Imperial General Staff, Field Marshal Sir Henry Wilson, were in favour of extending British commitments in Palestine. They were, however, ignored by the Prime Minister, David Lloyd George.

The British were not really interested in Syria, their interests lying elsewhere. But they did not want the French to extend their influence sufficiently far south to encroach on British interests in Palestine. For this reason they had excluded from the Sykes–Picot Agreement the desert and mountainous region east of the River Jordan from the rest of the province of Syria. This they named Transjordan. Closely involved with Palestine, from which it was virtually indistinguishable in both ethnic and economic terms, this part of the province of Syria had been reduced almost to anarchy as a result of the war. Seven-eighths desert, where the bedouin tribes roamed at will, the collapse of the Ottoman administration had left the settled inhabitants without administration of any kind. It had become a kind of no-man's land of warring tribes.

These tribes were divided between those who were nomads, wandering the deserts with their herds of camels and their flocks of sheep and goats, and those who were settled, dwelling in houses and cultivating the land. The former were bedouin; the latter *fellahin*, or peasants – or, in Jordan, *hadhari*. The bedouin called themselves *Ahl al-Arab* (the Arab people) and prided themselves on their hardihood and freedom. Their environment was violent, their lives were violent, and when they burst out of Central Arabia in AD 633 they became the harbingers of Islam. They are more usually referred to in Arabic as *al-bedu*, of which the singular is *bedui*. They have for some curious reason become greatly romanticised in the West, partly on account of two writers, T.E. Lawrence and Charles Doughty, who alternately glorified and denigrated them in their literary masterpieces, *Seven Pillars of Wisdom* and *Arabia Deserta*. Since the bedouin have played a very important part in the Hashemite Kingdom of Jordan, it will be necessary to consider them here in a little more detail.

Perhaps the most succinct definition of the bedouin has been provided by Lieutenant-General Sir John Glubb (Glubb Pasha),* who developed a remarkable empathy with them. 'We find', he has written, 'that a bedouin, in the strictest sense, is a camel-breeding nomad of certain specified tribes.'[2] These tribes, divided under their own shayks, to whom alone the bedouin would offer any kind of submission, and then only if they had earned their tribesmen's respect, were dependent almost entirely on the camel. A

---

* Pasha, pronounced Basha in Arabic, was an Ottoman title conferred on generals, governor-generals of provinces, and very senior government officials. It was abolished by Kemal Atatürk when he came to power in Turkey but has lingered on unofficially in some Arab countries, including Jordan. In Arabic it is always used in connection with an individual's first name, viz: Habis Pasha, rather than Habis Majali Pasha. A lesser title, that of Bey, pronounced Beg, is often used for ministers and for senior officers below the rank of general.

bedouin's wealth was judged by his herds, and much of his time was spent raiding other tribes for camels – *ghazzu* as they called it. The lives of women and children were sacrosanct in this kind of warfare, round which there developed a warrior tradition celebrated in the recital of heroic ballads and poetry round the coffee hearth. They scorned to sully their hands with a spade, despising the *fellahin* who did so, and stuffed their nostrils with rags to keep out the noxious fumes of civilisation whenever they entered the towns and villages that fringed the deserts. Their society was probably the most egalitarian on earth, but they were for the most part wild, undisciplined and virtually untameable, the true Ishmaelites. The settled Arabs regarded them with a mixture of fear and contempt, in much the same way as the original American colonists regarded the Red Indians.

Although each bedouin tribe had its own well-established grazing area, the constant need for pasture kept it regularly on the move. Great migrations were carried out annually. This had been going on for thousands of years, irrespective of the rise and fall of empires. International boundaries meant nothing to them. There was very little national consciousness until very recently. Their first loyalty was to the family, then to the clan and then to the tribe. Since they were deeply religious, however, bedouins treated the Hashemite family with great respect, both as descendants of the Prophet Muhammad and as Guardians of the Holy Places. In their turn, the Hashemites went out of their way to cultivate the bedouins, often sending their male children to spend a year or two with them to learn the lore of the desert. In Transjordan, which was largely desert, the two principal tribes were the Beni Sakhr and the Howeitat; and there were several other smaller ones. They were frequently at feud with each other, or engaged in raiding the villages along the desert periphery. Their principal means of livelihood had been the hiring out of camels for the annual pilgrimage from Damascus to Mecca and Medina, the *Hajj*, but the opening of the Hejaz railway from Damascus to Medina in 1908 shattered their precarious economy. Nor were matters improved by the lavish distribution of modern weapons and gold by the British during the war against the Turks. This provided an entirely new dimension to the ancient pastime of camel-rustling which, when conducted with spears and rusty old muzzle-loaders, caused far fewer casualties than when carried out with the modern rifle.

The bedouin were almost completely illiterate, quarrelsome, quick to take offence and intensely proud. 'The enemy of my enemy is my friend' can be taken as their motto, and they had many enemies. The blood feud was part of their lives. But their romantic nature, their attachment to traditional values, their hospitality, their hardihood and their endurance formed the other side of the medal. The explorer Wilfred Thesiger tells the story of Bin Kabina, one of the two bedouins who accompanied him on his crossing of the Empty Quarter in 1946–7.[3] Finding him asleep on the bitterly cold sand, wrapped only in his cotton loincloth, Thesiger asked him why he had not bought a blanket with the money he had given him. 'I don't care about the cold,' replied Bin Kabina. 'I am a bedui!' He wanted the money to buy camels, the basis of bedouin wealth, which the tribesmen sometimes treat better than their wives.

The deserts of Arabia were in a turmoil after the end of the First World War. This was due partly to the break-up of the Ottoman empire and to the provision of modern weapons, as previously described, and partly to the emergence in Nejd, in Central Arabia, of a fanatical and puritanical Muslim sect, the Wahhabis, who called themselves Al-Ikhwan (the Brotherhood). They had been skilfully utilised by the Emir of Nejd, Abdul Aziz bin Saud, a remarkable man, to help him achieve his ambition to become 'King of the Bedouins' and master of Central Arabia. The Wahhabis, who observed the strictest tenets of Islam, conceived it to be their mission to punish those of their co-religionists who did not observe their own strict rules. This they did in the most ruthless fashion, covering vast distances to swoop upon unsuspecting bedouin encampments, where they slaughtered all males regardless of age. Conventions which had for centuries governed bedouin warfare were swept aside, the very word Ikhwan inspiring terror wherever the bedouin pastured their herds.

The settled districts were equally disturbed after the ravages of war. There had been a rebellion in Iraq against the British in the summer of 1920, requiring 30,000 troops before it was quelled. In Syria the French, after forcibly occupying Damascus, drove Emir Feisal into exile, outraging the entire Arab world. In Palestine Sir Herbert (later Lord) Samuel, as the first High Commissioner, was setting up a mandatory administration intended to include both Palestine and Transjordan. Everywhere the Arab population, deeply affronted by the failure of the British and French to keep their promises, and gravely concerned about the consequences of the Balfour Declaration, were uneasy and discontented.

To add to the confusion that November 1920, there came the news of the arrival in Ma'an, then in the Hejaz but now in Jordan, of the Emir Abdullah, second son and right-hand man of his father, Sharif Hussein. He had left Mecca ostensibly to carry out a tour of inspection of the northern Hejaz, taking with him a small force of regular troops (al-Jaysh al-Arabi), and considerably more tribal levies. His principal companion was Sharif Shakir bin Zeid, who had come to the fore during the Great Arab Revolt; he was the father of Field Marshal Sharif Zeid bin Shakir, the present Commander-in-Chief of the Jordanian armed forces. Abdullah was given a warm welcome in Ma'an, receiving an invitation to continue his journey to Amman by the Hejaz railway, which happened to be operable between the two towns. En route, Abdullah stopped at Kerak to meet the notables, among whom was a young Lieutenant Alec Kirkbride, who had served under T.E. Lawrence during the war, and who was serving as the adviser to the short-lived National Government of Moab in Kerak. The two men were later to become firm friends.

Arriving in Amman on 2 March 1921, Abdullah received an even warmer welcome. He lodged in the house of Said el-Mufti, leader of the local Circassian community, who was later to become one of his prime ministers. Amman had fallen far from the position it had enjoyed under the Romans as Philadelphia, one of the cities of the Decapolis. It was now little more than a large village, of around 2000 souls, the majority of them Circassians settled there by the Turks after being driven out of the Caucasus by the Russians in the 1870s. Abdullah had let it be known that the purpose of his mission was to recover Syria for his brother Feisal, but the message he sent to Herbert Samuel in Jerusalem to explain his presence was much less bellicose and more placatory. It was, he said, to restore law and order where none existed at that time.

Abdullah had grown to manhood in the cosmopolitan society of Istanbul where his father, suspected of having Arab nationalist sympathies, had been exiled by Sultan Abdul Hamid in 1893. Abdullah was then eleven years old. Although the impression given by some writers is that Abdullah and his brothers were little more than bedouin shaykhs, this is far from being the truth. By the time his father Sharif Hussein returned to the Hejaz in 1908, Abdullah was already a member of the Turkish parliament and his father's right-hand man in the affairs of state. He played a prominent part in negotiations with the British which culminated in the Great Arab Revolt, and he commanded an Arab army in the war that followed. He was fluent in Turkish and knew more English than he chose to reveal. Abdullah was both a soldier and a diplomat, a combination that was to be characteristic of his grandson Hussein. He also possessed great personal charm.

He had married his first cousin Sharifa Musbah in 1902, by whom he had a son, Talal, born in 1909, and a daughter, Haya. In 1912 he married a Turkish woman by whom he had three children, a son, Naif, born in 1914, and two daughters, Maqbula and Munira. Many years later he married Nahida, a Sudanese, by whom he had no children.

The British government was concerned lest Abdullah's arrival in Amman should cause them trouble with the French, who would certainly oppose any further advance by Abdullah towards Syria. Fortuitously, it happened that a conference of all the most important British representatives in the Middle East was taking place at the time in Cairo, under the chairmanship of the Colonial Secretary, Winston Churchill. As a consequence of the new commitments undertaken in the Middle East, the British were overstretched both militarily and financially, while at the same time their wartime conscripts were clamouring for demobilization. It was essential to find some easing of the load.

It had been decided prior to Abdullah's arrival in Amman to offer the throne of Iraq to Feisal, as a sop for his eviction from Syria by the French, although it had been intended originally to offer Iraq to Abdullah. In order to cut down on the military manpower bill, the RAF were given responsibility for the internal security and defence of the newly mandated territories; and it was also decided to establish a military occupation of the region east of the River Jordan, which was to be called Transjordan. This was to be an Arab province under an Arab governor, who would be responsible to the British High Commissioner in Jerusalem. When Churchill left Cairo for Jerusalem on 26 March 1921, the favoured candidate for the governorship was the Emir Zeid, the youngest son of Sharif Hussein.

Abdullah was invited to meet Churchill in Jerusalem on 28 March. He repeated his statement to the High Commissioner that his object in coming to Amman was the restoration of law and order. At the same time he proposed that Palestine and Transjordan should be joined together under an Arab king. He was to repeat this proposal three times, an alternative being to link Iraq and Transjordan; but on each occasion it was politely rejected by Churchill. Instead, he suggested that Transjordan should become a Hashemite principality, at the same time offering it to Abdullah. This was a very different proposition from Iraq, which Abdullah had thought to have, Transjordan being virtually all desert without any revenues. Moreover, there was the Balfour Declaration to be considered. Abdullah was having no truck with Jewish settlement. He had already accused Samuel of uprooting the trees in Palestine in order to make room for Jewish immigrants. Samuel had replied that there was no reason to uproot trees since there was plenty of room in Palestine for the planting of more trees as well as for the immigrants.

Churchill then offered Abdullah a British subsidy, and also undertook to exclude Transjordan from the provisions of the Balfour Declaration. As a further inducement, he hinted that Transjordan might well turn out to be a springboard for the throne in Damascus, provided Abdullah could come to terms with the French by curbing the activities of the Syrian nationalists, who had taken refuge in Transjordan. He said that certainly His Majesty's government would look favourably on the prospect of a Hashemite on the Syrian throne.

One of Abdullah's attractions for the British, apart from the warm rapport he struck up with Churchill, was his insistence that he could establish control without the help of British troops, although he had said that some form of 'aerial support' would be helpful. Since military manpower was the burning issue, Abdullah's assurance was doubly welcome. He did not, however, accept the offer of Transjordan unreservedly, but undertook to form an administration for a trial period of six months. This was very much in line with the views of his brother Feisal who, after his bitter experience in Syria, was rather more conscious than Sharif Hussein of the weakness of the Arabs' negotiating position. As Feisal wrote to his brother Zeid on 19 January 1921, 'the wisest course is to take everything we can take and wait for tomorrow, because nights are pregnant and might give birth to miracles.'[4]

The Zionists were furious over the exclusion of Transjordan from the provisions of the Balfour Declaration, blaming it all on Churchill. Nor were the French happy at the prospect of a Hashemite on their southern border. They considered the Hashemites to be British stooges, and Abdullah never did succeed in winning them over.

Abdullah formed his first administration on 11 April 1921. One of his first actions was to organise a military force with which to restore law and order. It consisted mainly of men who had served originally in the Ottoman army before transferring their allegiance to Sharif Hussein, and then fighting under the Arab banner on the long march to Damascus. The senior Arab officer in this Jaysh al-Arabi (Arab army) was Abdul Qadir al-Jundi, who became a general in due course. To command his army Abdullah obtained the services of a Captain F.G. Peake, a British regular officer who had spent many years with the Egyptian army, commanding an Egyptian contingent under Feisal in the Great Arab Revolt. Peake Pasha, as he came to be known, resigned his commission in the British army on taking service under the Transjordan government. He was responsible for the choice of the force's English title, the Arab Legion, which would one day acquire renown throughout the Middle East.

Abdullah was described by Abramson, the first British senior official in Transjordan, as being 'lovable, considerate and generous', but, unfortunately, he was plagued throughout his life by a chronic shortage of money, among a people who count hospitality and generosity among the highest of human virtues. Indeed, it has been said of the Arabs that they are seldom grateful, but always generous. In those early days of his rule, when Abdullah had to establish himself as the ruler, his expenditure invariably exceeded his income. This exasperated the British government, which was subsidising Transjordan.

It is true that Abdullah could be very impulsive on occasions. His nickname as a child was al-Ajlan (the hasty one), and his friend Kirkbride was later to say of him that he was the most impatient man he had ever met. This caused endless friction with the British, who sent Colonel Henry Cox of the Palestine administration to Amman as Resident, with instructions either to curb Abdullah's extravagance or to get rid of him. Abdullah and Cox never did succeed in establishing close relations; and in 1924, when the Emir was in Mecca on the pilgrimage, arrangements were made to move a British cavalry regiment to Amman as a prelude to action that would prevent Abdullah's return. However, this happened to coincide with the successful repulse of a Wahhabi raid, which managed to get to within fifteen miles of Amman before a combination of the RAF and the Beni Sakhr tribe stopped it in its tracks. The general rejoicings which followed led to Abdullah's shortcomings being forgiven, if not forgotten, and he returned to his capital from Aqaba without another word being said. This was followed by the successful outcome of negotiations with Saudi Arabia, as a result of which Ma'an and Aqaba were incorporated into Transjordan, in return for certain border rectifications in the Wadi Sirhan in favour of the Saudis.

The story of the Hashemite–Saudi conflict must be briefly told. When Turkey entered the war against Britain and France in October 1914, the British government was anxious to enlist the aid of the Arabs. There were, however, two schools of thought concerning this. One based in Cairo favoured enlisting the support of Sharif Hussein in Mecca – the Hashemites. The other, based in Delhi, where the government of India was anxious to preserve its influence in the Gulf, favoured the Sauds, as represented by Abdul Aziz bin Saud, who had recently established himself as Emir of Nejd. In the end, those supporting the Hashemites prevailed, leaving Abdul Aziz bin Saud to consolidate his hold on Central Arabia with the help of his Wahhabis. This hold was later extended to include the Kingdom of the Hejaz, including the Holy Cities of Mecca and Medina, in 1924–5. Sharif Hussein, King of the Hejaz since 1917, abdicated in favour of his son Ali, who was in turn driven out of his kingdom by the triumphant Abdul Aziz.

The unfortunate Sharif Hussein has fared badly at the hands of several British writers, not least T.E. Lawrence's. He has been made out to be querulous, mean, hair-splitting and, towards the end of his life, barely sane. But an unbiased examination of the evidence clearly demonstrates that, although he could be difficult, Sharif Hussein was more sinned against than sinning in his relations with the British government. That it did not fulfil the pledges that it had made to him is now a matter of history. And so is Sharif Hussein's prediction of the consequences of the Balfour Declaration which, where the Arabs are concerned, has been proved correct time after time. As Emir Feisal was to write to his brother Zeid on 25 January 1921: 'We cannot compel England to fulfil her pledges to the letter; we cannot abandon our heritage; we cannot fight England and take what we want by the sword. This is the bitter reality.'[5]

It was not only Abdullah's feud with Abdul Aziz that concerned the British government. They were equally worried by Abdullah's ambition to become King of Greater Syria. He always argued that the Arab provinces of the Ottoman Empire had been split up solely to satisfy the interests of the Turks' imperialist successors. It made no sense, and the sooner they were reunited under one Arab ruler the better. This brought him into conflict not only with Britain and France, but also with virtually every other Arab government. He and King Fuad of Egypt were barely on speaking terms. The Saudis were furious when Abdullah, visiting Riyadh for the first time in order to patch up relations with King Abdul Aziz, expressed surprise that there was anything to see other than desert. His own relations in Baghdad viewed his activities with considerable suspicion – with the kind of benevolent irritation accorded to a respected but eccentric uncle. The Syrians, mostly republicans and always suspicious of the Hashemites, regarded him with a mixture of suspicion and fear. Who could guess what he was up to? Nor were they willing easily to forgive him for remaining on the sidelines during their rebellion against the French in 1925-7. Only the Druse never forgot the sanctuary he provided for the Al-Atrash, hereditary shaykhs of the Syrian Druse. (The Druse are an important, secretive and powerful Muslim sect who live mainly in Lebanon, Syria and Palestine. They make excellent soldiers and waged a long and bitter war against French occupation of Syria. Their stronghold, the Jebel Druse, lies immediately north of Jordan. In 1954, when Sultan al-Atrash fell out with his colleagues in the Syrian government, Jordan again provided sanctuary for him and his followers.)

Whenever Abdullah's thoughts strayed from the prospect of Greater Syria, or the Guardianship of the Holy Places, so rudely wrested from the Hashemites, they turned to Jerusalem, Islam's third holiest city, and the problem of Palestine. For centuries Palestine and the lands beyond the Jordan had been virtually one; traffic passed unimpeded between the two. Palestinians played an important part in the official and commercial life of Transjordan. Three of Abdullah's prime ministers – Tawfiq abu al-Huda, Samir Rifai and Ibrahim Hashim – were Palestinians. Although the more sophisticated, and on the whole better-educated, Palestinians affected to despise their country cousins across the Jordan, both Palestinians and Transjordanians had more in common than just their language and their religion. There were also twenty centuries of shared history.

Palestine and Transjordan were mandates of the League of Nations, placed under British tutelage. The British High Commissioner was represented in Amman by an official from the Palestine administration. He was called the British Resident. In 1926, quite arbitrarily, the High Commissioner converted Transjordan's Arab Legion from a military force into a gendarmerie, reducing it in strength to less than 1000 and restricting its activities to the policing of the settled areas. In its place there was formed the Trans-Jordan Frontier Force (TJFF), organised on typical British colonial lines, with British officers filling all the executive posts, and with Arabs holding only subordinate appointments. The TJFF, based in Zerqa in Transjordan, contained both infantry and cavalry, and was charged with Transjordan's defence, in co-operation with the RAF. Since the TJFF recruited almost entirely from among the settled Arabs, it was hardly well placed to deal with the desert, which takes up seven-eighths of Transjordan's land area. And as it happened towards the end of the 1920s, the situation in the desert was causing increasing concern to Abdullah and his government.

Abdul Aziz's Wahhabis had been creating mayhem along the border of Nejd with Iraq and Kuweit. They terrorised the tribes, preventing them from taking their flocks and herds out to pasture. But the situation was transformed in 1928 by the arrival on the scene of Captain John Bagot Glubb, a fluent Arabic speaker, who had resigned from the British army in 1926 to join the mandate administration in Iraq. Glubb, who established a remarkable rapport with the Iraqi bedouins, formed an armed desert police force of bedouins, possibly the first time bedouins had ever been employed in this role, and by a mixture of force and example put an end to the Wahhabi raids. Abu Hunaik, as he was nicknamed on account of a jaw wound received in France in 1917, soon became known as far afield as Transjordan. The Arabic means 'father of the little jaw'.

The Wahhabis had not confined their murderous activities to Iraq. The Transjordan tribes had also suffered from them, notably the Howeitat, who pasture their herds in Transjordan's southern desert. The TJFF were powerless to protect them from such raids, although they were able to prevent the Howeitat from seeking revenge by raiding back into Saudi Arabia themselves. In desperation the Transjordan government asked for the services of Glubb, who arrived in Amman early in November 1930. He was taken on to the strength of the Arab Legion and made 'OC Desert'. By employing much the same methods that had worked in Iraq, first gaining the confidence of the Transjordan tribes, and then forming a small elite force of bedouin camel police (Al-Badia, or the Desert Patrol), Glubb succeeded in pacifying the desert in two or three years. He then set about militarising his bedouin policemen, probably with the connivance of Emir Abdullah and the British Resident, Sir Alec Kirkbride, but certainly without the blessing of Peake Pasha, who thought policemen should be trained and equipped as policemen and not as soldiers. Glubb, who was appointed by Abdullah to command the Arab Legion on Peake's retirement in March 1939, proceeded to transform the force from a gendarmerie into a small but efficient army. He first formed a mechanised infantry battalion round the nucleus of the Desert Patrol, leading it alongside the British Army in the 1941 campaigns in Iraq and Syria. Later, the Desert Mechanised Force was increased to three battalions, 90 per cent of them bedouins, with a contingent of British officers on loan.

The Arab Legion's reputation was such that it was called upon to raise numerous infantry companies to guard British military installations scattered throughout the Middle East, and by the end of the war it had reached the strength of 12,000 officers and men, paid for by the British. By 1948, however, during the first war between the Arabs and Israel, the Arab Legion had been reduced in strength to around 4500. Abdullah took the keenest interest in his Arab Legion, seldom missing an opportunity to visit the troops. He and Glubb Pasha got on well together. Glubb has himself told the story of the Arab Legion in his two books, *The Story of the Arab Legion* and *A Soldier with the Arabs*.[6]

Transjordan, a British creation, needed to acquire legitimacy in accordance with international law, and Abdullah was anxious that this should be achieved early in his reign. He had appointed a commission as early as 1924 to draft a constitution, but in the event an agreement was drafted in Jerusalem which was in effect a treaty between Britain and Transjordan, which Abdullah signed on 20 February 1928. It proved to be unpopular with public opinion, which felt the Treaty had been imposed by the British, although Abdullah had been involved in the drafting from the outset. It preceded the British treaties with Iraq and Egypt; and it was followed by an Organic Law on 16 April 1928, which provided Transjordan with a constitution. An Electoral Law followed, passed after fierce debate, but nevertheless again resented as having been imposed by the British.

Abdullah's powers under the new Constitution were considerable but the unpalatable fact remained that Britain controlled his purse strings. This could not be said to have added to his popularity since Britain was held to be largely responsible for the disaster in Palestine. This dependence on British aid irked Abdullah as much as it did some of his subjects, but there was little that could be done about it. Happily his relations with the chief British representative in Amman, Sir Alec Kirkbride, were both close and affectionate.

Abdullah will long remain a controversial figure both in Arab and in other eyes. Many still believe that he entered into negotiations with the Zionists for his own personal aggrandisement. The truth, however, would appear to be that almost alone of all the Arab leaders at that time Abdullah recognised the power that would be exerted by the Zionists with the massive support of the United States behind them. Abdullah had little faith in the willingness of the Arab countries to sink their differences and present a united front to thwart the Zionist aim, although he did his best to persuade them to do so. In the circumstances, therefore, he sought to achieve the aim by diplomacy, particularly with regard to Jerusalem, which had for him almost a mystical attraction.

The first war between the Arabs and the Jews was fought in 1948. It owed its origins to the United Nations General Assembly vote on 29 November 1947 which partitioned Palestine between the Arabs and the Jews. The Islamic states voted unanimously against Partition, but this was the only point of unity for the Arabs. They had no concerted solution. As for the Jews, Abba Eban was to say in a BBC interview in June 1982, 'Partition was the principle which enabled Israel to be born.' The British government, despairing of ever finding a solution to the problem, announced that it was abandoning its mandate, and intended to withdraw from Palestine on 15 May 1948. This decision shocked many people, including General Glubb in Jordan, the more so since it was clear that the British had no intention of keeping the peace while the Jews and the Arabs took over that part of partitioned Palestine which the UN had allocated to them.

King Abdullah, who had been proclaimed King of the Hashemite Kingdom of Jordan when the Anglo-Jordanian Treaty that marked Jordanian independence from British tutelage was formally ratified on 22 March 1946, was deeply disturbed by the turn of events. He was well aware of Jewish strength and had no wish to put it to the test. He tried twice by secret negotiations with the Jews to reach agreement with them, but to no avail. In both instances the Jewish emissary was Mrs Golda Meir, which was perhaps unfortunate since Abdullah was not accustomed to negotiating with women; but there was in fact hardly any meeting of minds. Glubb too, through his own channels, tried to reach agreement that there would be no clash with the Hagana when the Arab Legion moved forward to occupy that part of Palestine allocated by the UN to the Arabs, but to no avail. The Hagana was the Jewish 'Defence' Force.

Prior to the British withdrawal, Abdullah sent his Prime Minister, Tawfiq abu al-Huda, accompanied by Glubb as his interpreter, to meet the British Foreign Secretary, Ernest Bevin, in London. When Tawfiq Pasha explained that his government intended to send the Arab Legion across the Jordan to occupy that part of Palestine allocated to the Arabs, Bevin replied, 'It seems the obvious thing to do,' adding the rider that the Arab Legion should not enter areas allocated to the Jews. Abdullah had therefore every reason to believe that his plan had British blessing; and accordingly, on 15 May 1948, the Arab Legion crossed the Allenby Bridge into Palestine. On that same day the Egyptian army entered Palestine from the south; a small Iraqi force reached the River Jordan opposite Beisan; and the Syrians attacked Samakh and then withdrew, never to appear in the fighting again.

There was in fact no co-ordinated Arab plan. An Arab League meeting was held in Amman to discuss war plans prior to the British withdrawal. It ended by the Iraqi representative congratulating himself that each Arab army would fight in accordance with its own plans, and not in conjunction with anyone else! For the sake of unity King Abdullah was proclaimed titular commander-in-chief, but his authority, apart from the Arab Legion, was nil.

The war that followed was disastrous for the Arabs. Only the Arab Legion, which was less than 5000 strong, distinguished itself. It saved the Old City of Jerusalem for the Arabs, and in conjunction with the Iraqis was able to secure the rest of the West Bank. The Egyptians were soundly defeated. It was Abdullah who insisted on sending the Arab Legion into the Old City to defend it from the Jews, who were on the point of seizing it. There was a truce on 11 June 1948 negotiated by the UN mediator, Count Fulke Bernadotte, who was to be murdered by the Jews on 17 September. During the truce the Arabs did little except talk, whereas the Jews bent every effort to acquire arms from abroad. Fighting broke out again on 9 July when the Jews seized Lydda and Ramle, but could not take Latrun, which was gallantly defended by the Arab Legion's 4th Regiment under Habis Majali. As Count Bernadotte commented at one stage: 'There are plenty of people fighting in Palestine but only one army – and that is the Arab Legion.' Bernadotte had put forward proposals for a ceasefire prior to his death, and on 18 July a second truce was agreed. This was followed on 23 October by a ceasefire demand from the UN.

The Arab League, which at Egypt's urging had rushed so heedlessly into war, laid down their arms without any thought for each other. Egypt agreed to an armistice in February 1949. Lebanon soon followed suit. Syria had long played no active part. In February Jordan was invited by Dr Ralph Bunche, Bernadotte's successor, to discuss armistice terms at Rhodes. On 11 March 1949 these terms were agreed by the Jordanian and Israeli delegations. Only Iraq refused to enter into armistice negotiations but withdrew its 19,000 troops unilaterally. On 3 April 1949 the Jordan–Israel armistice was formally agreed, leaving Jordan in occupation of what has come to be known as the West Bank. It was formally incorporated into the Hashemite Kingdom of Jordan in 1950.

Although King Abdullah has been vilified time and again for his policy towards the Jews, two facts are incontrovertible. The first is that he was the only Arab leader who made an honest attempt to resolve the Arab–Jewish problem before the fighting started; he was under no illusions about the strength of the Zionists and despised those who glibly announced their intention of driving the Jews into the sea. Secondly, it was King Abdullah who secured the Old City for the Arabs, despite the advice of his military commander, Glubb Pasha, who feared his small force would be swallowed up in the labyrinth of streets which make up the Old City. It can therefore be said, without fear of contradiction, that Jerusalem would probably have been lost had it not been for King Abdullah.

He was an Arab aristocrat of great charm and dignity. He loved the old ways: poetry, chess and the courtesy owed to lesser men by those of his station in life. His ambition was limitless but his field was narrow. He never ceased trying to extend it. When the former Lebanese Prime Minister, Riad as Sulh, was assassinated in Amman on 16 July 1951, it was rumoured that he had come to discuss Abdullah's plan to unite Jordan with Iraq, he to have the crown until his death, after which the young Feisal would succeed him. The debate for and against Abdullah will long continue but the fact remains that he was a remarkable man, one of the great Arab figures of his times. He was a *grand seigneur* who did his best with limited means to fulfil the Arab tradition of hospitality and generosity. On one occasion two of his servants asked him for money with which to buy new clothes for their wives and children before one of the great feasts. Abdullah had no money at that moment. Then he noticed the handsome carpet on his floor and told them to take it and sell it in order to buy clothes for their families. It was by actions of this kind that the King endeared himself to those who served him.

Kirkbride has called him the 'King with a twinkle', as quick to anger as he was to forgive.[7] Glubb Pasha wept when he heard of his death. Ibrahim Hashim, one of his prime ministers, said that 'to be in his presence was to feel the sun on a winter's day.'[8] According to his grandson he was 'a full-blooded extrovert who did not lightly brook refusal. . . . He was a wonderful old man, fierce and sometimes autocratic, who transformed Trans-Jordan, as it was, into a happy, smiling country.'[9] However, his importance in this study concerns not the services he rendered to Jordan, or for that matter to the Arab cause, but the influence he exerted on the character of his grandson, whose fate it would be to succeed him far sooner than anyone could possibly have imagined.

CHAPTER ONE

The Succession

'Ay, every inch a King!'[1]

King Abdullah's eldest son, Talal, had a sad life, despite his gentle nature and upright character. From early manhood onwards he was afflicted with a mental illness for which at that time there was no amelioration, and certainly no cure. This was to some extent aggravated by Talal's inability to get on with his extrovert and sometimes overbearing father, who had little patience with him. Abdullah was said to favour Naif, his son by his Turkish wife and Talal's half-brother, a sturdy but spoilt child. Talal was sent to England in 1926 when he was seventeen years old, the intention being to coach him for the Oxford and Cambridge entrance examination. His guardian, a Mr F. Ezechial, found him to be 'a lad of quiet and contented disposition, and an exceptionally nice fellow'. Unfortunately, however, his lack of a sound educational background proved difficult to overcome, and instead of a university he was sent to the Royal Military College at Sandhurst. Talal spent three years altogether in England, returning home only once. He was provided with very little pocket money, seven shillings and sixpence a term hardly allowing for any extravagance.

On his return from Sandhurst, Talal spent several months in Cyprus on the staff of the British High Commissioner, Sir Ronald Storrs, who was a great friend of his father's. He was then sent to the Iraq Military Academy for six months, returning to Transjordan in 1931 for the funeral of his grandfather, King Hussein bin Ali of the Hejaz. By then he had spent five of the most formative years of his life away from his homeland and his family.

In 1934 Talal married his mother's niece, the Sharifa Zein, an attractive and intelligent young woman who had for some years enjoyed the sophisticated life of Cairo. The old-fashioned ways of Abdullah's court must have come as something of a shock to her, but she soon acquired favour with her autocratic father-in-law when she presented him with a grandson in November 1935. Hussein was her firstborn, to be followed by two other sons, Muhammad and Hassan, and then by a daughter, Basma. Talal and Zein enjoyed a happy and united family life, despite a chronic shortage of money and Talal's unhappy relations with his father. Abdullah made little or no attempt to give his eldest son worthwhile employment, although Talal was intelligent and anxious to be of use to his country. Naif, who had been reported as 'ineducable' at Victoria College in Alexandria,[2] easily found favour with Abdullah, although his boisterous and extrovert character was always getting him into scrapes that infuriated his father.

Unlike most heirs to a throne, the young Hussein grew up in relatively straitened circumstances. His father's income was not much more than £1000 a year. The family lived in a modest five-bedroomed villa, far less grand than those occupied by Amman's wealthier citizens. It could certainly not be said of Hussein that he has never known 'how the other half lives', since for most of his childhood his family was part of the 'other half', despite their royal status.

One of the most attractive aspects of Transjordan during Hussein's boyhood was its simplicity. It was still a desert kingdom, its values very much those of the desert, where rich and poor alike lived in tents and slept on the ground. Amman was a modest little town, without the handsome houses and crowded boulevards that characterise it today. Abdullah liked nothing more than to retire to his black tent, pitched at Shuneh beside the Dead Sea, where he entertained in bedouin fashion, every man eating from the same dish, kneeling on one knee and eating with only his right hand. The entertainment was likely to be chess, or the recitation of poetry. Abdullah invariably rose early, had a bath and read the Holy Koran, and said his prayers. He would eat a light breakfast, always with company, inspect his horses, of which he was very fond, and then go to his office to receive visitors. On most days his official work had been finished by the time most government employees were starting their work day.[3]

There was, however, much to worry him. The Arabs in Palestine had been in rebellion against the British, in protest against British policy. This had been followed by the outbreak of the Second World War, during the earlier years of which Transjordan's British ally had suffered defeat after defeat. Britain had no stauncher ally than Abdullah, and there was a time when Transjordan was the British Empire's *only* ally, a fact insufficiently recognised by the British people today. Closer to home, there was the obvious deterioration in Talal's health, for which his father never seemed to make sufficient allowance. One of the bones of contention between the two was the young Hussein's education, Talal insisting that his son's grounding in Arabic should be sound, Abdullah emphasising the importance he attached to religious education. The unfortunate child was moved from school to school until he had attended six schools in all, from kindergarten upwards. He was a perfectly normal little boy, more attracted by his bicycle than his books, and fond of playing with children of his own age. His grandfather loved him dearly, a love that was certainly returned by his grandson, but he could not forbear from meddling in Hussein's upbringing, which inevitably led to argument within the family.

Abdullah would have liked his grandson to go to Harrow School, Winston Churchill's *alma mater*, but in the end it was decided to send him to Victoria College in Alexandria, which was run on British public-school lines, and where there was tuition in both Arabic and English. Hussein liked Victoria College, where his fees were partly paid by Abdullah. He enjoyed the games, and the requirement to mix with all kinds of boys. His memories of Victoria College are happy ones, but all too soon he was to be taken away and sent elsewhere.

King Abdullah – he had been proclaimed King instead of Emir (Prince), on 25 May 1946, when Transjordan became the Hashemite Kingdom of Jordan – was very devout. His devotion to Jerusalem was one of his most marked characteristics. He used to make a point of attending the Friday Prayers in the Great Mosque whenever he could, after what remained of Arab Palestine had been joined together with Jordan in 1950. His insistence on attending this ceremony worried his ministers and friends, who knew the King was blamed by many Palestinians for his efforts to resolve the Arab–Jew confrontation without bloodshed; it was not the first time in history that statesmanship and common sense had been stigmatised as betrayal. This attitude was not improved by Abdullah's known antagonism towards Haj Amin al-Husseini, the ex-Mufti of Jerusalem, who had committed the mistake of supporting Hitler during the Second World War, on the assumption presumably that Germany would win. Moreover, Abdullah felt, and with reason, that it was only his own Arab Legion which, at his own insistence, had held the Old City, and with it the Haram es Sharif,[4] against every Jewish attempt to seize it. His conscience at least was clear.

The assassination of political opponents has been a recurring theme throughout Arab political history. The fact that it has seldom resulted in any worthwhile change in policy has failed to influence those who have been willing to die in the attempt. Abdullah's supreme faith in God as his protector worried those close to him. When the former British Resident and now Ambassador, Kirkbride, besought him to be careful, Abdullah replied, 'Until my time comes, no one can harm me; and when my time comes, no one can guard me.' The assassination four days previously in Amman of the former Lebanese Prime Minister Riad as Sulh had made everyone nervous, political assassinations being previously unknown in Jordan. Abdullah's Prime Minister, Samir Rifai, begged him to take care. 'I believe in God. My life is in His hands,' the King replied. The Americans, who had got wind of a plot, added their warnings. Abdullah was not to be moved. He was a fatalist – as is his grandson after him.

It may seem surprising that he should have chosen to take with him that

grandson on what was to prove to be his last journey on this earth. He might
have thought it prudent to have prayed alone on that occasion. But it was
not to be. Several others whom Abdullah had invited to accompany him
declined. Abdullah had told Hussein this, and when he asked his fifteen-
year-old grandson, 'Would you like to come with me, my son?' Hussein had
replied, 'Certainly I would! You know, Sir, my life is worth nothing
compared with yours.'

They left Amman on Thursday afternoon, 20 July 1951, to sleep the night
in a house belonging to the Nashashibi family in the Jerusalem suburb of
Sheikh Jarrah. Hussein was still wearing the uniform of a captain in the
Arab Legion, after attending a ceremonial presentation of 'wings' to the
first batch of pilots in the Arab Legion Air Force (today the RJAF – Royal
Jordanian Air Force). They were accompanied by Abdullah's Court
Chamberlain, a young Palestinian called Nassir Nashashibi, who was also
responsible for the Broadcasting Station at Ramallah, near Jerusalem. The
Nashashibis and the Husseinis were the two leading Arab families in
Palestine, but it was unusual at that time for a Palestinian to hold such
a confidential appointment in Abdullah's court. Nashashibi, who later
became a prominent journalist and editor of *Goumouriyeh* in Cairo, says that
neither Kirkbride nor Glubb Pasha approved of his position.[5]

Abdullah and his entourage left Jerusalem early on Friday, 21 July, to
visit Nablus, where Abdullah was to pass the time before the noon prayer
with the Mayor, Suleiman Touqan. When, however, Hussein appeared at
breakfast in a civilian suit, his grandfather asked why he was not in uniform.
Hussein said he had sent it to Amman to be pressed. 'But you must wear
uniform,' the King insisted. 'Get it back at once!' This was done and
Hussein changed into uniform before leaving for Nablus. There the time
passed pleasantly until the King rose to go. 'There is hardly time for you to
reach Jerusalem in time to pray, *Sidi*,' protested the Mayor. 'Why not pray
in Nablus instead?' But the King was insistent.

They returned to the Nashashibi house, and while Hussein was momentarily out of the room, Abdullah told Nassir Nashashibi, 'He is the elite of
the elite. He is the continuity of my dynasty.' There then arrived a certain
Dr Musa Ali Husseini to pay his respects. He was related to the ex-Mufti,
was a graduate of London University, and was both the owner of a travel
agency and a journalist in Jerusalem. Aged forty-two, charming and
sophisticated, he had come to assure Abdullah of his loyalty, which the
King was pleased to acknowledge. Perhaps, however, Abdullah may have
had some premonition of what was to befall. Before they left for the Mosque
he told his companions of those he had invited to accompany him to
Jerusalem, but who had made excuses not to do so. 'They were afraid,' said
Abdullah, adding, 'When I have to die, I should like to be shot in the head

by a nobody. That's the simplest way of dying. I would rather that than become old and a burden.' He was sixty-nine years of age.

Shortly before noon the royal party entered the Haram es Sharif, which was thronged with worshippers and onlookers. The 10th (Hashemite) Regiment of the Arab Legion provided the bodyguard under the command of Lieutenant-Colonel (later Field Marshal) Habis Majali, a scion of one of Transjordan's most distinguished families who had ruled over Kerak for centuries. Habis, who was under the strictest orders from Glubb Pasha to guard the King well, had proved his military qualities when commanding the 4th Regiment in the defence of Latrun in 1948.

Abdullah had driven through streets lined by troops, and on his arrival at the Haram es Sharif, the car-door had been opened by Musa Ali Husseini, bowing obsequiously low. Within the enclosure the presence of the troops was so marked that Hussein asked one of the escorting officers if it was a funeral procession. The King must have felt the same because he said to Habis Majali, 'La tahabasni, ya Habis!' ('Don't imprison me, Habis!'). He also made plain his disapproval of the Guard of Honour drawn up outside the Al Aqsa Mosque, commenting that it was inappropriate in such a holy place. Then he entered the Mosque, to be greeted by the Shaykh, who bent to kiss his hand.

Simultaneously, a man appeared from behind the great door. There was a pistol in his hand and a shot rang out. Abdullah never saw his assassin, although he was less than six feet away. The King fell instantly, his turban rolling away across the floor. He was dead. Hussein, only a few paces from his grandfather, was momentarily stunned. Then shooting broke out all around him. He saw the assassin with glazed eyes pointing the pistol at him. There was a shot, but fortunately the bullet was deflected by a medal the Prince was wearing right over his heart. The assassin then fell to the ground, riddled by bullets from the escort. In the meantime Abdullah's companions had scrambled helter-skelter for cover, their one desire to save their own lives. It was a pitiful exhibition of human weakness which Hussein was never to forget.[6]

Some hours later, after being treated for shock, Hussein in crumpled uniform and shaken by grief, still only a boy, stood by the airstrip at Kolundia, outside Jerusalem, scarcely knowing what to do next. A British officer in Arab Legion uniform came up and saluted. He was Squadron Leader Jock Dalgliesh, second-in-command of the fledgling Arab Legion Air Force. 'Come with me, sir,' he said. 'I'll look after you,' and he flew Hussein back to Amman. It was the beginning of a friendship which has lasted down the years. King Abdullah's body was flown back to Amman in an aircraft piloted by Wing Commander Bill Fisher, who was then commanding the air force.

A military court was established, presided over by Abdul Qadir al-Jundi, deputy commander of the Arab Legion. The members were Lieutenant-Colonels Habis Majali and Ali Hiyyari. The assassin, Mustafa 'Ashu, was dead. Kirkbride has said he was a 'notorious terrorist', but he was more likely a hired killer. The plot was revealed by a Mahmud Antabla, who turned state's evidence. It involved one of the Arab Legion's most promising officers, Abdullah el-Tel, who had distinguished himself in the defence of the Old City in 1948, and who had signed the ceasefire agreement for Jordan; Moshe Dayan had done so for Israel. Abdullah el-Tel was a Jordanian, not a Palestinian, but he nursed a grudge against Glubb Pasha, who had refused him promotion to brigadier because he was too young and lacked experience. Whereupon he had left the Arab Legion in a huff and had gone to Cairo, from where he had engaged in anti-Jordan activities. Abdullah el-Tel has always denied complicity in Abdullah's assassination, claiming that he was 'framed' in order to add an East Bank flavour to what was predominantly a West Bank plot. He was sentenced to death *in absentia*, but was pardoned some years later and permitted to return to Jordan.

Four other plotters were found guilty and were sentenced to death. They were two brothers, 'Abid and Zakariyya Ukah, a cattle broker and a butcher; Abd-el-Qadir Farhat, at whose café the plot was hatched; and Dr Musa Ali Husseini, who pleaded his innocence throughout. Nevertheless, he was hanged with the three others on 6 September 1951.

The weeks that followed Abdullah's assassination were dominated by political intrigue over the succession to the throne. The Crown Prince, Talal, was out of the country at the time undergoing medical treatment. His condition was such that there were many who doubted his ability to contend with the stresses and strains of kingship. In his absence his half-brother, Naif, was proclaimed regent, at once taking steps to ensure that the Coronation took place as soon as possible, the intention being quite clearly to deprive Talal of the throne. Naif was not as well liked and respected as Talal, but he did have his supporters, including certain officers in the Arab Legion. Were he to succeed in his plans, it seemed likely that he would at some later stage have himself proclaimed king, which would probably destroy the young Hussein's chances of succeeding to the throne. As his mother Zein saw it, they would have vanished. She therefore fought a lonely battle for Abdullah's funeral to be postponed until Talal's treatment had been completed and he could return to Jordan to be crowned king. Fortunately for Jordan, she succeeded.

There was anxious debate over Talal's fitness, and there was undoubtedly some kind of a plot on Naif's behalf, but in the end the government decided for Talal. Two bedouin regiments were moved into Amman from Zerqa, and Naif, getting the message, left the country. He never returned until his death in 1983, when his body was given a royal funeral in the Hashemite burial ground above Amman. Talal arrived back in Jordan on 6 September 1951 and was proclaimed king.[7]

King Abdullah lost his life as a result of a Palestinian plot. There were many on the West Bank who hated him. The Egyptians were continually attacking him as a 'traitor to the Arab cause'. The truth was, however, that the Arabs, who had made mistake after mistake in their handling of the Palestine problem, needed a scapegoat, and many of them were keen that it should be King Abdullah. The tragedy was that he had died at a time when his country needed him most. Jordan had been overrun by more than 650,000 refugees from Palestine, drastically altering the balance between the East and West Banks. The problem of assimilating them into a country that was largely desert, had few industries and was largely dependent on a foreign power (Britain) for financial support must have seemed insuperable. What is more, Jordan now found itself with a border of more than 400 miles with Israel, but with an army less than 20,000 strong with which to defend it; and there was virtually no air force. Everywhere one looked, there seemed to be difficulties. Talal was not to be envied for his inheritance.

CHAPTER TWO

Crown Prince

'Hussein had marked charisma even as a boy.'[1]

It was at this critical juncture in Jordan's history that the British Ambassador, Sir Alec Kirkbride, applied to the Foreign Office for a new posting. Glubb Pasha said the reason was Abdullah's death. 'The light went out of Kirk's life when the King died,' said Glubb.[2] Kirkbride had been in the country on and off since 1918, and continuously since his appointment as British Resident in 1939. He knew everyone of importance, and a great many others of no importance. Abdullah and Kirkbride were genuine friends, although no doubt they quarrelled from time to time as friends do, but never with any real acrimony. Kirkbride was unequalled in explaining Britain's policy to Jordan, and Jordan's to Britain – a true diplomat. His influence was considerable but he preferred to keep it unobtrusive. A man of few words and a pawky sense of humour, he understood and loved the Jordanians, who understood and loved him in return. In Glubb's words, he was 'irreplaceable' in Jordan at that time.

So was Hussein's grandfather for Hussein himself, who had loved and deeply admired Abdullah, tinged sometimes probably with awe, since the King was not a man lightly to be crossed. The brutal suddenness of his death in one of Islam's most holy places was bound to have a psychological effect on a young and impressionable boy. Abdullah had been for Hussein the personification of all that he understood of the Hashemite tradition – their descent from the Prophet, and the part they had played in throwing off the Ottoman yoke. Abdullah was a rock among men, a true leader and the father of his country. The love Abdullah had had for Hussein had been returned in full measure. There could never be anyone else quite like him.

What is more, Abdullah's death completely changed Hussein's life. Whereas before he had been free to come and go more or less as he pleased, now he was the Crown Prince, heir to the throne, hemmed in by protocol and always on show whenever he appeared in public. As he was to learn as he grew older, for royalty there is no incognito; always, somewhere around, there will be some photographer waiting to trap the unwary, or some reporter anxious to file some statement or opinion, however garbled in the transmission. Not yet sixteen years old, and no different from thousands of other boys of that age, he could no longer grow up like them, however much his parents would have liked him to do so. As a first step they had to take him away from Victoria College, since Egypt was suspected of having had a hand in Abdullah's assassination, and send him elsewhere to complete his education. The choice fell on Harrow School in England.

The British public-school system has both its supporters and its detractors. Foreigners find it particularly difficult to understand. It must come as a severe shock to those who have not undergone initiation in British preparatory schools, in which conditions used to be even more rugged, with even less privacy, than was the case in the public schools. Hussein had not had this experience, and he was at sixteen older than usual for entry into Harrow. He must have found it very difficult to settle down in such a strange environment, and to adjust to the queer customs and traditions that govern a boy's behaviour in a school like Harrow. Even the food was different from Victoria College in Alexandria, wartime rationing still being strictly enforced in the Britain of the early 1950s. Fortunately Hussein's cousin, Feisal, heir to the throne of Iraq, was also at Harrow, where the two young Arab princes struck up a firm friendship.

They were, however, very different characters, as this story may demonstrate. Sir Winston Churchill, himself an Old Harrovian, was very fond of attending the annual occasion when the boys sang the school songs, Sir Winston joining in with great vigour. He sometimes took with him his Private Secretary, John Colville, also an Old Harrovian. On one such occasion Colville found himself talking with the Headmaster, and asked about the two Arab princes. How were they getting on? The Headmaster said that Feisal was a very well-behaved and quiet boy, never in trouble and rather unassuming. He would make an excellent constitutional monarch provided the conditions were right, which he thought unlikely since Iraq had a rather turbulent reputation. Hussein on the other hand had a much more vigorous character, and could be headstrong as well as determined. He would thrive on difficulties since they would bring out the best in his character, and he would prove himself to be a strong ruler. As time would show, the Headmaster's judgement was remarkably accurate.[3]

'It may seem a trifling reason for being a fish out of water,' Hussein has written, 'but Feisal and I were about the only two boys at Harrow who did not have surnames. English schoolboys are sticklers for protocol (much more rigid than we are in our palaces in Amman!) and they could not accustom themselves to switching from Smith minor or Brown major to just "Hussein" – so they very rarely called me anything at all.'[4]

Hussein's House at Harrow was the Park. His Housemaster, Mr Stevenson, thought Hussein had considerable determination, but his educational progress was hampered by the lack of a sound basic grounding when he was younger. This is hardly surprising considering the number of schools he had attended in Amman after leaving the nursery. But his interests never were of the bookish kind; he much preferred an active outdoor life, spiced wherever possible with challenge and just a touch of danger. It was probably his youngest brother, Hassan, who got the most out of Harrow, both intellectually and physically. Hassan's Housemaster, Mr Laborde, recalls him as being 'a splendid boy in the House',[5] but Hassan was of course spared Hussein's traumatic experience when their grandfather was assassin-ated. Hussein's House Matron, Audrey Miskin, found him to be highly strung and sometimes lonely. He often came to her for help, advice and consolation. She says he was very simple at heart and high-spirited at times, but noticeably weighed down by the thought of the responsibilities that lay ahead of him. He was however immensely proud of his heritage, and of being an Arab.

Hussein's great joy at Harrow was his car, a Rover given to him by a friend of his father's, although boys at Harrow were forbidden to have cars during term-time. His Housemaster was therefore not let into the secret, and matters were better kept that way. The car had of course to be garaged within easy distance, but somewhere where it would be out of sight and out of mind, at least as far as his Housemaster was concerned. It was as a result of searching for such a garage that Hussein first met Maurice Raynor, who owned a small garage near the school. 'Raynor was a man whose passion in life was cars,' Hussein has written. Raynor found in the young prince an equally ardent disciple. Hussein and Raynor struck up a friendship which was eventually to take Raynor and his wife out to Jordan, where Raynor's job was to look after Hussein's stable of cars of every kind and description. A skilled mechanic himself, Raynor found Hussein to be an excellent pupil. In the years to come, after he had come to the throne, Hussein often resorted to the Raynors' modest house in search of the quietness and domestic peace he found it hard to find in the protocol of court life.

The Jordanian Ambassador in London at the time was Fawzi al-Mulki, who went out of his way to ingratiate himself with the young Crown Prince. Hussein's Housemaster used to complain about this. Fawzi was a graduate of London University where he had managed to acquire some very left-wing views. He was also very ambitious, going out of his way to be charming to Hussein, who not surprisingly found parties and dances at weekends in London infinitely more fun than staying at school to play games or study his books. Any boy of Hussein's age would feel exactly the same.

It is entirely natural that any young man whose pocket permits it should find enjoyment in driving fast cars fast and in dancing with pretty girls. Hussein was popular among his fellows, and invariably generous and considerate. It was certainly just as well that for some part of his life he should be free from responsibility. It would not last for very long. It was said of Hussein's great-uncle, King Feisal I of Iraq, by his Prime Minister Jaafar el-Askari, that his two driving impulses were 'work and worry'. Hussein would discover all too soon that this was the fate of every ruler who sought to do his best for his country.

Hussein says in retrospect that he enjoyed Harrow, although some of those who knew him at the school say that he found the restrictions irksome. And so they must have been for anyone brought up as he had been in the domestic cosiness of Talal's household. Life in a British public school at that time was hedged round with rules and regulations, less so perhaps at Eton and Harrow than at most others, but inhibiting nonetheless. Hussein has also been critical of the curious British practice of segregating boys from girls.

Times have changed since Hussein was at Harrow. His belief in the advantages of the British public-school system, despite the obvious disadvantages, has been demonstrated by his support for Harrow. His youngest brother, Hassan, has benefited from this, and there are numerous other young Jordanians who have been fortunate enough to have enjoyed an education at one of Britain's finest public schools, entirely owing to Hussein's conviction that the education, and perhaps more importantly the character-building, is all-important in this modern age.

It is now time to consider the changes that were taking place in the Arab Legion, Jordan's army and air force, on the loyalty of which both the country's stability and the continuance of the Hashemite dynasty so largely depended. Before doing this, however, it is necessary to explain the vitally important role of the bedouin regiments in this connection. As has already been mentioned, the Hashemites have always cherished and nurtured their affinity with the desert, and with the bedouin tribes who dwell there; while the bedouins in their turn held the Grand Sharif in special reverence. It was natural when Glubb Pasha first began to militarise his bedouin camel police in the late 1930s that they should all have been bedouin tribesmen, most of them from Transjordanian tribes. However, as Glubb expanded this small nucleus, first into a desert mechanised regiment (battalion), and then into a Desert Mechanised Force (brigade), its fame became known all over Central Arabia; and tribesmen from tribes as distant as the borders of Iraq and Kuweit came to join. They had no loyalty to Transjordan as such, but only to the Emir Abdullah as a descendant of the Prophet and as one of the leaders in the Great Arab Revolt, in which the bedouins played such an important part. There was moreover a natural hostility between the nomads and their settled cousins, the origins of which have their roots far back in history.

When forming his force of desert policemen (later soldiers), Glubb was scrupulously careful to retain bedouin customs and traditions; he did not want a carbon copy of the British Army. For example, officers and soldiers ate from the same dish, as is the bedouin custom; and their uniform was copied from the bedouin style of dress, as can still be seen in the Desert Police today. Later in the 1939–45 war, however, the Desert Mechanised Force adopted the British Army's battledress, but always with the distinctive red and white Arab headdress (*khefiyyah*), always known in the Arab Legion as *shamagh*. The few British officers then serving in the Arab Legion were constantly exhorted to abide by the bedouin customs, particularly as they were dealing with people who are extremely touchy where their personal honour (*sharaf*) is concerned. No bedouin officer or soldier, for example, should ever be dressed down in front of his fellows, but should be taken to one side for whatever rebuke was considered necessary.

In order to emphasise still further the kinship with the desert, Glubb elected to base the Desert Mechanised Force at Azraq, far out in the desert in those days, and certainly too long, bumpy and dusty a drive for any government minister to undertake voluntarily. The Emir, however, came frequently. He loved his little army and revelled in the soldier's life. In return his soldiers received him with both affection and respect. By forming what was in effect a body of Household troops, Glubb had created a kind of Praetorian Guard whose loyalty was given to the Emir and their commander, Glubb Pasha, and to no one else. Both Abdullah and Kirkbride, the British Resident, recognised this, and presumably approved, since otherwise Glubb could never have acted as he did.

The rest of the Arab Legion in those early days, recruited from the towns and villages of Transjordan, still performed the duties of mounted (*Darak*) and foot (*Shurta*) policemen, under the command of Glubb's deputy, Abdul Qadir al-Jundi. As British commitments in the Middle East continued to grow, Transjordan was asked to provide infantry companies to guard the many military installations scattered from Palestine to the Euphrates and Tigris valleys. These Guard Companies were recruited for the most part from the settled areas, their officers likewise, and later formed the nucleus of the non-bedouin regiments that fought alongside their bedouin comrades in the war against the Jews in 1948. At its peak in 1945 the Arab Legion, both soldiers and policemen, numbered about 12,000, the bedouin element comprising about 30 per cent, a proportion which is roughly the same today. Reduced to less than 5000 by the end of the British mandate in Palestine in 1948, the proportion of bedouin and non-bedouin units that took part in the fighting for Jerusalem was nearer fifty–fifty, but this was changed rapidly as the Arab Legion began to expand in 1950–1, the majority of the new units raised to meet the Legion's increased commitments being non-bedouin in composition.

After the end of the first Arab war against Israel in April 1949, it was clearly necessary that the Arab Legion should be expanded, since there was now the 400-mile border with Israel (the demarcation line) which needed to be defended. There was, however, very little money in the Jordanian Treasury with which to pay for such an expansion. Fortunately, the British government was in the process of reviewing its strategic commitments in the Middle East, the object being to reduce the number of British units stationed there, since Britain was virtually bankrupt at that time. Arab Legion units, in alliance with the British, cost a great deal less to arm, equip and maintain than their British equivalents. The British Treasury was therefore persuaded to increase the subsidy paid to Transjordan that had been provided since Abdullah had first set up his government in 1921. It was willing to do this, however, only on condition that the British Army played a much larger part in the command, training and general supervision of the Arab Legion. This eventually resulted in an increase in the number of British officers serving with the Arab Legion from a mere handful to one hundred or more by 1955, most of them on three years' loan from the British Army, but a few on direct contract with the government of Jordan. They naturally expected to be paid and accommodated, many of them having their families with them, in accordance with the standards then prevailing in the British Army, and relatively few of them had the same command of Arabic and understanding of Arab customs as was the case with Glubb and his handful of British colleagues during the war years. Both Abdullah and Glubb were uneasily aware of this, Glubb commenting in 1952 that he had much preferred the time when there were only two or three British officers serving with the Arab Legion; but the need for British financial support was such that they had to acquiesce.

As a first step an infantry division was formed in 1951, its commander Major-General 'Sam' Cooke (Cooke Pasha), a British regular officer. He replaced Brigadier Norman Lash, a Palestine policeman. Schools of Instruction were formed for Artillery, Engineers, Transportation, etc., and new infantry battalions and regiments of artillery were raised. Between 1951 and 1955 the strength of the Arab Legion grew to around 20,000, and there were the beginnings of an air force. Approximately 50 per cent of the command posts were held by British officers, overall command being exercised by Glubb Pasha as Chief of the General Staff. Glubb, who had the rank of lieutenant-general, was employed by the government of Jordan, and not by the British.

All this expansion, and the concomitant influx of British officers, was taking place at a time when the former colonial empires were fast breaking up, and when the 'winds of change', as Harold Macmillan chose to describe the phenomenon, were sweeping across the world. A spirit of nationalism gripped the minds of men everywhere, most notably among the young, and it would have been surprising indeed had it missed out the Jordanians, particularly after the disastrous mess the British had made of Palestine. Most young officers in the Arab Legion were ardent nationalists, as were their co-religionists elsewhere in the Arab world, anxious to stand on their own feet and to cut the leading strings with whatever foreign power they had formerly been associated. In the case of the Arab Legion, it is perhaps fair to say that they were not so much anti-British as pro-Jordanian (or Arab).[6]

Although still a schoolboy, Hussein was not unaffected by this spirit of the times. Fawzi al-Mulki in London was an ardent nationalist; he must certainly have passed on his feelings to the Crown Prince during their numerous social meetings at the Jordanian Embassy and elsewhere. Acutely conscious as he was of his Hashemite heritage and the part played by his family in throwing off the Ottoman yoke, Hussein certainly shared the feelings of his compatriots. He, too, wanted to see his country stand on its own feet. However, he was probably more concerned at that time by the news he was receiving from Jordan of the state of his father's health, which seemed to be deteriorating.

During Talal's brief reign, he showed himself to be both a liberal-minded and a progressive ruler. He introduced a new constitution early in 1952, reducing his own powers and making the Cabinet responsible to parliament. This would not have been possible without the agreement of his Prime Minister and the other ministers, but it nevertheless received a somewhat mixed reception in the country. Jordanians were very conservative in mind and habit, and any increase in the powers of parliament, which included many West Bankers, made the more traditionally minded feel uneasy. What was the King up to? Was he being influenced by the British with their craze for Westminster-style government? And why had Talal agreed to join the Arab League's Collective Security Pact? This was certainly a departure from previous policy. In the Arab Legion, too, there were beginning to be rumbles of discontent among the younger officers, as they saw more and more British officers coming out to join the Legion. None of this could have escaped the young Hussein as he drove at high speed along the narrow English lanes, scaring his passengers out of their wits (his reputation as a very fast but extremely skilful driver had yet to be established).

Sadly, his father's health continued to deteriorate as the months went by, and it was clear to those who were close to the King that the stress of governing was undoubtedly a contributing factor. Eventually it was decided by the Prime Minister, Tawfiq abu al-Huda, with the agreement of his

Cabinet, that the King should be examined by a panel of two eminent foreign doctors. Their verdict was that he was unfit to rule. This was later confirmed by a panel of three Jordanian doctors. After a long debate in parliament, it was finally, and reluctantly, decided that Talal should be called upon to abdicate in favour of his son, Hussein.[7] When confronted by this, Talal, like the gentleman he was, accepted the government's request. After thanking parliament and the government for their consideration, and asking God to bless Jordan and its people, he stepped down from the throne and left for Istanbul, where he died in 1972. He was buried in the Hashemite burial ground in Amman. He had been a king of much promise, but fate had been unkind to him.

Hussein was in Switzerland that August, staying in an hotel with his mother, Queen Zein, and his brothers and sister. He must of course have had some inkling of what was afoot. Nevertheless, it came as something of a shock when on 12 August 1952, a letter was handed to him on a silver salver by one of the hotel pages. 'His Majesty King Hussein,' he read, before he slit open the envelope. His schooldays were over. His 'work and worry' had begun. He was three months short of his seventeenth birthday.

CHAPTER THREE

The Profession of Arms

'The Fittest man to make a soldier is a perfect gentleman; for generous spirits are ever apt for great designs.'[1]

King Hussein is a born soldier. The profession of arms is a natural one for him. He had since childhood listened enthralled to his grandfather's stories of the Great Arab Revolt, in which Abdullah had played such an important part. The Arabs are a martial race and Abdullah's stories lost nothing in the telling. Hussein's father too had undergone long military training. He wore his Arab Legion uniform with real cavalry panache, a handsome man with a true military bearing. Hussein was still only in his early teens when his grandfather made him an honorary captain in the Arab Legion, not long afterwards appointing him a personal ADC to the King. Hussein wore his uniform with great pride, although acutely conscious that he had undergone no kind of military training. It was something that he had hoped would be remedied sooner or later by attending the Arab Legion Cadet School at Abdile, above Amman, or some foreign military academy like his father and his uncle Sharif Nasser, who had attended the Iraq Military Academy in Baghdad. But now, with his father's abdication and his own succession to the throne, he had to put it out of his mind. They would never send him away to learn to be a soldier.

It was a melancholy thought as he stepped off the plane that hot August afternoon at Mafraq airport. The host of dignitaries assembled to greet him were drawn up in line, and there was a Guard of Honour to be inspected. Then, with Prime Minister Tawfiq abu al-Huda seated beside him, Hussein set off on the long drive from Mafraq to Amman. Since the Prime Minister sat in respectful silence for most of the journey, and he himself was not the most talkative of men at the best of times, Hussein was left alone with his thoughts. 'This is how it will always be from now on,' he thought. 'People will never be able to relax.' But Amman was to show him the reverse side of the medal. The streets were crowded with cheerful, boisterous people who gave the young King a tumultuous welcome. He was quite overcome by it, telling Tawfiq Pasha how much he hoped to live up to the people's trust in him.

Hussein could not assume his royal prerogative until he was eighteen, more than a year away. The Prime Minister was concerned to know what to do with him until then. He could not be sent back to Harrow, and they did not want to have him hanging about in Jordan with very little to do. They sent him to tour the country at first, accompanied by his uncle, Sharif Nasser, and his cousin, Sharif Zeid bin Shakir, and everywhere he went he charmed people by his evident friendliness and pleasant manner. But there was obviously a limit to visits of this kind, and in the end it was Sharif Nasser who provided the answer. Why should not Hussein attend a course at Sandhurst, as his father had done before him? The Prime Minister welcomed the suggestion, and Glubb Pasha was able to make the necessary arrangements with the War Office in London. Hussein himself was delighted. He says he remembers his father telling him, 'No man can rule a country without discipline. Nowhere in the world do they teach men discipline as they do at Sandhurst.'[2] Sandhurst was also to provide Hussein with the freedom to come and go that he could never have had back in Amman. It also helped to lay the foundations of a career which has been as much military as civil. It certainly turned a boy into a man surprisingly quickly. Hussein looks back on his time at Sandhurst with genuine affection and gratitude. It would not have suited everyone by any means, but it certainly suited him. He was posted to Inkerman Company in the Old Building, cold, cavernous and draughty, where the prevailing smell was of stale cabbage and leather polish. He was taken on the Sandhurst strength on 9 September 1952 as 'Officer Cadet King Hussein'.

Many people played their part in instructing Hussein in the military art, but three of them require particular mention. One was his Company Commander, Major (now Major-General) David Horsfield; another was Major (now Colonel) David Sutherland of the Black Watch, a Highland regiment; and the third, and perhaps the most important, was the Academy Sergeant-Major, 'Jacky' Lord, of the Grenadier Guards. All three formed a high opinion of the young King, who took to soldiering like a duck to water. Horsfield has said that he did not seem to care much for the more academic side of the syllabus but shone to advantage in the practical part – drill, tactics, rifle shooting and mechanical engineering.

It was Sutherland's task to select from the syllabus those items that were felt to be of the most value in an abbreviated course of nine months. Additionally, Sutherland accompanied the King as a kind of ADC whenever he visited other military institutions. He formed a great affection for him, saying that one of his most marked characteristics was his consideration for others. He was surprisingly fatalistic for a young man of his age but nevertheless 'enormous fun'. He drove a Lincoln convertible at startlingly high speeds, his Jordanian pennant requiring replacement at very short intervals. On one occasion they visited the School of Infantry at

Warminster, arriving a little late to find the welcoming party of 'top brass' waiting for them at the top of the steps. The King was driving, and Sutherland found he could not open his own door. The King jumped out and went round to release Sutherland, who was leaning against the door. When the door opened, Sutherland fell out, landing on the ground with his kilt over his head. The waiting party tried hard to conceal their smiles, but Hussein was genuinely concerned at his friend's embarrassment. 'He went on about it for quite some time,' said Sutherland. 'It was typical of him.'[3]

Sergeant-Major Lord's influence on Hussein was less direct, but possibly the most pervasive. He was a considerable personality. Impeccable in appearance, tall and ramrod straight, he dominated the drill square on which the cadets spent so much of their time. He was fierce without being savage, sharp without being rude, and never, never sarcastic. He died, unfortunately, young, his reward being the admiration and affection in which he was held by generation after generation of cadets. One of them was Hussein. Some years later he returned to Sandhurst to take part in the television programme *This is Your Life*, which featured 'Jacky' Lord; the King was smuggled in by the Commandant's ADC in the back of his car, and Hussein's appearance on the programme gave Lord the greatest pleasure. He died not long afterwards.[4]

Life at Sandhurst was very different from Harrow School. During the week it was all go, the most heinous crime being 'late on parade'. Hours were spent polishing leather and steel until they shone like mirrors; and there were band nights in mess, wearing 'blues', with in Hussein's case the gold chevrons of a cadet corporal shining above the elbow. There were the field exercises, at which Hussein excelled, and many hours on the rifle range where he became a marksman, as his grandfather had been before him.

But it was not all work. At weekends, and in breaks during the course, there were all the attractions of London life, and frequently Paris too, where the Jordanian Military Attaché, Major Ali abu Nowar, went to great lengths to ensure that his young King enjoyed himself. Fawzi al-Mulki, still Ambassador in London, also made certain that Hussein had a good time. There was no lack of male companions, and London is after all full of attractive young women only too happy to be taken out to dinner and dance with a handsome and well-mannered young king. These were happy times that passed all too quickly.

On his return to Jordan, Hussein assumed his constitutional powers on 2 May 1953. On the very same day his cousin, Feisal, assumed his in Baghdad. In both cities the flags were out, the crowds were cheering in the streets, there were parades to be attended and dignitaries to be welcomed. It was a far cry from the Sandhurst drill square, and Hussein made the most of it. He went to bed that night a very contented young man, but ringing in his ears was his mother's warning never to let power and responsibility go to his head.

While in London, and when still a schoolboy, Hussein had met the Sharifa Dina Abdel Hamid, a great-grandniece of King Hussein of the Hejaz. She was seven years older than Hussein and intellectually inclined, having been at Girton College, Cambridge, and Cairo University. She was not only older, but also more sophisticated than Hussein, the two sharing hardly any tastes or interests; but Hussein and Dina had enjoyed dancing together and found they shared a common pride in their Hashemite ancestry. Queen Zein was keen on the match, probably because she hoped her son would settle down and produce a family. Hussein accordingly wrote to Dina to propose marriage, and she accepted. They were married on 19 April 1955, and Dina later bore Hussein a daughter, whom they named Alia. But the marriage was not a success, the discrepancy in ages and differences in interests proving to be too difficult to overcome. The King divorced Dina in the autumn of 1956 when she was in Cairo on holiday. Annoyed by the snide comments in the Cairene press, he refused to send Alia to her mother, but later relented, and mother and daughter have since seen much of each other. Dina married many years later a Palestinian 'commando', Salah Taamri, who distinguished himself in the fighting against the Israelis during their invasion of Lebanon. He was taken prisoner and Dina has recently published a book recounting the difficulties of his release.

The Jordan Hussein had inherited was no longer the gentle, smiling country his grandfather had so painstakingly brought to maturity. It was as open to the 'winds of change' as every other Arab country. Over and above the effects of nationalism, the problem of Palestine and the Palestinians had come to dominate the politics of every Arab country. It is Hussein's unhappy fate to have had to grapple with this problem virtually every day since he has been on the throne; and now, thirty-five years later, it is just as intractable as it was in the beginning.

Fawzi al-Mulki reaped the reward of his services while in London by a summons to return to Jordan to form a government. He was determined to put into practice the liberal–socialist ideas then popular in the West, particularly in the universities, and he set about freeing the press by removing the restrictions imposed during Abdullah's more conservative regime. The Communists and the Ba'athists[5] took full advantage of this new freedom to seek new converts wherever they could find them, not least in the Palestinian refugee camps, where dissidence was rife. This caused great concern, which was eventually shared by Hussein himself, who decided to replace Fawzi by Samir Rifai, a more cautious and conservative politician, who soon shut down the Communist newspaper, and made the others toe the line. Fawzi was, however, made Chief of the Royal Hashemite Court, which did not signify any diminution in his influence with the King, whom he saw almost every day. It is the second most important political office in Jordan, after that of Prime Minister.

World politics were at that time dominated by the rivalry between the United States and the Soviet Union, and by the conviction in America that Russia, under Stalin, was determined to dominate the world. It followed that the world was divided into those who opposed Communism and those who supported it – or so it seemed at the time. Where Jordan was concerned, Hussein could have no doubts. Islam and the atheistic creed of Communism were incompatible, and on that he took his stand.

From the very day he ascended the throne, Hussein had to spend much of his working life in the company of men very much older than himself; his Prime Minister, his ministers and the Chief of the General Staff, Glubb Pasha. He did, however, gather around him an inner circle of friends and advisers, closer to him in age, and in some instances in interests. Perhaps the most influential was Sharif Nasser bin Jameel, his mother's brother, who was then a captain in the Arab Legion and Hussein's personal ADC. Another was his cousin, Sharif Zeid bin Shakir, then only a lieutenant, but close to the King, as his father the Emir Shakir had been to King Abdullah. A third was Major Ali abu Nowar, who as already mentioned had come to the King's notice when he was Jordanian Military Attaché in Paris. He appeared to be the rising star in Hussein's entourage. The King had asked for his return from Paris to be made his principal ADC but Glubb had politely declined, pointing out that Ali's Paris appointment was for three years. He did not add of course that he had personally sent Ali to Paris after receiving reports of his political discussions in an Amman hotel. Where Glubb was concerned, politics and soldiering went ill together. Eventually, however, he had to yield to Hussein's wishes, after pressure from the Prime Minister, and Ali returned to promotion to lieutenant-colonel and a comfortable position at court. It was one of the many brushes Hussein was to have with Glubb Pasha over the next two years.

Ali abu Nowar belonged to a well-known family from Salt. In his early thirties, he was a dapper and well-groomed man who smiled a lot. Some people found him ingratiating and his rapid promotion did not go down too well in the Arab Legion, nor for that matter with Sharif Nasser, who never did care for him. Ali had joined the Legion towards the end of the Second World War, had been to Sandhurst and had attended the British Army Staff College at Camberley. He was therefore reasonably well trained and experienced as a staff officer. His command experience, however, was limited to the command of an infantry company for a relatively short period. He was therefore looked at askance by those who had had more experience in command, particularly by the senior bedouin officers, who regarded Ali with contempt.

As the winds of change swept away the old empires, and with them both kings and presidents, the Arab countries were principally affected by the rivalry between Egypt and Iraq for the leadership of the Arab world. This rivalry was epitomised by the two leaders, Nuri as-Said of Iraq and Gamal abdel Nasser of Egypt. Both were military men but Nuri was much the older and more experienced, having distinguished himself when fighting on the Arab side during the Great Arab Revolt. Nuri had held almost every office in the Iraq government since the establishment of the state. Nasser had come to power by a military *coup d'état* which had overthrown King Farouk in 1952. He was immensely popular in Egypt for having ended the British occupation, thereby making Egyptians feel no longer second-class citizens in their own country. Neither Nuri nor Nasser were pro-Communist, but Nasser was a pragmatist and, as he was soon to demonstrate, he was prepared to enter into relations with the Soviet Union if he could not get what he wanted from the West. Nuri on the other hand was greatly concerned by the clearly aggressive intentions of Stalin's Russia, as was indeed Turkey – Nuri was half-Turkish. Turkey took the lead in forming a defensive alliance of Muslim countries which came to be known as the Northern Tier, or more usually the Baghdad Pact. Turkey and Iraq formally signed a pact of mutual co-operation at Baghdad on 24 February 1955, to which Britain adhered on 5 April, Pakistan on 23 September, and Iran on 12 October.[6] Nasser at one time thought of joining but the prominent position taken by Iraq probably dissuaded him from doing so. He then set about deliberately to wreck it, since he wanted Egypt, not Iraq, to be the leading Arab country.

As a soldier Nasser was well aware of Egypt's vital strategic position, but he had no intention of allowing his country to be dragged into war by the coat-tails of any other power, as had happened in 1914 and again in 1939. Therefore, he was not prepared to allow Britain to retain her bases in Egypt for the purpose of containing any Soviet threat in the Middle East, and he was active in undermining British influence elsewhere in the region. He was a Pan-Arab who aspired to the leadership of the Arab people, but never at the expense of Egyptian interests. For Nasser, Egypt always came first. In his view the Baghdad Pact might conceivably undermine Egyptian influence in the region, which was something he was determined to prevent.

Jordan was faced with a very difficult problem during the four or five years following Abdullah's assassination. The Rhodes Armistice in 1949 had left her with the ill-defined border with Israel that had to be defended. Moreover, after the joining of the West and East Banks in 1950, there was a considerable accretion of territory which had to be policed and protected.

Meanwhile, in the aftermath of the war with the Jews, there was continuous raiding across the border into Israel, mostly by peasants who had been cut off from their fields by the drawing of the demarcation line. The Israelis adopted a policy, to which they have adhered ever since, of launching massive reprisals in retaliation for such raids; such a reprisal was exacted at Qibya in October 1953 when an entire village was levelled to the ground. The British commander on the West Bank, and the local battalion comman-der, who was a Jordanian, were sacked, but this did nothing to lessen the resentment among the Palestinian population; nor were matters improved when Glubb later reinstated the Jordanian officer, much to Hussein's annoyance.

The Arab Legion, not much more than 20,000 strong and consisting of little more than three infantry brigades, was hopelessly overstretched, while at the same time it was trying to cope with the modest expansion that was in train. As some form of defence Glubb had established a kind of Home Guard (Haras al Watany), which consisted of arming the border villagers and providing them with leadership from the Arab Legion. This could only be a palliative when one considers the much heavier weight of metal the Israelis could bring to bear, and it was not particularly popular on either the West or the East Banks, some people fearing that the arms might be employed in an uprising against the Jordanian regime; the Haras al Watany was disbanded in the wake of Glubb's departure. It was clear to everyone, from the King down, that the Legion had to be expanded to meet its increased commitments, but where was the money to come from?

This debate was in progress when President Bayar of Turkey paid a state visit to Amman in the autumn of 1955. He told Hussein that only by joining the Baghdad Pact could Jordan expect to get the arms and the money it needed to expand and equip the Arab Legion. Unfortunately, he added, Turkey was in no position to help, but why not approach Britain, which was not only Jordan's ally but also a member of the Pact? Hussein was enthusiastic, although his Prime Minister, Said el-Mufti, was less so, fearing possible repercussions. Another supporter of the proposal was Wasfi Tell, a Prime Minister of the future and a lifelong opponent of Nasser. His brother, Mrwede, remains of the opinion that the whole history of the region might have been altered had Jordan joined the Baghdad Pact, but he says Nasser was determined to prevent it.[7]

If Hussein was enthusiastic, so were the British. They sent Field Marshal Sir Gerald Templer, the Chief of the Imperial General Staff, to discuss ways and means; it was even suggested that Hussein might be made an honorary field marshal in the British Army as an additional inducement. More practically, they presented Jordan with a squadron of Vampire fighter planes, and offered to increase the annual subsidy in order to provide an additional infantry brigade and more logistic support. It was not as much as Hussein had hoped for – he had been asking for an increase of three infantry divisions – but it was much better than nothing. Strangely, Templer had not found Glubb Pasha as enthusiastic as the King; Glubb appears to have thought that the Arab Legion was going to be expanded far too quickly, with a corresponding drop in efficiency.

All seemed set for Jordan to join the Pact when four ministers resigned on 13 December 1955. They were all from the West Bank. They were soon joined by the Prime Minister, elderly and unwell, who as leader of the Circassian community feared lest he be accused of betraying the cause of Arabism. Hussein appointed Hazza Majali, of the well-known Kerak family, as Prime Minister in his place. He was a strong man and a supporter of the Baghdad Pact. However, he had hardly formed his Cabinet before rioting began in Amman on 16 December. It spread with alarming rapidity right across the country, prompting Hazza Majali's resignation on 19 December and the King's dissolution of parliament. Templer had already returned home, advised to stay away until conditions had returned to normal.

Nasser's wrecking tactics had worked only too well. His agents had bought support throughout Jordan, more especially in the refugee camps, and in many places mob rule took over until the Arab Legion succeeded in restoring control. This did not happen until well into January 1956, and then only at the cost of many killed both in the Legion and among the rioting mobs. By the end of it all it was clear that there could be no question of Jordan's joining the Baghdad Pact without serious risk to the throne and to Jordan's stability; and the entire proposition was quietly dropped. Inevitably, however, there was a demand for a scapegoat to account for the disturbances that had occurred, and since the Arab Legion had played the principal part in restoring law and order, it was Glubb Pasha who was vilified in most Jordanian newspapers and of course on Cairo and Damascus Radios.

It was very unfortunate in the circumstances that Hussein's relations with his principal military adviser had been deteriorating over many months. A whole host of reasons have been advanced to account for this, but perhaps the most significant was the differences in age and outlook of an elderly English gentleman and a young and impressionable Arab king. Both had great respect for each other, but the gap was too wide to be bridged. In Hussein's case, the influences of Arabism and Arab solidarity played an important part in causing the friction between them. In Glubb's, it was the need to maintain the efficiency of the Arab Legion in order to defend the West Bank against possible Israeli aggression that loomed largest in his mind; he left the politics to others. Glubb loathed politics and saw his task as solely that of a soldier.

The Arab Legion plan for the defence of the West Bank was based purely on military considerations. This meant abandoning certain areas in order to ensure the security of the vital area, which was in this case the city of Jerusalem. This made military sense at the time, as it was again to do later, but unfortunately it was politically unacceptable. Nor could it be expected that a young King brought up in the Hashemite tradition could ever contemplate abandoning *any* of his subjects to the enemy. When Glubb tried to explain the plan to the King, Hussein dismissed it out of hand. There could be no abandonment of an inch of the sacred soil of Palestine to the Israelis, who had already got more of it than they deserved. After a somewhat stormy interview, the King left the room, suggesting that perhaps the time had come for the Chief of the General Staff to enjoy the retirement his services to Jordan had so richly merited. Unfortunately for both of them, however, the King did not follow this up with an official request for Glubb's retirement. Had he done so, Glubb would unquestionably have complied without further ado.

There was undoubtedly a feeling in the country, notably among the Palestinian element, that Glubb had too much power. In view of the nationalist feelings of the times, it was hard to accept that a foreigner should be in such a position. 'The real ruler of the country is Glubb Pasha,' wrote Anwar Katib, a journalist, to Colonel J.B. Slade-Baker, another journalist, in December 1954. 'People feel he is the real King and do not like it.'[8] Glubb himself has always insisted that he steered well clear of politics, for which he had a strong aversion, but his standing in the country was such that with the best will in the world people found this hard to believe. There was too a feeling among some of the Jordanian officers in the Arab Legion that Glubb unduly favoured the bedouin element in the army. Glubb used to explain his preference, if he had one, by pointing out that 'In every country rural or mountain districts produce the best soldiers and these are likely to be those least interested in politics.'[9] He was always afraid that the Arab Legion would become involved in politics, as had happened with the Egyptian and Syrian armies, and which would soon be repeated in Iraq.

The motives of those who sought to make trouble between the King and Glubb were probably mixed; some of them honestly believed that Glubb was too old and that the time had come for him to retire. He was in fact only fifty-eight, but his white hair and moustache, and his rather old-fashioned mannerisms, made him seem much older. The King's uncle in a revealing aside in 1952 said Glubb's military training had ceased in 1926 when he joined the British administration in Iraq as an Administrative Adviser, and that thereafter his experience had been confined to the tip-and-run tactics of bedouin warfare.[10] This was not in fact correct; Glubb had read and thought deeply about the military profession, but Sharif Nasser's view of him can be easily understood. And there were those like Ali abu Nowar, of course, who thought they knew all that was needed to become brigade and battalion commanders. Only Glubb and his British officers stood in their way.

The dispatches of the British Ambassador in Amman (Charles Duke) to the Foreign Office in London during 1955 are full of apprehension about the way things were going. It is clear that Glubb shared his concern but was at a loss to know what to do for the best. One of the Foreign Office's principal *bêtes noires* during this anxious period was Wing Commander Dalgliesh, who was commanding the RJAF. Dalgliesh was a fine pilot and an excellent flying instructor, and it was he who satisfied Hussein's burning desire to learn to fly. The Queen Mother, the Prime Minister and Glubb were violently opposed to it and put every obstacle they could in the King's path. Dalgliesh was the man who had flown Hussein back from Jerusalem after his grandfather's assassination and he enjoyed a friendly relationship with the King. He was therefore placed in an extremely difficult position. After yielding to Hussein's request to take him up for a lesson, he put the plane through a whole series of aerobatics before returning to the ground, hoping that the experience would put the King off flying for ever more. Hussein did in fact turn green, and when putting foot to ground was violently sick. But once this spasm was over, he turned to Dalgliesh and said, 'When is the next lesson?'[11] Dalgliesh had little choice than to continue with the flying lessons, although this brought him into conflict with Glubb, who accused him of being disloyal. Relations between the two men could hardly have been worse.

This came out into the open when the time came for Dalgliesh's loan service with the Arab Legion to end. This was in the latter months of 1955. Hussein wanted his tour to be extended but Glubb made no move to effect this. In a letter to the Foreign Office in October 1955, the Ambassador reported an interview with the Court Minister, Fawzi al-Mulki, in which Fawzi had said: 'The cause of the King's ill humour towards Glubb, he [Fawzi] thought, was probably our insistence on replacing Dalgliesh which he said had annoyed the King. . . .'[12] Prior to the receipt of this letter, Evelyn Shuckburgh of the Foreign Office had minuted on the file: 'Is W/ Cdr Dalgliesh impervious to our advice or could we ask him for help?' – presumably to improve relations between the King and Glubb. In reply it was minuted: 'W/Cdr Dalgliesh is a "King's man" and . . . it would really be useless to ask or expect him to influence the King in the way we want, unless that happened to coincide with the King's whim.'[13] Dalgliesh's return to the RAF followed soon thereafter but, fortunately for Hussein, Jordan had not seen the last of him.

As there continued to be no improvement in relations, Glubb wrote the Ambassador a very depressed letter in October 1955. Reporting this, Duke told the Foreign Office: 'I think it may well be that there are certain aspects of the running of the Arab Legion which date from the days when it was a small and more or less tribal force under the somewhat patriarchal administration of Abdullah and Glubb, and that some reorganisation is necessary to take account of the expanded size and less homogeneous character of the Legion now. . . .' He was undoubtedly right.

Cooke Pasha, Glubb's senior British officer, was clearly aware of what was happening when he commented at a private dinner party in May 1955, that 'The Pasha is having a very rough ride with the King and seems to be heading for a fall.'[14] It is therefore surprising that very few of the British officers serving with the Arab Legion at that time were similarly aware. This can probably be explained by the fact that the majority of them were living in the military cantonment at Zerqa, some miles from Amman, and only a very few spoke and read enough Arabic to read Jordanian newspapers and listen to Amman Radio. In any case, as is the tradition in the British Army, they did not involve themselves in political issues but concentrated on the training and the administration of the units under their command. There was, moreover, no visible change in the attitudes of their Jordanian subordinates, either at work or on social occasions, although the rioting against the Baghdad Pact at the end of 1955 had come as an unpleasant surprise. The Arab Legion had been stretched almost to breaking point to deal with it. The effect on Glubb himself similarly seems to have escaped them, although a British journalist who visited Jordan in the aftermath of the riots later told the British Ambassador in Cairo, Humphrey Trevelyan, that he did not give Glubb another three months in office, so low had his stock fallen.[15] The British Military Attaché in Baghdad, visiting Amman on his way to Beirut, had reached the same conclusion. Glubb, although outwardly composed and going about his business, was inwardly shaken. The future indeed looked gloomy.

CHAPTER FOUR

Dropping the Pilot

'. . . Glubb Pasha gave to this country great and distinguished service.' King Hussein[1]

The pilot in this case was General Glubb, whose relations with the King had reached the point of no return early in 1956. For some time talk of his replacement had been common gossip among Hussein's inner circle, according to Wing Commander Dalgliesh. He says he knew of the King's intention before leaving Jordan on posting back to the RAF late in 1955, adding that, had he told anyone, he would not have been believed.[2] Baron Alexis Wrangel, in Jordan as Director of the Tolstoy Foundation, also knew what was in the wind; he had been told by his Circassian friends. He did try to warn Glubb but failed to make contact with him.[3] It is surprising in the circumstances that Glubb's dismissal came as such a shock, not only to the British officers then serving in the Arab Legion, but even to the British Ambassador, Charles Duke, who was stunned by the news.

The decision to dismiss Glubb was taken by the King alone. He did not tell his Court Minister, Bahjat Talhouni, who had succeeded Fawzi al-Mulki, until the two drove to the Prime Minister's office on the morning of 1 March 1956. There Hussein confronted the equally surprised Samir Rifai with the royal edict, drafted by Hussein himself. He had taken the action partly on account of his sense of public opinion, and partly as a result of his commitment to Arabism. It was not in a fit of pique, as has sometimes been alleged, nor owing to pressure from his inner circle. One Arab writer attributes Glubb's unpopularity 'to the influx of the Palestinians into the political system of Jordan'.[4] This may have been so, but it had nothing to do with the King's conviction that in the cause of Arabism Jordan must be seen to be independent of British tutelage. That meant Arabising the Arab Legion, regardless of the services rendered by Glubb Pasha and the other British officers, to which the King paid tribute many times over when calmer times returned.

It has sometimes been claimed that Glubb's dismissal resulted from a conspiracy of young nationalistically minded Jordanian officers who were close to the King. This was not the case. There was of course a Free Officers Movement within the Arab Legion at the time. It had existed since 1954 and was modelled on the one in the Egyptian army headed by Gamal abdel Nasser, which had overthrown King Farouk. Hussein's friend and ADC, Ali abu Nowar, was a prominent member of the Jordanian Movement, and it can be taken for granted that Hussein as an ardent Arab nationalist was fully aware of this. But the King alone decided to dismiss Glubb; there was no one else. Glubb himself laid the blame at Nasser's door but, as Anwar Sadat has made clear, when the news reached Cairo it surprised Nasser just as much as it surprised everyone else.

The outcry in Britain over Glubb's dismissal astonished Hussein, who had not reckoned with such a storm of protest. He had acted in accordance with his constitutional prerogatives, as Glubb himself had been the first to recognise. The reaction of the British Prime Minister, Anthony Eden, was almost hysterical, to be described fifty years later as 'totally absurd' by Harold Macmillan, Chancellor of the Exchequer in Eden's Cabinet.[5] It is said that when the news of Glubb's dismissal first reached him, Eden exclaimed angrily, 'Why did the fellow allow it to happen?' – as though Glubb, as Chief of the General Staff of the Arab Legion, was in some fashion above the law.

It was not so much Glubb's dismissal as the manner of it that so outraged British public opinion. Glubb had come to be regarded as some kind of latterday T.E. Lawrence. Samir Rifai had at first proposed that Glubb should leave the country within two hours. When Glubb indignantly rejected this, pointing out that after twenty-six years everything he possessed was in Jordan, they compromised on seven o'clock the next morning, which was short enough in all conscience. Hussein was to make it clear later that he sympathised with Glubb over this.[6]

The need for haste on the Prime Minister's part probably arose from fear of some kind of sympathetic uprising in the Arab Legion in support of Glubb, particularly in the bedouin regiments, where he was regarded by many as a father figure. The longer he remained in the country, the more likely it was that there would be trouble. Glubb had in fact given the strictest instructions to General Cooke, the next senior British officer, that there were to be no manifestations of support of any kind. He wanted no Jordanian blood spilled on his account. The royal edict was to be strictly obeyed. This was faithfully observed by the British officers, bewildered though they were by the turn of events. They certainly succeeded in calming some of the wilder Jordanian spirits, many of whom believed that the King was acting under some kind of duress.

Further confusion was undoubtedly caused by some of the reasons advanced for the King's action. One was an alleged shortage in the ammunition reserves, owing to Glubb's policy. There was, however, no shortage, the reserves being calculated by the same method as the British

Army's. This has been confirmed by General Hutton, Glubb's Chief of Staff in the rank of brigadier, who had personally checked the ammunition a few months previously.[7] Glubb was in any case the last man who would economise in ammunition, having lively memories of the Egyptians' confiscation of ammunition destined for the Arab Legion at the height of the battle for Jerusalem in 1948. It had reduced the artillery to only a few rounds per gun. In this particular instance the King had obviously been misinformed.

Hussein had no intention of dispensing entirely with British assistance for his armed forces. He knew only too well how much they depended on the subsidy provided by the British government. But he did intend to remove all British officers from any kind of executive post, replacing them by Jordanians, while at the same time retaining a reduced number of British officers purely in a training capacity. A training mission was in fact formed in the wake of Glubb Pasha's departure, headed by Lieutenant-Colonel E.V.M. Strickland, who had until then been commanding one of the Arab Legion's armoured-car regiments. Strickland succeeded in establishing good relations with Ali abu Nowar, after Ali had been promoted major-general and appointed Chief of the General Staff in June 1956. However, the training mission proved to be short-lived. It was dissolved in October 1956 after the Anglo-French–Israeli attack on Egypt. For a time after the Suez Crisis Anglo-Jordanian relations were bad, Hussein feeling that he had been doublecrossed by Britain, Jordan's ally, when it went to war against an Arab state in collusion with Israel, Jordan's enemy.

It can be said, however, that Glubb Pasha emerged with the most credit from this unhappy episode in Anglo-Jordanian relations. Neither at the time, nor later, did he criticise King Hussein. He even wrote to defend him in a letter to the *Daily Telegraph*, in which he made it plain that the King was acting entirely within his rights in replacing him. The British government, after all the sound and fury, did nothing to compensate Glubb for his dismissal other than to confer a knighthood on him. It refused to provide a pension for him in his rank of lieutenant-general, and was not even willing to give him a gratuity. It did not offer him any employment and virtually washed its hands of him. It was left to King Hussein some years later to put the record straight, which he did in his usual generous fashion.

With the passage of time, most Jordanians have come to recognise Glubb Pasha's services to their country. This is particularly so in the case of the Jordanian armed forces. But the shadow of Palestine still hangs over Anglo-Jordanian relations, and although Glubb was entirely sympathetic to the Arab cause, there are still those who find it hard to forgive anyone who is British. One day, no doubt, there will be a Jordanian historian who will be able to set down Glubb's services in proper perspective, but until then it must be expected that he will have to bear some share of the blame for the British government's policy in Palestine. Although he retained his deep affection for Jordan until his dying day, as well as his great respect for the Hashemite Crown, Glubb, despite many pressing invitations, never returned to Jordan, preferring to retain his memory of the country as it was when last he saw it.

The plain fact is that Glubb Pasha had outlived his time in Jordan. Through no fault of his own, he had in a sense become an anachronism. He was however a great and a good man, whose legacy to Jordan was an army of which any country could be proud. That is not a bad epitaph.

Although the Palestinians greeted the news of Glubb Pasha's departure by dancing in the streets, it caused a good deal of consternation elsewhere. Glubb had been around for so long that he constituted something of a landmark. Although the Arabisation of the Arab Legion was marked by a change of title to the Jordan Arab Army, there were still those who hankered after the old title, of which they were proud; even today, many years after the event, there are still veterans who refer to themselves as having been in the Arab Legion. They are to be found in Britain as well as in Jordan. Meanwhile, in the world outside Jordan, the events in that country soon vanished from newspaper front pages as Britain and France drew nearer and nearer to a showdown with Egypt, as a result of President Nasser's nationalisation of the Suez Canal. Within weeks, 'l'affaire Glubb Pasha' had become history.

With the rift in relations with Britain, however, Jordan was now out on its own, at a time when the whole of the Middle East was in a ferment. Something had to be done about this and Hussein bent all his energies to securing friends for his country in the Arab world, to which he attached overwhelming importance. He paid visits to every Arab capital in order to demonstrate personally that Jordan now stood on its own two feet. Egypt had entered into a defence pact with Saudi Arabia and Syria which Hussein contemplated joining, only to discover in Baghdad that Prime Minister Nuri as-Said attached no significance to such a grouping, unless Iraq played the leading role, something to which Nasser could never agree.

It seemed to the Jordanians, as well as to the British, that Israel intended to take full advantage of the unsettled situation in Jordan by stirring up trouble in the West Bank. On 10 October 1956, they launched a particularly heavy punitive attack against Qalqilya, allegedly in reprisal for *fedayeen**

---

* *Fedayeen* means literally, 'Those who sacrifice themselves'. It has come to be associated with the Palestine Liberation Organisation as an alternative name for commandos or militia.

raids into Israeli territory. It was a typically heavy-handed Israeli reprisal for the deaths of two Israeli farmers. Hussein at once invoked the Anglo-Jordan treaty, asking for air support. The British government at the time was deeply involved in planning the attack on Egypt over the Suez Canal, and had no wish to become involved in a Jordan–Israel quarrel. It therefore referred Hussein to Iraq for support, at the same time bringing pressure to bear on Iraq to provide it. Nuri was not unwilling, but then the French intervened, fearful lest the presence of Iraqi troops and planes in Jordan might frighten off the Israelis with whom, as we now know, they were involved in the most delicate negotiations.

It is difficult to recall today the very complex situation in the autumn of 1956 in the Middle East, when Britain and France were planning the Suez operation. Despite the machinations taking place between London and Paris, it is clear that the British Chiefs of Staff were not fully aware of what was pending on the political level. Alarmed by reports of the military build-up in Israel, and unaware that this was directed against Egypt, the British Chiefs of Staff assumed that it was preliminary to an attack to seize the West Bank from Jordan. Preparations were made accordingly to go to Jordan's aid. Three aircraft carriers in the Mediterranean were put in a state of readiness; RAF fighter-bomber squadrons were positioned in Cyprus; and a parachute battalion was placed on full alert. All this was preparatory to an attack on Israel in support of Jordan! However, by 24 October, the British Prime Minister had agreed the plan whereby Israel would attack Egypt on 29 October, to be followed two days later by the launching of air attacks against Egypt by Britain and France. To complicate what was already a complicated enough situation, Jordan entered into a military alliance with Egypt and Syria on 25 October, which was entirely in accordance with Hussein's commitment to Arab solidarity.

The confused and gloomy political situation notwithstanding, Hussein at the time was riding on the crest of the wave. Although there were those who regretted Glubb Pasha's departure, and others in the army who bitterly resented Ali abu Nowar's meteoric promotion from major to major-general in less than three years, everyone could take pride in the fact that Jordan's army was now wholly Arab. Moreover, the replacement of the British had meant promotions all round, lieutenants and captains finding themselves majors and lieutenant-colonels almost overnight. They would have been more than human had they not welcomed this development. Hussein's obvious commitment to Arab unity and solidarity, as well as to the cause of Palestine, added enormously to his popularity; as did the trouble he took to travel round the country, talking with the people and visiting his soldiers. And now he came accompanied by his own Jordanian entourage, and not as before in the shadow of Glubb Pasha.

But it was not all euphoria. Those who in the public mind had become too closely associated with Glubb and the British found it expedient to retire into the background for a time, while others who chose to confound liberty with licence soon learned of their mistake. Hussein's uncle, Sharif Nasser bin Jameel, Queen Zein's brother, with an eye to possible trouble in the future, persuaded the King to form a Royal Bodyguard of picked men, most of them bedouins, with himself, Sharif Nasser, as their commander. They were to prove their worth in the troubled times ahead.

The six months between October 1956 and April 1957 were to prove to be Hussein's first real test. That he survived it successfully was due chiefly to his own courage and to the support he was given by his bedouin soldiers. The test began on 21 October when Jordan went to the polls for the first truly free elections to be held in the country. Hussein had insisted on this. Voting took place in an atmosphere of fury, whipped up by Israel's reprisal raids across the armistice line against West Bank towns and villages. Palestinians were clamouring for war, encouraged to do so by the media in Cairo and Damascus. Hussein was offered military support by Egypt, Syria and Iraq for any operation he chose to undertake against Israel, but he was wise enough to decline such offers with thanks. It was no time to go to war with a partially mobilised Israel. In the meantime the election results were announced. It was a victory for the left, headed by a West Bank lawyer, Suleiman Naboulsi, who was distrusted by the more conservative elements in the country. Naboulsi had a nimble mind, a quick eye for an opportunity, and a somewhat flexible political philosophy; Kirkbride observed that ten years earlier, when he first knew Naboulsi, he had been a staunch conservative. The King, however, despite some misgivings, invited him to form a government. This was applauded by General Ali abu Nowar, who had already managed to insinuate himself into Naboulsi's good books.

During his brief reign, King Talal had introduced a more liberal constitution in Jordan. This made the Cabinet responsible to parliament, instead of as previously to the King. Hussein probably favoured such a liberal approach and he therefore allowed Naboulsi to choose his own Cabinet, rather than as hitherto forming it with ministers of whom the King approved. Hussein also gave tentative approval to Naboulsi's proposal to terminate the Anglo-Jordan treaty, although this had not been in Hussein's mind when he set about Arabising the army. He was concerned about the British subsidy, but Naboulsi was confident that aid would be given by other Arab states instead. In this he was to be disappointed. It is also interesting that the British government was not so averse to the termination of the Anglo-Jordan treaty as has sometimes been assumed. According to Sir Charles Johnston, the British Ambassador in Amman at the time, the Foreign Office were as keen to terminate the treaty as Naboulsi was, saving thereby the cost of the British subsidy and avoiding the possibility of being dragged into a war with Israel at Jordan's side.[8]

Hussein has said that he assumed full responsibility for the new experiment in government. He felt the time had come to throw off Jordan's dependency on non-Arab assistance in favour of Arab solidarity; and at the same time to replace the older politicians by younger men with more modern democratic views. 'I had decided', he said, 'that younger and promising politicians and army officers should have a chance to show their mettle. I realised that many were very leftist, but I felt that even so most of them must genuinely believe in the future of their country, and I wanted to see how they would react to responsibility.' At the same time as taking this bold decision, but before inviting Naboulsi to form a government, Hussein concluded a new military pact with Egypt and Syria on 24 October 1956, whereby the armed forces of the three countries were placed under the command of the Egyptian general, Abdel Hakim Amer. As a gesture of solidarity, Amer flew to Amman on 25 October to attend the King's state opening of parliament.

Any rejoicing there might have been was quickly overtaken by events. On 31 October the Anglo-French assault on Egypt was launched by the bombing of Egyptian airfields. This had been preceded two nights previously by the seizure of the strategic Mitla Pass in Sinai by an Israeli parachute battalion. The collusion of the British and the French with Israel outraged Hussein. He immediately telephoned Nasser to offer Jordan's help, but Nasser advised him to stay out of the battle. He was aiming more for a political victory than a military one, in view of the odds against him. The British Ambassador received a frosty reception when he tried to justify Britain's action to Hussein. The British Army training mission was told to start packing, and the British became even more unpopular in Jordan. Syria and Saudi Arabia were invited to send troops to Jordan. The Iraqis, ready and waiting at Rutba, were also invited to enter Jordanian territory.

All seemed set for war when there was a surprising development. When the King ordered an advance from Jenin into Israel, the Cabinet refused to heed the King's order. Naboulsi considered that to do so would be absurd in the circumstances. He also criticised the King for having invited foreign forces to enter Jordan, particularly the Iraqis, who were not members of the new defence pact. In any case it was the government's prerogative, not the King's, to issue such an invitation. Naboulsi then announced his intention of opening diplomatic relations with the Soviet Union and Communist China, a proposal that cut clean across the King's often expressed opposition to Communism. Samir Rifai and other experienced Jordanian politicians like him regarded Naboulsi's policies with dismay. So did Hussein. Although Communist newspapers had long been outlawed in Jordan,

Naboulsi lifted the ban at the end of 1956 and *Al-Jamaheer* soon appeared on the streets.

Naboulsi was an intriguer and an opportunist with connections in both Egypt and Syria, neither of which was well disposed toward Jordan and the Hashemites. Hussein became convinced towards the end of 1956 that his Prime Minister, working in collusion with Nasser and the Syrians, was actively plotting against him. The Security Service was being infiltrated by Naboulsi, agents were being suborned, and every impediment was being placed in the way of Bahjat Tabara, the Head of Security (Mukhabarat). It was well known that certain army officers were being bribed. The division in the army between the bedouins and those recruited from the settled areas, which had always existed to some extent, became intensified, the bedouins resenting the fact that they were losing out to their better educated townsmen colleagues in the race for promotion. In January 1957 an Arab Solidarity Agreement was signed. This provided Jordan with an annual subsidy of £12.5 million for ten years, to be paid by Egypt, Syria and Saudi Arabia. At least one Jordanian officer did not believe the Agreement was worth the paper it was printed on. In the event it became increasingly difficult to extract the money, although at the time it was hailed as a remarkable manifestation of 'Arab Brotherhood'.

Hussein was more and more concerned by the increasingly leftward trend of Naboulsi's government. 'We'll all be Communists soon,' one bedouin officer commented.[9] Jordan's stability depended almost entirely on the loyalty of the army, already strained in some instances as a result of Glubb Pasha's dismissal; and rumours that some of the officers were being suborned intensified the King's anxiety. Sharif Nasser was equally concerned, passing on his fears to his nephew. There seemed to be a black cloud hanging over Jordan that might turn into a hurricane at any moment. When President Eisenhower submitted a resolution to Congress on 5 January 1957, by which he would be authorised to commit American troops in defence of any Middle Eastern country threatened by overt Communist aggression, Hussein acted swiftly. Although the Eisenhower Doctrine, as it came to be known, was not endorsed by the Congress until March, Hussein wrote a letter to Naboulsi on 2 February in which he clearly expressed his fears to his Prime Minister. Immediately thereafter he released the contents of the letter to the press.

The King made it plain that he was unhappy with the measures being taken by Naboulsi's government. He complained about the strange beliefs and views that appeared to be current. He feared lest Jordan, having broken off the chains of one kind of imperialism, might find itself 'enslaved' by another. He was referring of course to Communism, to which he was unalterably opposed. Quite apart from the religious aspect, Communism was directly contrary to the spirit of Arabism, setting country against country, class against class. He required stern action to be taken by the government to stop the rot. 'The standing laws and regulations of this country will provide you with ample opportunity to act,' he wrote.

The letter infuriated Naboulsi and his closest colleagues, who included General Ali abu Nowar. In an audience with Hussein, Naboulsi tried to persuade him to withdraw the letter. Hussein refused. The Prime Minister then took steps to leak to the press the fact that the King and his ministers were in disagreement. This was flashed all over the Arab world. The banning of the Soviet daily bulletin followed, by the King's command, resulting in the close-down of the Communist *Al-Jamaheer* after only two months of publication. Both King and Cabinet were preparing for a showdown.

CHAPTER FIVE

A Coup that Failed

'Courage is the thing. All goes if courage goes. . . .'[1]

Hussein's chief concern was his army. He was also worried by the reports he was receiving of the increasing involvement in politics of his recently appointed commander of the army, General Ali abu Nowar. He and some other senior officers were reported to have held talks with the Soviet Military Attaché in Damascus. Other officers were enjoying a lifestyle in Beirut that their army pay would certainly not have permitted. It looked as if the army might begin to fall apart as a result of opposing political factions inside it. This had after all happened elsewhere, and not only in the Arab world. Jordan's stability depended on the army and the King was right to feel concern.

After his appointment as Chief of the General Staff, Ali abu Nowar had lost no time in reorganising the army. He broke up the previous divisional organisation into five separate infantry brigades under his direct control from GHQ (Qyada) in Amman, wherever possible placing officers who shared his views in the important posts. His deputy, for example, was General Ali Hiyyari, an experienced officer but Ali's cousin. Another close associate, Muhammad al-Mai'atar, was to take over the key appointment as Head of Security from Bahjat Tabara. Similar changes were being made in the command of regiments and battalions, resulting in discontent among those who found themselves being passed over. Naturally Hussein came to hear of this discontent but was reluctant to interfere with the man he had so recently promoted to be his chief military adviser.

Jordan's principal military base was at Zerqa, a small town about eleven miles from Amman on the main road to Mafraq and the Syrian border. It had permanent water from the Wadi Zerqa and had been one of the watering stations on the Pilgrim Road (Darb al-Hajj) from Damascus to Medina and Mecca. In the 1870s Sultan Abdul Hamid had settled there the Chechen, a Muslim tribe driven out of the Caucasus by the Russians, to protect the watering places from marauding bedouins and to cultivate the fertile lands. Later Zerqa became the main cantonment of the Trans-Jordan Frontier Force until its disbandment in 1947, when the Arab Legion took over the military installations, consisting of workshops, stores, schools of instruction and quarters for officers and soldiers. Alongside the numerous military camps there had grown up since 1948 a large refugee camp occupied by several thousand Palestinians, driven from their homes and farms across the River Jordan. Most of them could find only menial employment in the military cantonment and were inevitably discontented and ripe for trouble.

More than half the army was on the West Bank, but Zerqa still contained a substantial garrison which included the Emira Alia infantry brigade, and one tank and two armoured-car regiments. Of the infantry brigade's three battalions, one was bedouin, as were both the armoured-car regiments. The tank regiment was non-bedouin, as was the artillery regiment in support of the infantry brigade. The 1st Armoured-Car Regiment was fiercely loyal to the King, considering itself a *corps d'élite*, and resenting the fact that its new commanding officer appointed by Ali abu Nowar was not a bedouin. Lieutenant-Colonel Ma'an abu Nowar was the brigade commander. Although a cousin of Ali's, Ma'an has always insisted that he was not a member of the Free Officers Movement, although of course he knew of it; but his very name was to make him an object of suspicion at a time when the bedouins were convinced that some kind of a plot was afoot to get rid of the King.

Hussein was the first to act by sending a message to Presidents Nasser and Quwatly (of Syria) emphasising the need for all the Arab states to stand shoulder to shoulder to combat any threat to their religion. He was obviously referring to Communism. Naboulsi responded by delivering a fiery address in Amman, with a well-known Communist standing beside him. This was followed by a riot during which the police were not very effective in restoring order. Conditions were deteriorating so fast that Hussein was virtually isolated in his palace. It was his belief in the Hashemite mission, his dedication to Islam and his devotion to Arabism which sustained him in that dark hour. Several army officers, outraged by Ali abu Nowar's behaviour, had resigned their commissions. They included Sharif Nasser. The mob appeared on the streets, orchestrated by Naboulsi's supporters, and Cairo Radio incessantly plugged Nasser's support for Naboulsi. The general impression seemed to be that Hussein could not possibly survive.[2]

On 8 April he was surprised to learn that the approaches to Amman had been blocked by the 1st Armoured-Car Regiment. Ali abu Nowar explained that it was only a routine check, but Hussein was furious. He was not taken in by the explanation and ordered the soldiers' withdrawal. They were mystified by the entire affair, not having any idea of what was happening. The following evening, 9 April, Sharif Nasser and several other members of the Royal Family saw the King. The news was grave. The army was uncertain, the police virtually useless, and the mob was standing by. 'Are you going to stand and fight, or should we all pack our bags?' they asked. Everyone knew that Arab revolutions could be bloody. But Hussein's courage did not fail him. 'I am going to stand and fight,' he replied, 'whatever the consequences.'

It was the month of the Ramadan Fast, one of the most trying of all religious observances, when not a morsel of food nor a sip of water may pass the lips from dawn to sunset; tempers become frayed, the digestion suffers and the simplest decisions become difficult. The Fast provided an additional complication, and it seemed to some that the stars in their courses were fighting against Hussein. On the morning of 10 April he received an intercepted cable from Nasser to Naboulsi. 'Do not give in,' he read. 'Remain in your position.' It was clear whom Nasser was backing.

On that same morning Hussein sent Bahjat Talhouni, the Court Minister, to demand the government's resignation. Naboulsi had ordered the retirement of Talhouni and the Chief of Security on the previous day without consulting the King. He did not comply with Hussein's demand without first consulting Ali abu Nowar, who advised he should resign. Ali probably saw himself as Prime Minister in a matter of days. Naboulsi's departure was followed by riots in the main towns. In Zerqa the army was restive. Cairo Radio excelled itself in vituperation. All the King's efforts to form a new government failed. First, Hussein Fakhri Khalidi, a West Banker, and then Abdel Halim Nimer had been unable to gather the necessary support. Finally the King turned to the veteran Said el-Mufti, a Circassian who had greeted his grandfather to Amman in 1921 and played a prominent part in the country's politics ever since.

As soon as Ali abu Nowar learned of this he invited Said el-Mufti to a meeting at an army camp in Amman, where Said was told that the army's preference was for Nimer. He should return at once to the King and acquaint him of this fact. He was also to tell the King that unless a government had been formed by nine o'clock that evening, Ali abu Nowar and his colleagues (Ali Hiyyari and Muhammad al Mai'atar were also present at the meeting) would not be responsible for anything that might happen that night. It was an ultimatum – repeated later by Ali abu Nowar personally to Talhouni.

It was while Hussein was struggling to form a government acceptable both to himself and to the army that a letter was delivered at the Palace. It was from a body of loyal officers who admitted themselves worried and puzzled by the orders they were receiving. They had heard that certain units were to surround Amman. They lacked confidence in some of their senior officers. This letter was followed on 13 April by the arrival of an officer from the 1st Armoured-Car Regiment, Abdul Rahman Sabila, who reported a meeting held by Lieutenant-Colonel Nazir Rashid with certain of his officers. Rashid had told them that the regiment must be ready to move at the shortest notice to Amman, where it was to surround and capture the Royal Palace, and with it the King. In answer to a question by Hussein, Abdul Rahman Sabila replied that there were traitors everywhere, but not in the 1st Armoured-Car Regiment. Its officers had met in secret and sworn an oath of loyalty to the King. They would pretend to go along with their commanding officer, at the same time keeping the King informed. Hussein thanked him warmly and advised him to return to his regiment. He and his fellow officers were not to reveal their real feelings until the last, vital moment. After dismissing the officer, Hussein sank back in his chair. It seemed to be the last straw. Who could he trust?

Bedouin can be very secretive. They can also be very impulsive. The two words most often on their lips are Allah (God) and sharaf (honour). For weeks on end the bedouin units in Zerqa and elsewhere had been debating among themselves. Their honour was at stake. If they allowed the King, direct descendant of the Prophet, to go under, their names would be blackened for ever. As the long, thirsty day drew to a close, and men listened for the evening gun, the call to prayer, and the meal that would follow, minds were being made up. They would fight *for*, and not *against* the King, and to hell with their commanding officer!

Back in the Palace Hussein was feeling jaded and dispirited. All the news was bad. He had not slept well for days. He longed for the first cup of tea of the day and a cigarette. He had no real idea of which way to turn. Earlier in the afternoon Baron Wrangel had called on him, making his way with difficulty through the crowded streets packed with shouting and excited crowds, among whom he says he recognised several well-known Egyptian agitators. Wrangel, who had been friendly with the King during the good times, wanted to assure him of his friendship during the bad. That was the purpose of his call on Hussein. On the previous evening he had had a meeting with two of the army's senior Circassian officers, Izzat Hassan and Fawaz Maher, both of them brigadiers. They had asked Wrangel what he thought of the situation. Wrangel had replied: 'In a similar situation in 1917 the Russian Tsar abdicated and threw Russia into chaos and Communism. Some hundred years before that a French general, Napoleon Bonaparte, trotted out his artillery and blew the crowds off the streets!' Wrangel says that evidently his remarks were not lost on his Circassian friends, since within twenty-four hours Amman was ringed by bedouin soldiers.[3]

Shortly after Wrangel had left the Palace, where he had received a warm welcome from Hussein, Ali abu Nowar arrived to see the King. Angrily the King began to cross-question him. Then the telephone rang. The call was for Ali from Ma'an abu Nowar in Zerqa. Ma'an's voice was very agitated.

The situation there was out of control, Ma'an told Ali. 'The whole brigade believe that their King is dead, or will be tonight. Their officers cannot control them. They are trying to move on Amman. Nothing can save the situation but the immediate presence of His Majesty.'

Ali seemed to be paralysed; all the bounce had gone out of him. He looked at the King, who snatched the telephone from him. 'I'll be right over!', he told Ma'an. Telling Ali to wait, Hussein ran out of the office. He told Bahjat Talhouni to get a car quickly. Then he sent two of his ADCs, his cousin Sharif Zeid bin Shakir and Majid Haj Hassan, who commanded his personal escort, ahead of him to Zerqa, where they were to report the King's well-being and his intention to visit Zerqa that evening. In the meantime all troops were to return to barracks. Hussein changed into uniform.

He took Ali abu Nowar with him to Zerqa, and also Sharif Nasser. Hussein sat in the front with the driver. He has said he had never felt so angry in his life. On the way, at Ruseifa, they met a lorry-load of troops and civilians, all clamouring to be led to Amman. When Hussein jumped out to be recognised, they went berserk, mobbing and kissing him as they swore they were his men. Hussein persuaded them to go back to Zerqa before returning to his car. He found Ali cowering behind the vehicle lest he should be recognised. He begged Hussein to let him return to Amman. He said the soldiers had been yelling for his blood and he had his family to consider.

Hussein dismissed him contemptuously. Ali was told to return to the Palace and wait there for the King's return. Hussein drove on to Zerqa, uncertain of the kind of reception he would receive in the gathering darkness. He found a milling mass of shouting and excited men, soldiers and civilians, firing shots into the air and calling for the execution of all traitors. Nothing so far in Hussein's reign has become him more than his conduct at that moment. It was like a reincarnation of the Arab Revolt when Feisal had swept into Damascus. Moving freely among the excited soldiery, shaking innumerable hands, embracing and being embraced, Hussein tried to calm them by his mere presence. He was perfectly all right, he told them. They were to return to barracks and resume their duties. Searching for the two ADCs he had sent ahead of him, he found they had been placed under guard. It had been assumed they were among the conspirators! With some difficulty Hussein had them released. By then it was midnight and the excitement was dying down.

He returned to find the Palace ringed by the 1st Armoured-Car Regiment. The wretched Ali was waiting in Hussein's study. He had told Bahjat Talhouni that the King had sent him back to reassure Bahjat and the rest of the Palace staff. When the armoured-car regiment had arrived, Ali, doubtless thinking they were part of the plot, had gone out to greet them.

He was confronted by a senior NCO, sten gun in hand, who ordered him back inside. Had it been anywhere else than the King's Palace, he told Ali, he would have blown his brains out. The Palace corridors were thronged with troops, shouting 'Death to Communism! Death to abu Nowar and all traitors!' Ali had broken down under the strain and was in very poor shape.

The event that had triggered off the army mutiny in Zerqa and brought about Ali's downfall was an order for the bedouin battalion in the Emira Alia infantry brigade to move out into the desert forty miles east of Zerqa. According to Ma'an abu Nowar these manoeuvres had been planned for some time, but suspicions had been aroused by instructions that no ammunition was to be taken. In view of the tension then prevailing among the troops, this was a sensible precaution, but it led to the inference that Ma'an's bedouin unit was being kept out of the way *without ammunition*, leaving the field clear for the non-bedouin units to deal with the King. Throughout the morning and afternoon of 13 April Zerqa camp buzzed with rumours, until finally towards evening the bedouin soldiers took up arms. Fighting broke out between them and the artillery, and it spread rapidly, hooligan elements from the refugee camp joining in to make hay while the sun shone. Shops were looted, the cinema was set on fire and shooting became general. Ma'an, surrounded by angry soldiers in his headquarters, completely lost control. Hence his telephone call to the Palace. He insists to this day that he had no idea what caused the mutiny, and that if there was a plan for a coup he was certainly not party to it.

Although Hussein was not convinced of Ma'an's innocence, the fact remains that at the subsequent court-martial Ma'an was acquitted, although many other officers were found guilty and sentenced to death. The King commuted their sentences to long terms of imprisonment. Ma'an says his trial was entirely fair but he was rearrested after acquittal and tried for a second time, again being found not guilty. In such unsettled times, doubtless the opportunity was being taken to settle old scores, and no member of the abu Nowar family could expect to be given the benefit of the doubt. But after a period in the wilderness Ma'an was honourably reinstated in the army, in which he rose to the rank of major-general, later going on to be Jordan's Ambassador in London, a government minister and Mayor of Amman. Many of the officers who had been judged guilty at their court-martial were similarly reinstated in due course. Hussein never allowed feelings of revenge to sway his judgement. Had it been Baghdad or Damascus it would have been a different story. In those cities there would certainly have been a bloodbath.

Hussein was almost at the end of his tether when he returned from Zerqa. He summoned Ali to his private study, thinking of the friendship they had enjoyed, the long talks on Jordan's future, the shared confidences. Now the trim young General was a broken man, begging for his life as the tears streamed down his cheeks. The young King felt nothing but contempt for his former friend and confidant. He deserved to die for treason. Might that not make him a martyr? Far better to throw him out like an old shoe. Let him go on leave until things had settled down. 'All right,' said Hussein. 'Go!' He sent Ali to spend the night with Said el-Mufti's brother, Shawket el-Mufti, a doctor, who to his disgust had to spend the night plying Ali with whisky and cigarettes until a plane could fly him to Egypt. Some years later Hussein granted him a free pardon and Ali returned to Jordan, where he took up a commercial career with some success. He probably made a better entrepreneur than a soldier. However, it is only fair to say that Ali abu Nowar has always maintained that he had never intended to carry out a *coup d'état*. It is also fair to say that some of the evidence points to the contrary.

There was still a great deal to be done before the country could return to normal. The Syrian brigade in the Mafraq area, deployed there since the Suez imbroglio, was making threatening movements, presumably in support of the supposed coup. Hussein made Ali's cousin, Ali Hiyyari, CGS, despite some misgivings. Ali Hiyyari was a more experienced officer than Ali, but much less sure of himself. Hussein sent him to the frontier to enquire into the Syrian movements, whereupon Ali Hiyyari promptly decamped to Damascus. There he held a press conference at which he denied there had been a plot to oust Hussein, accusing the King of manufacturing the whole business in order to discredit honest patriots like himself. He was to admit later that, aged only thirty-two when made CGS, he did not feel up to the job. He also denied that there had been any plot against the King, but said that Nasser's propaganda had filled the heads of many young officers like himself with romantic ideas about Arab unity. He too was later recalled to Jordan with a royal pardon and filled a number of important posts.

It must have seemed to the King, and to those who wished him well, that he might never regain control. The upheaval in the army had left behind a legacy that was to plague it for several years to come. Hussein could no longer count without question on the loyalty of his officers. Was Jordan to become another Syria, where the making or unmaking of governments seemed to be the principal preoccupation of most officers above the rank of major? A new Cabinet formed by Khalidi, with Naboulsi as Foreign Minister, appeared to be increasingly Communist-orientated. Naboulsi continued to press for diplomatic relations with the Soviet Union, convincing the King that Jordan would rapidly go Communist unless he intervened to stop it. These fears were increased when a National Congress held in Nablus on 22 April denounced the Eisenhower Doctrine, called for federal union with Syria and Egypt, and passed other left-wing resolutions. It demanded the reinstatement of all officers who had been dismissed for their conduct on or before 10 April. One of the delegates was Dr George Habash, of whom we shall hear a good deal more later. Jordan Radio was forbidden to publish the Congress's demands but Cairo Radio did so with the maximum publicity. Hussein, refusing to consider any of the Congress's resolutions, dismissed Khalidi on 24 April.

Strikes and demonstrations were the immediate result. They had died down in Amman by midday, but Hussein's search for a Prime Minister to succeed Khalidi continued until late in the night. His choice fell on Ibrahim Hashim, a former Prime Minister and elder statesman, and a loyal servant of the Hashemite Crown. Samir Rifai became Foreign Minister. Neither were men who would truckle to the mob and they answered the King's call reluctantly, feeling that only a military government could save Jordan from disaster. Hussein refused to give up, the arguments continuing until very late at night, and when finally Hashim and Rifai agreed to form a government, Hussein was completely exhausted. When he told Talhouni, his Court Minister, that he was going to bed, Talhouni respectfully suggested that the King should first get down on his knees, recite a verse from the Holy Koran, and thank God for his grandfather, without whose training there would have been no ministers willing to form a government. Hussein followed Talhouni's advice and slept the sleep of a contented man.

It soon became evident that within Ibrahim Hashim's velvet glove there was an iron hand. This was Samir Rifai, a Palestinian from Safad of right-wing views, but a politician to his fingertips. Martial law was proclaimed. Military courts were established. Curfews kept the mobs off the streets. Major-General Habis Majali, the hero of the defence of Latrun in the 1948 war, who had suffered a temporary eclipse in 1951 when he had supported Emir Naif's candidature instead of Talal's, was made Commander-in-Chief. Political parties were banned. Army units whose loyalty had been proven were stationed at key points on both the East and West Banks. Those officers in both the army and the police who were considered unreliable were quietly purged. For quite some time to come the prisons became uncomfortably crowded with officers who had allowed their ambitions, or political views, to take precedence over their oaths of loyalty to the King.

General Habis Majali was a character in his own right. His family had been *grands seigneurs* in Kerak for centuries and had been among the first to welcome the Emir Abdullah on his first arrival in the country. Their loyalty to the Hashemite Crown since then has been unquestioned. Habis Pasha was a *beau sabreur* in the old cavalry tradition. His sister was married to his cousin, Hazza Majali, who had been Prime Minister at the time of the abortive negotiations for Jordan to join the Baghdad Pact. The Majalis had governed Kerak in their own style, frequently rebelling against what they chose to describe as 'oppression'. They had rebelled against the Turks in 1912 when the Turks introduced conscription, the then Shaykh dying in Turkish captivity. As Hazza Majali was later to tell the British Ambassador, Johnston: 'We Majalis are used to killing and being killed.'[4]

The most pressing requirement was for money. The British subsidy had stopped; and, for all their brave promises, neither Egypt nor Syria had produced a single piastre of the money due from them under the Arab Solidarity Agreement. Fortunately King Saud, who had offered to send a Saudi brigade to support Hussein on 16 April, also promised to pay the £5 million that was the Saudis' share. This was done and was manna from heaven, since the Jordanian Treasury was empty. Hussein did not forget. As soon as the situation was sufficiently restored to make it possible for him to leave the country, he flew to Saudi Arabia to express his thanks in person. On his return to Amman on 29 April, he received the American Ambassador, who brought the welcome news that the US was providing $10 million in recognition of Hussein's success in maintaining the 'independence and integrity' of his kingdom.

Hussein called it 'Zerqa – The Final Round' in his autobiography. It had made three things clear. Firstly, that Hussein was a good deal tougher and much braver than people had previously realised. His courage earned him admirers not only among his own people, but all over the world. It had certainly altered his image in the United States, which was to stand Jordan in good stead in the future. It had also made him a personality to be reckoned with among the Arab rulers. Secondly, it was sadly apparent that King Talal's 1952 Constitution would have to be kept in abeyance for some time to come. This naturally led to criticism, particularly on the West Bank, but the King and his advisers were firm. These were certainly not the times for political experiment. And thirdly, the role of the bedouin regiments in rallying to Hussein's side had been of paramount importance. Hussein was never to forget this.

It is unlikely that the true story of the coup will ever be known. Hussein was convinced at the time that Ali abu Nowar was plotting to become Prime Minister, possibly with a view to overthrowing the monarchy and establishing a republic. Ali has always denied this, although how much credence can be attached to his denials must remain a matter of opinion. It has been claimed that Nasser was implicated, but Naboulsi has said that all the advice he received from Cairo was to remain on good terms with the King. But whatever the truth of it, it is certain that Sir James Barrie was right when he told his university audience in Scotland that 'Courage is the thing.' Fortunately, it is a quality in which Hussein has never been lacking.

CHAPTER SIX

A Coup that Succeeded

'Nuri told me that a dog could not bark in Baghdad without his hearing of it.' General Glubb[1]

The year 1958 began well, with Ibrahim Hashim and Samir Rifai in firm control. But Jordan was uncomfortably isolated in the Arab world. Egypt and Syria were openly hostile. Saudi Arabia, following its policy of sitting on the fence, could only be described as an uncertain ally. Nasser was determined to assert Egypt's leadership, at the same time drawing ever closer to the Russians, to whom he was indebted for the re-equipment and retraining of the Egyptian armed forces. Hussein was convinced that it had been Nasser's meddling in Jordanian affairs that had come so close to losing him his throne. He also resented the malevolent attacks made on him by Cairo Radio. At a time when he was beginning to feel increasingly hemmed in, it is not surprising that he should have turned to Iraq, where his cousin and schoolmate, Feisal, was now the King.

Although King Abdullah had at one time expected to be offered the throne of Iraq, he had little regard for the Iraqis, whom he used to describe as 'the bloody slayers of the Prophet's grandson Hussein'. There may, of course, be an element of sour grapes in this expression of Abdullah's feelings, because Iraq was as rich as Jordan was poor. The Iraqi branch of the Hashemites were inclined to patronise their poor but proud cousins in Amman. This was particularly true of the Emir Abdul Illah, the son of Abdullah's elder brother, ex-King Ali of the Hejaz. Abdul Illah was Regent of Iran from the death of King Ghazi in a car accident in 1939 until Ghazi's son Feisal came to the throne in 1953.

Abdul Illah throughout his regency had maintained a very close relationship with General Nuri as-Said, who had dominated Iraqi politics for almost a generation. Nuri had left the Ottoman army in 1917 to join in the Arab Revolt, in which he had distinguished himself. He had held high office in Iraq ever since its liberation from the Turks and much of Iraq's rapid development was due to his skilful manipulation of the country's oil revenues. Nuri was however too closely associated in the public mind with the Regent Abdul Illah, who was very unpopular. Hussein had disliked Abdul Illah ever since his Harrow schooldays. He resented his condescension and the way he treated the unassuming young Feisal, to whom Hussein was devoted. Nevertheless Iraq and Jordan had much in common, despite differences in the character of the people and Iraq's much greater wealth.

This became more apparent when President Nasser of Egypt and President Quwatly of Syria signed an agreement in Cairo on 1 February 1958, which united the two countries as the United Arab Republic (UAR). Egypt and Syria were very different in character and history, leading many people to doubt whether the union could ever work, but they kept their feelings to themselves in the wave of Arab nationalist euphoria that greeted news of the union. The fact that the new union was to be based on socialism made it particularly attractive to the young men and women who were starting to emerge from Arab universities. For many of them monarchies held out very little attraction, as Hussein was well aware.

His problems seemed to multiply as the months passed. Nasser's hostility led to a temporary severance of diplomatic relations. Syria, which had always been anti-Hashemite since Abdullah's time, was now lined up with Egypt. Despite Hussein's belief in Arab solidarity, Jordan had hardly a friend left. The one glimmer of light was a change in American attitudes. In the previous September there had been a much needed American gift of arms and ammunition. It had been delivered by US transport aircraft which had been compelled to use a circuitous route to avoid flying over Egypt and Syria. Nevertheless it had provided a welcome boost to Jordanian morale.

For some time there had been a discussion at ministerial level with Baghdad regarding a possible union between Jordan and Iraq. When King Feisal visited Amman on 10 February, shortly after the Egypt–Syria union was announced, it was possible to take matters further. The proposed union was to be one between two equal partners, but this failed to take into account the great disparity in wealth and population between the two countries. Iraq moreover, which had the least to fear from Israeli aggression, claimed to be the most implacable of Israel's enemies and had never concluded an armistice agreement with Israel. Jordan on the other hand was in the very front line, at risk from Israeli attack at any time. Not surprisingly, this resulted in a somewhat different approach to what was in Arab eyes the most pressing of all problems.

At Abdul Illah's insistence, Feisal was to be head of the combined state. Hussein would be his deputy. The capitals would alternate every six months. Foreign policy, finance, education and diplomatic representation would be unified. The union parliament would have the same number of deputies from each country. Ibrahim Hashim went to Baghdad as Deputy Prime Minister. Major-General Sadek Shera'a became Deputy Chief of the Combined Staff. It looked well on paper but was more romantic illusion than practical politics. The two countries were at heart unsuited to each other, notwithstanding the close connection between the two ruling families. The British Ambassador, Sir Charles Johnston, who attended the signing ceremony, compared the two young kings and concluded that Hussein was much the stronger character.[2]

'This is the happiest day of my life, a great day in Arab history,' Hussein told his people in a broadcast after the signing ceremony on 14 February 1958. 'We are under one banner, the banner of Arabism, which our great-grandfather, Hussein bin Ali the Great, carried in the great Arab Revolt.' The black, red, white and green flag chosen for the union was in fact a replica of the flag carried by the Emir Feisal from Mecca to Damascus forty years before. Nasser's telegram of congratulations to King Feisal II as the new head of state was effusive in its compliments. 'These glorious days for the Arab nation' seemed to carry the great man's imprimatur, although Hussein warned Feisal not to be fooled by it.

Abdul Illah's attitude towards the new union is interesting. In early July, while visiting Istanbul, he was interviewed by King Abdullah's former Chamberlain, Nassir Nashashibi, now a prominent journalist. Abdul Illah enquired how things were going in Jordan, and how Hussein was doing. Nasser told him that things were improving, but Abdul Illah disagreed. He said Hussein had no policy and was afraid of being swallowed up by Abdul Illah, raising his hand to his mouth and making the motion of swallowing. He said Hussein was wrong; he had no such ambition. All Abdul Illah wanted was for Feisal to marry and produce an heir; after which Abdul Illah would retire and settle in London. He said Hussein's trouble stemmed from the fact that 70 per cent of his subjects were Palestinians with no loyalty to the throne; the balance of 30 per cent were tribesmen who would sell their swords to the highest bidder.[3]

Abdul Illah was ignoring the trouble simmering in the Iraqi officer corps.* Iraq was no more proof than Jordan against the national socialist ideas prevalent in the Arab world at that time. Nasser was the young officers' hero. The Jordanian secret service had been working to uncover plots for many months. They had discovered one against the regime in Amman that was to take place simultaneously with one in Baghdad. It had come to light as the result of an interrogation of a young Jordanian cadet, Ahmed Yessef el-Hiari of the 4th Tank Regiment. He had admitted that he was to assassinate the King and Sharif Nasser. He had made a full confession. The plot was Egyptian-inspired and would take place at a public ceremony in July, in Baghdad as well as in Amman. Hussein immediately telephoned Feisal and asked him to send over a senior Iraqi officer who could be fully briefed.

* Less than a week after this meeting with Nassir Nashashibi, Prince Abdul Illah was brutally murdered in Baghdad.

The Iraqi emissary was General Rafiq A'rif, who commanded the Arab Union forces. His attitude throughout was one of polite boredom, as if the whole business was a waste of his time. He pointed out that the Iraqi army was considered to be one of the best in the Middle East; it had not been subjected to the same strains as the Jordanian army. The Iraqi authorities had everything under control. Far from worrying about Iraq, the Iraqis were much more concerned about Hussein and Jordan. He begged the King to take care. Despairing of pricking General A'rif's pompous self-esteem, Hussein besought him to repeat to Feisal and Nuri all he had been told in Amman. This A'rif said he would do. It was 11 July 1958 – a Friday. Over the weekend Hussein again spoke to Feisal, who was about to leave on a state visit to Turkey. The Turks, who had also got wind of a possible plot, added their warnings to Hussein's. They fell on deaf ears.

Coups, if they are to succeed, require careful planning, but this in itself is not enough. They also depend quite outrageously on luck. The circumstances must be just right; the troops on whom the conspirators depend must be in the right place at the right time. This is what happened on Monday, 14 July 1958 in Baghdad. The tragedy was triggered by events in Lebanon, where a civil war was beginning that has yet to reach a conclusion. Nuri, concerned by developments there, decided to move the 3rd Infantry Division to the Iraq–Jordan frontier where it would be conveniently placed, either to reinforce the Iraqi contingent sent to Jordan at the time of the Suez incident, or to move through Syria to help President Chamoun in Beirut.

The 3rd Infantry Division was commanded by Major-General Ghazi Dhagestani, a royalist and a brave man. There had been rumours of coups over many years but Dhagestani was to say later that he had never had any reason to doubt the loyalty of the two leading conspirators. They were Colonels Abdul Karim Kassem and Abdul Salam Arif, both commanding brigades in the 3rd Infantry Division. Kassem was a quiet, well-behaved officer, who had been through Sandhurst and was well regarded by the authorities. Arif was a different type, loud-mouthed and blustering. It was his brigade that was to launch the coup, Kassem agreeing to follow on close behind him. The first objectives were to be the radio station and the Royal Palace.

Both Kassem and Arif were radicals, and as such they were anti-monarchy, which they associated with the corruption notorious among the government ministers, not least with Nuri. They were republicans at heart, as indeed were the majority of Iraqi career officers, who were for the most part recruited from the petty bourgeoisie. The soldiers were mostly conscripts with little heart in their job. The 3rd Infantry Division was stationed at Baquba, about forty miles east of Baghdad. Its route to the frontier with Jordan would take it through Baghdad. It was motorised, with tanks. Standing orders forbade units or formations to pass through the capital with ammunition, a wise precaution against a sudden military coup, but on this occasion the rule was waived. The division might find itself going into action after it had reached the frontier and would have to be prepared to fight. This was the conspirators' first stroke of luck. The other was that Feisal and Abdul Illah, with some of the royal ladies, were to leave for Istanbul early on 14 July; had they gone twenty-four hours earlier the coup would probably have misfired.

Around 6 a.m. on 14 July, Arif's tanks and armoured cars seized the radio station, after which they pressed on to the Royal Palace. At this time Kassem was still at Baquba with his brigade. The Royal Bodyguard put up some resistance but were overpowered. Feisal and Abdul Illah came down into the garden to parley with the soldiers, only to be gunned down. There are various accounts of how it happened, one being that an officer offered them safe conduct, only to turn and machine-gun them as they walked. The royal ladies were similarly dispatched. In less than thirty minutes the Hashemite House in Iraq was virtually wiped out. The search for Nuri then began.

It is said that Nuri, hearing the gunfire and then receiving reports of what was happening, disguised himself as a woman in a *burqa* and tried to flee across the river, only to be betrayed and shot. His and Abdul Illah's corpses were dismembered and dragged through the streets the following day, accompanied by howling and shrieking crowds, all execrating Nuri and the Hashemites. The Baghdad mob has long had a reputation for being brutish and blood-crazy. It took revenge on Jordanians also. Ibrahim Hashim, Jordan's respected elder statesman, who was in Baghdad as Deputy Prime Minister of the Union, was murdered, as was Suleiman Toukan, Minister of Defence of the Union. General Sadek Shera'a, the Deputy Chief of Staff, was lucky to escape with his life. He was placed under arrest and threatened with a firing squad, but Kassem eventually relented and sent him back to Jordan. The British Embassy was looted and burned.

The news came like a thunderclap in Amman. Hussein, already fearful for his cousin's safety, was almost distraught. His first thought was to avenge Feisal. Sharif Nasser was nothing loath to lead the avenging force. He was after all a Hashemite too. The King sent Nasser to the frontier, but as reports began to come in from Baghdad it became clear that this was no ordinary coup. Kassem and Arif were in control and they appeared to have the army behind them. Most senior officers and government officials were either under arrest or were co-operating with the rebels. The behaviour of the Iraqi troops already in Jordan nauseated Hussein when they openly celebrated the murder of members of his family. But he resisted the urge to deal severely with them, contenting himself instead with taking some of their more senior officers into protective custody, to serve as hostages for the safety of Jordanian officers caught in Iraq. Eventually all were released unharmed.

As the deputy head of state, Hussein might have intervened to claim the vacant throne, but wiser counsels prevailed. There was no reliable information about what had happened but it seemed certain that King Feisal and other leading figures were dead. It would be foolish to dispatch troops without better intelligence. He was in any case averse to setting Arab against Arab, as would be the case if he intervened militarily in Iraq; and it had to be admitted that the Iraqi army was both larger and better equipped than the Jordanian. So Hussein called off the hunt and recalled Sharif Nasser, by then 150 miles into Iraq.

President Nasser was quick to take advantage of what must have seemed to him a remarkable stroke in his favour. Relations between Egypt and Iraq had never been easy, for which the Egyptians put most of the blame on Nuri, now dead. Despite the warm words with which he had greeted the Iraq–Jordan Union, Nasser had no wish to see a rival Arab power bloc threatening his ambition to speak for all the Arabs. He therefore recognised Kassem's new government on the evening of 14 July, and warmly welcomed the revolution. He was to regret this later when he discovered that in Kassem he had a wild cat by its tail.

The haste with which the new regime was recognised caused Hussein real anguish. Turkey recognised it on 31 July, the USA and Britain on 1 August. There were protests against doing so in Britain, notably by the former Prime Minister Anthony Eden, but the world as a whole seemed content to shake the bloodstained hands of murderers. This was, however, the least of Hussein's worries. It had been Nasser's deliberate policy to establish a cordon round Jordan. By this means he had prevented the importation of oil and other essential goods, except through Aqaba or by the desert road from Iraq. The same difficulties applied to flying to Jordan. But the frontier with Iraq was now closed, cutting off a certain number of large oil-tankers that were loading in Baghdad. Hussein and his ministers were frantic, since without oil everything in Jordan would come to a grinding halt. He applied to the Americans, who were willing to fly oil across Saudi Arabia to Amman. But the Saudis, in pursuit of their policy of keeping out of trouble, refused permission. Even when Hussein appealed personally to King Saud, the answer was the same. Hussein was more saddened than anything else. The dregs in a cup are always bitter. When finally some oil did get through, it came from the Lebanon, the planes crossing Israel. The rhetoric about Arab solidarity was reduced to a mockery.

On the night of 16 July Hussein took a step which probably saved him his throne. It required great moral courage but fortunately he did have the support of his ministers. He may have been inspired to act by the fact that by a matter of only a few hours a *coup d'état* similar to the one so successful in Baghdad had been nipped in the bud in Jordan. Calling together cabinet, parliament and senate at short notice, Hussein announced that the situation was so grave that he intended to ask for British or American troops. If anyone had views to the contrary, they were welcome to speak up. The King's proposal received unanimous approval.

Hussein lost no time in summoning the British and American chargés d'affaires, both ambassadors being out of the country. He requested the immediate support of British or American troops; he did not mind which. 'We need them for a limited time only,' he told them. 'I look upon this move as a symbol of the ties that bind free peoples in times of crisis.' Heath-Mason for Britain, and Wright for the USA, promised to consult their governments as quickly as possible.

There was a debate on the Middle East that night in the House of Commons. The Prime Minister, Harold Macmillan, wound up the debate for the government. He was preparing to go home when the cable from Amman reached him. Summoning immediately a full Cabinet meeting, Macmillan's first instinct was to consult the US Secretary of State, Foster Dulles. 'I was determined to do all I could to help Hussein,' he said, nearly thirty years later, 'but I first had to know what the Americans proposed doing. We had burnt our fingers over Suez and I had no intention of doing so for a second time. Fortunately Foster was anxious we should help over Jordan since the Americans were already going into Lebanon to help Chamoun. I then summoned the Chiefs of Staff.'[4]

Military men take a much less romantic view of going out on a limb without much hope of support than would seem to be the case with most politicians. Their views are conditioned by logistics. Any troops sent to Jordan would first have to get there. But how? Flying over Syria, Egypt and probably Saudi Arabia was out of the question. That left only Israel. Would they agree? There was the 16th Parachute Brigade in Cyprus on full alert. Two battalions under Brigadier Tom Pearson could be flown in, but they would be very much on their own. If the situation deteriorated – if for example the Jordanian army went the same way as the Iraqis, or if for example the Syrians or the Iraqis intervened in Jordan – Pearson's force would be a hostage to fortune. The British generals and air marshals were uneasy. They wanted to help but disliked the risks. Meanwhile the 16th Parachute Brigade was placed on standby.

After a virtual all-night session, the Cabinet agreed at 3 a.m. to order the Parachute Brigade to Amman; and the necessary instructions were flashed to Cyprus. Some little time previously Hussein's friend and flying instructor, Wing Commander Jock Dalgliesh, then serving at RAF Head-

quarters at High Wycombe, had been ordered to fly out to Jordan. A
Canberra bomber landed him at Akrotiri in Cyprus at 7 a.m. on 17 July.
There he found the first wave of paratroopers boarding their Beverly
aircraft. Dalgliesh was to accompany them. Operation Fortitude was
about to start.

'Unfortunately,' said Harold Macmillan,

> the Foreign Office had been terribly slow in obtaining clearance to
> overfly Israel. The first wave was over Israel when the Israelis said they
> were not cleared to overfly. Luckily the commander decided to go on and
> reached Amman safely but there was no question of course of the rest of
> the force doing the same. There was a frightful pause while we wondered
> how Pearson and his 200 troops would manage on their own. But in the
> end I cleared it up by a personal call to Ben Gurion. It was in Israel's
> interests, just as much as in ours, then and now, to have a stable Jordan.
> But it was a tricky situation while it lasted.[5]

For a moment the Chiefs of Staff must have felt their worst fears had been
realised; but within forty-eight hours Pearson was dug in round Amman
airfield with two parachute battalions and some light field artillery, supported by six Hunter fighters of 208 Squadron RAF. His mission was to
secure the airfield and protect King Hussein and his government. It was a
tall order nearly 6000 miles from home, with the bulk of the Jordanian army
still an unknown quantity, and with the British entirely dependent on the
goodwill of the Israelis to maintain communications with their base in
Cyprus.

Hussein's chief difficulty was his uncertainty regarding the loyalty of his
army. Deployed round the Royal Palace in Amman were Sharif Nasser's
Royal Guards, all handpicked, and the 1st Armoured-Car and 9th Infantry
Regiments, all bedouin. But in Zerqa there were the artillery, tanks and the
2nd Infantry Brigade, whose loyalty was uncertain. Moreover, the Syrians
were reported to be moving troops to the frontier. 'After all one can only die
once,' Hussein told the British Ambassador, who had returned from leave
on 17 July after a somewhat complicated flight from London via Cyprus.

It required a man of unusual strength of character to stand up to the
succession of blows which had been aimed at Hussein. The murder of Feisal
had wounded him deeply. Why Feisal? he thought. Why not me? Feisal
would not hurt a fly, and in any case he had no power. The discovery that
one of his own ADCs had been involved in the coup timed to take place
shortly after the Iraqi one was also a shattering blow. Whom *could* he trust?
The British Ambassador has said that for some weeks 'people expected to
wake up each morning to hear that the King had been assassinated.'[6] There
were plots, and rumours of plots. Nasser's propaganda machine went into

action, broadcasting a personal attack by Nasser on Hussein. Radio Damascus joined in the 'war of nerves' with zest. When the full report of the Baghdad horrors reached Amman on 23 July, together with photographs of the victims, both Hussein and Samir Rifai were badly shaken. 'Not a single foreign observer in Amman outside the British Embassy believed that, even with British and American help, the Jordanian Monarchy had a chance of surviving,' wrote Charles Johnston.[7]

According to those in Amman at the time, it was astonishing how the situation began to improve, little by little, and almost imperceptibly. Hussein, following the old military tactic that offence is better than defence, launched an outspoken attack on Nasser and Egyptian policy. He then began to visit army units in Zerqa and elsewhere. This, knowing as much as he did, required courage of the highest order, but it paid him very handsome dividends. He was warmly applauded by the soldiers, many of whose officers were known to be disloyal. More bedouin units were moved into Amman, where they got on famously with the British paratroopers manning the airfield perimeter. Amman gradually began to return to normal. Hussein gave a few parties. An additional British battalion arrived from Aden via Aqaba. The horrifying events in Baghdad were no longer front-page news.

The improvement was due not only to Hussein's own actions and the firm stance taken by his Prime Minister, Samir Rifai. World opinion, as represented by the General Assembly of the United Nations, had swung over to Hussein's side. A resolution calling on all member states to respect the sovereignty of others was unanimously adopted on 21 August, somewhat to Hussein's surprise. There was no mention in the resolution of withdrawal by the Americans from Lebanon, nor by the British from Jordan. The United Nations debate was followed by a visit to Amman by UN Secretary-General Dag Hammarskjöld, between 27 and 29 August. He was surprised to find the country so quiet. He admired Samir Rifai and was impressed by the King. It was agreed that there should be a United Nations presence in Jordan; this was followed by the arrival of Signor Pier Spinelli, an Italian diplomat, as the Secretary-General's special representative.

Perhaps more important was the announcement by the US that budgetary aid to the tune of $50 million would be provided. The British said they would provide up to £1 million, which would be in addition to the £1 million already agreed. They also undertook to pay the Jordanian share of the pensions due to former members of the Palestine administration.

There was no evidence, however, to show that there had been any change of heart in Cairo. Broadcasts from Cairo and Damascus continued the war of words but Jordan internally seemed to have settled down. Both the King and Samir Rifai were anxious that the British should withdraw as soon as possible; by their doing so, the propaganda line that Hussein was solely dependent on foreign troops could be disproved. The British government was equally anxious to remove the troops. It was agreed that the King would announce the proposed withdrawal in his speech from the throne to parliament on 1 October, and that the withdrawal would start on 20 October and be completed by early November. Many people, Jordanians and British, felt that the withdrawal was premature; the British Ambassador admitted in retrospect that he had 'underestimated the vitality and resilience of the Jordanian monarchy'.[8] Hussein was learning fast, every day and in every way, and this combined with his personality, charm, energy and above all courage went a long way towards converting the doubters and the disaffected.

The withdrawal was completed by 2 November, when the last British battalion embarked at Aqaba for Kenya. Hussein, with a bevy of generals, ministers and other notabilities, flew down to say farewell. The British presence, although made as unobtrusive as possible, had strengthened the faint hearts and encouraged the strong ones. Hussein was fully aware of this and expressed his thanks in a speech, referring to Jordan and Britain as 'partners', a word he was to use on other occasions in the future when speaking of the Jordanian–British relationship.

The swift reaction to Hussein's original request for military aid had involved Harold Macmillan and his colleagues in considerable risk. Had anything gone wrong, they would have received short shrift from the British electorate, whose recollections of the Suez fiasco were still fresh. The same is true of Hussein, and of his supporter, Samir Rifai, who had taken an equally great risk by welcoming back British troops so soon after they had been withdrawn from Jordan. They had no means of knowing how the people would react and, had the mobs taken to the streets in protest, they could not have been certain of the army's ability, perhaps even its willingness, to restore law and order. It was a measure of the King's despair after the Baghdad massacre that he should have felt compelled to seek British or American assistance; and equally it was a measure of his character and courage, as well as of his ability to judge the temper of his people, that Operation Fortitude passed off without the firing of a single shot.

At least some of this success was due to three of the British officers who were involved. The choice of Dalgliesh, for example, to command the RAF contingent was an inspired one. His already firmly established friendship with Hussein ensured the closest possible co-operation between the RAF and the RJAF. Brigadier Tom Pearson too, who commanded the Parachute Brigade, was ideally suited to a role that required as much diplomacy as military judgement. His panache and open friendliness smoothed the path with his Jordanian colleagues, who also valued his military experience.

Finally, there was Brigadier Michael Strickland, appointed to head the British Training Mission which remained after the Parachute Brigade had departed. Strickland, whose own war record was impressive, was well acquainted with the corridors of power, having spent several years on the staff in the War Office in London. He had also served in the Arab Legion for nine months prior to General Glubb's departure. Most of this period had been spent on the West Bank and he had not been involved in suppressing the anti-Baghdad Pact riots, having been sick at the time. He therefore had a clean slate where Ali abu Nowar and his friends were concerned and they had welcomed his appointment to command the British Training Mission set up in the wake of Glubb's departure. Although Strickland was no Arabist, he was a skilled diplomat who succeeded in getting on good terms with both the King and Ali abu Nowar. Unfortunately, however, Strickland's Mission was wound up as a result of the Suez affair in October 1956, but his return to Jordan almost exactly two years later was welcomed on all sides. During the twelve months he spent in Jordan in 1958–9 as Military Adviser to the King, Strickland did a great deal to repair the rift in Anglo-Jordanian relations that had followed the abrupt dismissal of Glubb Pasha, and so indeed did Dalgliesh. They were both the right men in the right place at the right time.

CHAPTER SEVEN

Ringed Round by Enemies

'There were times in those early years when I used to wonder from which direction the next blow would fall.' Sir Charles Johnston[1]

Hussein could have been forgiven if his early years on the throne had made him a cynic. That this was not the case was due to his faith in his religion, his confidence in the Hashemite destiny, and a readiness to forgive and forget which is such a marked feature of his character. But this does not mean that he was not hurt in times of betrayal by those he had trusted, nor that he accepted with equanimity the stream of abuse that was poured out on Cairo and Damascus Radios, or the filth of the gutter press. He resented it bitterly. His personal reputation was torn to shreds while he was still little more than a boy. Every inducement was offered to those willing to murder him – by bullet, bomb, poison or dagger. It changed him from boy to man surprisingly quickly, moulding his character and developing his natural shrewdness. If it did not curb his impatience, it did at least make him think twice before taking his decisions and choosing his inner circle of counsellors. Even then he was often let down.

Although one might not have thought so from the outpourings of Cairo Radio, the quick response by the British government to Hussein's request for help was very much to Nasser's advantage. Had Britain refused, and had Hussein been assassinated or overthrown, it is virtually certain that Israel would have taken over the West Bank; it might not even have stopped there since the supporters of Eretz Israel (the Land of Israel) also laid claim to what had been Transjordan, parts of Syria and southern Lebanon. Nasser well knew that, if that did happen, Egypt was in no position to go to Jordan's rescue. His newfound friend, the Soviet Union, might rattle the sabre but it had no intention of risking a confrontation with the United States. It is therefore likely that, as the British paratroops flew in to Amman, there were sighs of relief in Nasser's inner circle of advisers.

For three critical months, July to September 1958, Hussein had been on a knife edge. The slightest mistake or miscalculation might have swung the country against him. It was Samir Rifai's political skill and firmness that brought the civilian population under control. Likewise in the army,

General Habis Majali made it plain where its loyalty lay, and he dealt ruthlessly with those whose loyalty was in doubt. Worse was the atmosphere of distrust that permeated all levels of government; this took some time to dispel. The Security Service was efficient in uncovering plots, but the mere fact that the plots were continuing, and that some of the conspirators held positions of trust, filled Hussein with despair.

By October it was clear that the corner had been turned, for the time being at least. Hussein badly needed a break. He decided to join his mother in Switzerland for a three-week holiday. There remained the problem of how to get there. Fortunately information was received from the UN that air flights over Syria were back to normal. Plans were accordingly made for the King, accompanied by Dalgliesh as co-pilot, to travel in a RJAF Dove, a plane of moderate speed and carrying capacity, but very manoeuvrable in the hands of a skilled pilot. Hussein took with him his uncle, Sharif Nasser, Maurice Raynor and two RJAF officers to fly the plane back from Switzerland. The flight plan was logged with air-traffic control in Beirut, but not through diplomatic channels with Syria. At 8.20 a.m. on Tuesday, 11 November 1958, the Dove took off with Hussein at the controls, and headed north-east. Hussein, who was to be twenty-three in three days' time, was in holiday mood, laughing and joking with the small party of ministers who had come to bid him godspeed.

Air-traffic regulations required Hussein to report his position to air-traffic control at Damascus, which he did after thirty minutes' flying time from Amman. He was given permission to proceed, turning north-west towards Damascus and dropping as required from 9000 to 8000 feet. All seemed to be going well until they were suddenly called up by Damascus and told: 'You are not cleared to overfly. You will land at Damascus.' Johnston said later he was convinced that the Syrian government, suddenly aware that their arch-enemy was in their clutches, intended to force Hussein to abdicate once they had got their hands on him.[2] The same suspicion must have flashed through the minds of Hussein and Dalgliesh. They quickly decided to return to Amman, turning through 180 degrees and dropping almost to ground level. As soon as this information had been passed to Amman, they switched off their radio to avoid being tracked by the Syrians.

They were fifteen or twenty minutes' flying-time from the nearest point in Jordan, flying at 200 m.p.h., and at little more than a few feet above the ground. Dalgliesh took over the controls as two Syrian MiG-17 fighters appeared overhead, diving on them without first making the conventional visual signals that they should force-land. Had the Syrians opened fire, Hussein could not have escaped. But perhaps it was thought in Damascus that to shoot down a reigning monarch on a peaceful flight would be hard to explain away at the UN. More likely, the Syrians believed that the best way to deal with the problem would be to force Hussein into the ground. With all of them dead, it would be easy to say that it was an ordinary flying accident.

Dalgliesh was an extremely skilful and experienced pilot whose plane could turn in much tighter circles than his pursuers. The MiGs kept overshooting as they dived time and again, once nearly colliding as they pulled away. They did not abandon the pursuit until well inside Jordan. Dalgliesh did not rate their flying abilities particularly highly, but this would seem to downgrade his own high performance at the controls that day. He certainly saved Hussein's life, and of course his own.

Back in Amman, Hussein found himself a popular hero. The crowds, who had heard of the attack on Amman Radio, turned out to cheer him. There were protests to the United Arab Republic, and at the UN. The wilder spirits clamoured for war with Syria. Hussein, with the adrenalin still flowing, decided not to go abroad on holiday after all. In his auto-biography he has written:

> The scrape with the Syrian MiGs was the narrowest escape from death I have ever had, and I must admit that at one time I felt, to use the Air Force jargon, that I had 'bought' it. It is old history now and times have changed since those bitter days of 1958. Even so, the Syrian MiG incident was an attack on a head of state as yet unparalleled in history, and it will take me longer to forget it than it has taken me to forgive those responsible.[3]

Dalgliesh, in his characteristically modest account of the incident, pays high tribute to Hussein's calmness and quiet courage throughout. After the Syrian MiGs had abandoned the pursuit, he says,

> Drenched in perspiration from the exertions and nervous tensions of the last twenty minutes, I suggested we have breakfast. This was impossible. The manoeuvres we had subjected our aircraft to had smashed every piece of crockery on board. But Maurice Raynor, like a true Englishman, came to the rescue. He had nursed a thermos of tea throughout all the buffeting and using some plastic cups we were able to refresh ourselves with some of the finest brew ever tasted and, along with a Lucky Strike cigarette, there could be no sweeter moment.[4]

There can be no doubt that the incident was pre-planned on Syria's part. The Prime Minister told Dalgliesh two or three days afterwards that more than 200 Jordanian opponents of the regime, living in Syria in exile at the time, had assembled at Damascus airfield. 'They had been there since 6 a.m. on the morning of the flight having been informed that the King was overflying and would be forced to land at Damascus. If anything portended more of a kangaroo court than that little lot it would be difficult to imagine,' said Dalgliesh.

Six months later there was further confirmation of the plot. Two strangers turned up at the Amman airbase, seeking an interview with Dalgliesh, who was living there at the time. They turned out to be Syrians, and as such immediately under suspicion, but Dalgliesh agreed to see them. They were young, well dressed and obviously nervous. Both spoke English. They told Dalgliesh they were seeking political asylum. They turned out to be the pilots of the MiGs which had attacked Hussein's plane. One of them was a Circassian. They said they had received their training in Russia. They were one of three pairs of fighters airborne that morning to force the King to land at Damascus. After intercepting the Jordanian Dove they were to force it to land – if necessary by opening fire on it, but only after receiving permission from Damascus.

When their efforts to force down the plane were frustrated by Dalgliesh's skill at the controls, they requested permission to open fire but received no response. Twice more they asked for permission but there was no reply. There was no alternative but to abandon the pursuit. During the weeks that followed the rumour grew that it was they, the pilots, who had refused to open fire. They were accused of having Jordanian sympathies. Life became intolerable for them and they had to leave Syria. 'After a week in their new environment,' writes Dalgliesh,

> the younger of the two became acutely depressed and finally he asked to be repatriated to Syria. I reasoned with him, warned him that I was certain the Syrian authorities would wreak vengeance on him for defecting. But no, he felt he wanted to go back to his family. He was quite confident nothing would happen to him. He had friends. I arranged for him to be taken back to the Syrian frontier. At midnight he crossed into Syria. He never saw the sunrise.[5]

Dalgliesh was as surprised as most other people by the extraordinary outburst of loyalty that followed Hussein's miraculous escape from a violent death. He says the vast majority of people were on Hussein's side. Sir Charles Johnston, the British Ambassador, felt the same. Whereas on his first arrival in Amman, Johnston had found few people willing to be openly pro-British, by the end of 1958 the situation had completely changed. He believed the fires through which the King had passed in 1957 and 1958 had to a great extent matured him. He was now the real power in the country, always provided of course that he had the backing of the army. He could still be impulsive, sometimes to the despair of his advisers, but much less so than formerly. He seemed to be growing more and more like his grandfather

Abdullah, the architect of Hussein's kingdom. 'Abdullah would have been proud of his grandson,' said Johnston.[6]

At that time there were in Jordan three distinct power blocs, with which every Prime Minister might expect to contend. First, there was the Palace, where the King called the tune, but was influenced by the Queen Mother, her brother Sharif Nasser, the Court Minister and a few personal friends who were close to him in age and in common experience. Second, there was the army. Third, there were the powerful country magnates and tribal leaders whose influence was such that they could not be safely ignored. Conservative in character and political opinion, they were keenly aware of the crisis through which Jordan had so recently passed and were concerned above all else to prevent any repetition. The Palestinian influence also had to be considered, even though it was then confined principally to the West Bank. It required constant juggling to keep all four balls in the air all the time. In many ways Jordan was reminiscent of an Italian Renaissance state, in which there were many different factions striving for the ruler's ear, but none certain of retaining it for long.

Since it had been the bedouin regiments that had rallied to the King's side during the so-called Zerqa Mutiny of April 1957, it followed that the weeding out of malcontents within the army was concentrated chiefly on the non-bedouin element. This caused serious discontent at the time, the opportunity being taken to settle numerous old scores. Criticism was voiced by Samir Pasha and several of his Cabinet, none of whom was bedouin. It also led to arguments between the Prime Minister and General Habis Majali, the former insisting that the army must behave in a proper constitutional fashion and that all cases must be proven beyond reasonable doubt before officers were imprisoned or dismissed. The Prime Minister was supported by the army Chief of Staff, Major-General Sadek Shera'a, well educated and intelligent, but not a bedouin. Sadek's loyalty was regarded with some doubt, both within the army and by the Palace.

He had for many years been considered the ablest staff officer in the army. A native of Irbid, he had been pushed on rapidly by Glubb Pasha. In 1954, aged only thirty, he was given command of the 8th Infantry Regiment. A colonel by 1956, Sadek had been deeply involved in Ali abu Nowar's plot to get rid of Glubb Pasha. He was reputed to hold strong anti-British views, although in a curiously ambivalent way he contrived to look more like a British officer than a Jordanian, the effect enhanced by the pipe he invariably smoked. He was clever, ambitious and inclined to political intrigue – 'too clever by half', some said of him. As we have seen, after the Iraq–Jordan Union Sadek was sent to Baghdad as Deputy Chief of Staff of the new Joint Command. He was lucky to escape with his life after Kassem's coup, when he was arrested and sentenced to death. He spent three uncomfortable weeks in the death cell awaiting execution, then he was suddenly pardoned and sent back to Jordan. There, aged thirty-four, he was made Chief of Staff to Habis Majali, although the relationship between the two men had never been close.

Early in 1959 Hussein left Jordan for a long overseas tour that included visits to London and Washington. Shortly before his departure a plot was uncovered involving a certain Brigadier Qasim who, together with other officers, was planning to overthrow the regime. It was known that Sadek too was included in the plot but Hussein nevertheless decided to include him in his entourage. Sadek made desperate attempts to remain behind but Hussein was insistent. Throughout the trip the King was kept in touch with events as conspirator after conspirator was arrested. The hapless Sadek was frantic with worry at the absence of news regarding the coup. At one stage in the tour, in Chicago, he vanished for several hours and Hussein concluded that he had decamped. He returned eventually, only to beg permission on arrival in London to enter hospital for an urgent operation. This was refused. On the King's return to Jordan on 21 May, Sadek was arrested and tried by court-martial. He has always insisted that he was innocent of any attempt to overthrow the King, but the evidence against him was thought to be overwhelming. He was sentenced to death, later commuted to life imprisonment, spending what must have been several extremely worrying weeks in yet another death cell. He was pardoned in 1971 and taken back into government employment.

There are those who believe that Sadek was the victim of a move to get rid of Samir Rifai as Prime Minister; he was a supporter of Samir in the struggle with Habis Majali for control of the army. Although Samir could claim to have played a leading part in the restoration of stability in Jordan, his health was poor, he was more than a little tired, and his critics said he was losing his grip. Soon after Hussein's return from his overseas tour, Samir Pasha submitted his resignation, probably reckoning that the King would ask him to carry on. Hussein did not do so. He had an alternative Prime Minister waiting in the wings, Hazza Majali, aged only forty-four (Samir was fifty-nine) and eager for office. Hazza Majali had been Prime Minister when Jordan's entry into the Baghdad Pact was under discussion. He had been in favour of the Pact and had lost office as a result. Now he came back into power, a strong man with a powerful backing in his Kerak stronghold; and of course with the army's support through his cousin and brother-in-law, Habis Majali, the Commander-in-Chief.

It is evidence of Hussein's increasing political skill that he refused to be stampeded by Samir Rifai into keeping him in office. In effect he called Samir's bluff. Hussein had been hard at work behind the scenes getting another government together under Hazza Majali. But Samir had served Jordan well and no man more richly deserved a rest. He came from Safad in Palestine, although the Rifais were originally from the Hejaz. He had been trained in the strict tradition of the Ottoman civil service. A brilliant politician, who was up to all the tricks of his trade, Charles Johnston said of him that in 'life, as in bridge, he was a confirmed over-bidder'.[7] This may have been so, but when the time came for him to go, he went, like Glubb Pasha before him, with great dignity and without rancour.

Hazza Majali was an entirely different type, an Arab aristocrat and a clever political manipulator with a wider following in the country than Samir's; to that extent he was less inclined to endorse some of Samir's more repressive measures. Many internees were released and an attempt was made to patch up relations with the United Arab Republic, but without success where Nasser was concerned.

Personal security had never been a problem in Jordan until the Palestinian diaspora. Only then did the King, Glubb Pasha and other important officials need personal bodyguards. From the years 1948 to 1955, despite the influx of thousands of embittered refugees, there never seemed to be a requirement to carry personal weapons. Even when visiting the refugee camps, the hospitality was gracious and the welcome cordial. The change began after King Abdullah's assassination and Hussein himself never went unarmed thereafter. It is certainly the case that the Security Service was not very efficient until some years after Glubb Pasha's departure. He preferred to acquire information bedouin-fashion from those who came to drink coffee or tea with him, in his office or at home. The Arab Legion had much to be proud of, but its organisation for the gathering and dissemination of intelligence left a great deal to be desired.

This had to change after Monday, 29 August 1960, when the Prime Minister, Hazza Majali, was killed by a bomb, placed in his office by two accomplices. From then onwards, security in Jordan, as indeed elsewhere, has become one of the principal preoccupations of the state. It is difficult, however, to reconcile the requirements of security with the age-old Arab tradition of accessibility on the part of the ruler. It is extremely difficult to exclude from audience a man with a grudge, or a fanatic, or simply a man or woman hired to kill. Hazza Majali made a point of receiving petitioners on Monday mornings, a fact well enough known to provide those who plotted to kill him with an opportunity to do so.

The time-bombs had been placed in the Prime Minister's building, one in a drawer in Hazza Majali's desk, the other in a room on the ground floor, to the right of the entrance. They were reportedly placed there by two employees in the Prime Minister's office who were in Syrian pay. Just before 11.30 a.m., Hazza Majali was discussing various matters with a junior official, Zeid Rifai, the former Prime Minister's son, who would one day himself be a Prime Minister. Zeid left the office to fetch a certain file and was on his way back when the explosion occurred; fortunately he was not injured. The force of the explosion killed Hazza Majali instantly, blowing out the walls of his office and sending the debris crashing through the floor into the room below, where it killed Zaha Eddin Humud, Under-Secretary for Foreign Affairs, and Asim Taji, Director-General of Tourism. It also killed two members of Hazza's family who were visiting him, and a ten-year-old boy who was waiting to present a petition. Twenty minutes later the second bomb exploded, killing a wounded victim of the first bomb who was resting in the room. Had the King been in the building, as could easily have been the case, he too might have been killed or injured. Perhaps the assassins had planted the second bomb with this in mind.

Hussein had been resting at his country palace at Hummar, some distance from Amman, when he heard the news of the Prime Minister's murder. He set off for Amman, driving as fast as only he could. On the outskirts of Amman he was intercepted by the Minister of Defence and Habis Majali. Both men insisted that the King should not visit the scene of the explosion so soon after the event; they feared lest there might be other bombs set to explode. After some argument Hussein let himself be persuaded to go directly to the Palace and take charge of events. He ordered an immediate meeting of the Cabinet at which Bahjat Talhouni, the Court Minister, was appointed Prime Minister. Bahjat had been leaving Hazza Majali's wrecked office when the second bomb exploded, fortunately without hurting him.

Hussein's immediate reaction was one of horror and revulsion that anyone should contemplate such a crime; disposing of one's political opponents by the use of time-bombs was not such a common occurrence then as it has since become. He was particularly revolted by Cairo Radio's description of Hazza Majali as 'an imperialist agent'. Cairo sang the assassins' praises. Horror and sorrow were soon replaced by anger. It seemed clear that Syria was behind the assassination, probably with Egyptian support. Indeed, wherever Hussein looked, he seemed to see the burly figure of Gamal abdel Nasser lurking in the shadows and planning his destruction. He felt that sooner or later he must act to pre-empt the armed attack he was convinced was being planned against Jordan and his throne. Hussein talked a great deal during the weeks following Hazza's murder of taking up arms; so much so that the British Ambassador felt compelled to warn the King against the consequences of an attack on Syria. He sympathised with Hussein's feelings, but the King would be starting something of which no one could possibly foretell the outcome. Whether or not the King was influenced by this advice, wiser counsels certainly prevailed, and the troops massed close to the Syrian border were quietly returned to barracks.

Hussein never entirely forgave Nasser. The murderers were never caught and brought to justice. Hazza Majali's Director of Information was arrested and accused of complicity in the plot, but the real motive was never discovered. If it had been assumed that the assassination would be followed by a popular uprising against Hussein, or by political disturbances of a lesser kind, these never materialised. Jordan remained on an even keel, and under firm control.

Hussein was himself to have a narrow escape shortly after Hazza Majali's death. A plot to kill him was uncovered, the agent apparently being a member of the King's personal staff. A conversation had been taped by a Jordanian security officer who had become friendly with one of the staff of the UAR Embassy in Amman. When the tape was played back to the King, he heard the man saying: 'Within a short time Hussein will get the same treatment. We've recruited somebody in his residence to finish him off, and it won't be long now. If he had only stuck to a proper routine, we would have got him days ago.'[8]

It was thought expedient that the King slept elsewhere than in his Palace for the next few nights. He chose to spend the first night with his friends the Raynors, whose house was in the Palace grounds, while the plot was being further investigated. Raynor was sent to collect Hussein's clothes and personal effects from the Palace. Hussein told him to collect some new nose-drops for him, at the same time asking Mrs Raynor to get rid of the half-empty phial he had been using. She accordingly poured the drops into the sink and was horrified to see the liquid frothing and bubbling as she did so. She called the King to come and watch. He was appalled. The drops contained acid strong enough to peel off the covering from the chromium fittings. Had he used them, he would have died in dreadful agony. The culprit was never discovered, but Hussein wisely decided to make wholesale changes in his household staff, and to acquire a new medicine chest.

There followed the strange case of the poisoned cats. Semi-feral cats abound in Amman, the royal Palace having more than its fair share of them. One day Hussein came across several dead cats while walking in the grounds. When he casually mentioned this to one of the Palace officials, the official was seriously alarmed. It appeared that several other dead cats had been found, obviously poisoned. A plot to poison Hussein's food, again planned in Damascus, was uncovered. Ahmed Na'ana, one of the assistant cooks in the Palace kitchen, had been suborned by Syrian intelligence to do the deed. He had been under surveillance for some time and as a precaution had not been allowed near the King's food. However, in the expectation of a substantial reward if he succeeded in his task, Ahmed had been trying out the poison on cats in order to establish the correct dosage. This had led to his undoing. He went to prison, but some time later his daughter petitioned Hussein for his release on one of the great Muslim feasts. Hussein, magnanimous as always, gave way to her pleas, and Ahmed was freed to celebrate the Id with his family.

In those early years of his reign, before his natural impulsiveness had been tempered by experience, Hussein believed in the old military maxim that attack is the best form of defence. He was not prepared to sit back and accept with equanimity the scurrilous attacks made on him by Cairo and Damascus Radios. Nor did he agree with Nasser's role as spokesman for the entire Arab world. He was strongly opposed to Communism. As a fervent believer in Islam, he was just as determined to fight for his faith as he was to fight for Jordan. He therefore took the bold step soon after Hazza Majali's murder of flying to New York to address the General Assembly of the United Nations.

As might have been expected, the UAR placed every obstacle in his path. His intended flight by BOAC to London was refused permission to cross Syria. Hussein had instead to charter an Air Jordan plane to fly via Khartoum, Libya and Malta to London, the journey taking twenty-three hours instead of the seven hours by BOAC. From London he flew on to New York.

Hussein took immense trouble over his speech, preparing most of it himself. Some of his staff wanted him to tone it down, advice which he rejected, saying he had not travelled as far as the United States merely to utter platitudes. He spoke on 3 October 1960, following immediately after a furious tirade against the UN and its Secretary-General Hammarskjöld by Nikita Khrushchev, who was heading the Soviet delegation. Shortly before Hussein began to speak, Khrushchev, together with the UAR delegation, ostentatiously walked out, an act of gratuitous rudeness that won Hussein many supporters.

Speeches delivered thirty years ago read strangely today, a great deal of water having flowed under the bridge since they made the headlines. Nevertheless it is worth quoting the preamble to Hussein's speech since it makes plain the reason why he chose to address the General Assembly in the first place.

'There are four reasons why I am here,' he told his audience.

First, I was deeply concerned over what seemed to be an obvious attempt to wreck the United Nations. Second, I wanted to be sure that there was no mistake about where Jordan stands in the conflict of ideologies that is endangering the peace of the world. Third, as the head of a small nation, I felt it was my duty to the other small nations of the world, particularly to the new members of the United Nations, to share with them our experience in preserving the freedom which we, like they, fought so hard to win. Fourth, and finally, I believe it to be my duty to express my views on three vital problems in the Middle East affecting the peace of the world – namely, the growing tension between Jordan and the United Arab Republic, the independence of Algeria, and the still unanswered problem of Palestine. . . .[9]

Hussein went on to say that 'In the great struggle between Communism and freedom, there can be no neutrality.' Many of those listening agreed, and it won him much support in America. As for Palestine, he warned, 'The world's conscience seems to have closed its eyes in a rather shameful manner and for far too long on this tragedy of humanity. . . . The original failure of the United Nations to permit the people the right of self-determination in 1947 has left in its wake an unresolved situation. . . . The world is too prone to accept a *fait accompli* as a basis of policy. . . .'

The speech was something of a personal triumph. It converted many doubters, and won Jordan – and Hussein – many friends. The young man of twenty-five coming almost directly from the violent death of his Prime Minister, and from his own almost miraculous escapes, struck some of his listeners as being almost a knight errant, standing up boldly to be counted in a forum where far too many people were unwilling or afraid to state publicly their fundamental faith in humanity and their belief in freedom. It touched the hearts of many of his hearers, including Mr Nehru's, not a man usually inclined to put any trust in princes. President Eisenhower and Prime Minister Harold Macmillan personally congratulated Hussein, as did Hammarskjöld. The visit to New York was followed by one to Washington, where Hussein had valuable talks with Eisenhower, who was greatly impressed by the young King. Hussein's courage in making the trip had been rewarded. He had put Jordan on the map.

CHAPTER EIGHT

Palestine, the Palestinians and the PLO

'We make fun of ourselves, Palestinians; we say every two Palestinians need three chairs. All of us are leaders.'[1]

The problem of Palestine and the Palestinian refugees has been King Hussein's abiding concern since he ascended the throne. He has lived with it day and night ever since, remembering that his great-grandfather King Hussein bin Ali always refused to agree to the alienation of Palestine from the Arab homeland, and that his grandfather lost his life on account of it. It also has its bearing on Hussein's belief in Arab unity, since whatever else may divide the Arab countries, on one thing they are resolutely united: there must be a solution to the Palestine problem that will provide the Palestinian people with the self-determination they claim as the birthright of free peoples everywhere.

When Hussein first came to the throne there was a certain ambivalence towards the Palestinians on the part of their cousins on the East Bank. Although sharing their outrage at the way they had been driven out of their homes and lands by the Israelis, and although sympathising with their harsh lot as refugees, it was hard for a small country like Jordan, which was mostly desert, to absorb successfully what amounted to a virtual doubling of its population. There were too, among some people, doubts about their loyalty to the Hashemite regime, since it was well known that by no means all of them had approved the joining together of the West and East Banks in 1950 to form the Hashemite Kingdom of Jordan; moreover, there were those who considered King Abdullah to have been in league with the Jews in pursuit of his own aggrandisement. Relatively few Palestinians, for example, were enlisted into the Arab Legion in those days, and then only into the technical corps, the 'teeth' arms being reserved almost entirely for the East Bankers.

King Hussein has never subscribed to this view. His aim has been to weld together the two halves of his realm into one nation, as part of his concept of Arabism. It is also true to say that the Palestinians have made a major contribution to Jordan's economy since 1948, with their natural flair for commerce and their skills as engineers and technicians of all kinds. No one has tried harder, nor with more honest intentions, to solve the problem of the Palestinians than Hussein, by no means invariably helped by the Palestinians themselves, for whom unity of purpose has all too often been lost in a welter of words and internecine squabbling.

The disunity of the Palestinians was in many ways a reflection of the state of the rest of the Arab world in 1961. The short-lived union of Egypt and Syria was tottering towards collapse, the quick-witted Syrians resenting Egyptian arrogance and the inefficient Egyptian bureaucracy. President Nasser was at the same time feuding with Iraq and encouraging dissent in Jordan. His relations with Saudi Arabia were at best cool, and he was aiding the opponents of the Imam in the Yemen. He would soon complicate matters by sending a substantial number of troops to the Yemen in support of the republicans against the royalists. Many years later Hussein was to describe Nasser as a great Egyptian patriot, but accuse him of causing disunity among the Arabs by his determination to make Egypt great.

This was in the future. In 1961 Hussein felt sufficiently secure, after the uncertainties of the previous five years, to begin rebuilding his bridges with Nasser. He wrote in February proposing the restoration of good relations between Jordan and Egypt. Nasser responded in the same vein. The two years that followed were easier ones politically, as well as in a purely personal sense. Jordan, too, was beginning to pick up after years of internal discord. Industry was expanding, albeit slowly, and the tourist trade, one of Jordan's few earners of foreign currency, was given serious attention by the government. The port at Aqaba was developed, communications within the country were improved and expanded, and the armed forces were largely re-equipped as a result of aid from Kuwait, Saudi Arabia and the USA. Most significant of all, perhaps, was the great increase in education, with the opening of new schools and the university in Amman. Women were not excluded from these educational reforms that were to pay handsome dividends in the years to come.

A great deal of this improvement in Jordan's economy derived from the skills and enterprise of the Palestinians who had settled in Jordan. But there were others too who played an important part: Iraqis fleeing from the oppressive regime in Baghdad, and Lebanese who could see the writing on the wall in their own country and who flocked to Amman, which began to take on the shape and size of a great city, far different from the modest market town in which Hussein was born.

Hussein's gradually increasing self-confidence had in itself a certain infectious quality. Until now the impression that many people had had of him was that of the playboy. No one doubted his courage, but he was most often to be pictured at the wheel of a car, in the cockpit of a plane, or on waterskis behind a fast launch – and frequently, too, dancing in a nightclub with his arm round the waist of a pretty girl. None of this was the slightest bit unusual for a high-spirited young man with the means to indulge his tastes, but it had set tongues wagging both in Jordan and in the West. It could be said that Hussein provided plenty of copy for the gossip columnists, much of it reported inaccurately. But he would have been unrepentant were this ever brought to his notice. After all the difficulties he had successfully surmounted, he felt he had earned some relaxation among young men and women of his own age.

But Jordan is a conservative country and many a grey beard wagged disapprovingly. There was criticism in the newspapers, avidly seized upon by the King's opponents. King Abdullah, it was said, would never have approved of such goings-on. His court was renowned for its solemnity and protocol. Women seldom appeared there, and then never with bare arms and décolleté dresses. The appearance of women wearing shorts in public is still frowned upon in Jordan today; it was even more so thirty-five years ago. Collars and ties were *de rigueur* in the Arab Legion on the hottest day; no one ever saw Glubb Pasha in shirt sleeves and an open-necked shirt. There was some relaxation after Hussein came to the throne, but not to any marked extent. Most of his ministers had served King Abdullah and they behaved and dressed accordingly. It could be irritating for a young man in a hurry. Hussein tells of an occasion when he was late for a meeting and came bounding down the Palace stairs, only to encounter Queen Zein at the bottom of them. She told her son sternly that kings did not run from pillar to post. It is possible that Hussein took her admonitions to heart since punctuality has never since been among the Hashemite virtues.

It was not only the more conservative members of Jordanian society who regarded Hussein's lifestyle with some disapproval. It caused great concern in Washington and London, where King Farouk's fall from grace in Egypt was still very much in mind. But the problem was how to allow the King to live the active life he so clearly enjoyed, without at the same time endangering the stability of the monarchy. The Americans were sufficiently alarmed to post to their Embassy in Amman an official with the task of getting close to the King and helping with his popular image. He may have done some good, but it is more likely that it was Hussein's falling head-over-heels in love that really did the trick.

Scottish dancing was then all the rage and Hussein greatly enjoyed it. He used to hold parties at Shuneh, where he had a house beside the Dead Sea. The normal convention was that the King could not ask a lady to dance with him; she had to make the first move. One of the King's regular partners was Mrs Helen Tunnel (now Thompson), whose husband was a junior diplomat at the British Embassy. She was getting ready for a party at Shuneh when she was telephoned by a young RAF officer stationed in Amman. He had been invited to attend the King's party and wanted to take as his partner a Miss Antoinette Gardiner, who had recently arrived in Amman. Would Mrs Tunnel be kind enough to chaperone her? The answer was yes.

Miss Gardiner, usually called Toni, was barely nineteen. Her father, Lieutenant-Colonel Walker Gardiner, was a British officer who had been serving with the British Training Mission until it had been broken up at the end of 1959. Jordan was suffering from a severe drought at that time and Gardiner, who was an engineer by training, had stayed on at the Ambassador's request to assist the Jordanians in tackling the water shortage. He and his wife have made their home in Jordan ever since.

Their daughter was very blonde, short in height and very pretty. She possessed a vivacious personality but was still very shy. When Mrs Tunnel took her across the dance floor to be introduced to the King, the poor girl could hardly speak. It was only after frequent nudges that she could bring herself to invite him to dance. Hussein responded with alacrity, and from that moment onwards danced with hardly anyone else. Toni was very much an outdoor girl, fond like the King of swimming, horseback riding, water skiing and go-karting. And like him she enjoyed dancing and parties. They made a handsome pair, being of much the same height, and they were soon seeing a great deal of each other. Toni, who had only recently left school, had no aspirations to be considered an intellectual. Nor, for that matter, had Hussein. They were extremely well matched. Soon Hussein had fallen in love with her, and she with him.

Although Anglo-Jordanian relations had greatly improved by 1961, the prospect of their king marrying a British girl was not welcomed by some of his advisers. Nor was the Foreign Office in London altogether certain that it would not lead to complications. Hussein, however, was determined, and so was Toni. The young couple behaved with exemplary tact, and when the marriage took place there was widespread rejoicing throughout the country. Hussein gave his bride the Arabic name Muna al-Hussein, which means Hussein's wish. She converted to Islam and naturally became a Jordanian; she also studied Arabic. Above all she gave Hussein domestic companionship at a time when he was becoming increasingly lonely.

Muna, who was essentially simple in her tastes, did not wish to be called Queen but preferred instead to be called Princess Muna. Her pleasant and simple manner soon endeared her to the Jordanian people, and she provided Hussein with the domestic anchor he so badly needed at a time when his public duties were growing increasingly complicated and difficult.

One of his counsellors who had doubted the wisdom of the marriage was Wasfi Tell, a farmer–politician from Irbid who will figure prominently later in this narrative. He was a convinced King's-man of wide experience and strong personality. Born in 1921, he was the son of a famous poet. Wasfi attended the American University in Beirut, then a hotbed of Arab nationalism, and tried to join the Arab Legion in 1942, only to be turned down by Glubb Pasha – it was said on account of the fact that he was a university graduate. Wasfi joined the British Army instead, attaining the rank of captain and acquiring the habit of pipe-smoking; in later years he was seldom to be seen without one. He was demobilised in 1945 and the interest he showed in nationalist politics brought him into conflict with King Abdullah at one stage. Wasfi understood psychological warfare and knew how to manipulate radio, through which he became involved in government, and grew close to Hussein, who liked the way he spoke his mind. He first became a minister in Hazza Majali's Cabinet in 1959, and thereafter served for a time as Jordanian Ambassador in Baghdad. Wasfi's wide experience of men and affairs had made him suspicious of Nasser and of the Egyptian President's motives in trying to become the leader of the Arab world. He was unwavering in his hostility to Nasser's meddling in Jordan's affairs, and said so, frequently and unequivocally. His influence with the King was considerable and he was an excellent man of business.

Hussein was well aware of the importance of his armed forces, and he was never happier than when visiting his military units and talking with the soldiers and pilots. A fanatically keen flier himself, he had recently qualified as a helicopter pilot; he enjoyed the jargon of the young men and took the keenest interest in aeronautical matters. He devoted a great deal of time to building up the RJAF, and also to Jordan's civil airline, then limited to a handful of De Havilland Doves and ageing Dakotas. Wing Commander Jock Dalgliesh, who had taught him to fly, remained a friend for life, as also has Erik Bennet, who played an important part in developing the RJAF and who went on later to become an air marshal in the service of Sultan Qaboos of Oman. The RJAF owes a great debt to its King, and to his two British advisers, Dalgliesh and Bennet.

The ex-Mufti of Jerusalem, Haj Amin al-Husseini, had from his refuge in Cairo played an important part in keeping the Palestinian cause alive at a time when so many others were doing their best to forget it. He had his reward when the Arab foreign ministers met at Shtura in 1960 and agreed that there was a 'Palestinian Entity' on the West Bank. At the same time they made approving noises about the formation of a Palestinian Liberation Army (PLA), although Hussein, as King of the West Bank, could hardly be expected to approve; it must surely be the Jordanian armed forces who bore the responsibility for the defence of the West Bank against Israeli aggression. Moreover, this singling out of the West Bank as part of the concept of a Palestinian entity hardly conformed with Hussein's contention that the East and the West Banks were as one, in forming the Kingdom of Jordan. The

Shtura agreement was in fact the first small cloud on the horizon that would eventually swell into a tempest.

Unfortunately, Hussein's concordat with Nasser lasted only until the end of 1962. In September 1961 there had been a 'quiet revolution' in Syria which resulted in the end of the short-lived union with Egypt. Nasser's viceroy in Damascus, Field Marshal Abdel Hakim Amer, was put on a plane and sent home to Cairo. The United Arab Republic, so loudly proclaimed as an example of Arab unity, now consisted only of Egypt. Nasser's discomfiture gave Hussein the opportunity to point the moral, which he was unwise enough to do. He accused Nasser of arrogating to himself the leadership of the Arabs, of trying to impose Egyptian rule over the Syrians, and of causing disunity among the Arabs as a result. This was unwise because Nasser still had an enormous following among the Arabs. But Hussein continued his attacks, possibly at Wasfi's instigation, souring relations with Nasser, which reached their nadir when Jordan established a Joint Military Command with Saudi Arabia in August 1962. This was to lead to trouble.

There was a revolution in Yemen on 26 September 1962. An attempt by the republicans, backed by Egypt, to kill the Imam al-Badr failed. He escaped to raise the flag in the mountains among his Zeidi tribesmen. Nasser sent troops to assist the republicans. The Saudis provided the royalists with aid. As Sultan Fadhl bin Ali, Sultan of Lahej, once commented: 'Whoever tries to interfere in the internal quarrels of the Yemenis will sooner or later regret it.'[2] Hussein was soon to discover the truth of this. He sent a squadron of fighter planes to help the royalists. On arrival at Najran, near the Saudi border with Yemen, Hussein's air force commander, together with two other pilots, defected with their planes to Cairo. Wasfi had to be hurriedly sent to Najran to recall the rest of the squadron to Amman. The Saudis, as is their wont, kept a lower profile. They provided the arms and the money to the Imam, but no troops. It suited them for Nasser to become increasingly embroiled in Yemen, without any obvious advantage to Egypt. But this was of little use to Hussein, whose relations with Nasser began to go from bad to worse. They were soon as bad as they had ever been. How far Wasfi's influence was responsible for this deterioration in relations is difficult to establish, but it must have played some part. It helped to make Hussein unpopular on the West Bank, where Nasser had a considerable following. Nor was this feeling confined only to the West Bank. There was a certain amount of discontent in the army, due mainly to pay and allowances, that led to disturbances in Zerqa. Hussein's personal intervention, when his willingness to listen to genuine grievances impressed both officers and soldiers, soon settled the matter, but it was certainly a straw in the wind. Very soon thereafter Jordanian support for the Imam of Yemen was quietly allowed to wither on the vine.

There had been a further complication during 1962 when Israel announced its intention of drawing off water from the River Jordan to irrigate the Negev. This had been a bone of contention as far back as 1955 when Eric Johnston, a US official, had chaired a conference to discuss the Jordan waters. Johnston had allocated 60 per cent of the water to Jordan, Syria and Lebanon, and 40 per cent to Israel, but the agreement had never been ratified by the Arab states for fear they might be thought to be recognising Israel. Israel, with no such inhibitions, went ahead with its plans, whereas Jordan, with an urgent requirement to irrigate the Jordan valley, stayed its hand in the interests of Arab solidarity. The year of decision was to be 1964 when Israel would begin to draw off water from Lake Tiberias. It was with this in mind that a summit conference was arranged to be held in Cairo, in order to devise some means of dealing with the Israelis.

Prior to the Cairo Summit, however, the Arab world had been convulsed by events in Iraq, which had repercussions far beyond Iraq itself. In February 1963 President Kassem, who had deluded himself into believing that he was proof against overthrow, was attacked in the Ministry of Defence, which he had turned into a mini-fortress. The coup was masterminded by a former comrade, Colonel Abdul Salam, and Kassem died in the storming of his headquarters. Salam had the support of the Iraqi Ba'athists, and no sooner were the Ba'athists established in Baghdad than talks were opened with their Ba'athist former opponents in Damascus. Although the two parties had exchanged little other than insults for some considerable time, now it was all sweetness and light. The beguiling theme of union was discussed and there was an interchange of compliments, proposals and hot air between Baghdad and Damascus. Nasser, whose relations with Kassem had been bad, at once welcomed the new regime in Iraq and seized the opportunity to make a comeback into the centre of the Arab stage. It happened that Abdul Salam had Pan-Arab ambitions and welcomed the prospect of an Egypt–Iraq–Syria union. On 17 April 1963, an agreement to this effect was signed, as worthless a piece of paper as any signed by Arab heads of state or their foreign ministers since the end of the Second World War. Since there was to be an interval of twenty-five months before the Union came into being, there was plenty of time for reflection.

Jordan, which had not been invited to join the Union, was suddenly torn apart by riots. That mystical word 'union', which can be calculated to set most Arab hearts aflame, soon had the mobs demonstrating in Jordan's schools and universities and on the streets. The worst demonstrations were in Jerusalem, where the Jordanian flag was pulled down and burned, the police were attacked, and the mob rampaged through the streets screaming 'Nasser!' Hussein had replaced Wasfi Tell by Samir Rifai, Wasfi's known views being considered provocative, but Samir failed to get a vote of confidence in parliament. A motion supporting Jordan's adherence to the new Union was debated with acclamation, and at one stage it looked as if there was going to be a repetition of July 1958.

But Hussein was learning fast. He made his uncle, Sharif Hussein bin Nasser (not to be confused with another of the King's uncles, Sharif Nasser bin Jameel – brother of Queen Zein – who was a soldier), Prime Minister, and instructed him to act with vigour. The army was ordered into the streets and acted without fear or favour. Calm was quickly restored, helped greatly by Nasser's rapid disillusionment with the Syrian regime. Almost before the ink was dry on his signature, he withdrew Egypt from the Union on 23 July, describing the Syrians as 'fascists'. Syria and Iraq then tried to go it alone, but it was a case of oil and water. The Syrians got on the nerves of their Iraqi partners, who were as brutal and direct as the Syrians were smooth and devious. In November, President Abdul Salam threw the Syrians out of Baghdad, and yet another Arab attempt at union had vanished in smoke.

The ill-fated attempt had, however, given Hussein cause for thought. Like every other Arab, he favoured unity. But he wanted a union which would permit every Arab state to preserve its separate identity within the united whole. He had already stated his willingness to co-operate with the Egypt–Iraq–Syria Union, but he was not prepared to go any further than that. He could see the danger of allowing a small state like Jordan to become absorbed in a union. It would soon lose its identity – and the Hashemites risk their throne. Most of the East Bankers, apart from the refugee element, agreed with him. On the West Bank it was generally agreed that only after complete Arab unity would the Israelis be defeated; and in order to achieve this unity the Palestinians were perfectly willing to jettison Hussein, and Jordan too for that matter.

It was during these troubles, that lay scattered in Hussein's path like boulders in a *wadi*, that Muna gave birth to a son in February 1962. Every Muslim hopes that his firstborn will be a son and Hussein was overjoyed. The child was named Abdullah after his great-grandfather. He was to be followed in due course by another boy, Feisal, and then by twin girls, Zein and Aisha. The day after Abdullah was born, Hussein received a letter from an unknown Englishman asking whether he intended sending his son to Harrow. Hussein replied that he supposed that he would; but in the event security considerations led him to send both his sons to the USA for their college education. However, Abdullah did follow his father to Sandhurst, as did his sister Aisha. Feisal, who has inherited his father's love for flying, attended the RAF College at Cranwell, passing out in July 1987 with five of the seven awards. Hussein's daughter by Dina, Alia, was brought up by Princess Muna as one of her own family.

Hussein worried a great deal over the succession. When Abdullah was born he named him Crown Prince, but as one turbulent year followed another, different considerations began to prevail. Were anything to happen to Hussein, it was essential that the succession should be quick and firm. This was hardly likely to be the case when the Heir Apparent was still in the nursery. Moreover, the successor, whoever he might be, must be a Hashemite and have the army's support. Hussein's second brother, Muhammad, was next in line after Abdullah, but after anxious consideration it was decided to make Hassan, Hussein's youngest brother, Crown Prince, by royal decree. Hussein has said that it was not an easy decision, but Hassan was more politically adept than Muhammad, and was a strong character. In Hussein's opinion he possessed the characteristics that would be necessary in the event of his own assassination.

Hassan, who was twelve years younger than Hussein, was at Harrow at the time, where he had a most successful career, his Housemaster reporting on him as being 'quite outstanding'. He then went on to Christ Church at Oxford University, where he read Hebrew and Arabic. He is decidedly the intellectual of the family, an excellent public speaker with a great interest in science and economics. Hassan was proclaimed Crown Prince in 1965, after ratification by parliament, and has been Hussein's right-hand man ever since. His wife, Princess Sarvath, is the daughter of the late Sir Muhammad Ikramullah, one of the architects of Pakistan, and Pakistan's outstanding Ambassador in London for many years. She and Hassan have three daughters and a son.

Taking this difficult decision was typical of Hussein's no-nonsense and pragmatic approach to matters of state. Jordan's welfare and the continuance of the Hashemite house must have priority over all other considerations. He says it gave him a great deal of anxious thought. He has since named Ali, his son by Queen Alia, as next in line of succession after Hassan, and this has been ratified by the Council of State. Ali is still a minor.

Hussein's marriage to Muna, coinciding as it did with a relatively tranquil period in his turbulent reign, brought him a great deal of happiness. He discovered the joys of family life, playing with his children, nieces and nephews, picnicking in the desert or down by the Dead Sea, driving go-karts or relaxing in the sea at Aqaba. But he lived perforce a life of great tension, fending off Jordan's enemies, and doing his best to keep the country going, with very little industry and the crippling requirement to maintain a military establishment that so poor a country could ill afford. It meant constant juggling with finances if money were to be found to improve the country's infrastructure, and if at the same time its defences were to be strengthened. To some who knew Jordan in the reign of King Abdullah, when all was pastoral peace east of the River Jordan, it is astonishing that Hussein has managed to do as much as he has done.

In those early years on the throne, when he was learning statecraft by trial and error, Hussein naturally made mistakes. He could be short and abrupt with those he felt were not pulling their weight; and, like his grandfather Abdullah before him, he could be coldly courteous to those out of favour. But he tried always to be fair and it was Jordan that concerned him, not himself. Experience had shown him that by no means all men were to be trusted, nor were all men loyal or honest. Intrigue and politics would seem to be inseparable, and there are no greater intriguers, nor politicians, than the Arabs. For much of the time as he learned his trade, Hussein walked a tightrope, only too well aware that there were many who would delight if he lost his footing and fell. Sometimes he very nearly did, but he always managed to regain his balance. Yet it was a testing life, and he is surely not to be blamed if at times he was short of temper. Like all men who work hard, and who play hard, he expected others to do the same, and not surprisingly some could not stay the pace.

One who served him during those early years in his reign has had this to say of King Hussein:

> He was still learning his trade at that time, and it was interesting to see how, as his experience increased, he grew into the job. By the end of it all he had been through so much, had suffered so many disappointments, even disasters and betrayals, had met so many world statesmen and had survived so many crises, that he had become one of the world's most experienced and wisest leaders. By then everyone had heard of Hussein, and because they had heard of the King, they had heard of Jordan. It was a wonderful achievement. But only those of us who were with him during the tough times can really know how much he put into it, and what a tremendous man he is.[3]

In the forest of difficulties that Hussein had to traverse, one tree stood out. It was Palestine and the Palestinians. Although it was the ex-Mufti who first conceived the idea of forming some kind of organisation to co-ordinate Palestinian activities during their diaspora, it was undoubtedly President Nasser who was the midwife who produced the Palestine Liberation Organisation, better known by its initials, PLO. This took place at the first Arab Summit held in Cairo in 1964, which was designed to discuss the action to be taken by the Arab states when Israel began to divert the Jordan waters in order to irrigate the Negev. In fact, however, Palestine and the Palestinians came to dominate the meeting. In this Nasser was motivated not so much by concern for the Palestinians as by fear lest the *fedayeen* raids which were being carried out against Israel resulted in massive reprisals against Egypt. That could lead to a war with Israel, for which Nasser knew Egypt was ill prepared.

It has been alleged that it was the Americans who first put into Nasser's mind the possibility of bringing the Palestinians together into one comprehensive resistance movement, over which he, Nasser, might expect to assert control. The Americans were at the time quite close to Nasser and knew that he wanted to avoid war with Israel until Egypt was ready for one. That would be some considerable time in the future. Nasser therefore sponsored the creation of the PLO, at the same time ensuring that its headquarters would be in Cairo and that its chairman would be a Palestinian of Nasser's choice. This turned out to be a Jerusalem lawyer, Ahmed Shukairy, who had strong links with Syria, and who was a demagogue of the first water, violent in expression and hasty in judgement. He was not to prove a success.

Hussein had some doubts about the wisdom of establishing the PLO, but he went along with it in the interests of Arab solidarity, only stipulating that 'the PLO had to co-operate with Jordan without a trace of friction.'[4] He feared, with some justification, that Nasser might deflect *fedayeen* activities from Egyptian territory to Jordanian; the King had certainly no wish to resurrect the border war with Israel, which had temporarily cooled down. Hussein also agreed at that same summit to the formation of a Unified Arab Command (UAC) in order to consolidate 'Arab armed forces in the face of expansionist Zionism'. The UAC was to be headed by General Ali Ali Amer, an Egyptian officer. As a result of this, Jordan was to receive financial help from Egypt and Saudi Arabia to help with the re-equipment and expansion of its armed forces. Unfortunately, in the long run the UAC was to prove to be little more than a paper tiger, but its formation seemed to Hussein to be yet another step on the road to Arab solidarity; he therefore welcomed it warmly.

The PLO is an umbrella title for a variety of organisations with differing philosophies, aims and tactics. The most effective of these splinter groups has proved to be the Movement for the National Liberation of Palestine; in Arabic, Harakat al-Tahrir al-Watani al-Falastini. By reversing the important initial letters we get the acronym Fatah, by which it is best known. It was founded in 1957 by Yasser Arafat (Abu Amar) and Khalil al-Wazir (Abu Jihad), and it remained an underground organisation until 1965, when it came out into the open and took control of the PLO; some time later Arafat became the Chairman of the Organisation. The principal problem of the Palestinians, however, is their inability to agree among themselves. As one Jordanian has described them, 'they are all chiefs with no Indians.' Policy is debated endlessly and agreement is difficult. Fatah has, for example, spawned the Popular Front for the Liberation of Palestine (PFLP), a more violent organisation headed by George Habash, a Palestinian doctor; and the Popular Democratic Front (PDF) headed by Nawaf Hawatmeh, even more violent, who broke away from Habash in

1969. There is also the Popular Front for the Liberation of Palestine General Command (PFLP–GC), Syrian-sponsored and headed by Ahmed Jabril, who had originally formed the Palestine Liberation Front (PLF). If this welter of initials serves any purpose, it is to emphasise the disparate nature of the Palestinian Resistance Movement, united perhaps only in their determination to achieve self-determination for the Palestinian people.

Arafat, who was born in Cairo on 24 August 1929, is of humble origins, although distantly related to the Husseini clan, of which the ex-Mufti was a leading member. Trained as an engineer, largely as a result of his own efforts, Arafat subsequently worked in Kuweit where he amassed a considerable fortune, which he has dedicated to the Palestinian cause. A skilled conspirator and good organiser, he is a firm believer in consensus politics, which, given the stresses and strains within the PLO, means that he has all along been unwilling to go against the minority view. This has led many of the Arab leaders, notably King Hussein and President Hafez Assad of Syria, to doubt his ability to comply with any agreement that may have been reached with him. He has, however, a certain charisma, despite his often unkempt appearance, and there can be no doubt about his personal courage. He is certainly a man to be reckoned with.

One of Hussein's many endearing characteristics is his sense of humour, as this story which he has told against himself may demonstrate. When first he paid a visit to King Abdul Aziz bin Saud in Riyadh, that great man was far gone in decline, and confined to a wheelchair. After greeting Hussein and inviting him to inspect the guard of honour, King Abdul Aziz beckoned to the young King to accompany him into the Palace. A wheelchair was promptly provided for Hussein, which he smilingly declined, only to realise suddenly that protocol demanded that King Abdul Aziz could not be wheeled into the Palace with his guest walking by his side. Hussein accordingly accepted the offer and the two kings, young and old, were solemnly wheeled into the Palace side by side.

The Saudi Royal Family have their own way of arranging the succession to the throne from among King Abdul Aziz's numerous sons. Towards the end of 1964 their patience ran out with Abdul Aziz's successor, King Saud, whose extravagance and incompetence could no longer be endured, although Hussein blamed this more on Saud's advisers than on Saud himself. However, Saud had to abdicate in favour of his half-brother, Feisal, an entirely different character, who had been Saudi Foreign Minister for many years. An austere and deeply religious man, Feisal's bogey was Communism, which made him anti-Russian and *ipso facto* opposed to President Nasser, who was at the time deeply involved with the Soviet Union for the re-equipment and retraining of the Egyptian army. Feisal set about forming an Islamic pact among the Arab countries, which Jordan joined after Feisal's visit to Amman in January 1966. This caused a furore in Cairo.

There had been a brief period in 1963 and 1964 when most of the Arab countries were on speaking terms with each other. This solidarity had been brought about chiefly as a result of Israel's announcement at the end of 1963 of its intention to divert the Jordan waters. The decisions of the Arab Summit that resulted have already been recorded above. But Feisal's Islamic Pact put an end to this brief harmony. Nasser was furious and concentrated his venom against Hussein. The two were soon again at loggerheads, Cairo and Amman Radios adding fuel to the flames. This was unfortunate because there had been a marked change among the Arabs, particularly with Nasser, who no longer seemed to be hostile to the conservative monarchical states but instead sought their co-operation. The Islamic Pact changed this.

Hussein was also concerned by the activities of the PLO Chairman, Ahmed Shukairy, with whom his relations were no more than correct. Shukairy had based himself at the PLO office in Amman, from where he did his best to inflame the situation by his oratory. He was a rather uncouth man whose personal appearance and reputed lifestyle did little to endear him to the King.

Nineteen-sixty-six was to turn out to be a very different year. It was not only that it had begun with the Islamic Pact and the reopening of the Nasser–Hussein feud. In addition Fatah stepped up their *fedayeen* raids into Israel that spring and summer. They were not very successful and were easily handled by the Israeli security forces, but they did once again raise the possibility of Israeli reprisals against Jordan. The clamour for such action, chiefly against Syria, soon began to appear in the Israeli newspapers and on the radio. This caused Hussein great concern since it was well known that Fatah commandos were using Jordanian territory on their way to and from Israel. Wasfi Tell, who was Prime Minister at the time, advised Hussein to demonstrate his disapproval of the Fatah raids by closing the PLO office in Amman and sending Shukairy packing. The King followed this advice, and Shukairy was dispatched, on this occasion, to Gaza. Meanwhile, the war of words by radio increased in volume and in virulence.

The Syrians were mainly responsible for the fast-deteriorating situation. Their artillery on the Golan fired on the Israeli settlements below whenever they felt inclined, leading Wasfi Tell to comment, 'It is only a matter of time before the Israelis retaliate far more effectively than the Syrians ever could.' He was soon to be proved right, but he was wrong in assuming that the Israelis' wrath would fall on the Syrians. They struck instead at the remote hamlet of Samu, at the extreme southern end of the Jordan–Israel demarcation line, some ten miles south of Hebron. It was 13 November 1966. Samu, which was four miles inside Jordan, was chosen presumably because it was within easy reach of the Israeli security forces, and suitably distant from the nearest Jordanian military garrison. A relieving force was sent from Hebron as soon as reports of the raid were received, but it ran headlong into an Israeli ambush. Twenty-one Jordanian soldiers were killed and thirty-seven wounded. The Israelis had evicted all the inhabitants from Samu before the ambush and had dynamited all the houses.

There followed a furious outcry in Jordan. 'Too little and too late' was one comment. Hussein was blamed for refusing to permit the PLA to operate on the West Bank, and for disbanding the Home Guard and leaving the villagers to depend on the army. There were the inevitable riots, on this occasion inflamed by Shukairy's rantings and ravings. He called for the establishment of a Palestinian republic in Jordan, presumably with himself as President. Cairo and Damascus Radios vied with each other in their attacks on Hussein and Wasfi Tell. With or without Nasser's endorsement, the Jordanian armed forces were openly encouraged to overthrow the King. It was only another example of the Arabs' tendency to blame everyone except themselves for their own shortcomings. The Unified Arab Command proved to be completely ineffective; it merely provided employment, and improved promotion, for officers of the Egyptian army. No plans existed to deal with the kind of situation that had arisen at Samu, nor was any attempt made to rally to Jordan's side. Amid the charges and counter-charges in the press and on the radio, no one paused to consider that it had been Fatah whose activities had in the first place resulted in Israel's attack against Samu; nor did anyone mention that Fatah could have done nothing without Syrian support. The general impression was that it had all been Hussein's fault.

The Syrians certainly showed no signs of remorse. They criticised Hussein instead for putting down the rioting in Jordan with such a heavy hand, and then went on to kill a Jordanian border guard four hundred yards within Jordan. Hussein was so angry that he expelled the Syrian Ambassador. This led to even more vitriolic abuse on Damascus Radio. It was clear by the end of 1966 that the short-lived rapprochement between Hussein and Nasser had come to an end. Nasser grew closer to Syria as he pushed Hussein farther and farther out into the cold. Only the Israelis could have drawn any comfort from this. Should it ever come to war, they did not want to fight Egypt and Jordan simultaneously.

The reprisal raid by the Israelis on Samu proved to be the watershed in the run-up to the third Arab–Israel war. In the first place the Israelis, by choosing as their target a Jordanian village, when they knew well enough that it was Syria that was encouraging and arming Fatah, convinced

Hussein and his ministers that their own moderate policies would be no guarantee against an Israeli attack, should it ever come to war again. Since Hussein was convinced that Israel's long-term ambition was the seizure of the West Bank and Jerusalem, and since he felt certain that Israel would not let slip any opportunity to achieve it, it followed that Jordan in the event of war could not afford to go it alone and stay on the sidelines. She must ally herself with the other Arab front-line states.

There was another outcome to the Samu raid. It greatly inflamed the situation within Jordan itself. There were cries for vengeance, and for a time it seemed as if the country might be plunged into civil war. Only the army's steadiness, and its loyalty to Hussein, brought things under control. There was a great deal of wild talk, and in the refugee camps in particular there were some ugly incidents, ominous evidence perhaps of troubles to come. But Wasfi Tell was firm, and the agitation gradually subsided.

Samu had, however, placed Hussein in an extremely difficult position in relation to his loyalty to Arab solidarity. His refusal to retaliate by attacking Israel to avenge the destruction of Samu caused this loyalty to be questioned, particularly on the West Bank. He had managed by the skin of his teeth to get away with it over Samu, but he could not afford a repetition; and, unfortunately, one was waiting for him in the wings, only seven months away.

CHAPTER NINE

The Unnecessary War

'Don't make war. You will create a Palestinian nationalism, and you will never be able to get rid of it.' General de Gaulle to Abba Eban[1]

Churchill, when asked by Roosevelt to find a name for the Second World War, promptly replied, 'The Unnecessary War'. He said there had never been a war that could more easily have been prevented. This was equally true of the Arab–Israeli war of June 1967. No one on either side, apart from the hawks, wanted war at that time; but the Israeli hawks included a body of influential generals who felt the time had come to deal effectively with Egypt and Syria, although Jordan did not come into their calculations during the planning stage. On the Arab side the hawks were chiefly confined to Syria, which behaved at times in a highly irresponsible fashion. The war party in Israel did not include the Prime Minister, Levi Eshkol, nor the Foreign Minister, Abba Eban, who bent every effort to prevent war. De Gaulle may not have been strictly correct in warning Eban against creating a Palestinian nationalism, since as we have seen Palestinian nationalism had been steadily increasing in strength since 1960 and the meeting of the Arab foreign ministers at Shtura; but there can be no doubt that the 1967 war provided a considerable impetus to this process, as well as considerably increasing the number of Palestinian refugees in Jordan and elsewhere in the Arab world. The war was an unqualified disaster for Jordan since it cost Hussein half his kingdom.

The slide towards war began with the coming to power in Damascus of the Ba'athists in 1963, who showed themselves no more capable than their predecessors of providing Syria with a stable government. Their foreign policy appeared to be based on creating as much trouble as they could for the so-called 'reactionary regimes' in Jordan and Saudi Arabia. As part of their anti-Hashemite policy they lent their full weight to the PLO, encouraging Shukairy in his extravagant oratory, until in the end (as we have seen) an exasperated Hussein had to send him and the PLO packing. Nor were the Syrians particularly well disposed towards Nasser, memories of the brief Egypt–Syria Union being far from happy ones. They were also fully aware of Nasser's supposedly secret relations with certain Americans, the

US in Syrian eyes being almost entirely responsible for the establishment of the State of Israel.[2]

Although the Soviet Union was providing Egypt with arms on a large scale, it too was worried by American influence on Nasser. The Russians therefore began to establish closer relations with Syria. This caused Nasser considerable concern, as did Syria's encouragement of the PLO and Shukairy. Fatah was at this time still working under cover, but both the Egyptian and Jordanian security services were hot on its tracks. It was disturbing to think that Syria might provide both a base and the weapons for the more militant Palestinians to conduct operations against Israel, thereby increasing the likelihood of another war between the Arabs and Israel. Therefore, when Fatah launched the first *fedayeen* raids into Israel in 1965, Nasser took swift action to make his feelings plain. He instructed Field Marshal Abdel Hakim Amer to issue an order through the Unified Arab Command which described Assifa, the codename under which Fatah was operating, as an enemy of the Arab cause. Everything was to be done to discredit it among the Arabs.

The Arabs were divided in their approach to the Palestine problem. Nasser is said to have recognised the truth of the American conviction that Israel was a *fait accompli*, and that therefore little could be done for the Palestinians. The only way to prevent them in their misery setting the whole of the Middle East ablaze before Egypt was ready for it was by maintaining a tight control over the activities of the PLO. This in its turn meant putting some kind of a brake on Syria, never easy to accomplish. Ever the pragmatist, Nasser set about doing this by entering into a mutual defence treaty with Syria on 7 November 1966. It was a case of poacher turning gamekeeper.

Nasser needed as much reassurance as he could get as 1966 drew to a close. The unpopular war in Yemen dragged on, involving the cream of the Egyptian army. The fact that they lost their additional pay and allowances when they returned to Egypt had resulted in discontent among the troops, on whom Nasser greatly depended for the security of his regime. Meanwhile Egypt's economic problems multiplied – the rising birthrate saw to that – and, despite every effort on the government's part, the lot of the ordinary Egyptian was still one of the most miserable on earth. The last thing Nasser wanted was war with Israel, which would complicate matters still further.

It would not have mattered so much had the Arabs been able to agree on a common policy. As it happened, however, they could hardly have been more disunited. Nasser's attempts to reach agreement with King Feisal for an ending of the Yemen war had got nowhere, leaving Feisal with the feeling that he had been doublecrossed. Saudi Arabia and Egypt were barely on speaking terms. Admittedly relations with Iraq had improved since Kassem's overthrow, but President Aref in Baghdad was a conservative who believed Arab unity had to be based on Islam, although he was prepared to co-operate with Nasser's socialism. As for Jordan, the short-lived Nasser–Hussein honeymoon had come rapidly to an end. Hussein had plenty of evidence to show that many of the attempts to destabilise his regime, and even to bring about his assassination, had their origins in Cairo. As conditions inside Jordan settled down, it occurred to Hussein that perhaps the moment had come for him to counterattack Nasser. He was undoubtedly encouraged in this view by Wasfi Tell, with his profound suspicion of Nasser and his motives. Wasfi's previous experience of psychological warfare made him a powerful opponent, even for Nasser's formidable propaganda machine, Saut al-Arab (the Voice of the Arabs), which broadcast from Cairo.

Wasfi's chief target was Nasser personally. Neither Hussein nor Nasser can be held responsible for some of the more outrageous accusations broadcast from Amman and Cairo, but, in Jordan's case at least, some of the accusations can be seen in retrospect as having been counter-productive. For example, Jordan accused Nasser of sheltering behind the UN Emergency Force (UNEF), which had been deployed in Sinai since the 1956 war with Israel. This touched Nasser on the raw, and at a time when he wanted to avoid a war. The air became thick with mutual vituperation, Nasser denouncing Hussein as the 'whoremonger of Jordan'.

There was quite an influential body of opinion in Jordan which wondered if it made sense to attack Nasser at such a time. Surely it would be in the interest of Arab solidarity if Hussein and Nasser were to patch up their quarrel? This pro-Nasser party became more vocal after Wasfi's resignation as Prime Minister in December 1966. Wasfi always maintained that it was American-inspired, mainly by Richard Murphy, who was serving at that time in the US Embassy in Amman. With the exception of the hawks, however, no responsible official in Cairo, Amman or Tel Aviv wanted war. But the Israelis, with their pathological concern for their security, began to take the prospect of war far more seriously, and much earlier, than the Arabs. The generals were busy reviewing their war plans, believing as they did that this was the moment for which they had been waiting; they believed their political leaders must be stupid if they did not share this view. Yitzhak Rabin, Chief of Staff of the Israeli Defence Force (IDF), was particularly bellicose, and willing to put pressure on the Prime Minister should the need arise.

The Syrians were to give the Israeli hawks the opportunity for which they had been waiting. They opened artillery fire on Israeli settlers who had begun ploughing in the so-called Demilitarised Zone at the foot of the

Golan, a hangover from the Rhodes Armistice Agreements of 1949. They caused few casualties but created an enormous uproar in Israel. The Israelis sent a few tanks to encourage the settlers, whereupon the Russians for some unknown reason deemed this provocative. They told Syria that this might be a prelude to a full-scale attack on the Golan. This sent the Syrians hurrying to Cairo to enlist Nasser's support. In view of his mutual defence treaty with Syria, Nasser had no other option than to promise it.

As the winter months gave way to spring in 1967, tension in the Middle East increased. Although Nasser assured the Americans there would be no war 'except at a time and a place of our choosing', adding that Israel was much stronger than the Arabs, the Syrians continued with their sabre-rattling from Damascus. They appeared to be supported in this policy by the Soviet Union, for what purpose is hard to discern. The Russians seemed to be over-estimating the Arabs and under-estimating the Israelis. Hussein himself grew more and more uneasy. He suffered no illusions where the Israelis were concerned. As a trained pilot, who was struggling hard to build up his own small air force with little enough money with which to do this, he particularly feared the Israeli Air Force (IAF), which greatly outnumbered his own. He knew the powerful effect it could have on the land battle.

The IAF was soon to demonstrate its effectiveness. At 8 a.m. on 7 April 1967, Israelis began to plough a strip of Arab land south of Lake Tiberias. This was a deliberate provocation and produced the desired result. Syrian guns and mortars immediately opened fire, whereupon the IDF unleashed the guns, tanks and aircraft they had secretly assembled in anticipation of the Syrian reaction. A fierce air battle followed, which extended as far as the skies over Damascus. Six Syrian MiG-21s were shot down by Israeli Mystères with no loss to themselves. Israeli shellfire also caused many casualties; they lost only one man. There was an outcry in the Arab capitals that well suited the Israeli generals: it focused attention on Syria and the Golan.

Concentration of force is one of the principles of war. Every General Staff seeks to deal with one enemy at a time, dispersion of effort often resulting in defeat in detail. In dealing with the enemy forces deployed along her periphery, Israel has the advantage of interior lines. It is far easier for her to switch troops from south to north, or from east to west, than it is for the Arabs. Israel is moreover a small country and the distances are not great. But her generals wanted if at all possible to avoid having to fight Egypt and Syria simultaneously. They hoped to deal with Egypt first, before turning their attention to Syria. They did not include Jordan in their battle plan, hoping Hussein would stay out of the war, as he had done in 1956. This was conveyed to Amman by various means.

There were few hawks there. Hussein and his advisers were convinced that war would be to no one's advantage, except perhaps Israel's. Neverthe-less, no attempt was made that April and May to tone down Amman Radio's propaganda war against Nasser; if anything, it was stepped up. Nasser hit back on 1 May, accusing the King of being 'an agent and slave of the imperialists'. Meanwhile, in Israel, the duel between the hawks and doves was rapidly reaching a climax. The hawks, who included Moshe Dayan, recently appointed Defence Minister, were afraid lest the Prime Minister and Foreign Minister were going to 'do a Munich' on them. They could see their chances of smashing Egypt and Syria in quick succession fast slipping away, due to Eshkol's and Eban's conviction that it could all be settled by diplomacy. This was not at all what Rabin and his colleagues were planning.

It was an entirely unexpected, and unpredictable, move by Nasser that set the cat among the pigeons. UN Secretary-General Dag Hammarskjöld's diplomacy had been chiefly responsible for the setting up of the United Nations Emergency Force in Sinai in the aftermath of the Suez war in 1956. It was deployed in certain key areas such as Gaza, Sharm as-Sheikh and along the Negev border. Israel had refused to permit the establishment of posts on her territory, and Nasser had at first only reluctantly agreed. He made the proviso that UNEF must withdraw if Egypt requested it to do so. UNEF, like all peace-keeping forces of its kind, had had its successes and failures, but by and large it had fulfilled the Secretary-General's hopes. It had kept the peace in Sinai. UNEF was commanded by an Indian army major-general, Indar Rhikhye, whose headquarters were in Gaza and who took his orders from the Secretary-General in New York. The Secretary-General in 1967 was U Thant, a distinguished Burman.

General Glubb has written that there are today three different kinds of war. The first is global war, which speaks for itself. Then there is a localised war between two or more countries, like the Iraq–Iran conflict. And thirdly there is a United Nations war. In the case of the UN war, the Security Council was certain to intervene, probably sooner rather than later. The aim therefore was not necessarily to destroy the enemy's forces, but rather to seize territory which might be used as a bargaining counter at the UN, when the fighting had died down. This predicated a short, sharp war with limited objectives. Israel's in 1967 were the Sinai and a foothold on the Golan. The capture of Jerusalem and the seizure of the West Bank were not included in Israeli calculations, although Hussein was convinced that these were Israel's prime objectives.

For the kind of war envisaged by the Israeli General Staff, it would be essential to knock out the powerful Egyptian Air Force at the outset. Otherwise Israel's towns and cities would be pounded to pieces. The elimination of Egyptian air power was to be followed by a *Blitzkrieg* of tanks, supported by aircraft, all the way through Sinai to the Suez Canal.

With this phase of the operation completed, attention could be switched to Syria and the Golan. Mobile operations of the kind intended required commanders who led from the front, ready to seize the fleeting chance and willing to take great risks. The Israelis had already shown that these were the kind of operations in which they excelled. The Egyptians on the other hand were at sea in the fluid battle; their *métier* was a battle conducted from behind fixed defences; but there were no fixed defences in Sinai other than those erected by UNEF for an entirely different purpose. These were certainly never intended to withstand the kind of *Blitzkrieg* the Israelis had in mind.

Syria has been accused of entering into a secret agreement with Israel prior to the outbreak of war, utilising the good offices of the Spanish government for the purpose.[3] Syrian involvement would be limited to an exchange of artillery fire, in return for which Israel promised not to attack Damascus. The truth of this would be hard to establish but Syria was curiously slow in embarking on hostilities, and that at a time when both Egypt and Jordan were under great pressure. King Hussein certainly had his doubts about Syria. 'At least Jordan will enter this war with honour,' he said, when informed of Syrian hesitation.

Nasser was worried by the deteriorating situation. Syria claimed that Israel was massing tanks in Galilee. A Soviet delegation arriving in Cairo on 13 May confirmed this; they also said there were eleven brigades in Galilee, when there were in fact only twelve infantry companies. The Israeli Prime Minister offered the Soviet Ambassador facilities so that he could see for himself, but this was declined. The Soviet attitude throughout remains a mystery. Nasser's own position was at stake. Something like a war fever was sweeping Egypt. He had to do something to demonstrate his support for supposedly threatened Syria. On 15 May he ordered a state of alert and sent two divisions across the Canal into Sinai. On the following day he made his cardinal mistake. Despite the advice of his Foreign Minister, Mahmoud Fawzi, that any request for the withdrawal of UNEF should come only *after* the Egyptian armed forces were ready for combat, on 16 May an Egyptian officer arrived with a message for General Rhikhye at his headquarters in Gaza: 'For the sake of complete security of all UN troops which install OPs [observation posts] along our borders . . . you [should] issue your orders to withdraw all these troops immediately.'

It has since been claimed that Nasser was seeking a face-saving gesture rather than anything else. He wanted only a token withdrawal of UN troops, certainly not from the more sensitive places such as Sharm as-Sheikh at the entrance to the Gulf of Aqaba, which he knew the Israelis would regard as an act of provocation. Secretary-General U Thant, however, was not willing to oblige. Egypt could have all UNEF, or none of it. There was no middle course. U Thant subsequently explained the reasons for his action in a lengthy report to the Security Council, but he has been bitterly criticised by Foreign Minister Mahmoud Fawzi for complying with Nasser's request; he says Hammarskjöld would never have done so.[4] U Thant, however, emphasised the difficulties that would confront General Rhikhye if there were Egyptian troops milling about in Sinai, in or around UNEF posts, in the event of an Israeli attack. This predicament did in fact arise in Gaza, where UNEF suffered several casualties.

Nasser was in a cleft stick. If he withdrew his request for the removal of UNEF, he would again be accused of hiding behind UNEF's skirts. If he stuck by his request, he would have to occupy the posts vacated by them. This must include Sharm as-Sheikh, which the Israelis would regard as a *casus belli*. For once the cautious Nasser had overstepped the mark, and there could be no drawing back. He was to pay a terrible forfeit for his misjudgement.

The war hysteria sweeping Egypt and the rest of the Arab world may have influenced that judgement. Like a gambler constantly increasing his stake in the hope that the right card will turn up, Nasser poured more and more troops into Sinai until they amounted to seven divisions, which included nearly 1000 tanks. However, they were mostly second- and third-line formations, the best of the Egyptian army being far away in Yemen; these were mostly reservists or newly conscripted, mere cannon fodder. On 18 May Nasser finally took the plunge. He asked U Thant to withdraw UNEF. Hussein was horrified when he heard the news. 'From the day the United Nations troops were withdrawn from Gaza,' he says, 'I foresaw the consequences of this decision. To me it was obvious; war with Israel was inevitable.'[5] U Thant hastened to Cairo, arriving on 23 May, only to be told that Nasser had closed the Strait of Tiran the previous day. Nasser told U Thant that he had made his decisive statement prior to the Secretary-General's arrival because to have done so afterwards would have been an insult to him. U Thant made it clear that this must lead to war, but Nasser was not to be budged. He was on the slide to war and could neither stop it nor get off it.

The feeling in Amman was more anxious than bellicose. Wasfi Tell was no longer Prime Minister but he still retained great influence with the King. He wanted Jordan to stay out of any war, at least until it could be seen how the Egyptian Air Force was faring. He thought Nasser was bluffing, as indeed did the King, but that the Israelis would call Nasser's bluff. But what about Arabism and Arab solidarity in the face of the common enemy? And what about the West Bank, which Jordan certainly could not hold on its own? Jordan had to have allies. No one had anticipated that Nasser would act in such a hot-headed fashion, nor that U Thant would give in so easily to his request for the withdrawal of UNEF. It is true that U Thant has been made the scapegoat for the outbreak of war, but Sir Brian Urquart, who as one of U Thant's officials was in a better position than most to judge the issue at UN headquarters, does not agree. He considers that U Thant had little choice, given the conditions agreed by Egypt for the establishment of UNEF in the first place. Urquart reserves his criticism for the Great Powers, who did nothing to prevent the outbreak of war, but who then sat back and blamed U Thant for letting it happen.[6]

The pressures within Israel for or against war were not of course generally known in Amman at that time, although they may have been suspected. Left to themselves, Nasser and Eshkol might have been able to work out a deal, helped by U Thant, although this would seem to be unlikely. But the hawks in Israel were determined to seize the opportunity so foolishly offered them by Nasser. All they required was a *casus belli*, with which he was shortly to present them.

Wasfi Tell was not the only Jordanian advising caution. Sharif Nasser, then Deputy C-in-C, begged his nephew to do nothing hastily. He too had his reservations about Nasser. Zeid Rifai, then as always closer than almost anyone else to the King, had serious doubts. But Hussein's real worry was the West Bank; he reminded his advisers that he ruled over more Palestinians than any other Arab head of state. They were clamouring for war with Israel. If Hussein stood out against this outcry, it might even cost him his throne. Day and night he wrestled with the problem, as the war clouds rolled up from the western horizon.

The Jordanian armed forces formed part of the Unified Arab Command, then commanded by the Egyptian General, Ali Ali Amer. There had however been virtually no communication between the Egyptian and Jordanian armies for many months. Jordan had not been included in the defence agreement drawn up between Egypt and Syria the previous September. But if it came to war, it was essential that Jordan should have some knowledge of how the UAC intended to conduct operations. In order to discover this, if at all possible, Hussein sent the Jordanian Chief of Staff, Major-General Amer Khammash, to Cairo to consult with General Ali Ali Amer. Amer Khammash, aged forty-two, was one of the brightest of the Jordanian generals. A Gunner by training, he had joined the Arab Legion in 1940, and later as pilot of a spotting plane he was the first Jordanian to gain his wings. He was a trained staff officer with a deep interest in his profession. Hussein had great faith in him, and with good reason.

Khammash returned from Cairo on 18 May, a very worried man. The UAC was barely functioning and appeared to have no plans. Moreover, if it came to war, he was told, it would be a bilateral matter involving only Egypt and Syria. The UAC would play no part in it. Khammash tried to see

Nasser, but was told the President was too busy. He came back with virtually no information other than the Egyptians' conviction that they were well able to deal with the situation themselves. Nor were the Syrians any more co-operative. With the perversity that seems to be a Syrian national characteristic, they chose this moment (21 May) to place a bomb in a Jordanian bus. It exploded, killing fourteen people, just inside the Jordan border. Hussein was infuriated, and the Syrian Ambassador in Amman packed his bags yet again.

On 22 May the die was cast. Nasser announced the closure of the Strait of Tiran. Hussein was 'stunned' when he heard the news. The closure was to be effective from midnight on 23 May. Egypt announced a general mobilisation. Israel soon followed suit. In Amman, Hussein anguished over the course he should take. He knew as well as everyone else the arguments *against* going to war. But, equally, he was aware of the arguments *for* joining with Egypt and Syria. He had believed all along that Nasser did not want to go to war; Nasser might even have thought he could get away with it without war. But in Hussein's view war was inevitable. The Israelis would see to that. There was also, in the back of Hussein's mind, the short Arabic word *sharaf* (honour). When it came to the crunch it would be a matter of honour where Hussein was concerned – not only Jordan's but his own. He was also profoundly influenced by his concept of Arabism and Arab solidarity.

As the pressures mounted the suspense became almost unbearable. Hussein spent hours closeted with his generals going over war plans or endeavouring with his ministers to reach a decision on the course Jordan should follow. But he did not forget his soldiers, visiting them whenever he could and being received enthusiastically, almost rapturously. He was at his most relaxed when with them, delighting in their shouts of 'Hussein! Hussein!' By 29 May the King had made up his mind. Summoning the Egyptian Ambassador, he told him he wanted a meeting with Nasser. He said that if there was to be an Israeli attack on Jordan, which he considered likely, Jordan must co-ordinate its plans with Egypt. Nasser's reply was received around midnight. 'Come to Cairo as soon as you can,' he said.

Hussein took off for Cairo at 7 a.m. on 30 May in a chartered Jordanian Airlines Caravelle. Hussein, in combat dress, was at the controls. He wore a pistol at his hip. With him was Prime Minister Saad Juma'a, Foreign Minister Ahmed Toukan, General Khammash, Saleh al-Kurdi, who commanded the RJAF, and an air force ADC. Two RJAF fighters escorted the plane as far as Aqaba, from where Hussein flew on alone. On his own initiative he was flying to meet the man with whom he had been exchanging insults for many months past.

At Cairo airport Nasser was there to greet him, together with Egypt's four vice-presidents, the Prime Minister and General Ali Ali Amer. Nasser was wearing civilian clothes and pointed jokingly at Hussein's pistol. Hussein said they had been wearing uniform in Amman for more than a week. Nasser was rather stiff – there was no embrace but only a handshake – and before he let loose the photographers he asked Hussein if he wanted the visit kept secret. 'What's the point?' said Hussein. 'It will be found out sooner or later.' Nasser then asked, if the visit was kept secret, what would happen if the Egyptians arrested Hussein. The King replied that the possibility had never crossed his mind. Then he got into the waiting car lest the conversation should take an even more awkward turn.

Nasser thawed considerably during the journey from Almaza airport to the Koubbeh Palace. Hussein told him that it was vital they should co-ordinate their action since war seemed inevitable. The UAC should be revived. He continued on this theme in the Palace, where Nasser and he had a long private conversation before being joined by Field Marshal Abdel Hakim Amer and Prime Minister Saad Juma'a. Both Nasser and Hakim Amer seemed confident that Egypt and Syria could deal with Israel. There was in any case little point in reviving the UAC because Egypt and Syria already had a defence agreement. Why should not Egypt and Jordan sign a similar agreement, asked Nasser? A copy of the Egypt–Syria agreement was produced and Hussein hurriedly skimmed through it. 'If you put in Jordan in place of Syria,' he said, 'I am ready to sign.'

While the document was being prepared, Hussein took the opportunity to explain to Nasser the difficulties he was having with the PLO, and particularly with Ahmed Shukairy. Nasser told Hussein that he must rebuild his bridges with the PLO. Then, like a conjuror, he brought Shukairy into the room. Shukairy, unkempt and ungainly, had been unceremoniously wakened and flown down from Gaza that morning. He greeted Hussein effusively, and sat in the chair next to him during the signing ceremony. He then took it upon himself to address the gathering, calling Hussein the leader of the Palestinians, and saying he proposed to visit Jordan shortly. Nasser cut him short. Shukairy would not be visiting Jordan shortly, he said; he would be going there that very day, as a passenger in the King's plane. He went on to say that if Hussein had any further trouble with Shukairy, he was free to lock him up in one of his 'prison towers', with Nasser's blessing. This was greeted with a loud outburst of laughter, including Shukairy's, but in Hussein's case it was somewhat forced. However, his relief over the agreement with Nasser outweighed anything else.

Hussein had readily agreed that the Egyptian General Abdul Munim Riad, the Deputy Chief of Staff of the UAC, should direct operations in Amman under the overall control of General Muhammad Fawzi, C-in-C of the Unified Arab Command. Riad was due to leave shortly for Baghdad and

Damascus, where he could explain the new arrangements. Nasser had a short telephone conversation with President Aref in Baghdad, telling him of the new Egypt–Jordan agreement. Aref expressed himself delighted, and repeated this when Nasser handed the phone to Hussein. It was in fact a case of smiles all round, very different from the atmosphere that had greeted Hussein at Almaza airport on his arrival that morning. On the way back to the airport, Hussein paid a brief visit to the Egyptian GHQ at Heliopolis, where Hakim Amer told him how glad the Egyptians were to have Jordan back on their side. 'It strengthens our confidence,' he said. But General Khammash, who kept his own counsel, was not so confident. It seemed to him that the Egyptians were whistling in the dark to keep up their spirits, and were without any clear idea of how they should conduct operations.

When Hussein landed at Amman late that afternoon, it was to find that the tension he had left had been replaced by euphoria. Cairo Radio had announced the news at 3.30 p.m., bringing jubilant crowds on to the streets of every town in Jordan. Hussein descended the steps from his aircraft to the applause and clapping of the ministers and other dignitaries assembled there to greet him, most of whom had not known he had gone to Cairo until the news had broken. Even Zeid Rifai, despite his previous misgivings, says he heard the news with relief, although there were others close to the King who still had their reservations. One of the flies in the ointment was the appearance of Ahmed Shukairy, dressed in ill-fitting khaki but with smiles all over his face. He had conveniently forgotten his radio broadcasts insulting Hussein and calling for his overthrow. He managed to embrace a few of the welcoming party, but Hussein succeeded in avoiding any physical contact with a man he disliked and distrusted.

Despite the doubters, like Wasfi Tell, Hussein was convinced he had done the right thing. 'We felt the West Bank was a prime target,' he has said. 'We couldn't have survived an Israeli onslaught. Our only defence lay in coming together with the others.' It is quite possible that even at that eleventh hour Nasser believed he could avoid war. The Americans were working hard to persuade him to lift the blockade of the Strait of Tiran. It was rumoured that Hakim Amer had instructed the Egyptian commander at Sharm as-Sheikh not to interfere with the passage of Israeli vessels. The UN, as also Britain, France and others, was exerting every effort to prevent war. Nasser had even decided to send Zacharia Mohieddin, one of his closest confidants, to Washington on 7 June for talks. On 2 June, the US State Department told the Israelis that their discussions with the Egyptians were making progress; they were hopeful of a speedy result. They asked for more time to reach an agreement. They were certain Nasser did not want war.

The Americans may have been right over Nasser, but they badly underestimated the influence of the war party in Israel. As far back as 11 May, the Israeli Chief of Staff, Yitzhak Rabin, had said quite openly in a radio broadcast, 'The moment is coming when we will march on Damascus to overthrow the Syrian government, because it means that only military operations can discourage the plans for a people's war with which they threaten us.'[7] Rabin's views were undoubtedly reciprocated by Moshe Dayan, the hero of the 1956 war, who wielded great influence as Minister of Defence. They believed the moment had come to deal both Egypt and Syria a knock-out blow, and Jordan too if Hussein was foolish enough to intervene. The attempt by Levi Eshkol and Abba Eban to reach a peaceful solution infuriated the Israeli hawks. There was even talk of overthrowing them by a military coup if they continued to prevaricate.

Far away at Oxford University, where Hussein's youngest brother, Hassan, was about to take his Final Examinations, the news from Jordan became gloomier and gloomier. Hassan, at such an important stage in his university career, grew more and more worried. Should it come to war, he felt his place was either at his brother's side or in the firing line with the army. Eventually he telephoned Hussein, requesting permission to return home, but Hussein dissuaded him. After three years of study, it was only right he should take the examinations. It must have been a bitter pill for Hassan to swallow but he did as he was told. He therefore escaped a personal involvement in what was to turn out to be the most humiliating episode in Jordan's history.

CHAPTER TEN
June 1967

'We have fought with heroism and honour. Some day the Arab nations will recognise the role Jordan played in the war. . . .'
King Hussein[1]

The Six Day War between the Arabs and Israel in June 1967 must surely go down in history as an outstanding example of how every rule for the successful prosecution of war was broken by the Arab side. The Egyptian High Command was remarkable for the sheer ineptitude of its efforts; nor were the Syrians any better. Jordan, which had gone to war chiefly on account of King Hussein's determination to maintain Arab solidarity in the cause of Arabism, was to prove to be the principal sufferer, along with the Palestinians. Some of the failure was due to the virtual absence of any co-ordinated planning beforehand and to a complete absence of accurate intelligence about the enemy. Most of all perhaps, the defeat was owing to the surprisingly light-hearted way both Egyptians and Syrians went to war with an enemy whose prowess on the battlefield had been made abundantly clear during the Suez campaign eleven years previously.

Two well-authenticated instances of the blind folly of the Egyptian generals are to be found in the records. At a meeting with his top advisers held at the end of May, Nasser reminded them that the closure of the Strait of Tiran would make war certain. 'Are the armed forces ready, Abdel Hakim?' he asked. 'On my head be it, boss,' replied the Field Marshal, making the gesture of cutting his throat as he spoke. 'Everything's in tip-top shape.'[2] It was not true. The other example concerns General Sudki Mahmoud, commander of the Egyptian Air Force. He gave an interview to the newspaper *Al-Musawar* in which he said the Egyptian 'warning system and air defences are capable of discovering and destroying any air attack no matter how many aircraft are involved, nor from what direction they come'. He was soon to be forced to eat his words.

Although it was the Jordanians who came off worst, they had less control over their destinies than either Egypt or Syria. Hussein had in Cairo placed his armed forces under Egyptian command, which made sense in view of the existence of the Unified Arab Command, of which Jordan had formed part since 1964. However, from the moment he arrived in Amman on 1

June, it was obvious that General Riad would take his orders from General Muhammad Fawzi in Cairo, and from no one else. Nasser was of course Supreme Commander of the Egyptian armed forces, and Field Marshal Hakim Abdel Amer his deputy; Fawzi was C-in-C of the Joint Arab Command. Nor was Riad disposed to take advice from Lieutenant-General Habis Majali, the Jordanian C-in-C, nor from Habis's deputy, Major-General Amer Khammash. He intended to rely on the five Egyptian officers who had accompanied him from Cairo.

Amman is a long way from Cairo and in any case the problems confronting General Riad in a war against Israel differed vastly from those confronting the Egyptian Commanding General in Sinai. With this in mind it would have been better to have given Riad a free hand to do as he thought best instead of trying to control him from Cairo. But since this was apparently not the intention, it must be apparent that there had to be an efficient and secure means of communication between the two headquarters. There was in fact nothing of the kind. The Egyptians did possess an up-to-date communications system but had not got round to installing it. Instead there was only a public telegraph and radio telephone system that was systematically eavesdropped by the Israelis throughout. There was not even a Jordanian liaison officer at GHQ Cairo, an absolutely incredible oversight. This was not preparation for war – it was playing at soldiers.

The Jordanian General Staff had of course long made contingency plans for a war with Israel. As far back as Glubb's time it had been argued that the Arab Legion could not expect to defend every inch of the West Bank. Since then the plans had been refined, although for political reasons the King still insisted that he would not agree to giving up voluntarily any part of the West Bank. This entailed deploying the majority of the Jordanian army – five out of seven infantry brigades – along 400 miles of frontier between Jenin and Hebron. The two armoured brigades, 40th and 60th, mustering some 200 Patton tanks, were deployed in a counterattack role in the Jordan valley, around the Damiya bridge in the north, and near Jericho in the south. They were GHQ troops directly controlled from Amman. It was patently clear to the Jordanian generals that such a deployment of forces was a 'military nonsense' but they had perforce to acknowledge the political necessity. However, realising that the key to all the fighting on the West Bank was Jerusalem, both strategically and emotionally, they had drawn up a plan codenamed Operation Tariq which aimed to encircle and cut off the Jewish enclave from the rest of Israel. The object was to provide Jordan with a useful pawn in any negotiations after the cessation of hostilities for the return of territory seized by Israel. But if Tariq was to succeed, the plan must be implemented early in the campaign and be carried out with maximum force.

The Jordanian army was about 56,000 strong, all volunteers and with a high morale. Although short of equipment, what there was was good and reasonably well maintained. There was unfortunately very little anti-aircraft defence and the RJAF could muster only twenty-one Hawker Hunters for its striking force. There was also a grave shortage of pilots, many of them attending courses in Britain and the USA. The country was divided into two commands, Western and Eastern. Major-General Muhammad Ahmed Saleem was GOC Western Command with headquarters at Ramallah. Brigadier Mashour Haditha al Jazy was GOC Eastern Command with headquarters at Zerqa. He had only two infantry brigades to defend an area stretching from Irbid to Aqaba.

From the start most of the Jordanian generals regarded the prospect of going to war alongside the Egyptians with a marked lack of enthusiasm. They did not rate the Egyptian army, nor for that matter the Syrian army, very highly. They also considered Nasser's brinkmanship to be foolish. Some were more outspoken than others. Their advice would be to 'wait and see'. But others who were close to the King at the time, such as his cousin, Zeid bin Shakir, believe that Hussein had little choice. Ammer Khammash, perhaps the most intellectual of the senior Jordanian officers, holds the same view. He says Hussein was like a man who had swallowed a razor blade; either way it would have to be cut out, from his throat or from his stomach.[3] The British Ambassador in Amman at the time, Sir Philip Adams, also considers that Hussein had really no choice. He had either to swim with Nasser, or sink without him.[4]

Hussein was undoubtedly influenced by two principal factors: his belief in Arab solidarity, and his conviction that the West Bank must certainly be Israel's prime objective. Sooner or later they would be bound to contrive a situation that made war with Jordan inevitable. It was therefore better to fight as Nasser's ally now than to fight without him later. To a lesser extent he was influenced also by the support he had been promised by Saudi Arabia and Iraq; Syria seemed to be less certain. In the event, however, only Iraq made any real contribution, although their troops were cut to pieces by the IAF during their long march across the desert. The Saudis were so dilatory that they had reached only as far as Ma'an before it was time for them to return home. The Syrians were even slower; their behaviour was shameful.

At the series of conferences held before the opening of hostilities, it was agreed that Jordan should remain on the defensive until the promised reinforcements had arrived from Saudi Arabia and Iraq; only after that had happened would it make sense to go over to the offensive. In the meantime there would be harassing artillery fire and strikes against Israeli airfields. It was accepted that Israel would reply in kind, but probably only in low key because their attention would be directed against the Egyptians in Sinai, or against the Syrians on the Golan. Information had been received in any case from various sources that Israel had no intention of attacking Jordan unless it was forced to do so. General Munim Riad was fully aware of this, and so presumably was the Egyptian High Command in Cairo.

The story of the pre-emptive air strike against the Egyptian airfields by the IAF at 8.45 a.m. on Monday, 5 June 1967, has often been told. It was a remarkable feat of arms. The Israelis struck from an unexpected quarter and after flying at very low level to avoid the Egyptian radar. All General Sudki Mahmoud's proud boasts were seen to be hollow as the Israelis came screaming in from the west. In less than three hours the Egyptians were decimated, only 31 out of their 340 combat aircraft remaining serviceable. The skies over Sinai were now dominated by the Israelis, as would soon be the case over Amman and Damascus as well. Nasser was later to complain bitterly, 'They came from the west when we expected them to come from the east!'

On that Monday morning Hussein was at the Hummar Palace waiting to have breakfast with Muna. The phone rang around nine o'clock. It was Colonel Jazy, Hussein's senior ADC. Cairo Radio had just announced that war had broken out, said Jazy. After calling headquarters to check, Hussein jumped into his car and drove fast to Amman. It was the last he was to see of Muna and the children for nearly forty-eight hours. By the time he reached Amman a message from Hakim Amer had been received and was being decoded. It read as follows:

1. Israeli planes have started to bomb air bases of the UAR and approximately 75% of the enemy's aircraft have been destroyed or put out of action.
2. The counterattack by the Egyptian Air Force is under way against Israel in Sinai. UAR troops have engaged the enemy and taken the offensive on the ground. As a result Field Marshal Amer has ordered the Commander-in-Chief of the Jordanian Front to open a new front and to launch offensive operations according to the plan outlined the day before.

Inevitably it took some time before the full scale of the damage inflicted by the IAF could be established, but this does not condone the message sent by Hakim Amer at ten o'clock (Cairo time) that morning. It was totally false and misled both the King and Riad. It has been said in defence of Nasser, who was himself to repeat Hakim Amer's lie, that he did not know the truth until four o'clock that afternoon; but Anwar Sadat contradicts this. Sadat says he visited GHQ in Cairo at eleven o'clock that morning to find Hakim Amer wandering round his office like a man in a daze. Nasser then suddenly emerged from an adjoining office, whereupon Hakim Amer put all the blame on the Americans. He said it was their planes that had done the damage. Nasser rejected this. He was not prepared to accept it until Hakim Amer produced 'at least one aircraft with a wing showing the US ensign'.[5] It is perfectly clear from Sadat's account that Nasser had a fair understanding of the extent of the disaster before noon on 5 June. Nevertheless, it does not seem to have occurred to him to inform his Jordanian ally.

It is extremely difficult to establish who began the fighting on the Jordanian front. Chaim Herzog claims that the Jordanians opened up an artillery barrage around 11 a.m., about the same time as they launched air strikes against Israeli airfields.[6] General Khammash, on the other hand, insists it was the Israelis who were the first to open fire. In view of what was to transpire, the argument is academic. One Jordanian officer has said that the tension was such that almost anyone might have pressed the trigger – out of sheer excitement. But whoever it was who fired the first shot, the Israelis immediately implemented their battle plan under the command of Major-General Uzi Markiss, GOC Central Command. It was the moment for which they had been waiting – with Jerusalem their objective.

At Amman and at Mafraq the Jordanian pilots had been waiting to scramble since the news first came through from Cairo. But the Syrians with their MiG-21s, who were to provide the high cover, held everything up. Finally the Iraqis based at H-3* could wait no longer and took off, to be joined by the RJAF. The Syrians were late as usual, to Hussein's fury. The Jordanians on return reported good results, including four enemy planes destroyed without any Jordanian loss. It was about the only good news of the day. Just about the time of their takeoff Hussein received a message from General Odd Bull, the Norwegian commander of the UN Mixed Armistice Commission, which was based in Jerusalem. He was relaying to Hussein a message from Israel's Prime Minister. War had begun against Egypt, said Eshkol, but no action would be taken against Jordan provided Hussein stayed out of the war. 'They started the battle,' Hussein told Odd Bull, 'well, they are receiving our reply by air.'[7]

There was not long to wait before the IAF struck back. At 12.30 p.m. they caught the RJAF refuelling and rearming their planes. Major Firass Ajlouni, one of the RJAF's best pilots, was killed at Mafraq while taking off to intercept them. By 2.30 p.m. it was all over. The RJAF had been overwhelmed, with nearly all its planes destroyed. The fourteen pilots who survived the carnage were dispatched to H-3 where the Iraqis lent them some Hunters. In subsequent dogfights they accounted for nine Israeli planes but their influence on the land battle was nil. The Israelis rounded off their attack on Amman by rocketing and machine-gunning the Basman

* One of the pumping stations on the Kirkuk–Haifa oil pipeline which had been closed since 1948. H-3 was just inside Iraq, H-4 and H-5 inside Jordan.

Palace, one rocket actually penetrating Hussein's study and lacerating the chair in which he might well have been sitting. His escape brought to mind Muna and the children out at Hummar and he put a call through to her. She said all was well and he was not to worry about them. Abdullah and Feisal were having a marvellous time watching the planes attacking Amman. She was, says Hussein, 'very calm, in full control, very brave and clear-headed'.

Hussein had been fanatically air-minded ever since he came to the throne. He understood far better than his ministers that a country lacking a well-trained and well-equipped air force was in no position to defend itself. One of his complaints about Glubb Pasha had been Glubb's reluctance to expand the RJAF, although Glubb might well have argued that there was little enough money to equip the army, let alone equip an air force. Hussein was now to learn what it was like to conduct land operations against an enemy in full command of the air. The Jordanian soldiers were subjected to attack almost every time they moved; and when darkness fell, and it might have been thought that movement was safer, the IAF dropped flares to illuminate their targets. They were helped by the fact that so many of the roads and tracks on the West Bank ran through defiles, canalising movement and slowing it down. The Jordanian tanks, and even more their soft-skinned supply vehicles, were sitting ducks.

Nasser telephoned Hussein around 12.30 p.m. on 5 June. He repeated Hakim Amer's optimistic account of the Israeli air attacks and said the Egyptians had launched an attack on the Negev. At the same time he advised Hussein to seize as much territory as he could since the Security Council might well intervene that night. This was the first vague hint that Nasser might be in difficulties but he sounded cheerful enough. With exhortations of mutual encouragement, the two Arab leaders then rang off. It is difficult to understand what Nasser hoped to gain from such duplicity since the situation on the Egyptian front was reaching disaster proportions.

At 8 a.m. that morning the Israelis had launched their attack on Sinai, operating on three main axes. By midday they had penetrated the main Egyptian positions despite the optimistic reports put out by Cairo Radio on the instructions of Hakim Amer. Far from advancing into the Negev, as stated by Hakim Amer, the Egyptians were beginning to lose cohesion as the Israeli *Blitzkrieg* gathered pace. They were, according to General Khammash, only second- and third-line divisions hastily cobbled together when Nasser decided to move into Sinai.

None of this was apparent to Riad when he received his next instructions from Cairo. He was to move the 60th Armoured Brigade from its concentration area near Jericho to Hebron in order to join forces with the Egyptians advancing into the Negev.[8] Zeid bin Shakir, who was commanding the brigade, says he was given as his objective Beersheba. 40th Armoured

Brigade, commanded by Rakan Anad Jazy, was to move from Damiya to Jericho to replace 60th Armoured Brigade. These orders were issued at 12.40 and 1 p.m. respectively, but not before there had been a furious row between General Riad and the Jordanian staff. Riad's Director of Operations, the Jordanian Brigadier Ataf al-Majali, became so incensed that he put on his *shamagh* and tried to leave the operations room. It was all on account of Operation Tariq.

Major-General Muhammad Saleem, who commanded on the West Bank, and Brigadier Ataf al-Majali, were anxious to implement Tariq by seizing Mount Scopus to the north of Jerusalem, from where they could dominate and then capture the Jewish part of the city. Speed was vital, as also was the support of Zeid bin Shakir's tanks. But these were being sent on a wild-goose chase to Hebron, and by the time 40th Armoured Brigade had arrived to replace them it would be too late. Nor was this the only bone of contention. Riad did not agree with making Mount Scopus the objective. The Egyptians were advancing through the Negev to the south of Jerusalem and therefore the Jordanians should seize Al-Mukhaber, the hilly feature lying to the south of the city. Although Riad's knowledge of the terrain was virtually nil, and although he had the entire Jordanian General Staff lined up against him, he refused to budge.

Meanwhile the Israelis, reacting violently to the capture of Government House by the Jordanians, launched their first attacks against Jerusalem and Jenin, with a subsidiary attack against Hebron. With their planes acting as mobile artillery, the Israelis hammered the Jordanian defences, gradually forcing them back. The Jordanians fought with great courage, the battle for Ammunition Hill outside Jerusalem being particularly hard fought, but the odds were heavily weighted against them. By midday on Tuesday, 6 June, the Jordanians were surrounded and all troops moving up from the Jordan valley to reinforce them were caught by the IAF. The fighting inside the Old City was extremely bitter but on Wednesday, 7 June, at 10 a.m. the Israelis reached the Wailing Wall and their commander, Colonel 'Motta' Gur, was informed by the local Arab leaders that further Arab resistance would cease.

There was equally tough fighting for Jenin and Nablus. Although the Jordanians man for man, and tank for tank, gave as good as they got, and often better, they were simply overwhelmed by Israeli air power. As but one example, their 2nd Tank Regiment, under Lieutenant-Colonel Saleh Abdullah Suhair, deployed to cover the main Jenin–Nablus axis, was overrun in a night tank battle after having been pounded remorselessly throughout the daylight hours by wave after wave of rocket and napalm attacks. On the following morning, when the leading Israelis entered Nablus, they were surprised to be greeted by cheering citizens who had mistaken them for Iraqi troops supposedly coming to their assistance. Soon realising their mistake the people took up arms, but it could only be a last defiant gesture.

By the evening of 5 June it had become clear in Amman that unless the fighting could be stopped by political means, the West Bank would be lost. It became urgent therefore to arrange a ceasefire through the UN. This was easier said than done. When Ahmed Toukan, the Jordanian Foreign Minister, phoned the Jordanian Ambassador in New York, Dr Muhammad al-Farra, telling him that the war was going badly and asking him to obtain a ceasefire as soon as possible, the Ambassador flatly refused to do so. He had been listening to Cairo Radio's optimistic broadcasts and was convinced the Arabs were doing well. His Egyptian colleague was of the same opinion, having obtained his information from the same source.

General Riad, however, was in no doubt. He told Hussein that night that unless there was a ceasefire or a withdrawal within twenty-four hours, Hussein would have lost his army, and possibly Jordan as well. Hussein was appalled. He was not to know that Hakim Amer had already issued orders for a general withdrawal from Sinai by the time he had given orders to Riad to begin operations around Hebron. At about six o'clock on the following morning, 6 June, Riad got through to Nasser and told him of the serious situation. Nasser later called Hussein to suggest that Riad should cable a full report to Hakim Amer. Nasser appeared to be worried but he continued to claim that the Egyptian Air Force was raiding Israeli airfields. It was during this telephone conversation, on a very bad line, that Nasser and Hussein discussed the possibility of the Americans and British being in collusion with Israel. The Israelis listened to this conversation and later published a transcript of it to the world press. It made both men appear to be cheats and liars although there was a perfectly good explanation for the confusion.

At 6 a.m. on 6 June when he spoke to Nasser, who made no attempt to enlighten him, Hussein was still under the impression that Egypt had destroyed 75 per cent of the IAF. When therefore it was reported to him that a large number of unexplainable blips were appearing on the radar screen, and that furthermore they were coming from seawards, although the Israelis did not possess an aircraft carrier, it was too readily assumed that the blips were US and British planes on their way to reinforce the IAF after its 'catastrophic' losses over Egypt. To add to the confusion, the silhouette of the Mystère on the radar screen is very like the Hawker Hunter's, a British plane that the IAF did not possess. It was an easy mistake to make in the tense atmosphere of the Ops Room; and even though it could have been queried to Cairo, the likelihood is that the supposition would have been confirmed, since Hakim Amer at the time was doing his best to persuade Nasser that it was US aircraft who were doing all the damage.

As it was, Hussein was furious when he heard the news. He summoned at once the British, American and French ambassadors and confronted them with the accusation of collusion. They did their best to reason with him but the King was beyond argument. He was very close to losing his self-control and the ambassadors took the wisest course. They bowed themselves out. It was a most unfortunate incident which would probably have been soon forgotten, had it not been for the eavesdropped telephone conversation between Hussein and Nasser. Although there was no collusion where Britain and France were concerned, there is evidence, unconfirmed from official sources, that the USAF flew photographic reconnaissance missions from an airfield near Beersheba. If true, this must have been of great help to the Israelis in judging the effectiveness of their air strikes, and in estimating the progress of their ground troops.[9]

Nasser had concluded the telephone conversation by encouraging Hussein not to give up, and by telling him that Egyptian planes were still striking at Israel. This was of course untrue and very difficult to justify, unless Nasser himself was still in the dark. The wonder is that Hussein could ever bring himself to speak to Nasser again. Jordan was also badly let down by Syria, whose failure to take part in a joint offensive with Jordan on 5 June was a major contributory factor to the loss of the West Bank. Although Hussein had sought Syrian assistance, on Riad's recommendation, prior to the outbreak of hostilities, a Syrian brigade did not materialise in Jordan until 8.20 p.m. on 8 June. When Riad ordered the brigade to move to defensive positions at 10 p.m., the brigade commander refused to do so. Riad then sent him and his brigade back to Damascus. However, their treacherous prevarication did not save the Syrians. By 2 p.m. on 10 June, the Israelis were in Kuneitra and the Golan was theirs.

Throughout the short campaign Hussein spent every available moment with his soldiers and his pilots. Riad was commanding his army and there was little for him to do at headquarters. He hardly ate but drank endless cups of tea, chain-smoked and never slept; he was to comment ruefully later that Riad, despite the pressure, still found time for a quick nap. Hussein travelled miles in his jeep exposed to air attack, almost at times as if he was seeking death. Haggard, unshaven and red-eyed, he was welcomed enthusiastically by the troops. He had a very narrow escape when visiting Rakan Anad Jazy's headquarters near the Damiya bridge, when an Israeli plane swooped down as they were chatting by the roadside. Since Hussein made no move, Jazy seized him and forcibly threw him into a slit trench. 'We may have lost the war,' he told him, 'but we don't intend to lose our king.' During this anxious period Hussein managed to telephone Muna from time to time, but could snatch time for only a brief visit to Hummar. To her credit Muna never bothered him.

Late in the night of 6 June Hussein learned the full story of the Israeli air strikes the previous day. It was incredible. He also knew by then that the Egyptians were in full retreat in Sinai, and that the Israelis were fast closing on the Suez Canal, which they reached on 8 June. It had taken them four days. General Riad had already requested permission for a withdrawal from the West Bank, and Hakim Amer had agreed. The necessary orders had gone out, despite protests from Habis Majali and his staff in Amman, and from commanders in the field. As soon as Hussein heard of the order, he at once cancelled it. Naturally this led to more confusion, some brigades having already abandoned their defensive positions in preparation for withdrawal. The Security Council had ordered a ceasefire to be effective from 11 p.m. on 6 June. Additionally, General Riad told the King in blunt soldierly terms that to continue with the war was simply throwing away human lives. However, the fighting continued throughout the night, ending finally at midday on 7 June.

Hussein's army and air force had been crushed in little more than forty-eight hours, due very largely to the IAF. Jazy's armoured brigade could muster no more than eight tanks out of its original ninety; Shakir's brigade managed to get forty tanks back across the River Jordan. The killed and missing amounted to 6094 but most of the missing got back eventually to the East Bank. Riad's decision to withdraw from the West Bank was probably the most unfortunate decision of the entire campaign. It lost Jordan the West Bank, and the Arabs Jerusalem. It was decided against the better judgement of Hussein himself, Habis Majali and Amer Khammash, who thought the army should have regrouped and gone on fighting. Brigadier Mashour Haditha did not agree with the withdrawal. In his view it was unnecessary. 'I was not defeated,' he said. 'I did not even take part in the fight!'

It was a catastrophe – worse even than 1948. It swelled Jordan's refugee population by another 200,000, bringing the total to more than 850,000. The Palestinians could not believe it. 'I was turned completely upside down,' said Arafat. At least they had hung on to the Old City in 1948, thanks to the Arab Legion. Now it was occupied by the Israelis. Would they, could they, ever give it up? At 5 a.m. on 7 June General Bar Lev, Deputy Chief of Staff at Israeli GHQ, signalled the Israeli commander battling outside Jerusalem: 'We are already being pressed for a ceasefire [by the UN]. We are at the Canal. The Egyptians have been carved up. Don't let the Old City remain an enclave.'

There is no glory in defeat, but it was the more humiliating because it had come so quickly. Every man and woman in Jordan felt the shame of it, no one more than the King. All his allies, apart from the Iraqis, had failed him. Shukairy, whose mindless boastings had done so much to increase the tension beforehand, had taken himself off to Damascus. Nasser had made mistake after mistake. It was entirely due to his charisma that he managed to survive what would have been the justifiable wrath of his people. In Anwar Sadat's opinion, however, Nasser did not really survive the Six Day War. 'The events of 5 June dealt him a fatal blow,' wrote Sadat. 'They finished him off. Those who knew Nasser realised that he did not die on 28 September 1970, but on 5 June 1967, exactly one hour after war broke out.'[10] General Shakir, who accompanied Hussein on the visit he paid Nasser soon after the conclusion of hostilities, remembers vividly a comment made by Nasser to the King. 'At last I have realised', Nasser said, 'that the Egyptian army is full of braggarts who cannot fight.'

Hussein, as ever magnanimous, has been careful to avoid blaming Riad, whom he regarded as being a competent professional soldier. Field Marshal Habis Majali has been more critical. 'It was a great mistake to place the army under command of a foreigner who knew neither the ground nor the capabilities of the troops he was commanding,' he has said. 'General Riad refused to listen to or take into account views of Jordanian field commanders, and actually quarrelled with Brigadier Ataf Majali. He insisted on carrying out his orders to the letter despite the fact he was made aware of the dire consequences that would result.' General Shakir thought Riad was competent enough but lacked knowledge of the terrain and his troops. Khammash, a fellow Gunner, got on well with Riad but doubted his military ability. Wasfi is much more critical. He admitted that Riad was lively and intelligent but said his relaxed manner was really a form of mental paralysis.

In Riad's defence it has to be said that he was thrown in at the deep end by his Egyptian superiors and left to swim as best he could. He was as much misled by the reports from Cairo as the Jordanians. However, it was a grave error of judgement for him to alter the Jordanian operational plan from defence to attack without having any clear conception of where the Egyptian troops were, nor whether the promised reinforcements from Iraq, Saudi Arabia and Syria would in fact materialise. It was this change in plan that led Riad to throw away the Jordanian armour in what can only be described as the most crazy fashion.

When Riad received the false information that the Egyptians were advancing into the Negev and hoped the Jordanians would co-operate with them, Riad at once alerted 60th Armoured Brigade and ordered it to move to Hebron. At the time this order was issued, 12.40 p.m. on 5 June, Amman was under heavy air attack. It must surely have been apparent to Riad that Shakir's brigade, moving in broad daylight through several defiles, must be subjected to air interdiction. But apparently not. As soon as Shakir received the order he collected his Order Group and set off for Hebron, leaving the rest of the brigade to follow. Attacked from the air on the way, Shakir arrived in Hebron to discover that the route he had been directed to take from there to Beersheba was barely passable for jeeps, let alone for tanks. Meanwhile his tanks, moving up from Jericho, were under constant air attack, which was, he says, 'extremely efficient and ruthless'. The soft-skinned supply vehicles suffered the most, but the road was also littered with burning and burned-out tanks. Shakir says that the information they were receiving from Cairo was deliberately misleading; at the time when Nasser was telling Hussein that his planes were attacking Israel, he was simultaneously pleading with Boumedienne in Algiers for the loan of Algerian planes to replace his own.

Riad's mishandling of 60th Armoured Brigade, disregarding Brigadier Ataf Majali's advice to the contrary, was to be followed by a similar error with regard to 40th Armoured Brigade. Riad ordered this brigade to move in broad daylight from Damiya to Jericho to replace 60th Armoured Brigade. The dust thrown up by the tank tracks alerted the Israeli Air Force and led to several air strikes. Moreover, it was extremely hot and the tank crews suffered greatly from heat exhaustion during the move. No sooner had they arrived at their destination, however, than they were ordered to retrace their steps to Damiya. Hours of valuable time had been wasted, tanks had been needlessly lost through enemy action or mechanical break-down, and the crews had been exhausted as a result of this futile manoeuvre.

On arriving back at Damiya, Colonel Jazy was ordered to halt the advance of Israeli tanks into the Jordan Valley from the direction of Jenin and Tubas. The Israelis were closely supported by their air force, which struck with deadly effect against 40th Armoured Brigade. The Jordanian tank crews fought with great gallantry but all the odds were against them. By the time the fighting had died down 40th Armoured Brigade was left with only eight tanks that were battle-worthy. Meanwhile their sister formation, 60th Armoured Brigade, was strung out along the road from Jericho to Jerusalem and Hebron, its progress marked by burning and burned-out tank hulls. Long before it reached its destination, Riad ordered its return to Jericho, with instructions to counterattack for the relief of the hard-pressed defenders of Jerusalem.

It was a frustrating experience for the Jordanian staff officers at GHQ in Amman to have to witness such a blatant misuse of armour. Their efforts to influence General Riad and his handful of Egyptian advisers were simply ignored. It leads one to question how General Riad's high military repu-tation ever came to be established. Mohammed Heikal, however, insists that Riad was one of the best generals to be produced by the Egyptian army. He says Riad 'won the respect and affection of his subordinates in a matter of minutes'. The Jordanian officers who came into contact with him certainly liked him. Apparently Riad's popularity in the Egyptian army was such that some of Nasser's advisers feared that he might have political ambitions. When Nasser was told of this, he replied: 'If he is efficient and can command in battle, and if he can win the battle, I am ready to give him my job without waiting for him to stage a *coup d'état* – and he would be entirely entitled to have it.'

Riad, who was a bachelor with more than his fair share of Egyptian charm, was to be criticised later in Cairo for his mishandling of the battle in Jordan, but the excuse made for him was that he had been misinformed and misled by the Jordanian High Command. His Jordanian experience certainly had no effect on his subsequent military career. He went on to become Commander-in-Chief of the Egyptian army. He was killed during an exchange of artillery fire across the Suez Canal in March 1969.

Hussein was devastated by his army's defeat. It was hardly credible. In a voice hoarse with fatigue and emotion, he spoke to his people on Amman Radio. 'We have fought with heroism and honour,' he told them:

> Some day the Arab nations will recognise the role Jordan played in the war. Our soldiers have defended every inch of our earth with their precious blood. They were not afraid in the face of the total superiority of the enemy's air power which surprised and paralysed the Egyptian Air Force on which we had counted. Now what's done is done. My heart breaks when I think of the loss of our fallen soldiers. They were dearer to me than my own person. My brothers, I seem to belong to a family which, according to the will of Allah, must suffer and make sacrifices for its country without end. Our calamity is greater than anyone could have imagined. But whatever its size, we must not let it weaken our resolve to regain what we have lost. If in the end you were not rewarded with glory, it was not because you lacked courage but because it was the will of Allah. May Allah now be with our people.

Nasser sent Hussein a message on 6 June. 'When the history books are written,' he told Hussein, 'your courage and tenacity will be remembered. They will not forget the heroic Jordanian people who went straight into battle without hesitation, and with no consideration other than honour and duty. . . .' Since Hussein came in for a great deal of criticism after the war, it is as well that Nasser's tribute should be remembered. His joining forces with Egypt had been for Hussein a matter of honour. This was something that did not seem to concern the Syrians; and Hussein found it hard to forgive them for their lack of support in Jordan's hour of need.

The real scapegoat, if one needs to be found, must surely be Field Marshal Abdel Hakim Amer. From beginning to end he made mistake after mistake. Sadat even accuses him of changing the agreed plan of operations. 'On Monday, 5 June,' says Sadat, 'Amer accompanied by all commanders took an aircraft and flew off on a tour of inspection to Sinai. It was only natural that when the C-in-C was in the air, orders should be issued to all SAM and anti-aircraft batteries to hold their fire. And it was during that tour that Israel attacked all our airfields and hit our aircraft on the ground. We can say the war began and ended while Amer was still in the air.'[11]

Amer was of course a political general, albeit a well-liked one. He owed his high rank principally to his closeness to Nasser, who trusted him to keep the armed forces in line. There were other Egyptian generals who were better fitted than Amer to command in the field, as was to become evident when next the Egyptians went to war with Israel. Amer is supposed to have tried to commit suicide in the immediate aftermath of Egypt's defeat. It is said that he tried to do so a second time; alternatively he may have been killed by the regime. A doctor, however, who examined him during a brief visit to London at some time during this period, diagnosed his complaint as inoperable cancer. He may have died from this, but we shall never know.[12]

As a tailpiece to a campaign that was a disaster from start to finish for the Arabs, the part played by Nasser's propaganda machine, the Voice of the Arabs (Saut al-Arab), deserves a mention. In the effort to boost popular morale, Cairo broadcast the most mendacious reports which, as we have seen, actually misled the Jordanian and Egyptian representatives at the UN. The Egyptian broadcasters did even worse. By reporting the movements of the Iraqi troops from Iraq on their way to the front, they provided the IAF with the information they required to pinpoint the Iraqis and destroy them en route. Only a battered remnant eventually got as far as the Jordan Valley.

As another example of their hare-brained activities, Cairo broadcast the intention of the Jordanians to occupy Mount Scopus, the key feature in their plan to seize all Jerusalem in Operation Tariq. This information alerted the Israelis, who were able to reinforce Mount Scopus before the Jordanians could mount their attack, which not surprisingly was repelled. This is perhaps the outstanding example of the Arabs' failure to co-ordinate *all aspects* of their operations which, more than anything else, resulted in Israel's victory.

CHAPTER ELEVEN

The Trojan Horse

'. . . I think we have come to the point now where we are all *fedayeen*.' King Hussein[1]

The Six Day War left an indelible impression on Hussein. It seemed inconceivable that the army and air force of which he was so proud could have been wiped out in less than a week. Most of his tanks, planes and guns had been either destroyed or captured. Jordan's economy was in ruins, and it had been made amply clear that the other Arab states (with the exception of Iraq), although profuse in promises, were poor in performance. It was hard too to forgive Nasser for his blatant deceit; the King, with his customary magnanimity, did forgive Nasser in the end, but he did not forget.

The next three years were desperately difficult for Jordan and the King – probably the most difficult years in Hussein's reign. For a proper understanding of the background to Hussein's problem during those three years, it is necessary to go back sixty years. There were still men alive in Jordan in 1967 who could just remember the time when Palestine and the land lying east of the River Jordan formed one entity under the rule of Turkey. Men and goods passed freely from one to the other, and even farther beyond to Damascus and Baghdad. Throughout this vast region most of the people spoke the same language, followed the same religion and spoke of themselves as Arabs. Turkey's defeat in 1918 changed all this. They now called themselves Iraqis, Jordanians, Syrians, Lebanese and so on. It was as citizens of separate countries that they did business together, or went to war with each other. Such unity as they might have been expected to derive from a common language, religion and culture had been fragmented by the modern conception of the nation-state.

Out of all these divided peoples only the Palestinians had no country to call their own after 1948. All that remained of what had been for more than fourteen centuries a predominantly Arab country was a narrow strip of territory round Gaza, and the West Bank, which had in any case been incorporated with Jordan in 1950. The Six Day War removed even the rump of Gaza and the West Bank, leaving the Palestinians stateless, apart from those who had elected to become Jordanian or Israeli citizens – and the latter were very much of the 'second-class' variety. In the rest of the Arab world the Palestinians lived only on sufferance. Some of them made fresh careers for themselves in other countries, acquiring other citizenships, and in some instances considerable fortunes; but they were a minority among nearly two million Palestinians, the majority of them peasant-farmers or artisans, whose hearts remained in the land of which they had been dispossessed. Forced into refugee camps, dependent on charity, regarded with suspicion or distrust by those among whom they dwelt, the Palestinians, described by Kirkbride as being 'notorious for [their] habit of querulous complaint',[2] had plenty to complain about.

Wherever there were enough of them to constitute a threat, as in Jordan, Syria and Lebanon, the problem of their assimilation was a constant preoccupation of governments. The influx of 200,000 more of them, to add to the 650,000 or more already living in Jordan, was a cause of great concern on the part of Hussein and his ministers in the aftermath of the Six Day War. The most sensible solution would be to assimilate the refugees as ordinary citizens of Jordan, to which many of them had already contributed by their skills and industry; but this conflicted with the aim at that time of the PLO, which was the recovery of the lands taken from the Palestinians in 1948. The leaders of Fatah were convinced that none of the Arab regimes had wanted war with Israel in June 1967; given the slightest opportunity, they would have backed out. However, having fought and lost the war, their principal concern now was to recover the territory which had been taken from them; in return for this, Fatah believed, they would be willing to sign a peace treaty with Israel. Were this to happen, Israel would be left in possession of all the territory she had seized in 1948. The Palestinian cause would be lost. Arafat has gone so far as to claim that the greatest mistake made by Israel was the failure to withdraw from the Occupied Territories immediately after winning the war. Had Israel been prepared to do this, Arafat believes they would have obtained the peace treaty they so badly wanted from the front-line Arab states. This would have resulted in such rejoicing among the Arab peoples concerned that the cause of the PLO and Fatah would have been killed stone dead.[3]

This is of course hindsight. It is true, however, that one of the contributory factors to the outbreak of war in June 1967 was the largely ineffective guerrilla campaign waged by Fatah inside Israel beforehand. The war's consequences were as calamitous for the PLO as they were for Syria, Jordan and Egypt. Fatah was holding a conference in Damascus only two days after the war had ended. Most of its leaders were in despair. Even Habash, one of the most militant Palestinians, declared that all was lost. Only Yasser Arafat disputed this. Although not as yet the Chairman of the PLO, Arafat was nevertheless determined to wrest victory from defeat.

'This is not the end,' he said. 'It's the beginning. We are going to resume military actions.'[4] But few of his colleagues agreed with him.

The loss of the West Bank and Gaza Strip did however galvanise into action many Palestinians who had hitherto been sitting on the fence, hanging about the refugee camps for the most part and feeling sorry for themselves. Many of them joined Fatah, particularly from the West Bank and Gaza; Fatah then launched a guerrilla war inside Israel on 28 August 1967. This could only have been done with Syrian connivance but it was an amateurish business. By the end of the year Fatah was again on the run. The Israelis were much more efficient and ruthless than the Arabs. They captured more than 1000 commandos, many of whom talked. Fatah was also unpopular on the West Bank, whose citizens suffered from the Israeli reprisals. The West Bankers at the time believed that any settlement with Israel must be a political one; and for this reason they regarded Fatah's activities as counter-productive.

Arafat only narrowly escaped capture himself, while operating on the West Bank. Khalil al-Wazir called him back to Damascus towards the end of 1967; he was too valuable a prize to be allowed to fall into Israeli hands. The guerrilla campaign had failed and the fact had to be faced. Arafat acknowledged this but was not going to give up. He was determined to maintain the sense of Palestinian identity and saw clearly that this could only be done by keeping the struggle alive. It was the way in which he tried to do this that in the end led to his conflict with Hussein.

Although the King deeply sympathised with the Palestinians, and shared their aspirations to a great extent, he was after all king of a country which had as a result of war been cut in half. Moreover, of all the Arab rulers, he numbered among his subjects more Palestinians than the rest of them put together. His primary aim therefore was to recover the West Bank, which he regarded as being a sacred trust. He and Nasser were agreed that the only sensible way to set about achieving this aim was by negotiation, not by war. It followed that Fatah's attempts to stir up the situation inside the West Bank and Israel merely made the Israelis more intransigent when it came to negotiations. Moreover, it led from time to time to Israeli reprisals against Jordan. Hussein was therefore not in favour of Fatah's activities, which were doing the Palestinian cause a lot more harm than good.

When the June 1967 war ended there was an outcry in Jordan about its conduct. Habis Majali came in for a great deal of uninformed criticism, which led the King to replace him as Commander-in-Chief by Amer Khammash; Habis Pasha became the King's adviser on defence. General Khammash, a 'thinking soldier', at once instituted the most searching examination into every aspect of Jordan's military affairs – strategic, tactical, organisational and logistical. The outcome was a complete reorganisation of the armed forces. The first priority however was the replacement of the weapons lost in the war, both the King and Khammash knowing full well that 'an army has no pride in itself if badly armed'.[5] The problem was where to go for the arms.

They tried the United States and Britain first, telling both governments that the arms would be obtained from wherever they could be procured, including if necessary the Soviet Union. The US was unmoved. The British provided a few Centurion tanks and Hawker Hunter fighter-bombers. Hussein then decided to visit Moscow, taking Khammash with him. They were given a warm welcome in the freezing Russian winter. Hussein left Khammash to negotiate with the Soviet Minister of Defence and Chief of Staff, both of whom had joined the Red Army seven years before Khammash was born. They were friendly, but very tough. Yes, they said, Jordan could certainly have the weapons, but only for cash. Yet there was no cash.

They next visited Saudi Arabia, where the oil boom was about to start. General Khammash was most impressed by King Feisal, but he unwittingly offended protocol among the non-smoking Wahhabis by lighting a cigarette; he says this caused something of a sensation, although in the end it was Feisal himself who sent out for an ashtray.[6] After listening intently to Hussein's account of Jordan's parlous financial situation, in the course of which Hussein told Feisal that Jordan was 'Saudi's window to the west', Feisal agreed to finance the re-equipment of the Jordanian armed forces. He did not mind whether the arms were purchased from the US or Britain, but as a fervent anti-Communist he did not like the idea of dealing with the Soviet Union. In the event Jordan obtained the arms it required from both American and British sources. The Saudis paid for them. It did not happen overnight of course, but by 1970 the Jordanians were reasonably well equipped, and in some instances better provided for than before the June 1967 war. The army was certainly better organised and its strategy more clearly defined. For this General Khammash deserves great credit.

The Arab states held a summit conference in Khartoum in August 1967. Syria and Algeria boycotted the meeting. The other states agreed to employ only diplomatic means in order to secure Israel's withdrawal from the Gaza Strip and the West Bank. At the same time they passed a resolution that came to be known as the Three No's: 'No peace with Israel. No recognition of Israel. No negotiations with Israel'. They also insisted on 'the rights of the Palestinian people in their own country'. How this statement was considered to be compatible with the intention only to use diplomatic means to bring about Israel's withdrawal was never explained.

At this bleak time there was fortunately some improvement in Jordan's financial position. Kuweit, Libya and Saudi Arabia began to help in September; Western aid was also promised. But tourism, one of Jordan's chief sources for foreign exchange, was slow to recover; the loss of Jerusalem and the West Bank was a severe blow. Israel had formally annexed the Old City, and had decreed in July 1967 'that Jerusalem is one city indivisible, the Capital of the State of Israel'.[7] They then proceeded to 'Judaise' the administration, which in effect turned the Palestinian inhabitants into second-class citizens. Some continued to try and maintain a dialogue with the Israelis, but many others crossed over in despair to Jordan, leaving behind their property and land, which were appropriated by the Israeli authorities.

Israel's annexation of the Old City was not permitted to delay or interfere with the efforts being made in the UN to bring about peace between the Arabs and Israel. Working towards this end, the Security Council on 22 November 1967 passed Resolution 242, which has since been taken to represent the formula for achieving 'a just and lasting peace' between the Arabs and Israel. (The full text of Resolution 242 is given in the Appendix.) King Hussein played a vitally important part in the drafting of the Resolution, and thereafter in persuading President Nasser to support it; but he has never succeeded in persuading the PLO to do the same. The PLO argue that there is nowhere in the Resolution any reference to the *Palestinians*, whose problem becomes merely a 'refugee' one, the inference being: 'Only settle the refugees and the Palestinian problem will disappear.' The PLO have all along maintained that the Resolution is slanted in Israel's favour, and they complain that its acceptance by the Security Council effectively cancelled an earlier UN Resolution, which called for the Palestinians to be allowed to return to their homes.

All this may be fair comment; but the fact remains that had Israel abided by the Resolution, and had it withdrawn from the Occupied Territories at the end of 1967, the history of the Middle East in the following two decades might well have been less tragic. Gunnar Jarring, a Swedish diplomat, was chosen by the UN Secretary-General for the task of implementing 242; it was an impossible assignment. The Israelis declared they would not withdraw without first agreeing the terms of a peace settlement; the Arabs were not prepared to enter into negotiations with Israel until there was a withdrawal from the Occupied Territories. In the meantime the Resolution itself was subjected to a minute examination by experts in international law, one of whom concluded that it was open to as many interpretations 'as a dog has fleas'.[8]

This has been most unfortunate because there can be no doubt that at the time both Nasser and Hussein wanted peace. They were willing to go to considerable lengths in order to achieve this, but there was no reciprocity on Israel's part. Moshe Dayan certainly held out very little hope of Israel ever reaching agreement with the Arabs. 'We are doomed to live in a constant state of war with the Arabs,' he said, 'and there is no escape from sacrifice and bloodshed. This is perhaps an undesirable situation, but it is a fact. If we are to proceed with our work against the wishes of the Arabs we shall have to accept such sacrifices.'[9]

Although Dayan's statement could be considered a counsel of despair, his view is also echoed by many Arabs. Nasser always had serious reservations about 242, telling his generals in November 1967, 'What has been taken by force can only be recovered by force.'[10] But he required time to rebuild the Egyptian armed forces and acquire the weapons he needed from the Soviet Union. Hussein has always accepted 242 as a basis for negotiations, and he has never abandoned hope of reaching agreement with Israel through diplomacy. He could not possibly acquiesce in the occupation of the West Bank by Israel; it was after all half his kingdom. Had he accepted such a situation, it would have been to put at risk both the throne and his own life. He had to find a way round the logjam, however long it might take.

Hussein visited Cairo on 13 January 1968. He was given a warm welcome but Nasser told him that diplomatic contacts with Israel were unlikely to achieve anything. Hussein said he had refused to accept a letter from the Israeli Prime Minister sent to him through Ambassador Jarring. He believed Jarring was trying to arrange a secret meeting in Cyprus between Israel and the Arab states; Hussein had told him that this was outside the scope of Jarring's mission. Jarring had recently seen Abba Eban, the Israeli Foreign Minister, who had given him the Israeli interpretation of 242. It had been clear from this that the Resolution represented a series of bargaining points, each one of which would have to be negotiated separately with the Israelis. Nasser was able to confirm that the Egyptians had received identical information from Jarring.

The meeting in Cairo was extremely cordial. Always the realist, Nasser advised Hussein to obtain the arms he needed from Britain if he could, rather than from the Soviet Union. He thought it would be unfortunate if a situation arose where the Arabs were armed by the Russians and the Israelis were armed by the West. In arms as with other things it was wise to diversify. Nasser had no desire to see the Arabs become satellites of either of the superpowers, as had so obviously happened in Israel's case.

There could be no question of Fatah accepting the Israeli occupation as a *fait accompli*; to do so would mean abandoning the aim of keeping the Palestinian struggle alive. It was less easy, however, to determine how best this could be done. The West Bank population was cowed by an over-whelming Israeli military presence. The Syrians refused to permit *fedayeen* raids to be mounted from their territory. Lebanon was clearly heading for civil war. This left only Jordan as a base for operations, and Jordan contained tens of thousands of Palestinian refugees who sympathised with

Fatah's aims. There was also a large Iraqi Expeditionary Force in Jordan, sent there by President Aref to help defend Jordan against Israeli attack; Iraq had never signed an armistice agreement with Israel and had made plain its support for the PLO.

The main drawback to using Jordan as the base for guerrilla activities was the King himself. Hussein was determined that his efforts to recover the West Bank should not be jeopardised by Fatah activities over which he had no control. He remembered the border war of the early years of his reign and he had no intention of permitting a repetition. Nor did he want to provoke the Israelis into expelling their Arab population across the Jordan, something they were quite capable of doing in the opinion of some of his advisers. His policy was therefore to avoid provoking Israel while he tried to repair the ravages of the June 1967 war.

This policy had the support of most East Bankers, but not of many Palestinians. It was also clear that the Iraqis felt differently; and there were 25,000 of them camped around Mafraq and Zerqa. Hussein was in a very difficult position. There were those who believed he could not possibly survive. For Fatah, the King was expendable; all that mattered was the recovery of Palestine. But it was still necessary not to annoy the King, who had expressly forbidden the mounting of guerrilla operations on Jordanian territory. There was therefore no question of establishing training camps and ammunition dumps. But 'safe houses' could always be found for *fedayeen* inside the teeming refugee camps; and there were caves in the mountains where arms and ammunition could be stored. The first requirement would be to infiltrate into Jordan the men and weapons.

Here the Iraqis came to Fatah's assistance. Some 400 trained *fedayeen* arrived in Jordan disguised as Iraqi soldiers, transported in Iraqi trucks and bringing with them the arms and ammunition needed. Once inside Jordan, it was easy for the guerrillas to melt away among the refugees, keeping their Iraqi uniforms handy lest they were uncovered by Jordanian intelligence. Inevitably news of this operation eventually reached Hussein, who announced that the dispatch of *fedayeen* into Israel without his knowledge would be considered an 'unparalleled crime'. Strict orders were given for the interception of raiding parties but some got through, sometimes with the assistance of the Jordanian soldiers themselves. There were usually clashes, either going or returning, on these raids, turning the Jordan Valley into a 'Tom Tiddler's Ground' of gunfire and machine-gun fire every night. True to their policy of massive reprisal, the Israelis struck back with twice the weight of metal, deep into Jordan itself. This caused mounting concern in Amman.

There was some concern too over Hussein's health. The events of June 1967 seemed to have drained him. He looked drawn and haggard, he lost a lot of weight and he suffered from a jaw complaint. The constant stress brought on his sinus trouble. But he never let up, travelling all over the country to meet the people and to encourage his soldiers and airmen. His personal security was a matter for continual worry. Now that he had taken to travelling by helicopter, which needless to say he piloted himself, there was less risk of ambush, but even a helicopter is at risk from a surface-to-air missile.

Fatah soon discovered that their guerrilla operations across the River Jordan evoked very little response from the Arab population, who were thoroughly cowed. Moreover, the ruthless methods of the Israeli General Security Service soon rooted out any cells which Fatah had tried to establish. But Fatah did succeed in killing people and sabotaging installations – on no less than thirty-seven occasions, according to the Israelis. With six people killed and forty-four wounded the Israelis were fast losing patience. It ran out completely on 18 March 1968, when a school bus exploded a mine planted by Fatah. It wounded several children and killed a doctor who was travelling with them. The time had come, said Moshe Dayan, to teach the *fedayeen* a lesson they would never forget. In his capacity as Minister of Defence, he set about planning it.

Yasser Arafat's headquarters had for some time been established in the refugee camp at Karameh – the word means 'dignity' in Arabic – across the Jordan Valley from Jericho. Karameh is situated astride the main north–south road running down the valley. It is seven miles north of Shunet Nimrin, from where the Jericho–Salt road begins the 3500 feet climb out of the Jordan Valley and up the Wadi Shueib to Salt. There is a bridge across the Jordan at Damiya, fifteen miles north of Karameh. There is another bridge, the King Hussein, seven miles west of Shunat Nimrin. It can therefore be seen that Karameh can be approached from several different directions from the west. The Jordan Valley is from three to four miles wide in the area of Karameh, the mountains rising steeply behind to provide excellent observation across the plain to the river and beyond.

Karameh had been no more than a hamlet until 1948, when several thousand Palestinian refugees settled there. Some substantial buildings had been erected over the years – a mosque, a hospital, a school and so on; a few of the more well-to-do refugees had built themselves substantial dwellings. The refugee camp had taken on almost a permanent look, although the inhabitants had never abandoned hope of returning to their homes and farms in Palestine. They were reputed to be a fanatical crew, and they had welcomed Arafat with open arms. In the previous November the Israelis had shelled the village and killed several people, among them girls caught while leaving the school. This had infuriated the Palestinians, who complained that the Jordanian army had done nothing to protect them. 'Come and defend us,' they had told Arafat. Their spirit so impressed him that he decided to make Karameh his headquarters.

The Israelis did not attempt to conceal their intention of avenging the bus incident of 18 March. Guns and tanks were assembled openly, and there was talk of parading the captured *fedayeen* in Jerusalem afterwards. They would be smashed, as would the Jordanian army if it dared to intervene. Dayan forecast that it would all be over in a few hours. There could also be little doubt that the Israeli objective was Karameh.

If Arafat had followed the teachings of Mao, he and his followers would have melted away into the hills. Both Jordan and Iraq advised him to do this. George Habash's PFLP, some twenty of whose members were operating in Karameh, advised the same. Arafat and his loyal lieutenant, Khalil al-Wazir, thought differently. They knew perfectly well that with only 300 *fedayeen*, many of them mere boys, armed only with light and medium machine-guns and rocket launchers, they did not stand a chance against the Israelis. However, they were seeking not a military victory but a political one. They were determined, said Arafat, 'to prove there are people in our Arab nation who are ready to fight and to die. So I am sorry, we will not withdraw. We will fight and we will die.'[11] One need not like or admire Arafat in order to recognise the nobility of such a declaration.

Jordanian intelligence had of course been monitoring the Israeli build-up across the Jordan. The 1st Infantry Division had been deployed to cover the approaches from the Jordan Valley to Salt and Amman; it was reinforced by two armoured-car regiments and several infantry battalions. The divisional commander was Major-General Mashour Haditha al-Jazy. 60th Armoured Brigade under Brigadier Sharif Zeid bin Shakir was in support near Salt. A full alert had already been ordered, prior to the Israeli crossing of the river on a frontage of nearly fifty miles at 0400 hours on 21 March 1968. Simultaneously, Israeli paratroops carried in helicopters began to land behind Karameh.

Arafat had decided, contrary to Jordanian advice, to keep his men underground in their shelters until the Israeli tanks arrived on the scene; his aim was to knock out as many Israeli tanks as possible. But as the Israeli paratroops advanced into Karameh, the shelters became death traps. The Israelis quickly winkled out the *fedayeen* and shot them in batches. The Jordanian artillery shelled the tanks as they advanced across the plain, but by 0700 hours they had linked up with the paratroopers in Karameh. By then Arafat had withdrawn his *fedayeen* in order to regroup them behind Karameh. A second column of tanks, which had crossed the river at Damiya, was halted by Jordanian tanks and armoured cars, losing three tanks. The Israelis took up a defensive position but moved no farther forward.

There was a fierce artillery duel, under cover of which the *fedayeen* destroyed some Israeli tanks. It was also claimed that Israeli tank crews jumped out and fled. This may or may not be true; the confusion of battle often results in wild statements. The Jordanians were in a muddle themselves, because General Haditha's headquarters had been attacked from the air, leaving him dependent on his artillery radio net for the control of the battle. At 0800 hours the Israelis started to raze Karameh to the ground, a task for which they had had plenty of practice. They left only the mosque. Their air force had now begun to intervene actively in the battle, attacking Jordanian gun positions and the tanks which were moving down the defiles leading to the Jordan Valley.

The Israelis started to withdraw at 1700 hours, their mision presumably accomplished. Their withdrawal was harassed every yard of the way by the Jordanians, who claimed to have killed or wounded 250 Israelis; and to have knocked out twenty tanks and twenty armoured personnel carriers. Their own losses were 207 killed and wounded, with twenty-five tanks and APCs destroyed or disabled. Arafat reported his losses as ninety-three killed and many more wounded or captured. Israel later admitted to twenty-eight killed and two tanks abandoned. The discrepancies are such that the true state of the casualties is never likely to be known. When one of the Israeli tanks was exhibited at Amman, its dead driver still in his seat, a soldier who was looking on spat in the dead man's face. 'Don't do that,' snapped the King, who was also inspecting the tank. The soldier's action was not in keeping with either the King's or his army's honour.

Although Chaim Herzog in his book on the Arab–Israeli wars says the Israeli mission at Karameh was accomplished despite many mistakes, it is hard to understand on what he bases this statement. The Israelis had been given a bloody nose by the Jordanians, but much more significantly they had provided Arafat with a remarkable psychological victory, on which the PLO and Fatah were quick to capitalise. In next to no time the *fedayeen* were the heroes of the hour, and Arafat was the hero of heroes. Israel had unintentionally created a Trojan horse that would in time come close to costing Hussein his throne.

CHAPTER TWELVE

The *Fedayeen* Insurrection

'They were the most difficult years in my life.' King Hussein[1]

The battle of Karameh was followed by a remarkable upsurge in Palestinian morale. Few Palestinians stopped to consider that without the help of the Jordanian army Arafat and his followers would have been massacred. The PLO's propaganda was so skilful that those who propagated it actually came to believe it themselves. They were to some extent assisted by General Mashour Haditha's generous tribute to their courage. Even hard-headed men like Sharif Nasser and Wasfi Tell acknowledged it. Yasser Arafat became the man of the hour and was fêted like a conquering hero who had escaped death by a miracle. The 'martyrs' killed at Karameh were given public funerals in Amman to the accompaniment of hysterical acclaim. Volunteers from all over the Arab world flocked to join the *fedayeen*. Khalil al-Wazir, sitting under a tree outside Salt, signed up 5000 of them in only three days. Mostly they were Palestinians from the refugee camps, but many other races were represented as well.

As their numbers increased the *fedayeen* split up into several groups professing different ideologies and following separate leaders. Al-Nasr was one such group. There were numerous others all under the umbrella of the Palestine Resistance Movement (PRM). Although Fatah managed to maintain some kind of discipline, it was lamentably lacking in some other groups, notably those who followed George Habash or Nawaf Hawatmeh. They were a law unto themselves. This did not matter so much at the outset since the majority of the *fedayeen* (or commandos as they came to be called), as well as their activities, were confined to the Jordan Valley. But as the Israelis stepped up their reprisals to *fedayeen* raids by bombing, shelling and the use of napalm on Jordanian towns and villages, the vast majority of *fedayeen* moved back to Amman, Irbid and other towns and villages in Jordan. Some of them began to behave as if they owned the place, as one shopkeeper has described. 'No sooner had we opened the shutters,' he says, 'than a party of them would come swaggering in, Kaleshnikov in one hand and a collecting tin in the other, asking for contributions for the "Cause". One dare not refuse. The first arrivals would be followed by others throughout the day. We suspected that most of the money went into their own pockets.' The shopkeeper was a Palestinian.[2]

During 1968 and 1969 the increasing presence in their midst of the *fedayeen* began first to worry, and then to anger, the rest of the population. The *fedayeen* ignored the country's laws, carrying arms in public and setting up roadblocks to check the documents of passing travellers. Whereas Hussein and Nasser were agreed that if they were to recover the Occupied Territories it must be by patient diplomacy rather than by force, the PLO were determined to continue with the armed struggle. Inevitably this was leading to Israeli reprisals which did far more damage to the ordinary citizens of Jordan than to the *fedayeen*. Some of the PLO leaders believed that Hussein was an obstacle to the achievement of their aims and were prepared to overthrow him. Although Arafat himself was opposed to the overthrow of legitimate Arab rulers, others disagreed with him. Abu Da'oud, Fatah's field commander under Khalil al-Wazir, insisted they would not get anywhere without first removing Hussein. He said many Jordanian officers would join in a coup against the King.[3] It would be surprising if information of this kind did not get back to the King.

Hussein viewed with increasing concern the deterioration in relations between his people and the *fedayeen*. The comings and goings of the PLO leaders were equally disturbing. They travelled all over the Middle East drumming up support, almost as representatives of an independent state. In Amman they drove around like ministers, accompanied by armed escorts. Matters reached such a pitch that Hussein was petitioned to do something about controlling the *fedayeen*. 'I try to exert control,' he replied, 'but it's difficult to tell who is a commando and who is not. Besides, what do you expect me to do? What should I do to a people who have lost everything – who were driven out of their country? Shoot them? I think we have come to a point where we are all *fedayeen*.'[4] Most worrying of all, perhaps, were the increasing clashes between his soldiers and the *fedayeen*. He knew how touchy bedouin soldiers could be when it came to their personal honour. The *fedayeen* were behaving as if it did not matter any more.

The problem was further complicated by the conflicting advice being given to the King. Among his advisers were both doves and hawks. The former, among them Prime Minister Bahjat Talhouni, advised reaching an agreement with the PLO and avoiding clashes with the commandos; this meant virtually confining the army to barracks. The hawks, headed by Sharif Nasser and Wasfi Tell, who saw more clearly than most the threat to the throne, advocated tough action to bring the *fedayeen* to heel. This school of thought included several senior army officers like Sharif Zeid bin Shakir and Qasim Ma'aita.

Matters were not helped by the inability of the Palestinians to agree among themselves. Arafat realised that to overthrow the King would be to play directly into Israeli hands. It had for many years been Israel's contention that the proper place for a Palestinian state was Jordan. Once Hussein had been overthrown, and a Palestinian government substituted for the Hashemites, any hope of recovering the Occupied Territories and Jerusalem would vanish. Arafat was therefore in favour of co-operating with the King; but he wanted to keep the struggle alive by launching *fedayeen* operations across the River Jordan into the West Bank and Israel.

This policy was bitterly disputed by some of the more militant PLO leaders, notably by George Habash and Nawaf Hawatmeh. Habash openly advocated violence in order to draw attention to the Palestinian cause. Nor was he willing, as Arafat was, to restrict such action to Israeli territory. Habash, a Marxist, favoured indiscriminate action, provided the aim was to publicise the wrong done to the Palestinians. His colleague, Hawatmeh, soon broke away from Habash to form the Popular Democratic Front (PDF); it was another group dedicated to violence.

Habash's slogan was 'Unity, Freedom, Vengeance'. Like many Palestinian intellectuals, he despaired of bringing his people's plight to world attention by reasoned argument. It was under his aegis that the PFLP started to hijack planes, bomb airport lounges, assassinate opponents on the streets of London and other cities, and plant firebombs in stores like Marks and Spencer's. The logic behind these terrorist activities was simple. 'When we hijack a plane,' said Habash, 'it has more effect than if we killed a hundred Israelis in battle. For decades world public opinion has been neither for nor against the Palestinians. It simply ignored us. At least the world is talking about us now.'[5] There was of course an unfortunate side-effect. Although world public opinion was certainly alerted to the plight of the Palestinians, at the same time it concluded that they and terrorists were one and the same thing.

Arafat, a shrewd politician, was well aware of this. He insisted that the armed struggle must be kept alive, but not at the expense of harmless travellers and tourists. The place to wage it was inside Israel and the Occupied Territories. Raids of this kind were mounted throughout 1968 and 1969, rarely with much effect, but they did cause concern in Israel, which retaliated by bombing and shelling Jordanian towns and villages, sometimes deep inside Jordan. Inevitably this lost the PLO the sympathy of many Jordanians, who at the same time were becoming increasingly angered by the behaviour of some of the *fedayeen* in their midst. On 4 November 1968 the army, exasperated beyond endurance, launched an attack on Al-Nasr in the Jebel Ashrafiyeh and Jebel Hussein refugee camps on the outskirts of Amman. By the end of the action twenty-eight *fedayeen* had been killed, as well as four soldiers. The army complained that it had been called off before teaching the *fedayeen* the lesson they deserved. The *fedayeen* on the other hand went round boasting that they had given the army a bloody nose.

'It was quite remarkable how soon the *fedayeen* succeeded in alienating the people,' says one Jordanian of Palestinian origin.

> Whereas even Wasfi Tell after Karameh was pro-*fedayeen*, in a matter of months everything changed. At the beginning of 1968 there were not many of them to be seen in Amman; most of them were in the Jordan Valley or around Irbid. Then suddenly, almost overnight, the streets of Amman were crowded with them, behaving as if they owned the place. They quickly turned ugly if you remonstrated with them for any reason. We used to ask each other why the King permitted them to behave in such a fashion. I had many Palestinian friends, some of them very closely connected with Fatah and the PLO, and without exception they deplored the conduct of the commandos, or militia as they now seemed to be called. I know for certain that one of my friends complained directly to Abu Amar [Yasser Arafat] but he seemed powerless to do anything about it.[6]

This was Arafat's principal failing as a leader. He could not impose discipline on his followers but instead sought always for a consensus. As one of his critics has written, 'there was nothing consistent or constructive in decision making; rarely did one decision supplement or complete an earlier one; every session started from scratch. . . .'[7] This probably accounts for the fact that those who have had to negotiate with Arafat invariably complain that as a leader he cannot deliver. For all his undoubted courage, dedication and intelligence, Arafat seems to lack the steel necessary for the really tough decisions. It was this that was the cause of his failure to discipline the *fedayeen* between 1968 and 1970.

Arafat had had a meeting with Nasser in November 1967 which was to have far-reaching consequences for the PLO, Fatah and Arafat personally. The meeting had been arranged by Muhammad Heikal, editor of *Al-Ahram*, and during it Nasser accused the PLO of being 'romantics'. If they thought they were going to persuade the Israelis to give up Israel, it could only be a dream. If they thought they could drive them out of Israel, they must be mad. Their policy must be realistic if they were to have Nasser's support. On New Year's Day 1968, Fatah did come up with a policy that made sense, however distant or utopian its realisation might be. This was to create a democratic state in Palestine in which Jews and Arabs would live as fellow citizens. 'We were saying "No" to the Jewish state,' said Arafat, 'but "Yes" to the Jewish people.'[8]

This was very different from the intransigence of the PFLP, or even the PLO, but Fatah did not control the PLO in 1968 and their proposal was rejected. But the seeds had been sown in Nasser's mind and he decided to put his money on Arafat and Fatah. He even took Arafat with him on a visit to Moscow that summer, only to discover that the Soviet leaders were not willing to receive Arafat. At the time they said they were interested only in reaching agreement in accordance with Resolution 242. Although naturally disappointed, Arafat was still on the crest of the wave. He had succeeded in establishing excellent personal relations with Nasser, who was employing all his influence to secure Fatah a predominant position within the PLO. At the fifth Palestine National Congress in Cairo in February 1969, Fatah acquired control over the PLO, with Arafat as Chairman of the organisa- tion. He and his colleagues had out-manoeuvred Habash, Hawatmeh and the others. They were now in a position to dictate the PLO's policy.

Their principal weakness was a lack of funds. Until now their weapons had been provided free by Communist China, but many of them disliked the idea of being dependent on Communists. It was urgently necessary to place the PLO's finances on a firmer footing, but how? When Arafat approached Nasser he was read a lecture on Egypt's near-bankruptcy; but why did he not try King Feisal of Saudi Arabia? Accordingly Khalad Hassan (Abu Sa'ed), head of the PLO's Political Department and a member of Fatah, was sent to Riyadh in March 1969. After considerable difficulty he secured an audience with Feisal, which turned out to be a resounding success. Fortunately the two men got on well together. Moreover, although the Saudis are always cautious, they are solid in their condemnation of Israel. This was sufficient to lead them to support the cause of the Palestinians, although it required the diplomacy of Khalad Hassan to turn this support into something much more concrete.

Feisal in the first place imposed a 5 per cent tax on the salaries of all Palestinians working in the Kingdom, and there were many thousands of them, some drawing huge salaries. He then agreed to provide the PLO with an annual subsidy of $12 million. Finally, he said Saudi Arabia would provide the PLO with as much ammunition and as many weapons as could be spared from its own armoury. Two weeks later twenty-eight truckloads of arms and ammunition arrived in Jordan for the PLO. This transformed the situation for Fatah and revitalised the entire Palestinian Resistance Movement.

Although most Jordanians could understand and sympathise with the Palestinians' longing for a return to their own country, the behaviour of the *fedayeen* was making them more and more unpopular. 'It was more than I could stand,' said one long-serving NCO who was himself a Palestinian. 'We were the proper soldiers, not the so-called commandos, who couldn't hit a target at fifty paces if you gave them a hundred dinars. They insulted our women and said bad things about our King. I cannot understand why we ever gave them houseroom.'[9] The PLO too were acting almost as if they were an independent institution, organising their own army, as well as diplomatic representation abroad. 'This was by no means to our disadvantage,' an Israeli has commented, 'since there is a powerful school of thought inside Israel which has maintained all along that the proper place for a new Palestinian state is Jordan.'[10]

Now that the PLO were receiving aid in money and weapons from the Saudis, it had become possible to fire Katyusha rockets across the River Jordan against Israeli targets. This in turn led to savage reprisal attacks by the Israelis, resulting in more and more Jordanian civilian deaths. Hussein came under more pressure to do something about it, although he was doing his utmost to avoid an outright confrontation with the PLO. It can be said that he almost bent over backwards to avoid a clash.

He made some changes in the army's high command in July 1969. Amer Khammash became Minister of Defence and his place at the head of the army was taken by Sharif Nasser. No one had any doubt about his views. It was said that he had sworn an oath to his sister, the Queen Mother Zein, that he would lay down his life for the King should the need arise. Sharif Zeid bin Shakir was at the same time given command of the elite 1st Armoured Division, which contained many bedouin units. As a result of Kuweiti and certain other assistance it had recently proved possible to purchase twenty-four Hawker Hunters from Britain and forty M-60 tanks from the US, which gave the army's morale a welcome fillip, although the King continued to be disturbed by the reports he was receiving of the army's increasing dislike of the *fedayeen*.

However, with the army under the firm control of Khammash and his uncle, and with the striking force commanded by his cousin, the King was reasonably confident of his ability to control events. He was less certain of some of his ministers. Bahjat Talhouni, the Prime Minister, was not a particularly strong character, and if the King's difficulty in obtaining unprejudiced advice is to be understood, it is necessary to remember that many of Jordan's leading citizens were themselves of Palestinian origin. There had been little difference between Transjordan and Palestine prior to the ending of the British mandate, and people had relatives on both banks of the River Jordan. Loyalties were to that extent divided, and no doubt in some instances hearts were allowed to rule heads. In February 1970, with a view to introducing some steel into the Cabinet, Hussein appointed Rasoul Kilani as Minister of the Interior. Kilani at once banned the carrying or discharge of weapons within the limits of any town. He also insisted on the proper registration of all vehicles, which was a direct hit at the *fedayeen*. There were howls of protest.

The first major outbreak was the besieging of the police station on Jebel

Ashrafiyeh, where George Habash controlled the main refugee camp. The PFLP were the cause of this trouble, which was not put down for several days, and then only after limited army support. This was the first serious outbreak of lawlessness in February 1970, and from then on incidents became increasingly frequent. During the months that followed an attempt was made to combine the eleven major *fedayeen* groups into one military confederation, the Armed Struggle Command, which was dominated by the PLA and Fatah; but other groups maintained a quasi-independence whenever it suited them. As Hussein twisted and turned, anxious above all to avoid a shooting confrontation, good men had to be sacrificed. One of the first heads to roll was Kilani's, less than two weeks after his issuance of the firearms banning order.

Hussein had visited Cairo prior to Kilani's dismissal. Nasser had made plain his support for the PLO, declaring that he would react strongly were Hussein to use force to bring the PLO to heel. On the other hand, Nasser considered the PLO's activities were counter-productive if there was ever to be a chance of reaching a political settlement with Israel. Therefore, provided Hussein was circumspect, he would have Nasser's support. It was a classic case of 'Heads I win, tails you lose.' Hussein returned to Amman a very worried man.

Arafat may have done all he could to restrain his followers, but his authority was at best limited. Nor was he helped by the divergence of views among the leadership of the PLO. While Arafat was trying to reach agreement with Hussein, men like Abu Da'oud were arguing fiercely for Hussein's overthrow. Abu Da'oud, as commander of the Palestinian militias in Jordan, bore the chief responsibility for the lack of discipline in some of the *fedayeen* groups, which he chose to blame on 'the foolish and criminal activity of the leftists in our movement'.[11] This was probably true, but he was singularly ineffectual in restraining them. Hawatmeh's PDF were the worst offenders. They shocked the Jordanians by being free with women, and by broadcasting Marxist slogans from a mosque to mark the centenary of Lenin's birth.

Kilani's order banning the carrying of weapons in the towns had led to an outcry in Syria and Iraq. With all the inevitability of a Greek tragedy, Hussein was moving steadily along a path that must eventually lead to an outright clash with the PLO. The population was growing increasingly infuriated by the behaviour of the *fedayeen*; and the army had been confined to barracks in order to minimise the chances of a clash. Hussein's many meetings with Arafat produced only vague assurances. The refugee camps had become virtually 'no-go' areas for the police. At Khaw, near the main military base at Zerqa, a complete Iraqi brigade, with two PLA battalions under command, was busily fraternising with the militias. At Mafraq, the

King Hussein as Supreme Commander of the Jordanian Armed Forces.

The King's grandfather, King Abdullah
bin Hussein.

The King with his younger brother,
Prince Muhammad.

Back row: The King's youngest
brother, Crown Prince Hassan, and
Hussein. *Front row:* The Queen
Mother, Zein, and Princess Basma,
Hussein's sister.

The King's father, King Talal bin
Abdullah.

The Royal Family.

Arab unity: the King with President Hosni Mubarak of Egypt *(left)* and President Saddam Hussein of Iraq.

The King greets PLO Chairman Yasser Arafat, with Prince Muhammad looking on, Amman.

With Queen Elizabeth II.

The King greets a Bedouin Sheikh.

At the White House.

With the troops.

The boy king, aged eighteen, being briefed during a visit to an Arab Legion Artillery Regiment. General Glubb Pasha is on the right of the group.

The soldier king.

The King with his youngest daughter, Princess Raiyah, in 1986. Photo by Zohrab Makarian.

The King and Queen Noor.

air base close to the Syrian border, the remainder of the Iraqi division, which was supposed to be helping the Jordanians to defend the country, was in fact collaborating with the PLO. Meanwhile, Damascus Radio was working hard to increase the tension, praising the PLO and attacking Hussein and his government.

At the beginning of June matters began to go from bad to worse. A Jordanian paratrooper was attacked in Amman on 6 June. This was followed by clashes between the soldiers and the *fedayeen*. On 7 June an American diplomat, who had unwisely gone on his own to investigate the situation in the Ashrafiyeh refugee camp, was kidnapped. He was released the next day after an official approach had been made by the Jordanian government. Fighting broke out on 9 June between the *fedayeen* and the army, and also among various factions within the *fedayeen* themselves. It was close to anarchy.

On the same day there came the first direct attempt on Hussein's life. The *fedayeen* had been gradually infiltrating the vicinities of most public buildings and police stations, although they had left military installations severely alone. The King was out at Hummar when Zeid Rifai arrived posthaste, with the news that the *fedayeen* were firing on the intelligence headquarters. Despite Zeid's protests, Hussein insisted on going to see for himself. He sat in front of the car beside the driver, nursing an automatic rifle. Zeid Rifai and Sharif Nasser sat in the back. There were three Land Rovers full of troops, in front and in the rear, as escort. On reaching the Suweilih crossroads, they were halted by a barrier. Firing broke out as this was being raised, killing one soldier and wounding another. The rest of the escort took to the ditch, returning the fire.

Sharif Nasser jumped out, calling on the King to do the same. Hussein seemed to be oblivious to their cries and carried on shooting from the car window. Then, almost as if in a dream, he opened the door and made for the ditch. He was followed by Zeid Rifai and the escort commander, both of whom landed heavily on the King, straining his back. The firing continued for some time until it was considered safe enough for the King to return to Hummar, where he was greeted by the Royal Guard with passionate demonstrations of loyalty. The King had however to take to his bed for three days on account of his back. It was afterwards claimed that eight of his attackers had been killed. Both the PLO and PFLP denied having had any hand in the ambush. They even said it had been set up by Jordanian officers acting as *agents provocateurs*. The times were such that almost any excuse served.

When the news of the King's narrow escape reached the troops, there was an immediate outburst of anger. The PLO claimed the army had shelled the Jebel Wahadat and Jebel Hussein refugee camps in reprisal, but an

independent witness has denied the truth of this. The King, confined to his
bed, was growing increasingly anxious about his army. He was to say of this
period later:

> No one – adult or child – could be sure on leaving his house whether his
> family would see him again. Amman became a virtual battlefield. No
> Regular Army people could enter the city in uniform, as they would be
> fired on by the PLO. I tried my best. Twice, I was ambushed. And I
> almost lost control. The people in the armed forces began to lose
> confidence in me. A great part of my time was spent answering calls that
> we had failed to stop this Company or Battalion from leaving their
> garrison to fight the PLO, and that I alone could reason with them. The
> best I could do was to persuade them to stop where they were. At that
> point, some captain in the army might actually have been able to rally the
> rest behind him.[12]

There was a very real fear in Hussein's mind that the army might mutiny out
of sheer exasperation.

Despite efforts to arrange a truce, this internecine fighting between
various factions of the PLO continued on the following day, 10 June. It led
to the death of Zeid bin Shakir's sister Jozah, who was killed by a stray
bullet when she went on to the roof of the house to see what was going on.
Major Bob Perry, the US Assistant Military Attaché, was also killed at
point-blank range when he went to his front door to open it to some
fedayeen. They were driven off by some Fatah commandos. Later that day a
truce was arranged, but it was almost immediately broken.

For a proper understanding of Hussein's dilemma, it should be borne in
mind that every man, woman and child in Jordan regarded Israel as *the*
enemy, and considered the Palestinians to have been cruelly treated. It
simply made no sense to see these self-same Palestinians acting as if they
were the enemy. Many Palestinians themselves deplored the conduct of the
fedayeen and were infuriated by their behaviour. But many of Hussein's
counsellors believed that the only way to deal with the problem was by
negotiation with the PLO, despite the fact that it was becoming increasingly
obvious that the PLO exerted no control over certain of its factions.
Although tempers were fast reaching boiling point in the army, no one
wanted to force the King to act hastily. Zeid bin Shakir begged him not to be
influenced by his sister's death. He offered instead to resign his command,
if that would make negotiations with the PLO easier. Sharif Nasser did
likewise. Talhouni, as well as other ministers, urged the King to negotiate
in order to reach an accommodation with the PLO.

Although dubious of any result, Hussein reluctantly agreed to do so. He issued a message on 11 June to the armed forces in which he said that until now the army had stayed outside Amman where armed bands were now engaged in looting and murder. Their aim was to occupy 'our land' and to set up a mini-state within it. They were calling for the removal of Sharif Nasser and Sharif Zeid. Nasser, who had always been loyal, had been attacked and one of his bodyguard killed. Zeid's sister had been killed, but both men had throughout acted with restraint. Although the King had rejected demands for their dismissal, he had accepted their resignations with regret. A Joint Committee was then set up with the PLO to resolve problems and to allocate blame.

Hussein now assumed overall command of the armed forces as Supreme Commander. The army commander was to be Major-General Mashour Haditha al-Jazy, who had until then been Sharif Nasser's deputy. Mashour had commanded the 1st Infantry Division at Karameh and was well regarded by the *fedayeen* as a result. He was a man of impeccable bedouin ancestry, belonging to the al-Jazy section of the Howeitat tribe, with a pleasant but not particularly strong personality. He was the complete opposite in character to Sharif Nasser, who was both forthright and outspoken. This had made Nasser unpopular in some quarters, but his loyalty to the King was impregnable. Mashour too had his detractors, some of whom considered he was on too close terms with the PLO. To the extent that this was true, it was to prove useful later. Although his appointment was not universally welcomed in the army, it did produce a momentary calm. Some fifty tourists, who had been briefly prevented from leaving the Philadelphia Hotel in downtown Amman, were released; and on 14 June the Prime Minister announced that all was quiet again. This was endorsed by Arafat, but the peace was a shaky one. The PFLP and PDF by their irresponsible activities made certain of that. They had led to the evacuation of American subjects, which had begun on 12 June.

In a further attempt to reach agreement with the PLO, Hussein now changed his Prime Minister. Abdul Moneim Rifai, brother of the late Samir Rifai and a known moderate, replaced Bahjat Talhouni on 26 June. Meanwhile the state of affairs in the army continued to worry the King. Reports of discontent in the military garrisons flowed into the Palace, reinforcing the advice he was receiving in favour of tough action from his more hawkish counsellors. But Hussein was anxious if at all possible to avoid an outright confrontation. Added to his natural sympathy for the Palestinians was the knowledge that any such clash must result in many innocent civilian casualties. It has been suggested that the King was under such pressure from some of his generals that he did at one stage consider abdication, but this has always been denied. As one of those generals has said: 'It was not in His Majesty's nature to run away. Besides, he knew as well as the rest of us that every decent-minded man and woman in Jordan was behind him.'

A delegation from various Arab countries arrived in Amman on 27 June at the King's invitation. They had meetings with both the government and the PLO, after which an agreement was signed on 10 July. This confirmed Jordan's recognition of the PRM and accepted the 'legal' presence of the *fedayeen* in the country. In return the PRM agreed to remove their bases and depots from Jordan's towns and cities; furthermore, weapons were not to be carried within certain specified municipal limits. It was a sensible and workmanlike agreement that worked for a time. The trouble was that Arafat lacked the authority to enforce it. There was no meeting of minds within the higher counsels of the Palestine Resistance Movement, as George Habash and Nawaf Hawatmeh had already made abundantly clear.

When Habash had visited the tourists detained by the *fedayeen* on 12 June, he had apologised for the inconvenience caused them but had said their sufferings could in no way be compared with those inflicted over the years on the unfortunate Palestinian people. He doubted whether any one of his audience could have borne such suffering. As a parting shot, he told them that the United States was the real enemy. Habash was of course a convinced revolutionary. He believed that only by armed struggle could Palestinian wrongs be righted. He or Hawatmeh blocked, or sabotaged, every attempt to reach agreement between the Armed Struggle Command and the Jordanian government. Arafat even denounced Habash, although not by name, as an 'extremist demagogue'. Everyone knew to whom he was referring.

The situation did however quieten down in July. Wasfi Tell, who at the height of the troubles had been forced to take refuge at Hummar since his way home was blocked, went so far as to say in early July that the situation was 'copeable'. It was not to remain so for long, but at least it made it possible for the King to leave the country briefly. He flew to Rabat to congratulate King Hassan of Morocco on his survival of a *coup d'état* on 10 July. The coup had been launched on King Hassan's forty-second birthday and was thwarted only by the strong action taken by General Oufkir, Morocco's strong man. Hussein's gesture was typical of him. He never forgets his friends.

It was at this critical time in Arab affairs that the US government chose to come up with a new peace plan for the Middle East. Its architect was the Secretary of State, William Rogers, and it will be described at greater length later in this narrative. Suffice to say here that Nasser's reaction to the American proposals aroused violent Palestinian opposition. This greatly annoyed Nasser, who went so far as to refuse to receive Arafat when he visited Cairo at the end of July. Arafat had rubbed salt into the wound by first visiting Baghdad on his way to Cairo. There he had been assured of the support of the Iraqi Expeditionary Force, still stationed in Jordan. This was unlikely to be welcome news to Nasser, who was always jealous of Iraq. Although relations between Nasser and Arafat had been more or less patched up by the time Arafat left Cairo, Nasser saw fit to tell Hussein that it was high time the PLO was taught a lesson. This might have been taken as giving Hussein the green light for action against the PLO, although it is doubtful whether it was intended as such, Nasser always preferring to keep his options open. But Hussein had in fact little choice. He had either to assert his and his government's authority, or risk losing his throne. He knew the army's patience was fast running out.

At the beginning of August various tank and artillery units were moved to the vicinity of Amman as a precautionary measure. Zeid bin Shakir was recalled to active duty and made Deputy Chief of Staff (Operations). As such it was his task to draw up plans for dealing with the *fedayeen*. It came as a surprise to discover that no plans of this nature existed in the head-quarters. Shakir and his staff had to start from scratch and they worked day and night for two weeks to produce a plan. They were hampered in this by the virtual absence of any reliable intelligence regarding the *fedayeen*. 'No one knew their strength nor anything about their weapons,' he says. As a further complication the police had lost all authority, and there were Palestinian sympathisers even in army headquarters. This made it difficult to ensure effective security.[13] General Mashour Haditha was so anxious to avoid a confrontation with the Armed Struggle Command that he forbade a broadcast intended to extol the training and dedication of Jordan's Special Forces. He thought it might be considered provocative. The King had to intervene personally to ensure that the broadcast took place.

The uneasy truce was broken on 29/30 August when renewed firing broke out in the residential quarter of Amman. The troops in their efforts to get to grips with the *fedayeen* were greatly hampered by the deep trenches which had been dug as part of the project to install main drainage in the residential areas of the city. These trenches provided excellent cover for the *fedayeen*, and they afforded a means of communication that was safe against small-arms fire. This only added to the army's exasperation.

July and August are the hot months in Jordan, when the wind blows in from the desert, bringing not only sand but also shortening of tempers. In the army camps tempers were already short enough. Officers and soldiers alike found it hard to understand why the King seemed to be so reluctant to assert his authority. They found the behaviour of the *fedayeen* insupportable. They could not go on leave without first changing out of uniform lest the *fedayeen* subjected them to indignity, or even worse. And weren't these the people they had saved from massacre at Karameh? It is not surprising that the ordinary soldier should have found it intolerable. And so did his officers.

CHAPTER THIRTEEN

Black September 1970

'From the Battle of Karameh onward, it became apparent that whatever pride Arabs might take in the courage and dedication of the Fidayin, they posed a real menace to established governments.'[1]

On 1 September 1970 the King went to Amman airport to greet his daughter, Princess Alia. He had avoided driving through the centre of Amman but was ambushed all the same. His route must have been disclosed to his enemies. The motorcade was approaching a sharp bend when fire was directed on it from across the road. The majority of vehicles managed to round the bend before they were stopped and the fire was returned. Hussein had once again to take cover. Prince Muhammad, his younger brother, was travelling in a separate car. He says the ambush site was cleverly chosen. The road was narrow and was overlooked from the hillside above. The firing was heavy and almost continuous. Most of the party took refuge in houses but it was hard to see how they could get away without coming out into the open. It was getting dark and the situation was confused.

They succeeded eventually in turning the King's car and getting him away in the direction from which he had come. Reinforcements arrived and the noise of firing was deafening. Prince Muhammad managed to get away, thankful to have escaped unscathed. His personal escort, a bedouin sergeant, commented ruefully that it was one thing to be shot up by the Jews, but quite another when one's own kith and kin tried to murder one.[2] Hussein was furious but the army was even angrier. It required only one more incident to lead to a head-on clash between the soldiers and the *fedayeen*. It was not long in coming.

Prolonged firing broke out in Amman on 4 September. Then on 6 September, a Sunday, the PFLP brought off their most spectacular coup so far. This was masterminded by Habash's lieutenant, Wadi Haddad, Habash himself being away in North Korea at the time. It began with an attempt to hijack an El Al airliner en route from Amsterdam to London. It failed. The hijackers were a young Palestinian woman, Leila Khaled, aged twenty-six, who had hijacked a TWA Boeing en route to Damascus the previous year, and a young Latin American, Patrick Arguello. He was fatally wounded in an exchange of fire and Khaled was overpowered. The plane's Captain saved the situation by putting the plane into a steep dive, subsequently landing it at Heathrow.

That same day, around 6.45 p.m., a TWA Boeing en route from Europe was hijacked while in flight and talked down by an English-speaking commando on to a desert strip known as Dawson's Field near Zerqa. The *fedayeen* renamed the strip Revolutionary Airstrip. It was soon to receive another plane, a Swissair DC-8, which had been hijacked soon after takeoff. A third plane, a Pan Am jumbo jet, was hijacked soon after taking off from Amsterdam and flown to Cairo, where it was blown up at 2.23 a.m. on 7 September. The passengers and crew were given only three minutes to get clear. Meanwhile, at Dawson's Field, 310 passengers from the American and Swiss planes spent a cheerless night, guarded by *fedayeen* who were themselves ringed by a cordon of Jordanian soldiers. Three days later a British VC-10 with 115 passengers and crew was similarly hijacked to Dawson's Field. Hussein denounced the hijackings as the 'Shame of the Arabs'. Nasser was equally angry, but as a demonstration of what could be achieved, given the wit to plan and the ruthlessness to carry it out, the only word for the PFLP's operation is spectacular.

Widespread firing in Amman, which had started on 4 September, made movement in the streets dangerous. There was firing around Suweileh and Hummar on 8 September. An incident at Irbid, which was rapidly turning into a *fedayeen* town, caused great indignation and led General Mashour Haditha to demand an enquiry. He was to discover that the Armed Struggle Command exerted little influence with the PFLP. He also tried to secure the release of Leila Khaled in return for the relief of the British hostages, but at that moment no one knew whether there were any. With the hijacking of the VC-10 on 9 September there certainly were British hostages, which probably accounts for the hijacking in the first place.

Fighting in Amman grew in intensity, often between the *fedayeen* themselves. The conditions demanded for the release of the planes and passengers were threefold: the release of Leila Khaled held in Britain; the release of three guerrillas held in West Germany; and the release of three guerrillas held in Switzerland. On the other hand American and Israeli passengers would be released only in return for the freeing of an unspecified number of guerrillas held in Israeli jails. Failing any agreement on the above the planes would be blown up, and with them the passengers, by 3 a.m. on Thursday, 10 September.

Hussein and his government were virtually powerless. The army dared not intervene lest the *fedayeen* blow up the planes. Mashour Haditha conducted the preliminary investigations and succeeded in obtaining the release of 127 women and children, in return for which the army had to pull back just over a mile from Dawson's Field, but not without murmurings by the troops. 'All we talked about all day long was what we would like to do to those damned Palestinians,' said one officer. There was little the King could do about it since the negotiations were out of his hands. He had no influence with the PFLP, and Arafat's position was little stronger. He had only just returned from Cairo, where Nasser had told him that any more provocations would mean the loss of Nasser's support . . . and then had come the hijackings.

There was a slight lull on 10 September but many householders began to stock up in preparation for a siege. The King managed to stop one army column from entering the city but it had required all his powers of persuasion. The army was seething. On 11 September the PFLP prevented a food convoy organised by Fatah, and intended for the hostages, from reaching Dawson's Field. This led the Iraqi government to withdraw support for the PFLP. Attempts that were being made to secure the release of the British hostages were endangered by frequent inaccurate broadcasts by the BBC. This caused the British government to issue retraction statements at equally frequent intervals. Amman had now become the main focus for the world's press, whose many statements based on rumour as much as on fact did more harm than good in a situation that was tense to bursting point.

The British Embassy succeeded on 12 September in obtaining the release of the women and children. When this was followed some time later by an announcement of the release of Leila Khaled, the connection seemed obvious, but in fact there was none. Arafat too had been doing his best to secure the hostages' release. He knew the damage that would be done to the Palestinian cause were they harmed. He summoned a meeting of the Armed Struggle Command and demanded a majority vote in favour of the hostages' release. He is even reported as having threatened to resign if the vote went against him. But there was no need. After releasing all but sixteen of the hostages, whom they retained as a guarantee for their own safety (they were not released until 25 September), the PFLP destroyed all three planes. Arafat's reaction to this needless act of defiance was to suspend the PFLP from the Central Committee of Palestinian Resistance (CCPR), which caused Habash and his followers no concern.

Hussein did not know which way to turn. He was furious about the hijacking but reluctant to expose his people to the dangers that must undoubtedly follow a head-on clash between the army and the *fedayeen*. He had however been badly shaken by his experience when preventing an Air Defence artillery regiment from entering Amman a few days previously. On that occasion he had first sent his brother Prince Muhammad, accompanied by Zeid bin Shakir, to halt the column. They had been ignored. When

Hussein arrived on the scene himself, he had been treated almost with contempt. Seeing a brassière fluttering from a radio aerial, he had pointed at it enquiringly. In reply he was told that it was because their King was a woman who was afraid to take action against their country's enemies. Hussein spent nearly three hours arguing with the sullen soldiers before they reluctantly turned back. Yet these were men, as the King has since pointed out, who would have fought like tigers to win back their land for the Palestinians.

Arafat no longer exercised any real control. He had worked out with Prime Minister Abdul Moneim Rifai an agreement whereby the *fedayeen* would be permitted bases *outside* the main towns, from where they would be able to carry out attacks against Israel. But such an agreement had no reality. Arafat could not enforce it. He knew there were those in even his own Fatah who applauded the hijackings and were sorry Fatah had not thought of it first. Arafat's reluctance to discipline his own extremists had merely played into their hands.

This was fully understood by the King and his closest advisers, among whom were his two brothers, Wasfi Tell, Zeid Rifai and three army brigadiers – Zeid bin Shakir, Qasim Ma'aita and Maazen Ajlouni. There were other army officers too in close support. They were insistent that the *fedayeen* must be brought to heel. Whether they threatened to depose the King if he failed to move is difficult to establish, but it would seem unlikely. Hussein saw clearly that he had been left with little option, however much he loathed the prospect. Unless he restored the authority of his government, Jordan would be reduced to chaos. This must have been in his mind when he rejected the agreement reached between his Prime Minister and Arafat on 14 September. He had no faith in Arafat's ability to carry it out.

The Prime Minister told the King he had done his best and if the King was not satisfied then he should resign his office. Hussein temporised by refusing to accept Abdul Moneim Rifai's resignation for the time being; instead he went into conference with his inner circle of advisers, a meeting which did not end until 11 p.m. By then it had been decided to enforce with all the means at the government's disposal the agreement worked out with the PLO in the previous July, under the auspices of a committee containing members from Algeria, Tunisia, Sudan, Egypt and Libya. Jordan had then agreed to recognise the *fedayeen* CCPR; the Palestinians in their turn had agreed to disband their bases and depots and refrain from carrying weapons in the towns.

Once this had been decided, the King dismissed Abdul Moneim Rifai and his Cabinet and appointed a military government in their place. To most people's surprise the new Prime Minister was to be a virtually unknown brigadier, Muhammad Daud, whose chief claim to office was that he was the senior serving Palestinian officer, and a man of known moderate views. The King announced his appointment, and the formation of a military government, early on 16 September. 'We find it our duty', he told his people, 'to take a series of measures to restore law and order to preserve the life of every citizen, his means of living and his property.' By then the army had been ordered to surround Amman, and Mashour Haditha had been replaced as C-in-C by Field Marshal Habis Majali, who had been recalled from retirement. The new Cabinet contained seven generals and brigadiers, two colonels and two majors. Brigadier Daud went into immediate conclave with Arafat in a last desperate attempt to make the Palestinians see reason. He failed.

The odds seemed to be on the side of the army. It was much better disciplined, trained and equipped. It possessed much heavier weapons than the *fedayeen* and had the advantage of a centralised command structure. Jordanian intelligence estimated that there were 52,000 *fedayeen* in and around Amman, 12,000 of them full-time, the rest part-time. It was optimistically considered that they could be driven out of the city in two or three days. Tank columns supported by infantry and artillery would advance from north and south, meeting somewhere in the centre of the city. The plan was simple enough but its execution was to prove to be much more difficult.

The Jordanian army had had little experience of street fighting, which is essentially an infantry task. It had been organised for mobile operations, but tanks are vulnerable in cities, and artillery finds it hard to bring its weight of fire to bear. Street fighting is a slow, hard slog, when a few stout-hearted men in a strongpoint can hold up a whole company or battalion. An additional limitation was the need to restrict civilian casualties. Amman, moreover, was a natural tank trap, with stout stone-built houses covering the spurs which run east and west of the Wadi Zerqa. The ravines between the spurs are deep, some of them with steep sides, and adjacent to the residential areas were the refugee camps, rabbit warrens of narrow streets providing easy refuge for the *fedayeen*. To have dealt with the problem as quickly and as clinically as proposed would have required many more troops than the Jordanians had available.

Nor was Amman the army's only problem. The *fedayeen* were strongly based in Irbid, Jerash and Zerqa. Then there were the Israelis, who might take advantage of the army's preoccupation to move across the River Jordan. The riverline had to be defended. The Iraqi Expeditionary Force, 25,000 strong, posed a threat in the north around Mafraq and Zerqa. The Iraqis could, and did, make the RJAF base at Mafraq untenable. There was always the possibility that they might intervene on the side of the PLO. That they did not is attributed by Prince Muhammad to their Minister of

Defence, General Takriti, who visited the Iraqi troops just before the fighting began. He says Takriti was a sensible man who could see no advantage in destabilising Jordan. This did not make him popular with his colleagues in Baghdad, who forced him into exile. He was assassinated in Kuweit in 1971.

Syrian neutrality could not be relied on. Nureddin Atassi, the President, strongly supported the PLO. Two Syrian politicians, Salah Jedid and Yusuf Zuayen, were violently anti-Jordanian, constantly urging intervention on the side of the PLO. But General Hafez Assad, the Alawite air force commander, was more cautious, convinced that Syrian intervention would bring both the United States and Israel into the conflict. He advised neutrality but Jordan could not afford to ignore the threat to its northern flank.

The other question-mark was the army's loyalty. It counted many Palestinians in its ranks, some of them of senior rank. When it came to the point some 5000 officers and soldiers went over to the other side, or took off their uniforms and stayed quietly at home.[3] This was a far smaller number than the PLO had calculated. One senior officer did resign; he was Brigadier Bajahat Mohasein, commander of the 2nd Division, but he came from Tafila, not from Palestine.

The army was to enter Amman at 5 a.m. on Thursday, 17 September. When Habis Majali arrived at army headquarters on the previous night to study the proclamation to be broadcast in his name as Military Governor, he was annoyed that his new rank of field marshal had been omitted. Once this had been rectified the old soldier wrapped himself in his blanket and went to sleep on his office floor. He at least knew where his duty lay. Out at Hummar, which was in almost total darkness as a precaution against *fedayeen* shelling, the King was closeted with Prince Hassan and Zeid Rifai. The rest of the Royal Family were widely dispersed. Princess Muna was in London with her sons. Queen Zein moved from her town palace out to Hummar. Other members of the Royal Family were in Aqaba, or were already abroad in Europe and the United States.

Hussein knew that his decision to send in the army was certainly the most important one in his reign so far. The alternative could only be abdication since he could not share the power in Jordan with Arafat and the PLO. And yet he recoiled from the prospect of Arab fighting Arab and feared the consequences to his civilian subjects of battles in the streets of Amman. The very strong humanitarian streak in his character hated the thought of it, although he knew he had been left with no alternative. Throughout the daylight hours and far into the night of 16 September, the atmosphere in Amman was curiously tense as army and *fedayeen* prepared for the battle to come. One Amman resident has compared it with waiting for an earthquake. Another, out late that night in pursuance of his official duties, found the streets strangely quiet, and an equally strange absence of barricades, when he made his way home in the small hours.

The plan was for the 1st Infantry and 4th Mechanised Divisions, supported by the 60th Armoured Brigade, to move into the city from north and south. Their orders were to root out the *fedayeen* from the places they had occupied, and from the sprawling refugee camps dotted round the city. It was intended to be more of a police operation than a civil war, as it is sometimes (though erroneously) described. Neither description is in fact correct. It was not a civil war because a great many Palestinians took no part in it, nor did they even approve of the *fedayeen*. It was not a police operation because soldiers are not policemen at the best of times, and least of all when employing tanks and artillery in pursuance of their objectives. The fact that it was by the King's direct command that they were to use only 'minimum force' is neither here nor there. When soldiers start firing their weapons, someone is bound to get hurt. During that same day Arafat summoned his Central Committee to declare a general strike on 18 September. Its proclaimed aim was the overthrow of 'Hussein's fascist government'. Meanwhile the *fedayeen* prepared to resist.

One Amman resident recalls going to bed that night with the uneasy feeling that it could well be his last:

There were sporadic outbursts of firing, but that was nothing unusual. It had become a feature of life in Amman since the beginning of the year. But on this occasion it sounded more menacing, due perhaps to my imagination. I lay down in my shirt and trousers in case I had to get up in a hurry. Early next morning, around five o'clock, I woke to the sound of tank tracks in the street outside. I looked out of my window to see several tanks moving cautiously along the street from the direction of Salt. I thought the tank crews looked very grim and determined as they clattered past. I remember going straight to the kitchen and filling every receptable I could find with water. I had a premonition that it might turn out to be a long job. Just as well to be prepared, I thought.[4]

Having handed over to the army, Hussein could only wait. They told him it would all be over in forty-eight hours, which was far too optimistic. The tactics were simple. As the tanks advanced, supported by infantry, they would draw the *fedayeen* fire. They replied to it with devastating effect. The noise echoing between the stone-built houses was deafening. Dust thrown up by the tank tracks hung low in the sultry early-morning air, coating the tank crews as they searched for targets. All over the city people woken early from their beds fastened down the shutters; those with cellars hastened down to them. The streets were empty apart from those fleeing to relatives whom they thought lived in safer areas. At Marka airport the Air Force Regiment, reinforced by two infantry companies, manned the perimeter defences. The borders with Syria and Iraq had been closed; Jordan's only link with the outside world was by air. It was hoped that by nightfall on 19 September, the two armoured columns would meet close to the Roman amphitheatre in the centre of Amman.

As the news leaked out, there was an immediate outcry in the Arab countries. Libya's Muammar Gadaffi was the first to make his voice heard; he wanted assistance sent to the PLO immediately. Nasser, concerned but cautious, preferred to wait until the situation was clearer. He sent General Sadiq, his Chief of Staff, to Amman to arrange a ceasefire. Sadiq got nowhere in army headquarters, where the generals were determined to see the thing through. Meanwhile the *fedayeen* were fighting back fiercely, contesting every inch of the way. They had plenty of ammunition and their anti-tank rocket launchers imposed caution on the tanks. Zeid bin Shakir says they were surprised by the volume of the *fedayeen* fire. They shelled Hummar with a 122 mm gun, but without doing much damage. More and more troops were brought in, only to find that even more were required. Telephones and electricity had failed by 9 a.m. After fifteen hours of continuous firing the *fedayeen* were still full of fight by the end of the day.

The King was growing increasingly anxious as the fighting dragged on into 18 September. He was worried at the prospect of outside intervention. Syria was his main concern; but Iraq was not far behind. Progress seemed to be desperately slow. The large number of press correspondents who were cooped up in the Hotel Urdon got most of their news from PLO sources, which was to that extent contentious. All the news broadcast by the BBC was of the same kind.* The Iraqi brigade at Zerqa was reported to be moving towards Jerash and there were reports of fifty Syrian tanks concentrated at Deraa, close to the Jordan border. The British Ambassador, who had only managed to reach his Embassy in a Jordanian armoured car, was asked by the King about possible British intervention, although Hussein added that he hoped 'it would all be over by sunset'.

He was to be proved wrong, although there was a short lull on 19 September, when Hussein summoned British, French and American representatives with a request for medical aid. His concern at the delay in finishing the business mounted by the hour. He had no fear of the ultimate

---

* BBC reporting continued to be so biased that towards the end of the year the King was moved to protest to the British Ambassador. It was of course hotly denied by the BBC but Zeid Rifai, who by that time was Ambassador in London, had taped the offending broadcasts and was able to provide irrefutable evidence.

outcome provided there was no outside intervention, but the longer the fighting continued the more vulnerable he became. The need to avoid civilian casualties, as the King had commanded, added to the soldiers' difficulties. They could not just blast themselves from house to house as they could in a war. Nasser too was a problem. He supported Arafat and had no desire to see the PLO destroyed. All along he had advised Hussein and Arafat to be patient and was now shocked by the news reaching him.

There had been fighting at Zerqa, the military cantonment fifteen miles north-east of Amman. The *fedayeen* were well established in the refugee camp there. There were few active units in Zerqa and it had been necessary to form an *ad hoc* force of recruits, cadets and students attending the various schools of instruction. It was commanded by Brigadier Muhammad Idris of the School of Artillery. He did not find it easy to restrain the enthusiasm of his 'boy soldiers', who succeeded in clearing Zerqa by the evening of 19 September. The fighting flared up again the next morning when the two PLA battalions attached to the Iraqi brigade at Khaw came to the *fedayeen*'s rescue. Fighting continued sporadically for several more days with neither side gaining the upper hand. One of the Jordanian officers killed in Zerqa was Brigadier Qasim Ma'aita's son.

Hussein's fear of Syrian intervention was realised at 11.30 p.m. on 19 September when the Jordanian troops defending the frontier town of Ramtha were attacked in the rear. The press in Damascus and Baghdad had been screaming for intervention and on 18 September the two countries had held talks. The upshot was an agreement that the Iraqi force deployed around Mafraq would move eastwards into the desert after dark on 19 September, firing red and green flares to mark their progress. This would leave the way open for the Syrians to attack the Jordanians covering Irbid. The Iraqi intention to withdraw eastwards had of course been communicated to the Jordanian High Command, but the Iraqis did not disclose the fact that they had also informed the Syrians. At 5 a.m. on 20 September the Syrian 5th Division, containing two tank brigades equipped with Soviet T-54s and T-55s, together with a PLA brigade and a brigade of Syrian commandos, crossed the border into Jordan.

The Jordanians, with more than a third of their army tied down in Amman, and with another third defending the Jordan Valley, had little to spare in order to deal with such a massive attack. There was only the 2nd Infantry Division, which had already been involved in heavy fighting with *fedayeen* around Irbid. Its commander had resigned and his temporary successor, Atallah Ghasib, had been wounded by a mortar bomb; he was literally 'walking wounded'. Two tank regiments of 40th Armoured Brigade, and an infantry brigade, were hurriedly moved from the Jordan Valley, where they had been facing the Israelis. They were just in time to occupy the high ground overlooking the Ramtha–Irbid and Ramtha–Amman highways before the Syrian tanks appeared. 'I didn't give much for our chances,' one of the Jordanian tank commanders was later to confess.[5]

However, the Jordanians were helped by the inept handling of the superior Syrian force. The Syrians' reconnaissance was so bad that their advance towards Irbid was stopped abruptly by the Wadi Shallala, a natural tank trap which a brief study of the map would have disclosed, as would the fact that the entire route from Ramtha to Mafraq was dominated by a ridge behind which the Jordanian tanks were hull-down with excellent observation and fields of fire. This was a considerable Jordanian advantage, because their Centurion tanks with their 105 mm guns outranged the Syrian tanks by as much as 800 yards. They knocked the turrets off the Syrian tanks and the crews panicked. Nevertheless, there were many more Syrian tanks than Jordanian.

As darkness fell on 20 September the situation was critical. Only the exhausted Jordanian tank crews, and the equally exhausted infantry of the Khalid bin Walid Brigade, stood between the Syrians and a free run down the highway to Zerqa and Amman. The army was still bogged down in Amman, and the *fedayeen* were full of fight in Jerash and Irbid. The situation in Zerqa changed from hour to hour. Iraqi intentions remained shrouded in mystery. The Israelis were reported to be concentrating troops in Galilee, presumably to counter any Syrian move into the Jordan Valley. Jordan's situation looked very black indeed.

On 21 September the Syrians began to move forward and there was very heavy fighting throughout the day. By an unusual quirk of fate, the Centurion tanks that did such sterling work for Jordan had been lent by Iraq to make up for Jordan's tank losses during the June 1967 war. For six hours there was a tank battle in the open country south of Ramtha, but numbers eventually began to prevail. Also the Jordanians were short of artillery, with guns still to arrive on redeployment from the Jordan Valley. At 5 p.m. four RJAF Hunters on reconnaissance over the battlefield were fired on by the Iraqis when returning to base at Mafraq. This led Hussein to order the removal of all aircraft from Mafraq to H-5, seventy-five miles to the east.

Hussein was seriously worried throughout the day. He had already told the ambassadors of Britain, France and the Soviet Union and the American Chargé d'Affaires on 20 September that Jordan faced the gravest threat in its history, and that he would be interested to know what they intended to do about it. The Americans required no reminder of the gravity of the situation. They ordered a full-scale alert, moved the Sixth Fleet to the eastern Mediterranean, and placed some 20,000 troops at combat readiness. The Russians followed suit by reinforcing their fleet in the Mediterranean, at the same time leaning heavily on their Syrian ally.

The joker in the Syrian pack was the air force. So far on the orders of its commander, General Hafez Assad, it had not intervened in the battle. He believed that to do so would inevitably bring the Israelis into the battle, and possibly the Americans as well. This would not do the Syrians the slightest good. This strange action on the part of one of Syria's most senior generals was not of course known at the time, nor could the Jordanians possibly have reckoned with it, but it played a significant part in saving the day for them. Nevertheless by 6 p.m. the Syrians had taken the vital Mafraq–Irbid crossroads, and their further advance was only just held by a Jordanian counterattack supported by two Hunters. 'It is doubtful if we can hold,' said Hussein to one of his visitors.

On the following day, however, there was a remarkable change in the situation. After fierce fighting had begun soon after dawn, Jordanian tanks and artillery began to take their toll of the Syrian armour. Soon the RJAF joined in from H-5, flying sortie after sortie and wreaking havoc with their machine-gunning and rockets. Tank after tank, APC after APC, and truck after truck went up in flames. By nightfall the Syrians were more concerned to recover their tanks than to try to push any farther forward. They had in fact shot their bolt. That night, while Atallah Ghasib and his commanders were planning to launch a counterattack at dawn on 23 September, the Syrians crept home to lick their wounds. The Iraqis, whose part in this strange affair has still to be fully explained, lent them transporters for their tanks, but they left behind nevertheless sixty-two disabled tanks and sixty APCs. Hussein was later, as a goodwill gesture, to allow the Syrians to recover the tanks they had left littering the battlefield. Syrian casualties amounted to 600 killed and wounded, many of them (according to the Syrians) being Palestinians.

The new American Ambassador, Dean Brown, did not arrive until after the fighting had broken out. He had to be taken in an armoured car to the Palace in order to present his credentials. He acted as the intermediary for the many signals sent to President Nixon by the King. These had to be transmitted via the British Embassy since the American communications had ceased to function.

The evacuation of the women and children of foreign nationals began on 23 September; the first plane out was provided for women and children of all nationalities. The Americans had of course already left. There was fighting around the British Embassy that evening, and on the following day at the Terra Sancta convent. The *fedayeen* were still very much in evidence. The situation was equally confused in Irbid, where the army had yet to impose control after routing the Syrians. Hussein was to say later that the most difficult time was between 20 and 24 September. Libya had cut off financial support and had severed diplomatic relations. Kuwait soon followed. The cautious Saudis stayed on the sidelines but would probably follow suit if the fighting dragged on. Although the Amman suburbs had been largely 'liberated', the *fedayeen* were still strongly entrenched in the centre of the city. The King had forbidden an all-out assault for fear of civilian casualties.

Ceasefire messages were broadcast on 25 September, but firing began again next day. This was the day after the sixteen hijack hostages had been rescued. The President of Sudan, General Numeiry, had been trying to arrange a ceasefire on behalf of the other Arab leaders. One of his problems was locating Arafat, who took great care not to remain in any one place for any length of time. On 24 September Numeiry succeeded in meeting with him on Jebel Webdeh; not without considerable personal risk, according to John Bulloch, who says Numeiry was fired on 'by both sides'.[6] The army had given him a safe conduct, although he was later to accuse them of firing at him. This was hardly surprising in the circumstances since it is difficult when fighting in built-up areas to distinguish between friend and foe. The firing was just as likely to have come from the *fedayeen* as from the army.

Numeiry had agreed the terms of a ceasefire with Hussein. The *fedayeen* were to move out of the cities, after which the army would do the same. *Fedayeen* activities were to be strictly restricted to areas that were contiguous with Israel. Only the PLO would be regarded as their legitimate representative. Finally, they were to abide strictly by the laws of Jordan. Since Arafat could not be contacted, the terms were agreed in his name by Salah Khalaf (Abu Iyad) his closest friend and a member of Fatah since 1963. He later claimed that he had agreed only because he thought Arafat had been killed. When he came to hear of the terms, Arafat promptly disowned the truce. The PLO have since claimed that Hussein's generals would not agree to it.

Numeiry refused to accept defeat. With the Syrians in retreat and with his army steadily tightening its grip on Amman, Hussein was disinclined to make any further concessions. But he was under great pressure from Nasser to put an end to the fighting. Nasser told him that his patience was wearing out. He was of course a very tired and sick man, worried lest Arafat should be replaced by a firebrand like Habash. Nasser was also concerned about the casualties, which had been wildly exaggerated by the media, who were in no position to judge. The true figure will probably never be established but it would seem that between 1500 and 2000 dead is the most likely figure. The official Red Cross figure was 1600, which included the army's casualties.

Fortunately Arafat saw the futility of continuing the struggle; he therefore invited Numeiry to see him. Numeiry did so, although not without great difficulty, and he managed after long and patient talks to persuade Arafat to accept Hussein's ceasefire terms. Early in the morning of 25

September Arafat's message was broadcast to the *fedayeen* by Damascus Radio:

> Our great people, our brave revolutionaries, to avoid more innocent bloodshed, and so that the citizens may care for their wounded and get the necessities of life, I, in my capacity as supreme commander of the Palestine revolutionary forces, and in response to the appeal by the mission of Arab heads of state, agree to a ceasefire and ask my brothers to observe it provided the other side does the same.

There was not in fact an immediate ceasefire. Firing continued in parts of the city, notably in downtown Amman, where something like a 'no-go' area persisted near the Philadelphia Hotel. But people began to come out again into the streets, to assess the damage and to replenish their larders. There was no electricity, no telephones and very little water. Food was in short supply. There were dead to be buried and wounded to be attended to. For nearly a week Amman had been a city under siege and no one was entirely certain that it would not happen again. In the army there was a feeling that the job had been left unfinished.

Meanwhile Arafat was whisked off to Cairo where he was received like a head of state. According to one report he was smuggled out of Jordan by Shaykh Sa'ad of Kuweit, wearing Shaykh Sa'ad's robes, and carried to the airport in a Jordanian APC.[7] He had several hours in private with Nasser, who was horrified by his tale and concluded that Hussein must have lost control over his army. Nasser called Hussein the next morning and spoke of 'a horrifying massacre'. He is alleged to have threatened Hussein with the intervention of the Egyptian army if the killing did not stop.

This was not the first time Hussein had been rebuked by Nasser. He had been unable to attend a summit meeting in Cairo and had sent Brigadier Daud in his place. The Brigadier, sick and dejected by the course of events, had seized the opportunity to resign both his office as Prime Minister and his commission in the Jordanian army. Nevertheless, Nasser had at one stage congratulated Hussein on possessing 'the patience of Ayub [Job]' despite *fedayeen* provocation. He had now changed his tune. Nasser was worried lest the situation should escalate and bring Israel into the argument. This could lead to hostilities between Egypt and Israel, something that Nasser was determined to prevent. He felt Hussein had landed him in a mess by his attack on the *fedayeen*. After hearing Arafat's side of the story, he was more than ever convinced that Hussein was to blame. It must therefore have been with little expectation that Hussein would accept that Nasser invited him to attend an Arab heads-of-state meeting in Cairo on 27 September.

CHAPTER FOURTEEN

Expelling the PLO

'It had to be done but I wish they had not compelled us to drive them out.'[1]

When Hussein responded to Nasser's invitation by piloting his personal Caravelle to Cairo on 27 September 1970, he knew he was a Daniel flying into the lions' den. Several of his advisers were opposed to his visit. Arafat had had forty-eight hours' start on the King and had made full use of his time. His account of the so-called 'civil war' lost nothing in the telling, the PLO being depicted as wretched victims of Jordan's 'brutal and licentious soldiery'. Nasser readily accepted Arafat's story, although it has to be said that Nasser was at the time already a very sick man, and to that extent not as alert as he might otherwise have been. Gadaffi, who had been screaming for Hussein's blood ever since the fighting had started, was another who accepted Arafat's account in its entirety. Hussein knew of course that this would be so; it was therefore a very courageous act on his part to have gone to Cairo.

He had been at his country house at Hummar during most of the fighting. The defences were manned by the Special Forces, but at least one attempt had been made by the *fedayeen* to shell the residence. It had also been discovered that the King's personal driver had PLO sympathies, and that one of the royal cooks had tried to poison him; the cook was also caught in possession of a grenade. After the fighting was over the army captured detailed maps of Hummar which made plain that the King was by no means as secure there as had been thought.

Nasser was at Almaza airport to greet Hussein. There was no ceremony and Nasser's greeting was cool. He had been appalled by Arafat's graphic but exaggerated account of the fighting. He drove with Hussein to the Hilton Hotel, where Arafat had been treated like a conquering hero when he arrived there two days earlier. Hussein was in air force uniform, a pistol slung at his hip. He looked very strained, his manner abrupt. This was most unlike him, although understandable in the circumstances.

At 1.30 p.m. the Arab leaders attending the meeting filed into the hotel's main conference room where Arafat had already addressed them. He was the only man besides Hussein who was ostentatiously armed. He led the way into the room, to be followed by King Feisal of Saudi Arabia, Gadaffi of Libya, Shaykh as-Sabah of Kuweit, President Numeiry of Sudan, Bahi Ladgham of Tunisia, Es Shamy of Yemen, Franjieh of Lebanon, and Nasser himself. They seated themselves at a horseshoe-shaped table, with Nasser in the centre. Hussein and Arafat sat at the wings.

The discussion lasted for six˙hours, with a break in the middle for refreshments. Nasser adopted the role of peacemaker. He looked desperately tired. The others left most of the talking to him. Nasser began by expressing his sympathy for the Palestinians who had been, he said, 'massacred by Hussein's bedouin soldiers, who had run amuck'. At the same time he felt sorry for Hussein who had been humiliated in the eyes of the world by the misdeeds of the PFLP. He pointed out that it was only after the hijackings, and the negotiations carried out by the PLO with Britain, Israel, Switzerland and West Germany, in flagrant disregard of Jordanian sovereignty, that the King had lost his patience. But this was no excuse for the behaviour of his soldiers, who had caused quite unnecessary damage and suffering among the civilian population.

Numeiry was strongly anti-Hussein. He accused the Jordanians of carrying out 'a war of extermination against the Palestinian people'. Gadaffi was even more extreme, threatening to send his army to Jordan to support the PLO; how it was to get there was never explained. Hussein did not take these attacks lying down. He launched a bitter attack on the 'Syrian butchers', accusing them of 'cowardly aggression'. The meeting went on and on, the two principal protagonists defending their actions in the face of accusation and counter-accusation. Eventually some kind of agreement was reached. There was no formal censure of Hussein. There was, however, a great deal of rhetoric, without much common sense. None of the Arab leaders present was willing to relieve Hussein of the crushing burden of the refugees. Nor were they prepared to sink their differences in order to bring real pressure to bear on Israel.

The agreement reached was not the one Hussein had told Numeiry in Amman that Jordan was willing to accept. Some restrictions were placed on *fedayeen* movements, but the Jordanian army was similarly circumscribed. The *fedayeen* were not required to respect Jordanian sovereignty, nor were they reminded that they existed to fight the Israelis rather than the Jordanians. The agreement concluded with the high-sounding words: 'Full support of the Palestinian revolution is ensured to enable it to carry out its sacred duty, the liberation of its land.' As a final gesture of amity, King Feisal persuaded Hussein and Arafat to shake hands. It was futile, except as a gesture.

It might well have been asked what had actually been achieved. Although Nasser had been forced to admit that Hussein had undoubtedly been provoked, particularly by the PFLP, it was Hussein who had been put in the dock and not Arafat. Apart from the fact that his army was bound to win in the end, however desperately the *fedayeen* might fight against it, Arafat certainly seemed to have won the political battle. The trouble was that he exerted virtually no control over Habash and Hawatmeh. Although the fighting in Amman, and outside in the countryside, petered out early in October, it could in no way be claimed that the *fedayeen* problem had been satisfactorily resolved.

It has been said that Hussein owed it to Nasser that he got away comparatively lightly at the Cairo meeting. It had begun with scowls and had ended with smiles. It had been clear that Nasser's main concern was to pour oil on troubled waters. He had all along urged Hussein to try to bring about the return of the West Bank by diplomatic means; and in this context the conduct of the *fedayeen* in Jordan had been a great embarrassment to him. On the other hand he had no desire to see Arafat replaced in the PLO by one of the wilder spirits, who might by his actions involve Egypt in war with Israel, something Nasser had every intention of avoiding until he was ready for it. His main aim was therefore to bring about a reconciliation between Hussein and Arafat, ignoring the fact that conditions in Jordan, due almost entirely to the PLO, had made this virtually impossible.

In his heyday Nasser might have found a way through the maze, but in September 1970 he was a sick and prematurely aged man. He had worn himself out, first as a conspirator and thereafter by the appallingly difficult task of governing Egypt. His inclination to interfere in the affairs of the other Arab states had been equally wearing. Soon after returning from the airport on 28 September, where he had gone to bid farewell to the Shaykh of Kuweit, Nasser had a heart attack from which he died.

He was buried on 1 October amid scenes of hysterical lamentation. The other Arab leaders had barely had time to reach home before they were on their way back to Cairo again. The grief was spontaneous and genuine throughout the Arab world. For most Arabs Nasser was the embodiment of Arab nationalism. As the first true Egyptian to rule over the Nile Delta for nearly 2000 years, Nasser had done great things for Egypt. He had restored his people's pride in themselves after centuries of foreign domination. His influence had reached out far beyond the limits of Egypt to the remotest Arab hamlet, and there was a true sense of loss at his death. Although Hussein's relations with him had seldom run smoothly, the King would have been the first to admit his regrets. The pity of it was that Nasser never made use of his great influence to bring about the Arab unity to which Hussein had dedicated his life.

Hussein never really trusted Nasser. It was after all owing to Nasser that Hussein had lost half his kingdom. Nor was Hussein under any illusion regarding Nasser's views on monarchies. He had happened to be with Nasser on one occasion when news was received of the successful coup against King Idris of Libya. Recalling Nasser's delight at the overthrow of yet another Arab king, Hussein commented, 'That scene will be for ever engraved on my memory.'[2] He believed Nasser was a great Egyptian patriot whose principal motivation was to make Egypt great. The pursuit of Arab unity took second place to this.

At the Cairo meeting on 27 September it had been decided to set up a Truce Supervisory Commission in Amman. It was to be headed by Bahi Ladgham, the Prime Minister of Tunisia. In order to help with the restoration of normal conditions, Hussein dismissed the military government and appointed Ahmed Toukan as Prime Minister. Toukan was a professional politician, but he was in his seventies and was held in low regard by the PLO. He got on well however with the Bahi Ladgham, which was a point in his favour. Ostensibly his Cabinet was civilian, but it nevertheless contained six officers. There followed a short lull, although the *fedayeen* remained very much in evidence. Indeed the army complained that they had not been allowed to finish them off once and for all.

This is the time to dispose of the canard that Hussein had allowed his bedouin soldiers to 'run amuck'; the expression is Nasser's, largely as a result of the highly emotional information he had been given by Arafat and Numeiry. The troops were in fact kept on a very tight rein, as Hussein had ordered. His great fear was civilian casualties as a result of military action. Considering the fact that they felt their names had been blackened – a matter of great shame for the bedouins in particular – the troops did behave with great restraint. There were undoubtedly occasions when they did not, as must always be the case when men are fighting for their lives; but all things considered, these occasions were remarkably few.

Although naturally showing signs of strain, the King was much more cheerful and relaxed after his visit to Cairo. It had been the worst ordeal in his life so far, but he and most of his advisers believed they had got the measure of the *fedayeen*. Wasfi Tell was one who did not. He, and those who thought like him, were suspicious of the Truce Supervisory Commission, which seemed to be more pro-PLO than otherwise. Wasfi felt that although the *fedayeen* had been given a bloody nose, they were far from finished with. If the King's writ was to run throughout his realm, they would have to be rooted out. He did not believe in half-measures; and many of the generals agreed with him.

The King's uncle was probably one of them. His resignation as army commander had not been welcomed by the army. Although he was criticised from time to time, Sharif Nasser's loyalty was never in doubt. In the most critical moments in Hussein's reign, he was invariably to be found at the King's side. He was particularly popular with the bedouin troops, partly on account of his descent from the Prophet Muhammad, and partly as a result of the imaginative irrigation schemes he had initiated in the desert. These had permitted many of the tribesmen to settle on the land after centuries of nomadism.

It may seem difficult in retrospect to understand the irresponsible behaviour of the Palestinian leadership after the patched-up truce that followed after the meeting in Cairo. It can easily be explained, however. The factiousness that would appear to be inherent in the Palestinian character was faithfully mirrored in the Palestinian leadership. The PFLP and PDF simply ignored Arafat's attempts to reach a *modus vivendi* with the King; meanwhile their followers, arrogant to the last, continued to alienate the long-suffering Jordanians by their insufferable behaviour. And not only the Jordanians, it should be said; many of the Palestinians among them were sick and tired of those *fedayeen* who did nothing but bring the good name of Palestine into disrepute.

By October Hussein was sufficiently convinced that the time had come for the final act. He therefore replaced Ahmed Toukan by Wasfi Tell as Prime Minister. Everyone knew where Wasfi stood. Zeid bin Shakir was instructed to draw up a plan that would squeeze the *fedayeen* into submission to the country's laws. Bahi Ladgham and his colleagues continued to do their best for reconciliation but were quietly ignored by both sides. Yet Arafat and the King went on trying. In October they signed an agreement which Habash promptly repudiated. The same thing happened in January 1971. Meanwhile the two-stage plan devised by Zeid bin Shakir was put into operation.

The first stage, designed to last from November 1970 to April 1971, was intended to drive the *fedayeen* out of Amman, Irbid, Jerash and Ajlun. The second stage, lasting from May to July 1971, was to round up the *fedayeen* who had attempted to turn the rugged country between Jerash and Ajlun into a fortress. The pressure applied was unceasing and irresistible, particularly now that the *fedayeen* were beginning to run out of ammunition. They were even accused of collaborating with the Israelis in the sabotage of the Zerqa oil refinery, a charge which does seem rather far-fetched. The ineffable Gadaffi once again broadcast an appeal to Hussein's soldiers to overthrow him; he was treated with contempt. Another Arab summit was convened but Hussein refused to attend it. The PLO went on squabbling among themselves, forcing Arafat to admit later, 'During the revolt our Palestinian leadership was divided and rival groups fought each other.'[3]

An American airlift of arms and ammunition, which were landed at Dawson's Field, replenished Hussein's armoury and was welcome evidence of US support. In fact Hussein's courage in tackling the *fedayeen* had won him many allies in Washington, not least President Nixon and Henry Kissinger. The British also helped replenish the Centurion ammunition shot off against the Syrians. Attacks on police posts in the Irbid governorate could not be tolerated, and on 26 March 1971 the army struck back with maximum force. The *fedayeen* were driven out, and after months of anarchy the King's writ ran once again in Jordan's second-largest city.

On 6 April 1971 the King ordered the *fedayeen* to clear out of Amman. 'The land where the weapons should be wielded and resistance should be planted is the Occupied Territories,' he told them, 'so that every citizen here may live in peace and security.' They were taken in buses out of the city, many of them making their way to Jerash and Ajlun, where the *fedayeen* were still in strength. The King gave them two days to go and when the time came they went quietly. The army was in such overwhelming strength that they had little option. By then Bahi Ladgham had abandoned his task in despair and had gone home.

Some 5000 *fedayeen* were in the Ajlun area, dispersed in the small villages in that rough country. They were determined not to give in. Their vision might be limited but their courage could not be denied, since their chances were hopeless. But, as before, they soon succeeded in alienating the Jordanians among whom they were living. On 1 June 1971 they murdered a farmer in Jerash, leading Hussein on the following day to order Wasfi Tell 'to take bold and tough action against the guerrillas'.

What followed was a hard-fought battle among the rocks, dwarf oaks and underbrush of some of the most rugged country in northern Jordan. The *fedayeen* were well dug in, some of their positions being as high as 3500 feet above the Wadi Zerqa. The terrain was honeycombed with ravines, water courses and caves. These natural defences had been improved by the construction of redoubts, but the defenders were outnumbered, outgunned and outfought. There was much for the army, particularly the bedouin units, to avenge. So unrelenting was the army's pressure that some *fedayeen* preferred to wade the Jordan in darkness and surrender to the Israelis. By 18 July 1971 it was finished; and Jordan had been rid of a scourge which had come close to destroying the nation.

Much of the blame for the situation having arisen in the first place must be attached to the other Arab states, who did nothing to restrain the Palestine Resistance Movement. Instead they had supported it in its intransigence and folly by providing it with arms and money, and by encouraging it by wild rhetoric. Gadaffi, the wildest of them all, called a conference in Tripoli attended by Egypt, Syria and Yemen – and Arafat by special permission. It passed a series of resolutions condemning Hussein and requiring him to do penance. He took no notice. Syria and Iraq closed

their borders, as much to bar the way to the fleeing *fedayeen* as for any harm
they thought it might do to Hussein. The army, with its morale now sky
high, interpreted the diplomatic term 'close pursuit' as freely as it chose.
Shots were exchanged across the Jordan–Syria border, increasing the
tension between the two countries. There was a very real risk of war. The
Syrians once again closed their airspace to Jordanian aircraft, and in August
1971 war fever was rampant in Damascus and Amman. This was cooled
by the fortuitous visit of Nasser's successor President Sadat to Syria's
President Assad. It was no part of Sadat's long-term plan for the settlement
of Egypt's outstanding differences with Israel that Syria and Jordan should
fight each other.

'I think we lost Jordan because Arafat refused to discipline the leftists,'
said Khalid Hassan of the PLO after it was all over.[4] Another Palestinian
who supports the PLO and who admires Arafat has said much the same:

> We dug our own graves in Jordan. We were welcomed as heroes after
> Karameh and then driven out like thieves in the night three years later. It
> did not seem to occur to us that although we shared a common language,
> culture and religion with the Jordanians, they were in fact in some ways
> different from us. Some of them had been living in Jordan for centuries
> and resented our appropriation of their country – or so it must have
> seemed to them. The same thing was to happen in Lebanon. Our leaders
> failed to realise this. I suppose they were too busy squabbling and
> intriguing among themselves. We were split up into so many groups that
> poor Abu Amar [Arafat] was incapable of insisting on a common policy
> and imposing discipline. He and the other leaders were like twenty cooks
> quarrelling over what to put in the sauce. We needed a Head Chef to bang
> our heads together. Alas, Abu Amar was no Head Chef. He was a nice
> man, and a brave one, but he possessed no real authority. He was
> hopeless when it came to dealing with firebrands like George Habash and
> Hawatmeh. They thought they knew best and ended by doing the
> Palestinian cause untold harm in the eyes of the rest of the world. We
> should have followed the example of the Algerians. It was only after they
> had cleared out the wild men and imposed a very tough discipline that the
> FLN really began to gain ground.[5]

CHAPTER FIFTEEN

An Uneven Road

'We viewed the PLO as a potentially disruptive force . . . it presented itself to us largely as a terrorist group.' Henry Kissinger[1]

The most urgent requirement after the departure of the *fedayeen* from Amman was to get the main services operating again and the soldiers off the streets and back to barracks. Both were accomplished remarkably swiftly. The British lent Post Office and Electricity Board engineers to restore the telephone system and the electricity supply; this latter repair restored the water supply. The army helped with the distribution of food. Energetic action was taken to repair, and where necessary rebuild, damaged houses. Hussein had asked for medical assistance as soon as the fighting began, the first medical team to arrive, unannounced as it happened, coming from Abu Dhabi under Dr Horniblow; it saved many lives. Other medical assistance had followed later and worked hard to clear the hospitals of those wounded in the fighting. In Amman the situation soon returned to normal.

However, it took some time longer to rehabilitate the police, who had not shown to advantage in the struggle with the *fedayeen*. They had virtually collapsed, and their morale was low. Britain lent Sir Richard Catling, an experienced police officer, to advise on the reorganisation of the police force. Soon the police were back on the streets, reorganised and re-equipped. They had suffered for years from the chopping and changing of their senior officers; Catling strongly recommended that the new Chief of Police should hold office for at least five years. He was Colonel Anwar Muhammad, who had previously commanded the Royal Bodyguard.

The PLO were in disarray. Unwelcome in Syria, where they were kept under very strict control, the hard-core commandos mostly made their way to Lebanon, where the government of that unhappy country lacked both the will and the authority to keep them in order. Soon the Palestinians in exile were alienating the Lebanese, as previously they had alienated the Jordanians. Their leadership was divided and dejected, united only in placing the blame for their misfortunes on Hussein and his government. When Arafat was later to be asked whether he would act in any different way were the clock to be turned back to 1968, he surprisingly replied, 'No, I wouldn't deal with the situation in any different way.'[2]

The divergent views among the leadership were reflected throughout the Palestinian Resistance Movement. Only the commandos were united in their aim. This was the restoration of Palestine as a secular state. They were interested neither in partition, nor in Resolution 242, nor in the restoration of Hashemite rule. Splinter groups like the PFLP and PDF supported this line, although extremists like Habash and Hawatmeh saw the struggle in terms of world revolution. Arafat, who controlled the PLO's purse-strings, and who was therefore the source of patronage within the Movement, held much more moderate views than either Habash or Hawatmeh. He and Hussein could talk to each other, although there was not much love lost between them. Arafat has said he can trust Hussein, although not all his advisers.[3] But the differences between the two men lay in their approach to the common problem. Arafat spoke for the Palestinians of the dispersal, who had fled their homes and were now stateless refugees. Hussein spoke for those now living in Jordan as Jordanian citizens, and for those (he thought) on the West Bank who were still *de jure* Jordanian citizens. The King knew, of course, of the strong support for the PLO on the West Bank, but he still had hopes of a return to Hashemite rule. It was after all the Mayor of Nablus, Hatem abou Gazaleh, who had said: 'anything Arab is better than Israel.'

The PLO leadership was unable to decide what to do next. Arafat had at least a policy – to keep the dream alive. He was an excellent public-relations man who enjoyed the travel involved, commuting round the Arab world and being received in some Arab countries with all the formalities of a head of state. He knew that morale had been severely shaken by the events in Jordan and he wanted to avoid a repetition of them. This would certainly be the case if the *fedayeen* started to launch raids into Israel from southern Lebanon, as was being advocated in certain PLO circles. Arafat knew that Israel would respond by attacks on targets in Lebanon, which would involve the Lebanese. He wanted to avoid this, if at all possible. At the same time he was well aware that the feeling uppermost in the minds of most of the commandos was resentment against their leaders, and a burning desire for revenge against their enemy. Salah Khalaf (Abu Iyad), who had been prominent in Fatah counsels since 1963, stressed this often and forcefully. Some means had to be found to satisfy this demand for action if the young men, who made up the hard core of the Movement, were not to drift away or take matters into their own hands. Thus the concept of the 'terror' weapon came to be debated by the PLO High Command.

The trouble with terrorism is that it hardens, rather than softens, attitudes on both sides of the divide, particularly when it is employed indiscriminately. It may make 'martyrs' on one side, but is just as likely to make 'heroes' on the other. Moreover, terrorism is unlikely to prevail against a tough government unless it is supported by an internal uprising of the kind organised by the FLN against the French in Algeria. It is easy to see in retrospect that the PLO was unwise in adopting terror as a policy, since it has not only resulted in *all* Palestinians being labelled as terrorists in the minds of many people, but has also tied a label round the PLO's neck which it will find difficult to untie, particularly where Israel and the USA are concerned.

At the beginning the possibility of employing terror, against selected targets as well as quite indiscriminately, as a means of bringing the plight of the Palestinians to the world's attention, was no more than a state of mind. There was neither the money nor the weapons with which to carry out a campaign. Nor was there the intelligence necessary for the selection of victims and the planning of attacks. Moreover, the young men and women recruited to carry out these near-suicidal missions needed some kind of inspiration, someone to avenge, a talisman. They found one in Abou Ali Iyyad, the *fedayeen* leader who had stayed to fight alongside his comrades when the rest of the leadership had fled Jordan. A huge man, with a black patch over one eye, he had fallen to a hail of bullets in the last desperate stand. The movement created to avenge him came to be known as Black September; it was an offshoot of Fatah.

Salah Khalaf was Black September's godfather. Without him it could not have received the leadership's backing. He arranged for the finance and obtained the weapons. He also secured the co-operation of Fatah's intelligence organisation, which could suggest targets and provide the information concerning them. If in the end Salah Khalaf was to discover that he had released a jinn from the bottle that quickly passed beyond his control, its activities more counter-productive than otherwise, this was certainly not the feeling in Black September's early days. He had found a means whereby the commandos could find revenge for their injuries, boost their morale and publicise their cause. Arafat and some of his colleagues had their doubts, but they did not interfere.

Hussein was the most obvious target, but by the end of 1971 his personal security was extremely efficient. After him, Wasfi Tell was enemy number two. He was combining the office of Prime Minister with that of Minister of Defence and in the latter capacity was attending a meeting of the Arab League's Joint Defence Council in Cairo. On 28 November 1971, as he was entering the Sheraton Hotel for a meeting, he was gunned down by Black September. Something seems to have gone seriously wrong with the Egyptian authorities' security arrangements. It is even more difficult to explain why it was that the four young assassins, who were quickly rounded up, were never brought to trial; but four months later, when the hue and cry had died down, they were put on a plane and shipped off to Damascus. Hussein never really forgave Anwar Sadat for this inexplicable leniency, the more so since he was 'desolated' by Wasfi's death, according to Wasfi's brother, Mrwede, who was Hussein's Private Secretary at the time.

Wasfi had been very close to Hussein and his death caused the King real grief. He was honoured by burial in the Royal Hashemite Cemetery in the presence of everyone of consequence in the country. However, his body was later disinterred and buried on his farm. During the disastrous 1967 war, Wasfi and a few friends had been sitting near that very spot discussing the situation. Someone had asked what could be done. 'Stay here and fight to the death,' said Wasfi, 'and after I'm killed I hope they will bury me here!' His family consequently requested Hussein's permission to comply with Wasfi's wishes, and naturally it was granted.

Hussein appointed Ahmed el-Lozi Prime Minister in Wasfi's place, but Wasfi was in a sense irreplaceable. He had had great influence with the King, and had never been afraid to speak his mind when he thought Hussein was on the wrong track. He was also known to be incorruptible, by no means a universal virtue among politicians. Above all, he possessed the confidence of the army.

Wasfi Tell's assassination certainly produced the publicity desired by Black September. Their next target was to be Zeid Rifai, who had been sent to London as ambassador after virtually continuous service at the King's side. He had a narrow escape. His limousine was fired on while travelling through Kensington. The chauffeur stalled the engine. By then Zeid Rifai, crouching in the back, had been fired on several times. He was a sitting duck but escaped with a wound in the hand. The assassin apparently lost his nerve and took to his heels. Political assassinations were not then as common in Western capital cities as they have since become, and the attack on Zeid Rifai became something of a sensation. He was recalled to Jordan not long afterwards and made Prime Minister.

Black September had been built up on the cell system. No one, apart from a very few, could list its membership, least of all those who carried the guns and bombs. After its failure to assassinate Zeid Rifai, Black September chose targets other than Jordanian. Seizing the Saudi Embassy in Khartoum, they murdered two Americans and a Belgian diplomat. There was a bungled attempt in Bangkok, followed by the hijacking of a Japanese jumbo jet and a massacre at Rome airport. Salah Khalaf had unleashed a monster which soon passed from his control to extremists like Wadi Haddad. The final enormity was the Munich Olympic massacre, which aroused tremendous hostility to the Palestinian cause. As Arafat had feared at the outset, the Israeli reaction was predictable. They launched a series of massive air strikes on Lebanon, killing far more Lebanese than Palestinians.

It needs to be said, however, that despite the fear and loathing created by

the activities of Black September and similar groups, the aim that led to
their setting up has been to a great extent achieved. They have forced
the world to recognise that there *is* a Palestinian problem, however much
the Israelis would prefer the world to forget it. By their ruthless disregard
for the lives of innocent civilians, they have demonstrated that the conditions under which they have been compelled to live for forty years are
precisely those that breed desperation and contempt for the ordinary norms
that govern civilised life. They may represent only a small proportion of the
Palestinians in exile, but they do in their way make plain the burning desire
of every refugee to return to the home and the land from which he or she has
been driven.

Hussein's principal concern in the aftermath of the PLO's expulsion was
the state of his Treasury. It was virtually empty. The subsidies from Kuweit
and Libya were no longer forthcoming, while that from Saudi Arabia
seemed uncertain. Fortunately the Saudis did not withdraw aid, and the
Americans came forward with a generous contribution. Britain too
increased its already modest grant, and by what seemed like a miracle
Jordan was kept afloat financially. Since parliament had been prorogued,
more and more devolved on Hussein personally. The vast majority of
his subjects were content that this should be so, now that their days and
nights were no longer made hideous by indiscriminate bursts of machine-
gun fire.

The King never lost sight of his aim to liberate the West Bank, and did his
best to discover through third parties whether the Israelis were willing to
enter into realistic negotiations. This invariably foundered on the Israeli
reluctance to give up any territory. Since Hussein's willingness to reach
agreement was based on Resolution 242, there was an inevitable deadlock.
Such concessions as might be made by either side amounted to nothing in
the face of Israel's insistence on maintaining its military garrisons on the
West Bank and along the line of the River Jordan.

In March 1972 Hussein put forward certain proposals which he was
careful to emphasise could be implemented only in the event of an Israeli
withdrawal. He proposed that there should be a United Arab Kingdom
which would comprise a federation of the West and East Banks. Each would
have its own capital, governor-general and institutions, with its own courts,
and be generally autonomous. The King would be head of state and be
advised by a Federal Council of Ministers. Amman would be the federal
capital; Jerusalem capital of the West Bank. The armed forces would be
recruited equally from the East and West Banks. Hussein made it clear that
this could only be a blueprint for the future. It would need to be confirmed
or rejected by a referendum once conditions were right.

There was the inevitable outcry, the PLO claiming it was a sell-out. Mrs Golda Meir did not help by announcing that Israel had not been consulted. Hussein's honest attempt to find some way round the logjam had done him no good, but he was undaunted. He went on trying. He had acquired much more self-confidence as a result of his successful tussle with the PLO. He was slowly becoming transformed into a world statesman. He found his opinions were not only asked for but welcomed whenever he visited foreign capitals. If anything, his stature was enhanced when the Palestine National Congress, meeting in Cairo in January 1973, solemnly announced its intention to work for his overthrow. It rallied many to his side who had hitherto been lukewarm or indifferent, both in Jordan and abroad.

Among the King's many responsibilities was that of being head of the extended Hashemite family. He was the arbiter in all their disputes and their solace in times of distress. What is more he was head of the extended family which was Jordan. Everyone was a claimant for his favour or support; and in the age-old Arab tradition he had to make himself available to listen to suppliants of every kind and description. This constituted a heavy burden on a man who had at the same time to grapple with the problem of the West Bank, the PLO and all the other difficulties that seem inseparable from the Middle East. One Western ambassador, new to Amman, found it quite extraordinary that the King was able to deal with problems involving Jordan, the people and his own Hashemite family.

It came as a surprise to many people at the end of 1972 when the King divorced Princess Muna. She was well liked in Jordan and few had any inkling of marital problems between the two. In the event, everything was handled with the utmost discretion on both sides. Muna had never put herself forward as wife of the King and she had not been interested in politics. She was essentially an outdoor woman, fond of sport, riding horses and parties. Possibly she matured less quickly than the King. She has retained all her privileges and visits Jordan frequently from her home in the United States.

Some time before the divorce Hussein had met and fallen in love with Alia Toukan, daughter of a Jordanian diplomat, whom he married after his divorce from Muna. She came from a well-known Nablus family which had settled in Salt. She was a beautiful and very intelligent woman, who had been working for Air Alia. She was well educated and fitted in well in both Arab and Western society. She was of course much older than Muna had been when Muna was first married. She made the King happy, and as an Arab herself could confidently take on any minister or ambassador when it came to discussing political problems. She gave Hussein a son, Ali, and a daughter, Haya. A keen sense of humour was one of her principal characteristics.

Hussein's interest in technological advancement probably explains his interest in operating an amateur radio station, which has brought him friends all over the world. He has found it the ideal way to unwind. During the difficult days in 1970, when he was more or less cooped up at Hummar, he found it a great relief to call up his fellow enthusiasts. 'This is JY One – Hussein on the mike' was his call-sign. Maurice Margolis, another radio ham from London, often spoke with the King. He says Hussein spoke only of family matters and never tried to make propaganda. A couple in Pennsylvania, Charles and Mary Anne Crider, were told: 'Morale is high. I'm very well and in good shape.' They became friends of the King.

The struggle for survival had taken its inevitable toll. It brought on sinusitis and the severe headaches which accompany the complaint. Hussein had perceptibly aged, an effect that was enhanced when he took to wearing a beard for a time. He took plenty of exercise and kept himself in trim, but the never ceasing demands of his office left him little time for leisure. There was also the strain of the constant threat of assassination; the Middle East's reputation for violence provided little consolation in that respect. But the King was a fatalist, like his grandfather before him, and he was fortified in the belief that his life was in God's hands. He worried not on account of himself but rather on account of his family, and of the extended family which was Jordan.

In his biography of King Hussein, published in 1972, Peter Snow criticises the King for the personal style of his rule. He implies that it is undemocratic, unduly patriarchal and unlikely to be long acceptable to the well-educated young Jordanians now emerging in ever increasing numbers from Jordan's universities and colleges.[4] More recently, Walid Jumblatt, the Lebanese Druse leader, accused the King of suppressing all kinds of political parties by proroguing parliament in 1974, ruling since then by personal decree.[5] Jumblatt went on to say that all the Middle Eastern leaders are afraid of political parties, preferring self-rule, although if the Lebanese experiment is anything to judge by, whether confessional or otherwise, it holds out very little hope for the introduction of Western-style government in the Arab countries.

It is, however, a historical fact that in all the Arab monarchies 'the King, Amir, Shaykh or Sultan does not merely reign but rules.'[6] This has been the case throughout the centuries, as has been the requirement that the ruler must demonstrate his fitness to rule if he is to receive allegiance from his subjects. The unfortunate King Talal's abdication owing to illness is a clear example of this. This form of personal rule is attributable partly to the continuing tribal nature of Arab society, and partly to the absence of long-established political parties, which are such a feature of Western democracies. On the other hand, the Arab ruler is expected to conform with the ethics of Islam, and to consult with the tribal elders (or their equivalents) during the decision-making process. As King Hussein has said, 'To me rule was not merely a crown or a mace but an honourable service' – and here 'service' is the operative word.[7]

There was a short period in Jordan's history – during Naboulsi's premiership – when the Prime Minister and Cabinet considered *they* were the decision-makers. It was not a happy time, and from the late 1950s onwards the King played an increasingly important decision-making role, until by 1967 he was, and remains, the principal decision-maker in all fields of policy, particularly in foreign policy. Since Jordan is vulnerable to outside pressures, both militarily and economically, the state's survival depends very largely on diplomacy. King Hussein, with his wide experience of international relations, is Jordan's chief diplomat. He personally appoints ambassadors, some of whom may report directly to him, the Foreign Ministry executing the policy promulgated by the King.

Hussein likewise appoints the Prime Minister, whose Cabinet has to be approved by the King in accordance with the constitution. The Prime Minister will be chosen from the ruling elite, all of whom are known personally by the King. Arabs are great respecters of tradition, and throughout the centuries there have existed families that traditionally have played their part in the government and administration of their countries, irrespective of whether the Byzantines or the Ottomans held the reins of power. The Prime Minister will of course be consulted by the King in the formulation of policy, but it will be the King who finally decides on policy; the Prime Minister and Cabinet will execute it. This arrangement inevitably places the King in the forefront of the political battle, for which reason he has to possess an acute awareness of the state of public opinion on every issue. This played an important part in deciding the King to dismiss Glubb Pasha in 1956, and to throw in his lot with Egypt in May 1967.

Although Jordan's decision-making process is not institutionalised as in the West, the existence of a Chief of the Royal Diwan (Royal Hashemite Court), and also of a Minister of the Royal Court, plays a very important part in providing the King with advice on domestic and foreign affairs, as well as in monitoring the implementation of policy and acting as a bridge between the King and the Prime Minister. The appointment and the influence of the Chief of the Royal Court is somewhat analogous to that of the President's Chief of Staff at the White House. Those chosen to be Chief of the Royal Court are usually of prime ministerial timber.

One of the tasks of the Diwan is to keep the King informed of popular feeling. Since Jordan still remains at heart a tribal society, particularly where the bedouins are concerned, the Diwan contains a Tribal Council, the importance of which can be judged from the fact that it was headed for many years by the King's younger brother, Prince Muhammad. It ensures that the King always keeps in touch with tribal affairs, and ensures that the age-old bedouin tradition of the right to personal contact with the ruler (or shaykh) is always preserved.

Another difference from Western democratic practice relates to control over the armed forces. This control is exercised solely by the King as Supreme Commander. The Prime Minister is not in the chain of command, which runs directly from the King to the Commander-in-Chief, whom the King selects and who sees the King frequently. Members of the armed forces enjoy a privileged position in Jordan, the King devoting a great deal of his time to their supervision, although he delegates the everyday running of the armed forces to the Commander-in-Chief and the General Staff. The loyalty of the army is of paramount importance to the dynasty, and Hussein never misses an opportunity to visit his soldiers, many of whom he addresses by name. This loyalty is reflected in the fact that many senior generals never retire, but fill various diplomatic and other appointments until they are too old to carry on. General Amar Khammash, for example, was for many years Chief of the Royal Court after an outstandingly distinguished career in the army.

There is a parliament consisting of an elected house of deputies and a house of notables (the senate), whose members are appointed by the King. The house of deputies was recalled in 1984, after a ten-year absence, and elections are pending. Parliament can debate issues but has no power to implement its conclusions. It can, however, conduct votes of confidence in the government, and can impeach ministers. It also has some control over the government's fiscal policies. Its real power lies in its ability to represent to the King the extent of popular feeling on a particular issue, thereby playing a part in the decision-making process, although it will be the King who finally decides. He also has the constitutional power to dissolve parliament.

Almost certainly King Hussein would prefer to liberalise the political system in Jordan, but his earlier attempts to do so were hardly encouraging. Since the survival of the state must remain his principal concern, anything that may affect Jordan's stability requires the most careful consideration. This is why loyalty to the regime is the supreme virtue in Jordan, whether it be in the selection of ministers or in the promotion of senior officers in the armed forces. King Hussein has had to survive too many perils to make him anything else but cautious when it comes to political experiment. As he once commented to a British ambassador on the question of the selection of a new prime minister – 'Jordan is a very small country and I know my people too well!'[8]

CHAPTER SIXTEEN

The October War – 1973

'All warfare is based on deception.' Sun Tzu[1]

Nasser had lost no time after the shattering events of June 1967 in trying to establish the causes of Egypt's defeat. As a result of a searching analysis there followed a wholesale reorganisation of the Egyptian armed forces, and a complete re-equipment programme which relied almost entirely on assistance from the Soviet Union. The Russians were at the same time providing arms and advisers to Syria. The United States in its turn increased its aid to Israel.

As soon as Nasser considered that his forces were ready, he launched what came to be known as the War of Attrition across the Suez Canal, against the Israelis occupying Sinai. This had consisted of commando raids and artillery bombardments, which resulted in 20,000 Egyptian military and civilian casualties, and 3400 Israeli military casualties, until a ceasefire was agreed in July 1970.

The Israelis had responded not only by counter-battery fire across the Canal, but also by air strikes deep into Egypt itself. These had caused many civilian casualties and had given rise to considerable complaint among the long-suffering civilian population. As a consequence of these air strikes, Nasser had managed to reach agreement with the Russians for the provision of surface-to-air missile batteries (SAMs). These were deployed not only for the defence of airfields and vulnerable points within Egypt itself, but also for defence against air attack for a twenty-mile-wide strip running the entire length of the Canal. Moreover, Russian planes flown by Russian pilots were based in Egypt. They had several brushes with the IAF that led to much concern in Washington and Moscow. Neither of the two superpowers had any wish to escalate an already dangerous situation.

There was a conflict of views in Washington among those responsible for advising President Nixon on the Middle East. This arose from the rivalry that existed between the State Department, headed by William Rogers as Secretary of State, and the National Security Council which was headed by Henry Kissinger. It was accentuated by the President's lack of faith in the State Department, and by his tendency to play one of his advisers off against another. Nixon relied more on Kissinger than on Rogers, although the latter was a personal friend. More and more the conduct of negotiations with Hanoi, Moscow and Peking came to be entrusted to Kissinger, until only the Middle East seemed to lie within the sphere of operations of the State Department. Even here Nixon may have been influenced by the fact that Kissinger was a Jew, although he did not in fact practise his religion. Nevertheless, it was reasonable to suppose that Kissinger would be regarded as pro-Israel.

As it happened Kissinger did have strong views about the Middle East situation, but not because he was a Jew. He could see little prospect of reaching agreement between the Arab states and Israel; and he feared lest the United States become bogged down in sterile negotiations with them at the expense of a settlement in Viet Nam, the establishment of relations with Communist China, and the achievement of détente with the Soviet Union. Therefore it was inevitable that his views and Rogers' should be directly at variance.

With the possibility of superpower confrontation looming ever larger as the War of Attrition grew in intensity, the State Department became increasingly alarmed. Joseph Sisco, its expert in Middle Eastern affairs, was indefatigable in his efforts to relax tension between Egypt and Israel. It was largely as a result of these efforts that Rogers chose to launch a new initiative in pursuit of Middle Eastern peace in December 1969. He did so in the unusual forum of a Washington conference on adult education. He told his audience that American policy would be 'to encourage the Arabs to accept a permanent peace based on a binding agreement, and to urge Israel to withdraw from occupied territory when her territorial integrity is ensured'. He said that precise details would need to be worked out by Ambassador Jarring, the UN Secretary-General's Special Representative in the Middle East, but the intention was clear. Israel's withdrawal, given acceptable safeguards, from Egyptian territory. No mention was made of Jordan or Syria, but since the agreement was to be based on Resolution 242 it could be assumed that similar agreements were to be reached with those countries.

The Rogers' initiative was unwelcome to Kissinger, who regarded it as premature. Egypt's response was lukewarm. Israel rejected it out of hand, saying it amounted to 'an appeasement of the Arabs'. Undeterred, the Americans continued to seek support, in Moscow and elsewhere. On 25 June 1970, they came up with a fresh set of proposals that came to be known as the Rogers Plan. Rogers called on all the parties to 'stop shooting and start talking'. There should be a ceasefire for a limited period, in accordance with certain conditions put forward by Jarring to the Secretary-General.

Hussein at this time was deeply embroiled in the *fedayeen* problem. However, he had already told Nixon that both Egypt and Jordan were committed to Resolution 242. They were prepared to sign any document, other than a peace treaty with Israel. Unfortunately this commitment was not endorsed by the Egyptian Foreign Minister, Mahmoud Fawzi, who visited Washington three days after Hussein. This led Washington to assume that Rogers' second initiative would be no more successful than his previous one.

They were to be surprised. Nasser visited Moscow on 29 June 1970, and told an astonished Brezhnev that he intended to accept the Rogers Plan. His reasons were purely tactical. Egypt needed a ceasefire to cut down on civilian casualties and to give the army a breathing space. Above all, he needed time to complete the SAM zone along the Canal. Although he had little faith in Rogers' proposals, he intended to make use of them to serve Egypt's interests. Nasser announced his acceptance on 23 July in a speech which caused consternation throughout the Arab world, particularly within the PLO. He was violently denounced by Habash and Hawatmeh, and vilified in the Palestinian press.

Hussein flew to Cairo on 20 August, at Nasser's invitation, and the reasons for Nasser's acceptance were explained to him. However, when Hussein took the opportunity to raise with Nasser his problems with the *fedayeen*, he received cold comfort. Nasser told him that Jordan and the PLO must learn to coexist, and he specifically warned against the use of force. Arafat was given the same message when he visited Nasser on 24 August. It satisfied neither Hussein nor Arafat, who would be fighting each other within three weeks. In little more than four weeks, Nasser would be dead.

Israel only agreed to a ceasefire on 31 July after strong American pressure. The Israelis had no faith in the Rogers Plan; nor were they encouraged by the reports they were receiving of the installation of more and more SAM sites in the Canal Zone. In their efforts to beat the ceasefire deadline, the Egyptians were erecting dummy sites, which they intended to replace with the real thing when the missiles arrived from Russia. Israel protested again and again about these violations. When the Americans passed them on, Egypt blandly denied them. It is hardly surprising that Israel should have announced on 6 September that it would not take part in negotiations to be conducted by Jarring. By then, however, the focus of the world's attention had been shifted to Jordan, as a result of the hijackings by the PLO. It is nonetheless surprising that the Egypt–Israel ceasefire had continued to hold.

Nasser's successor, Anwar Sadat, was virtually an unknown quantity outside Egypt. He had been named Vice-President by Nasser almost as an afterthought. Although he had been one of the original members of the Free Officers conspiracy which overthrew King Farouk, his influence within Nasser's inner circle had not been significant. When the time came, however, he showed he could be both decisive and ruthless. Sadat possessed all the shrewdness and cunning of the Egyptian *fellah*, as well as the toughness of mind and body that came from living dangerously for most of his adult life. He was not afraid of making the hard decisions. He liked to think things through carefully, and then work to a calculated plan. Few of his colleagues could have imagined that he proposed to bring the Israelis to the negotiating table as a result of a defeat inflicted on them by Egyptian arms. This may have been Clausewitzian in conception but hardly conceivable in Egypt's case. Israeli superiority on the battlefield was taken more or less for granted by most military experts.

Sadat had lost patience with the Russians for their failure to provide Egypt with weapons in the time and quantity required; nor was he satisfied with their political support. There were 20,000 Russians in Egypt, and they were no more popular than the British had been before them. Sadat recognised that Nixon's election had marked a sea-change in United States foreign policy, and he believed that Nixon was annoyed by Israeli intransigence and the Zionist influence on American domestic politics. All this resulted in the conclusion that US support would be of more value to Egypt than Russian. On 8 July 1972, Sadat saw Soviet Ambassador Vinogradov and gave the Russians their marching orders. They were virtually all out of Egypt by 17 July, and Sadat set about mending his fences with the United States. He was to prove markedly successful.

Sadat knew that Egypt could not fight Israel on its own. He needed an ally, but Jordan did not fit the bill. In the first place he disapproved of Hussein's handling of the PLO problem; and secondly he knew that the Jordanian army was not ready for war. There was in any case a lack of rapport between Sadat and Hussein, whom Sadat suspected of trying to do a deal with Israel in order to get back the West Bank. Hussein has admitted he found Nasser easier to deal with than Sadat.[2] The former British Prime Minister, Lord Callaghan, records in his memoirs disparaging comments made to him by Sadat about Hussein.[3]

Syria, still smarting from the loss of the Golan, was the obvious partner. The country had become much more stable since Hafez Assad had come to power after a bloodless coup in 1970. The Syrian armed forces had been reorganised and re-equipped in the same fashion as the Egyptians, again with Soviet assistance. It was an additional advantage that both armies were organised and trained in accordance with Russian military doctrine. Their generals understood each other. Having decided to secure Syria as an ally, Sadat initiated secret negotiations that culminated in agreement in April 1973 for a joint plan of attack on Israel. Only D-Day and H-Hour remained to be decided.

The strictest secrecy was kept. Only those who 'needed to know' were included in the planning. Hussein was not one of them.

Kissinger says he had a long discussion with the Egyptian Foreign Minister, Muhammad el-Zayat, the day before the war began, and is convinced that the Egyptian had no knowledge of Sadat's plans. The UN Secretary-General, Kurt Waldheim, who had lunched with the Syrian Foreign Minister on the same day, is similarly convinced that he had been told nothing. Hussein was rather relieved that Egypt and Syria seemed to be so absorbed in their own affairs that they had no time to bother about Jordan. Not that the Arab world, frequently encouraged by Gadaffi, lost any opportunity to abuse Hussein for driving out the PLO. 'When we attended meetings in other Arab countries,' one Jordanian has said, 'we were treated like vagabonds or pickpockets. No one wanted to know us. . . .'

Nevertheless, Jordan's isolation had its advantages. It enabled Hussein to repair the damage left in the wake of his struggle with the PLO, and set in train an ambitious programme to extend and improve Jordan's infrastructure. The armed forces were re-equipped and reorganised; new roads were made; new hospitals and schools constructed; irrigation brought more land under cultivation; and the moribund tourist industry was revitalised. As Hussein was later to say, when inaugurating Jordan's 1975–80 Development Plan, 'Backwardness is the principal enemy and the natural ally of evil and oppression everywhere.' The remarkable development of Amman, which transformed it from a modest market town to a great city in the space of not more than fifteen years, was just beginning; and although Jordan had no oil to export it did possess a large number of well-educated young men and women with services to offer in the new oil-rich states in the Gulf. Jordan exported expertise, the remittances home making a significant contribution to Jordan's economy.

These were the years when Hussein really began to develop his relations with the United States. Until his courageous handling of the *fedayeen* problem evoked a responsive chord in the mind of President Nixon, Jordan had not counted for all that much in the State Department. Egypt, Iraq and Saudi Arabia were much more important. But Hussein had greatly impressed President Eisenhower when he first visited Washington; Eisenhower had told Nixon, then the Vice-President, that although Hussein was a very young man he was mature far beyond his years, and in terms of intelligence he ranked with the ablest of the leaders Eisenhower had met. Hussein was later to pay many visits to Washington, meeting every President, but undoubtedly the greatest impression he has made was on Richard Nixon. Nixon was particularly impressed by Hussein's 'high intelligence, wisdom, physical and moral courage', and has said that 'Hussein was and is without question a world leader rather than simply a parochial monarch of a small country'.[4]

When Hussein first met Nixon on 8 April 1969, he made an excellent impression. Kissinger described him as 'one of the most attractive political leaders I have ever met'.[5] However, it was not until his state visit to Washington in 1971 that Hussein really acquired the confidence he needed in order to deal directly with the leader of the world's most powerful nation. He was grateful for the American help and support he had received during his confrontation with the PLO in 1970–1, and he was anxious to thank the President in person. He also hoped to obtain both financial aid and weapons at a time when his other sources had dried up.

The President was waiting to receive the King on the White House lawn as he arrived by helicopter. Passing the Marines Band on his way to greet the King, Nixon told the Bandmaster, 'Strike up "Solid Men to the Front",' the Souza march certainly appropriate for the occasion. Later in the Oval Office, one of those present thought the King was rather overawed by the occasion. He asked for only two regiments'-worth of artillery pieces when he had been briefed to ask for three. Nixon immediately replied, 'But my advisers tell me you require three regiments'-worth, Your Majesty,' and that was the number provided. Commenting on Hussein's love of speed and skill at the wheel, Nixon has said that he is like Brezhnev in this respect, although the Russian had scared Nixon when driving him round the narrow and twisty Camp David lanes in the Lincoln with which he had just been presented. But when Hussein drove Nixon out to Hummar for dinner, Nixon experienced no qualms since he says he knew the King was a 'very competent pilot and expert driver'.

The King's state visit was to prove very important for Jordan since it resulted in what came to be known as the M-60 Program. This was virtually the rearmament of the Jordanian armed forces with US help. American military advisers helped to reorganise the army and air force and there was an extensive re-equipment programme. It can be said that with the completion of the M-60 Program, the Jordanian armed forces were as well trained and as well equipped as they have ever been, with their morale correspondingly high.

This was as well because on 6 October 1973, after nearly three years of silence, the sound of artillery fire again reverberated around the Middle East. The fourth Arab–Israeli war began a little after midday with a Syrian offensive in the Golan and an assault crossing of the Suez Canal by the Egyptians, with the aim of obtaining a lodgement on the east bank. This is sometimes called the Ramadan War because it was fought during the Great Fast, or the Yom Kippur War because the battle began on the holiest day in the Jewish calendar. It was in fact codenamed Operation Badr by its chief architect, Anwar Sadat.[6] It took almost everyone by surprise, including Hussein. Sadat telephoned him soon after H-Hour to ask him not to intervene, at least not in the early stages. Hussein, with memories of June 1967 still in mind, was content to wait. His air force was in no position to take on the Israelis, nor was the army deployed to attack the West Bank. It is also unlikely that either he or his advisers had much confidence in the chances of the Egyptians penetrating the strong Israeli defences along the Canal. The Egyptian army had hardly distinguished itself in the previous wars against Israel; and bitter experience had shown the Jordanians that the standard of their staff planning was not very high. They were soon to revise this opinion.

The most interesting aspect of this war is that it was fought for a strictly limited *political* objective, at least where the Egyptians were concerned. The operational plan had been masterminded by Sadat, but the detailed planning had been entrusted to Field Marshal Ahmed Ismail Ali and his Chief of Staff, Major-General Saad el-Shazli. Sadat's aim was to break the political deadlock caused by Israel's reluctance to enter into peace negotiations which might entail Israel's withdrawal from the Occupied Territories. In a directive issued on 2 October 1973, Sadat made his aim clear: 'I believe that if the enemy's theory of the permanent superiority of its forces can be successfully challenged, both the short-term and the long-term repercussions will be incalculable. In the short term it should make possible a peaceful and honourable solution to the Middle East problem and in the long term it will create a cumulative modification in the aggressive psychology of Zionism.'[7]

Sadat, in other words, wanted to destroy once and for all the Israelis' belief in their own invincibility, thereby compelling them to come to the negotiating table. But it is doubtful, however, whether his ally, Hafez Assad, saw things in quite the same light. Israeli occupation of the Golan after the 1967 war posed a constant threat to Damascus and was hard for Syria to bear. In May 1973 after allying himself with Sadat, Hafez Assad had set about removing the large numbers of Palestinians who had lodged in Syria after their expulsion from Jordan with the PLO. He encouraged and financed their removal to Lebanon, ridding himself thereby of an incubus while at the same time protecting Syria's western flank. With Arafat and his commandos firmly established in Tyre, Sidon and Beirut, harrying the Israelis with weapons liberally supplied by Syria, Hafez Assad was able to turn his entire attention to the Golan.

Egypt's and Syria's initial successes were remarkable. They astonished the world. Their soldiers fought both bravely and skilfully and the Israelis suffered enormous losses in *matériel*. This was chiefly due to the sophisticated anti-tank weapons supplied by Russia and the courage of the tank-hunting squads. But although the Israelis had been caught badly on the wrong foot, they managed to recover quickly. By 14 October they were engaged in one of the greatest tank battles in history against the Egyptian armour, a battle which involved about 2000 tanks. There were similarly fierce tank battles in the Golan where the Syrians succeeded in capturing the summit of Mount Hermon. The losses in weapons were such that both the United States and the Soviet Union airlifted large quantities of weapons and ammunition in support of their protégés. This caused worldwide concern lest the two superpowers should be drawn into the fighting. Indeed, just before midnight on 24 October, the United States placed its armed forces at a high state of alert, a move which had the desired effect of cooling off the Russians. But the situation while it lasted was extremely menacing to world peace.

Hussein, with his belief in Arab unity and solidarity, was in a difficult position. He did not like to stand on the sidelines when Egypt and Syria were fighting the common enemy; on the other hand his memory of both Egyptian and Syrian conduct was still clear in his mind. He did not want to incur a repetition. Neither Sadat nor Hafez Assad had taken him into their confidence when planning the war, and he was unhappy about the air situation should the IAF turn its attention on Jordan. However, he sent General Amer Khammash to Cairo on 11 October with a message for Sadat. In it Hussein said that it would be unwise for Jordan to intervene without adequate air support. By then, however, Sadat's initial optimism was starting to wane as the Israelis hit back, and he was keen to draw Jordan into the battle. Hussein's message was unwelcome – as was a report three days later from Arafat, who had suggested sending Palestinian units to fight alongside the Egyptians in the Negev. In order to do this, they would have to traverse Jordan, and permission for them to do so had been refused. Sadat was later to tell James Callaghan that he had even offered to guarantee the Palestinians' conduct by sending Egyptian officers to command them, but Jordan still remained reluctant. The reason was obvious. The Israelis were bound to find out about the Palestinians, and the battle would undoubtedly spread from the Negev to the Jordan Valley, dragging in the Jordanians willy-nilly; that is probably what Sadat, with the Israelis across the Canal and his Third Army surrounded at Suez, would have liked.

The arguments for and against Jordanian intervention went on for days. Crown Prince Hassan had witnessed from the Jordanian side of the border a battle between the Syrians and the Israelis for the communications centre at El Al in the Golan; he had come away unimpressed. Later, when one of the King's advisers declared that Jordanian blood must be spilt, Prince Hassan interjected, 'So long as it is not yours, I suppose?'[8] There was, moreover, the problem of the Iraqis, who had sent their 3rd Armoured Division across the desert to support the Syrians. The movement of this division was a considerable logistic feat, but by 11 October Syria was fighting desperately to hold the Golan, and there could be no question but that Jordan had to intervene, without relaxing its guard against an Israeli attack across the River Jordan. This inevitably restricted the number of troops that could be spared to go to Syria's assistance.

In the event the 40th Tank Brigade under Colonel Khalid Hajhouj Majali moved into Syria on 12 October. It was followed by the 3rd Armoured Division (Brigadier Alawi Jarrad), but it did not arrive until 22 October, only a few hours before Hafez Assad agreed to a ceasefire. Only the 40th Tank Brigade became involved in heavy fighting, losing twenty-seven killed and fifty wounded. Fourteen of its tanks were disabled beyond repair. This did not compare of course with Syrian losses, but the Israelis were impressed by the professionalism of the Jordanian tank crews and their tactical handling. Security Council Resolution 338 of 21/22 October calling for a ceasefire was accepted by Jordan at 2 a.m. on 23 October, some time after the other parties involved had accepted the UN Resolution (see Appendix). Although the guns had stopped firing, there was still a long way to go before any kind of settlement was reached. Hafez Assad felt particularly aggrieved with Sadat who had, he felt, sought a ceasefire for Egypt without much thought for his Syrian ally, who was still fighting strongly. This was to colour Syrian–Egyptian relations for many years to come.

Israel, Egypt and Syria had all suffered astonishing losses in equipment, but the war had at least partially achieved Sadat's aim. It had demonstrated conclusively that the Arabs could plan a war successfully, and conduct their operations skilfully and bravely. There was no longer any reason for accepting Israel's supremacy on the battlefield, although it is true that the Israeli speed of reaction after the initial surprise was formidable. Once again Israel's advantage in the possession of interior lines was made clear. It is extremely difficult to co-ordinate Arab offensives in sectors as far apart as Sinai and the Golan, whereas Israel can switch troops from one sector to the other very rapidly.

One important outcome of the war was the opportunity afforded to the remarkable Henry Kissinger to bring about a dialogue between the contending parties. Kissinger has been bitterly criticised both by the Arabs and by Israel, but no one can deny the energy he brought to his task; nor the astonishing nimbleness of mind that enabled him to chart a course through a veritable forest of difficulties. His 'shuttle diplomacy' captured the world's imagination and led eventually to both an Egypt–Israel and a Syria–Israel disengagement, although by no stretch of the imagination can it be said to have resolved the long-standing problems of the Middle East.

Kissinger's negotiations extended throughout most of 1974, having begun with a conference at Geneva in December 1973, at which all the contending parties were represented. Most of the negotiations were bilateral, between Egypt and Israel, and Syria and Israel, with Kissinger acting as honest broker between the parties. Hussein was not personally involved, although in retrospect Kissinger has said that perhaps he could have done more for Jordan.[9] This may have been so; but it would seem unlikely that Israel would ever have agreed the conditions necessary for any agreement with Jordan – viz withdrawal from the Occupied Territories and the Old City of Jerusalem. Meanwhile Hussein was concerned lest Sadat should do a deal with Israel at Jordan's expense in order to recover Sinai. Hafez Assad was similarly suspicious of Sadat's motives. It was always possible that Jordan's claim to the West Bank might be overruled in favour of the PLO as part of a larger deal. Zeid Rifai, who had known Kissinger at Harvard, made this clear to him.

Hussein insisted that the West Bank was Jordanian territory, which he was under an obligation to recover from the Israelis. Nor could he overlook his responsibility for the Muslim and Christian parts of Jerusalem. He said the real question was who represented the Palestinians. This had been complicated ever since 1964 by the introduction of the PLO, with whom the Israelis had said they would never negotiate. It therefore made sense for Jordan to do the negotiating, although Hussein was perfectly willing to discuss some kind of self-determination for the West Bank once it had been recovered.

Kissinger, reflecting the views of most other Americans, considered the PLO to be entirely disruptive. Their policy was the destruction of Israel. Added to which, in the sole high-level contact the US had had with them, it had been made plain that they were determined to destroy the Hashemite Kingdom of Jordan. In the climate of American opinion at that time, there could therefore be no question of the Americans entering into any kind of dialogue with the PLO. This is an interesting example of the negative effect of the policy of terror, as adopted by the PLO. But, as John Bulloch has pointed out, it did have its positive effect as well.

The Palestinians, he writes, 'achieved no real successes as a result of their operations, and even in the years of their military heyday, between 1968 and 1969, the Israelis were never in any danger from guerrilla action,' but the PLO had nevertheless succeeded in keeping 'the idea of Palestine alive', and had forced 'Arab and world leaders alike to take their aspirations into consideration'.[10] This had been no mean achievement, given the apathy into which the Palestinians were sunk in the earlier years of their dispersal. Indeed, 1974 was to turn out to be Arafat's year. Driven out of Jordan ignominiously three years previously, and soon thereafter forced on to the defensive as a result of the infighting within the Palestinian Resistance Movement, he was now well established in Beirut with money pouring into his coffers from Saudi Arabia, Kuwait, Libya and the Gulf states. And while his young commandos trained with the weapons he could now purchase for them, Arafat himself travelled far and wide publicising the Palestinian cause. He was even invited to address the General Assembly of the United Nations that November, appearing in combat fatigues and making his famous 'gun and olive branch' speech.

'I have come', he told the Assembly, 'bearing an olive branch and a freedom fighter's gun. Do not let the olive branch fall from my hand.' He had talked of the Palestinians' dream to have a homeland of their own, but he added that he faced the reality of Israel's existence. It all sounded very reasonable and the speech was received with considerable applause. Sir Brian Urquart, who in his capacity as a United Nations official has met Arafat many times, respects Arafat's courage and resilience, but nevertheless regards him as being to some extent a 'play-actor'. He doubts his ability to deliver in the event of his being accepted by Israel and the US as a negotiator.[11] Such acceptance might strengthen his position inside the Resistance Movement, but it would at the same time lay him open to a charge of treachery from his more fanatical followers.

His oratory nevertheless impressed many among his audience on 13 November 1974. On 22 November, by UN Resolution 3236, the international community acknowledged the rights of the Palestinians to 'self-determination, national independence and sovereignty'. By Resolution 3237 the PLO was granted Observer Status at the United Nations. Although neither the USA nor Israel voted for the Resolutions, the entire performance was a considerable triumph for Arafat, and moreover one that would have been inconceivable three years previously.

The General Assembly had in effect endorsed the resolution passed at the Arab Summit held at Rabat the previous month. This recognised the PLO as the only legitimate representative of the Palestinian people, and required King Hussein to hand over the West Bank to the PLO, if or when he had succeeded in recovering it. This came as a complete surprise to Hussein. He had of course known of the resolution to be debated but was confident of the support of King Hassan of Morocco and President Sadat, both of whom in the event voted in favour of the resolution. Hussein argued strongly against it but without making any headway. If the intention of the Arab leaders was to help the Palestinians rather than to snub Hussein, their decision was a shortsighted one because it destroyed Hussein's powers as a negotiator on behalf of the Palestinians. When, much later, Hussein was asked whether he thought Sadat's intention was to keep him out of the negotiations which Sadat was already conducting secretly with Israel, he replied that he had often wondered. There was little chemistry between him and Sadat. Sadat was a man of fixed ideas who did not want anyone to get in his way now that he seemed to have won Kissinger over to his side.

According to one of Hussein's closest aides, many Palestinians in Jordan expressed dismay over the Rabat resolution. He said they blamed the King for accepting it. But, although they were asked why they did not make their views public, they preferred to grumble behind the scenes. They did not want to stand up to be counted.

CHAPTER SEVENTEEN
The Search for Peace

'We have followed every avenue, exploited every opportunity, and bent over backwards to accommodate friend and foe alike to see a just and lasting peace in our troubled region.' King Hussein[1]

Hussein has been entirely consistent in his efforts to regain Arab lands, in the pursuit of his belief in Arab unity and in the mission of the Hashemites to promote this unity. It has even been alleged, although this is denied by the King, that he did at one time negotiate personally with Israel, but without effect. He has however met leading Israeli personalities, such as Moshe Dayan and Shimon Peres, in the course of his search for peace. Hussein has said that Dayan was one of the most reasonable of the Israeli leaders until the October 1973 War, after which he seemed to have joined the hardliners.

Although Hussein has been politically hamstrung since the Rabat Summit resolution, which deprived him of the authority to negotiate on behalf of the Palestinians in favour of the PLO, Jordan underwent something of an economic miracle during the following decade. This was due largely to generous aid from abroad, and to a series of five-year plans, imaginative in their conception and skilfully overseen by Crown Prince Hassan and his team of advisers; it was during this period that Prince Hassan created Jordan's Royal Scientific Society, to keep Jordan abreast of scientific developments elsewhere in the world. Meanwhile, in Saudi Arabia and in the Gulf, the oil boom was about to bring hitherto backward areas into the modern age, with the consequent need for engineers, teachers, doctors and many other professions and trades, to help develop the infrastructure of the new rich. Here Jordan was in an excellent position to contribute, with its young and well-educated population, both men and women. Their remittances home were a welcome addition to Jordan's exchequer; and they made a powerful contribution to Arab solidarity. As another manifestation of this solidarity, Jordan supplied a contingent to fight alongside the Omanis in suppressing a Communist-inspired rebellion against Sultan Qabous in the Dhofar province of Oman. Both Britain and Iran also took part in this campaign.

At the Geneva Conference in December 1973, Hussein had proposed that Israel and Jordan should withdraw to a depth of five miles from the banks of the River Jordan. He described this as 'disengagement', in line with the negotiations Kissinger was conducting with Israel for a withdrawal from Sinai. Hussein believed it would reduce the possibility of frontier incidents, but the Israelis turned down the proposal. He raised it again in March 1974, but Mrs Golda Meir would not hear of it. Her successor, Yitzhak Rabin, was more receptive, but the Rabat resolution, which soon followed, clearly undercut Hussein's authority to conduct negotiations affecting the Palestinians. However, this did not prevent the King from seeking every opportunity to free the Palestinians from Israeli military occupation, and he travelled the world in order to explain the Palestinian case. In this endeavour, his sincerity and moderation won him both friends and admirers. Meanwhile, Israel continued to tighten its grip on the Occupied Territories, appropriating Arab land on the West Bank and encouraging settlement on it by Israelis, many of them belonging to extreme right-wing organisations.

Whereas there might have been just a chance in December 1973 of an Israeli withdrawal from the West Bank, at the time of the Geneva Conference, as the years went by the likelihood became increasingly remote. The PLO's adoption of terror as a policy did nothing to promote this objective nor did the coming to power in Israel on 21 June 1977 of Menachem Begin as leader of the Likud coalition government. Begin was a fanatical believer in Eretz Israel, claiming that the West Bank, which he insisted on describing as Judaea and Samaria, was historically part of Israel. He was equally adamant that Jerusalem, including the Old City seized in June 1967, was inalienably for evermore the capital of Israel. Despite every effort by Hussein to sustain the Arabism of the West Bank by treating its Palestinian inhabitants in every way as he treated the inhabitants of the East Bank, the Israelis continued remorselessly to tighten their grip. Former President Jimmy Carter has described in his book, *The Blood of Abraham*, the marked contrast between his first visit to the Allenby Bridge across the Jordan in 1973 and a further visit ten years later.[2] In 1973 there had been a constant stream of travellers passing to and fro across the river, with only perfunctory checks by a handful of border guards on either bank; in 1983 there were Israeli uniforms everywhere, there were long queues of vehicles and people were being subjected to the most rigorous examination; the atmosphere was acutely depressing. One Jordanian woman, who feels it incumbent on her to visit her family near Nablus every year, describes the searches to which she is subjected by the Israelis as 'humiliating'. She submits to them only for the sake of filial piety.[3]

Hussein's metamorphosis into a statesman over the decade was marked by a noticeable change in his appearance and manner in public. The young, dashing and perhaps impulsive image of earlier years was replaced by an altogether steadier and more deliberate one. The welcoming smile and ready laugh still remained, but his expression was more thoughtful and his manner more restrained. He had inherited his grandfather's ability to evoke both loyalty and devotion in those who worked closely with him. Although he drove them hard, and expected a high standard, he was always generous and thoughtful. He was not aloof like the Shah of Iran, but as much at ease when chatting with a young fighter pilot as he was when talking with one of his generals or ministers. Whenever there were matters of great importance pending he would, after discussing them in great detail with his advisers, often retreat to his study for one or two days to consider in seclusion how best to tackle the problem. Wherever he went in the country, he never lost an opportunity to talk with ordinary people; among the tribes he was as likely to be addressed as 'Hussein' or 'Abu Abdullah' (Father of Abdullah) as 'Sayyidna' (Our Lord) or Sidi (Sir). This was as he would have wished. He never forgot the Hashemite connection with the Arab people.

As always he gave a great deal of his time to the armed forces, being probably at heart a soldier or an airman. He would find time in his busy schedule to attend such a mundane affair as a regimental sports meeting, giving away the prizes with a cheerful word to officers and soldiers alike. When with his air force he was never happier than when discussing technical matters, of which he had considerable knowledge, with the pilots and technicians. Although the armed forces are no longer the country's chief source of employment, as was the case forty years ago in the time of the Arab Legion, they are still regarded in Jordan with considerable respect. Conscription was introduced in Jordan in 1976, partly in order to provide a reserve of trained manpower which had previously been lacking, and partly to bring together the youth of the country at a formative period in their lives in the interest of nation-building. Exemption is made for only sons. It cannot be said that conscription is universally popular, any more than national service was in Britain, nor the draft in the United States, but it does have its credit side. The Commander-in-Chief is the King's cousin, Field Marshal Sharif Zeid bin Shakir. He was at Sandhurst with the King and has been close to him over the years. Zeid's father, Amir Shakir, took part in the Great Arab Revolt and accompanied Abdullah on his journey to Transjordan, becoming later Abdullah's adviser on bedouin affairs.

President Sadat's hopes that Egyptian success on the battlefield in the October 1973 War might bring Israel to the negotiating table with Egypt ran into the sand when Israel came close to annihilating the Egyptian army in the closing stages of that war. From then onwards Sadat bent every effort towards unlocking the door by diplomacy, in the course of which he succeeded in establishing very warm relations with the Americans, who liked his character and style. Finally, with the object of demonstrating Egypt's true concern for peace, Sadat made his remarkable visit to Jerusalem in November 1977, incurring as a result the bitter criticism of his Arab allies, but receiving the plaudits of most of the rest of the world. This led Carter to initiate the diplomatic moves that were to result in what have come to be known as the Camp David Accords.

The Camp David Accords, signed on 17 September 1978 by President Anwar Sadat and Prime Minister Menachem Begin, and witnessed by President Jimmy Carter, led to the signing of a peace treaty between Egypt and Israel, but also resulted in the exclusion of Egypt from Arab counsels for nearly a decade. There can certainly be no doubt about the good intentions of Carter as the chief architect of the Accords; it was only his singleminded determination to bring about agreement between Sadat and Begin that brought the discussions at Camp David to a supposedly successful conclusion. According to one American authority, Carter was 'unique among American presidents in the depth of his concern to find a peaceful resolution of the conflict between Israel and its Arab neighbours'.[4] This was so much the case that Carter made it almost the principal plank in his foreign policy during the first two years of his presidency.

Although President Carter has his critics, in Jordan as elsewhere, few will deny that he is a man of the highest moral principles and of deep Christian faith. As a practising Southern Baptist, he was brought up on the Bible. So it is hardly surprising that the continuing turmoil in the Holy Land should have aroused his concern long before he decided to run for the presidency. He studied the problem in great depth, bringing to it the trained mind of an engineer, as well as a remarkable capacity to absorb a quantity of memoranda on the subject that would have had only a passing interest for the majority of American politicians. Carter had had, however, very little experience of international negotiations prior to his election as President, unlike President Nixon, whose strength in the handling of foreign policy was his knowledge of the personalities involved. To Carter, both Sadat and Begin were virtually unknown quantities.

Carter's decision to invite Sadat and Begin to Camp David, where they would be to a large extent isolated from outside pressures, stemmed from his belief that men of honest purpose when working face to face must almost certainly arrive at a solution to their problem in the end. He believed in magnanimity and goodwill among men, provided that their cause was just. Although deeply religious, there was no fanaticism in his makeup. He could not understand a man like Begin, at heart a fanatic who would fight to the end to defend his cause, and for whom compromise was almost a dirty word. A master of language, with the ability of a lawyer to define the meaning of every word in a statement which he was expected to accept at face value,

Begin took Carter's measure very early on during the talks at Camp David. He had of course met him during meetings preliminary to Camp David, when he is reported as having expressed the opinion that Carter was soft – like a 'cream puff', according to one source.[5]

Sadat was a different story, although it did take a little time before he and Carter established a firm friendship. Sadat's personality particularly appealed to Americans. He was warm and outgoing, as are so many Americans; he had soon achieved a close rapport with Kissinger when Kissinger was Nixon's Secretary of State. Compared with so many of the Arab leaders with whom they had to deal, Sadat seemed to the Americans to be a model of common sense, open in conversation and willing to compromise. Talks with him at his house in Cairo beside the Nile Barrage, while the Egyptian President pulled thoughtfully at his pipe, were essentially civilised and down to earth. He believed, as did the Americans, that the key to peace in the Middle East was an agreement between Egypt and Israel. Once that had been achieved, the other Arab states would have to fall into line. Carter took at face value Sadat's assertion that he could easily deal with Hussein and the Saudis, perhaps also with Hafez Assad, an unfortunate and mistaken assumption since it led to the virtual exclusion of the other Arab states until after the Camp David Accords had been signed. This made it a foregone conclusion that any agreement reached at Camp David would not receive their imprimatur.

Begin and Sadat were poles apart. The same held true for Begin and Carter, to a large extent. Begin believed profoundly in Eretz Israel, which meant that his country's boundaries had long been established by Holy Writ. It was not for him, nor for anyone else, to take issue with what amounted to a sacred trust. Whereas Sadat professed to scorn detail, preferring the big picture and the large gesture, Begin subjected every comma to the minutest scrutiny. He was a complete master of his subject, steeped in the history of the Israelites and acutely conscious of the horrors of the Holocaust. Moreover, as the leader of a very fragile coalition government, Begin knew that anything he might agree at Camp David could easily be torn to shreds in the Knesset and lead to the downfall of the Likud government. Although always well mannered and courteous, Begin was a very tough negotiator.

Nor were matters helped when it became apparent early on at Camp David that Sadat and Begin were unable to negotiate face to face. There was between the two men a marked personal antipathy. This meant that the US President had to act as a go-between, conveying proposals from one side to the other, and often himself drafting proposed amendments to the documents under discussion. In retrospect the situation was a bizarre one. The most powerful man in the most powerful country in the world was acting the part of an honest broker between the leaders of two countries that were virtually American satellites, dependent almost entirely on American goodwill. Although this may have said a great deal for Carter's heart, it said less for his head. It meant that Carter was pledging his own political future on a successful outcome to the negotiations. So much of Carter's political capital had been invested in Camp David that he could scarcely have permitted the negotiations to fail, although there were times when they came perilously close to doing so.

This is not to suggest that Carter's motives were not of the highest. They certainly were. But he was like a man trying to guide two others through a minefield, neither of them entirely certain that he knew what he was doing. Begin at least had a fairly clear idea of the path, and he was not disposed to stray from it. Sadat, in order to ensure a safe passage, was willing to change direction, even if this meant abandoning strongly held convictions. One example of this was his virtual abandonment of anything that could be done for the Palestinians, in order to obtain the return of Sinai to Egypt. Begin, on the other hand, gave up nothing. He made no written commitment regarding the halting of settlements on the West Bank, and it is virtually certain that he never had any intention of withdrawing from the West Bank, which he regarded as historically part of the State of Israel. He was equally inflexible over Jerusalem. 'I personally felt his vision of Israel's place in the Middle East was profoundly flawed,' writes William Quandt, 'anchored more in the past than directed to the future.'[6] Flawed or not, Begin came away from Camp David with almost all of his aims achieved, whereas Sadat had thrown away nearly all his cards in order to get back Sinai.

It is easy to understand why in the end Sadat, Begin and Carter reached agreement at Camp David. No one wanted to be held responsible for failure by the rest of the world. Nevertheless Carter, despite his suspicion of Begin's motives, was prepared to take on trust oral statements that were not backed up subsequently in writing. He also accepted Sadat's assurance that he could deal with Hussein and the Saudis, although he knew that Hussein had considerable reservations about Sadat, as indeed Sadat had about Hussein. Carter should have known through his ambassadors that Sadat was not held in as high regard in Amman, Baghdad, Damascus and Riyadh as he was in Washington DC. He was considered to be something of a mountebank, and was disliked for his growing arrogance.

Hussein first met Carter in Washington on 25 April 1977, when the Americans were preparing the groundwork for what turned out to be the meeting at Camp David eighteen months later. Hussein made it perfectly clear that any participation by Jordan in negotiations with Israel was dependent on the return of the West Bank and East Jerusalem. Were Israel to agree to a withdrawal, it was perfectly possible that the West Bank could be placed under international control for a period, in order to allow the Palestinian people to determine their future government. Hussein told Carter that the US should take the lead in sounding out the various interested parties, but the time would come when the US should make certain concrete proposals. He warned against reconvening another conference at Geneva without first agreeing a plan for the settlement of the problem, since in Hussein's view failure to do this could lead to disaster. He was to repeat this in an interview with the *New York Times* on 27 April. Hussein had also emphasised the importance of including the PLO in any discussions, leading Carter to comment that he feared the PLO might adopt a pro-Soviet line.

There were of course further interchanges at official level between Amman and Washington. In addition, Carter met Hussein again in Teheran on New Year's Day 1978, when Hussein continued to be noncommittal. Sadat had by then made his famous journey to Jerusalem on 19 November 1977, which if anything increased Hussein's doubts concerning his motives. He was equally distrustful of Begin, almost as unknown a quantity to the Jordanians as he was to the Americans. Hussein had already met Moshe Dayan in London on 22 August, when he had made it perfectly clear that he would abide by the Rabat decision, which meant that the PLO had to be included in any discussion about the future of the West Bank. Moreover, he refused to accept any kind of division of the West Bank between Jordan and Israel. He insisted on Israeli withdrawal from *all* occupied territory, including East Jerusalem. Hussein could hardly have made his position more clear, either to Carter or to the Israelis.

The truth was that Carter and Hussein were on different tracks. Hussein could not accept a peace that ignored the legitimate aspirations of the Palestinians. Nor was he prepared to sidetrack the PLO in order to get back the West Bank; he knew this would result in disaster. Carter, on the other hand, as he became increasingly involved in the labyrinthine negotiations with Sadat and Begin, soon began to change his aims. The object of the exercise was no longer to resolve the problem of the Palestinians, but instead to achieve a peace treaty between Egypt and Israel. This certainly suited Begin, and as time went on it seemed that it would suit Sadat as well. It was a change of emphasis, however unstated, that Hussein could neither agree to nor condone.

That Camp David was an achievement cannot be denied, however flawed in Arab eyes it may be today. It owed almost everything to President Carter, who demonstrated what can be achieved by an American president if he is prepared to devote much time to preparing the ground, and then to overseeing the negotiations in the role of honest broker. In Carter's case, however, it lost him support in the USA, and not only among the Jewish community. Many people felt he was devoting far too much of his time to the Middle East to the exclusion of important issues nearer to home. He was also accused of being pro-Arab.

Carter has himself admitted that his most serious mistake at Camp David was his failure to get clarified in writing 'Begin's promise concerning the settlement freeze during the subsequent peace talks'.[7] He also regrets that neither he nor Sadat kept Hussein informed of the progress of the talks until too late, by which time Hussein had decided to join the majority of the Arab states in condemning the Accords. This failure is all the more surprising since Carter has written: 'Of all the countries in the Middle East, only Lebanon shares with Jordan such a deep concern about present circumstances, and Hussein probably worries more than any other leader about how his nation's own interests might be adversely affected by changes yet to come.'[8]

It was a major achievement on Begin's part to get so much by giving away so little. By neutralising Egypt with the signature of a peace treaty, Begin had made it almost impossible for the Arab states to go to war with Israel, since a war without Egypt was hardly conceivable. It also protected Israel's rear in the event of a war with either Lebanon or Syria. In return for this handsome bonus he had agreed to return Sinai to Egypt, and also to remove Israeli settlements from Sinai. He had lost the Sinai oilfields but had gained passage for Israeli vessels through the Suez Canal; and he had not budged an inch over Jerusalem, declaring in a letter to Carter (as we have noted), 'the government of Israel decreed in July 1967 that Jerusalem is one city indivisible, the Capital of the State of Israel.' He had also avoided committing Israel to withdrawal from the Occupied Territories of the West Bank and Gaza, other than in the most general terms. He had in fact no intention of abiding by them, and even if he had, it is most unlikely that the Knesset would have agreed.

There was, however, a wide gulf separating the signing of the Accords at Camp David and the conclusion of a peace treaty between Egypt and Israel. Begin was bitterly criticised by some of his supporters for conceding as much as he had done; Ariel Sharon was one of the most vociferous of his critics. Sadat was abused even more savagely throughout the Arab world. It looked at one stage as if the conclusion of a peace treaty would be indefinitely delayed. Then early in 1979 the revolution in Iran toppled the Shah, and US foreign policy in Iran became a mockery. The Middle East was shaken to its foundations, and it was judged all-important for the Carter administration that there should be success with Egypt and Israel. Begin, as might have been expected, was stubborn. Sadat was more accommodating. Carter concluded that Sadat was willing to let the West Bank go down the chute provided he could get something in Gaza.

There were tough negotiations with Begin in Washington, and in March 1979 Carter went to Egypt and Israel to try a little arm-twisting – without much success in Begin's case. By 13 March it seemed that the negotiations had reached an impasse; then Begin suddenly told Carter he was prepared to put the amended proposals for a peace treaty to the Knesset, provided Sadat agreed to an exchange of ambassadors. Carter flew immediately to Cairo, to be met at the airport by Sadat, who was willing to agree to almost anything in order to get a peace treaty, despite the views of his advisers, who were much less amenable. Having obtained Sadat's agreement, and after passing the news to Begin, Carter flew back to Washington. It had been quite a day, beginning in Jerusalem, then taking in Cairo, and ending with a triumphal welcome in Washington.

The Peace Treaty, on which Carter had set his heart, was signed by Begin and Sadat in Washington on 26 March 1979. Sadat was gunned down two and a half years later, while celebrating the anniversary of the 1973 war; Begin, having sent Israel's army into Lebanon on the ill-named Operation Peace in Galilee, resigned his office in October 1983, and retired into virtual seclusion; and Jimmy Carter was rejected by the American people in 1980, when he ran for a second term. It cannot be said that any of the three principals at Camp David derived any long-term personal benefit from all their efforts.

Nor in the long run have the Egyptians, the Israelis and the Palestinians done so. Egypt, the most powerful Arab country, was excluded from Arab deliberations for several vital years. Israel, freed from the danger of Egyptian attack, embarked on her disastrous foray in Lebanon. The Palestinians, meanwhile, have seen nothing of the autonomy on the West Bank which they were promised, but have instead had to witness the creation of many more Israeli settlements in the Occupied Territories, and have also been subjected to more and more Israeli military rule. However, for as long as American history is written, Camp David and the Egypt–Israel Peace Treaty will remain the highwater mark of Jimmy Carter's presidency.

Hussein, who had from the outset regarded the Carter initiative with more than a little scepticism, was careful to remain on the sidelines. When the President's National Security Adviser, Zbigniew Brzezinski, visited Amman with a high-level team to brief Hussein on the Peace Treaty, he arrived late and left early. Hussein was neither amused nor impressed. An extremely courteous man himself, it was the kind of gaucherie least calculated to win him over. Sadat's assertion that, once Egypt had concluded a peace treaty with Israel, the rest of the Arab world would follow suit proved wrong. There could be no peace treaty between the Arabs and Israel without agreement over the Occupied Territories and the rights of the

Palestinians. The Camp David Accords, where Jordan is concerned, have come to be regarded as a non-event.

The year 1977, which saw Hussein deeply involved in the complex negotiations that led eventually to Camp David, was also one which brought him a deep personal loss in the death of Queen Alia. She had been visiting a hospital at Tafila in the south of Jordan, and with her was the Minister of Health. It was 9 February, Jordan's winter, when the weather can change dramatically in a very short space of time. It was the late afternoon when they left to return to Amman in a helicopter piloted by Captain Badr Zaza, the King's personal pilot, who had flown him on many dangerous missions. He was the air force's most experienced and skilled helicopter pilot, as well as being the King's personal ADC and a close friend. They were accompanied by a second helicopter, acting as escort.

They were within five to ten miles of Amman when the helicopter suddenly vanished from the radar screen. The weather had closed in and there may have been a 'white-out', when the pilot's instruments fail to provide a true picture of height and direction. The terrain was hilly, but not unduly so, but for whatever reason Captain Zaza failed to estimate his height and crashed, killing himself and his passengers. Helicopters are notoriously difficult to fly when weather conditions interfere with the pilot's visibility, and it has to be assumed that this is what happened.

Hussein was devastated when he heard the news. His marriage to Alia had been a particularly happy and successful one; he was devoted to her. The public duties of the King in a country as small and as demanding as Jordan are never-ending and unceasing. Alia had helped Hussein to endure this burden by providing him with a happy home. She had also played her full part in the life of the nation, which was plunged into mourning by the news of her death.

For a time Hussein withdrew into a kind of monastic seclusion, profoundly depressed. His advisers were gravely concerned by his withdrawn manner and haggard appearance. He had lost his sparkle, seemed to be plunged into melancholy, and rarely smiled. Even his children, to whom he was devoted, failed to comfort him. He carried out his public duties of course – he would not have been Hussein if he had not – but without much enthusiasm. Much of his time was spent designing a tomb that would be worthy of the woman he had loved.

'His Majesty was completely shattered,' according to a friend and admirer. 'He withdrew into himself and for a time he seemed to have lost all interest in life. This became very worrying since there was a great deal happening all around us at the time. We did our best to cheer him but without any success until fortunately he met Queen Noor and fell in love with her. It was a great relief.'[9]

Hussein first met the young American architect Lisa Halaby when he was attending a ceremony to mark the arrival of the first jumbo jet to join Air Alia (now the Royal Jordanian Airline). This airline owed a great deal to Hussein's keen personal interest and initiative, ever since he had appointed Ali Gandour, an aeronautical engineer who had been Vice-President of Lebanon International Airways, to transform Jordan's ageing fleet of aircraft into a modern airline, able to compete with any other airline in the world. The project was first launched on 8 December 1963 by the purchase of one DC-7, financed by private subscription; there were many teething problems, all of which were overcome by Gandour's genius and the King's steady support. In the aftermath of the June 1967 war, when the tourist trade drastically declined, the state took over the airline and there has been a steady expansion ever since.

Among those presented to Hussein during the ceremony was a very striking young American woman, whose father, Najeeb H. Halaby, had filled many important government appointments in the United States; he had been at one time President of Pan Am. He was of Syrian origin. His wife was Swedish. Their eldest daughter, Lisa, was tall, blonde and very attractive. Aged twenty-six, she had studied architecture and urban planning at Princeton University, before arriving in Jordan in 1976 to work on a master plan for the creation of an Arab Air University. Her university days had coincided with the upsurge in student demonstrations as a result of the Viet Nam war; she was therefore no stranger to campus unrest. Widely travelled, with a mind of her own, Lisa Halaby was proud of her Arab ancestry, although in every other way she might have seemed typical of a young American woman of her background and education.

The King was at once attracted by her. Soon they were dining together almost every night. They fell in love and Hussein proposed marriage. She says she thought hard and long before accepting. She did not doubt their love for each other, but she wondered whether she was 'the wife he needed'. She hoped she could contribute to Jordan's future development, but realised there might be problems ahead. Hussein had already been married three times, and there were eight children, some of them almost grown up, others quite young. Alia had been a popular queen, with the advantage of having been born a Jordanian, whereas Lisa Halaby had been born an American citizen, her Arab blood notwithstanding; and the United States has taken the place of Britain as the whipping-boy of the Arab world. Individual Americans are welcomed gladly enough, but US policy in the Middle East is criticised as bitterly today as once British policy was. Although Arabs are remarkably free from the race and colour consciousness that has caused so much trouble in some other parts of the world, they are politically minded to an intense degree, which in extreme instances leads to xenophobia, and they are also great gossips. There is no more satisfying way of passing the time while sipping coffee in a café than discussing the misdemeanours of one's superiors and passing judgement on them, whether well founded or otherwise. Whatever goes on in 'the Palace', true or surmised, is an immediate subject for discussion.

The extended family is also part and parcel of Arab life. In the case of King Hussein it covers not only his immediate Hashemite family but the Jordanian family as a whole. Most look to him as the head of this extended family and there can be few families in which no discord of any kind is to be found. Wherever this may have existed, Hussein's Queen would have to walk delicately. After their marriage Hussein named her Lisa Noor Al-Hussein (Light of Hussein) and during their honeymoon in Aqaba all the children from Hussein's previous marriages were invited to share in their happiness. Queen Noor says she found no difficulty in adjusting to her new role. She had after all spent some time in Jordan and was intensely interested in the country and the people. She was determined to identify herself completely not only with her new country, but with her new extended family, and no one could have worked harder to make a success of this. She has been converted to Islam, has studied Arabic and continues to play an ever increasing part in public life.[10]

She has been encouraged in all this by the support she has received from her husband. Compared with America, Jordan is still very much a man's world, although women are now playing an increasing part in the life of the nation. Nonetheless, even in a country as progressively minded as Jordan, politics are still largely reserved for men, the more so in view of the fact that the King is no figurehead head of state but the actual ruler of the country. Consequently, Queen Noor confines her activities while in Jordan to projects intended to improve the quality of life of the ordinary Jordanian, based on the Noor Al-Hussein Foundation created by Royal Decree in September 1984.

She is an excellent public speaker and has been entrusted with several important missions in the United States and Britain, addressing audiences at Harvard, Georgetown University and Oxford University, and elsewhere, on the many problems facing Jordan in the complicated world of the Middle East.

Queen Noor is not only very attractive and charming; she also has her husband's gift of conveying the impression that whoever she happens to be talking with is the one person she really wants to meet. Deeply concerned with Jordan's historic traditions, she has at the same time devoted herself to giving Jordan a modern image in both a social and a cultural sense. The Royal Endowment for Culture and Education which she founded in 1980 is intended to assess Jordan's development needs in the fields of higher education, culture and the arts, and then to help meet those needs in a creative fashion. Prominent among Queen Noor's cultural activities has been the promotion of the Jerash Festival of Culture and Arts when annually there is held in the ancient Roman amphitheatre a festival at which Jordanian, Arab and international performing artists can interact and exchange ideas in an appropriate atmosphere. The Queen has also been instrumental in establishing a Music Conservatory to provide musically gifted Jordanian children with the opportunity to develop their artistic talents. Another project close to her heart has been the founding of the Jubilee School, intended to be an independent three-year coeducational secondary boarding school for 600 gifted young Jordanian scholarship students from all sections of society.

Queen Noor's interests range over a multiplicity of projects, by no means all of them concerned solely with culture and education. She is interested in child care, community development and the integration of women in the natural development of Jordan. All this is being achieved in a sensible and unobtrusive fashion without giving rise to opposition among a cautiously conservative and traditionally minded people. For those old enough to remember King Abdullah's times, progress has been truly remarkable. But for all the changes that have been made, and for all the advances that have been achieved, Jordanian society still remains strongly traditional in its attitudes. Girls are still expected to be modest in behaviour, however well educated, and sons are still expected to respect their fathers and mothers. How much longer this can be expected to continue is anyone's guess, but while it does it provides Jordan with a kind of social cohesion that should be the envy of many Western societies. Queen Noor, in her own way, exemplifies this attachment to the old values while at the same time acknowledging the need for change wherever necessary. It is a rare combination.

She manages to combine the refreshing frankness of an American with the innate dignity and respect for tradition of the Arab. She is also a devoted mother, having borne King Hussein two sons and two daughters – Princes Hamzah and Hashim born in 1980 and 1981, and Princesses Iman and Raiyah born in 1983 and 1986. She has also taken under her wing as mother Queen Alia's two children, Princess Haya and Prince Ali, and Queen Alia's adopted daughter, Abir Muheisen.

CHAPTER EIGHTEEN

Journey Up a Blind Alley

'Arafat is remarkably resilient and represents a necessary compromise and will continue to have the greatest influence on PLO policy for the foreseeable future.' President Carter[1]

'Arafat just cannot deliver.' Marwan Kasim[2]

When Prime Minister Menachem Begin sent the Israeli army into Lebanon on 6 June 1982, with the stated intention of destroying the PLO's military infrastructure in that unhappy country, he presented to the outside world a totally new image of Israel: no longer a David, surrounded by brutal Goliaths, but just another aggressor nation engaged in power politics by the use of the sword. This image was enhanced on 15 September by the massacre in the Shabra and Chatilla refugee camps of Palestinian civilians by Maronite thugs, while the Israeli army stood idly by. By then, however, the PLO had evacuated Beirut. This had taken place at the end of August, as a result of American and Saudi mediation and pressure, without however the PLO conceding defeat. The PLO were dispersed to those Arab countries which had agreed to accept them, Arafat himself moving part of his headquarters to Tunis. Hussein, who admits that he is baffled by the situation in Lebanon, did not intervene in the unhappy struggle; nor for that matter did any other Arab country, apart from Syria. But Hussein did accept that a contingent of the PLA should be stationed in Jordan, where it still remains.

On 1 September, the day after the PLO's departure from Beirut, the US President, Ronald Reagan, made a fresh attempt to initiate peace negotiations between the Arabs and Israel. 'The successful completion of Israel's withdrawal from Sinai,' he said, 'and the courage shown on this occasion by Prime Minister Begin and President Mubarak [Sadat's successor] in living up to their agreements, convinced us the time had come for a new American policy to try to bridge the remaining differences between Egypt and Israel on the autonomy process.' The President said this had been interrupted by events in Lebanon, but the opportunity had now come 'to resolve the root causes of conflict between the Arabs and Israelis'.

He said that recent events in Lebanon had shown that the military losses sustained by the PLO had not lessened the Palestinian yearning for a just solution of the claims of their people. Israel's successes in the Peace for Galilee military operation had on the other hand shown that overwhelming military superiority could not by itself bring 'just and lasting peace to Israel and her neighbours'. He called on Israel to recognise that she could achieve security only through genuine peace; and he called on the Arab states 'to accept the reality of Israel, and the reality that peace and justice are to be gained only through hard, fair and direct negotiation'.

The President said the time had come to move further in accordance with the Camp David Accords. This meant that over a period of time – he mentioned five years – the inhabitants of the West Bank and Gaza should have full autonomy over their own affairs. He explained that the purpose of the five-year period, which would begin after free elections for a self-governing Palestinian authority, was 'to prove to the Palestinians that they can run their own affairs, and that such Palestinian autonomy poses no threat to Israel's security'. He said that during the transition period the United States would not support the creation of any more Israeli settlements on the West Bank, adding that a freeze on such settlements would be more conducive to the creation of confidence than anything else Israel could do. At the same time he made it clear that the transfer of domestic authority to the Palestinians should not interfere with Israel's security requirements; nor would the United States agree to the creation of an independent Palestinian state. A compromise on this must be found. Possibly the best solution would be an association of the self-governing West Bank and Gaza with Jordan, as King Hussein had proposed more than a decade previously. The President concluded: 'It is the United States' position that, in return for peace, the withdrawal provision of Resolution 242 applies to all fronts including the West Bank and Gaza. . . . Finally, we remain convinced that Jerusalem must remain undivided, but its final status should be decided through negotiations.'

Hussein warmly welcomed Reagan's entry into the Middle Eastern arena, from which the King had felt himself excluded by President Jimmy Carter. The Reagan initiative may have been no more than a restatement of old principles, but it was at least an honest attempt to reopen the dialogue. Hussein therefore gave the Reagan Plan his cautious support. The PLO did likewise. However, the mere mention of Israeli settlements on the West Bank was sufficient to ensure an immediate rejection by Begin's government, which continued to press ahead with its settlement policy.

With Israel's rejection of the Reagan Plan, it was stillborn from the start, which no doubt accounts for the Americans' apparent reluctance to press forward with it. Within a week of the President's speech, however, there was an Arab summit meeting at Fez on 9 September 1982. There the Arab countries took the historic decision to give *de facto* recognition to Israel's pre-June 1967 boundaries. They also agreed the so-called Fahd Plan, proposed by King Fahd of Saudi Arabia and President Bourguiba of Tunisia. This contained the following principles:

1. Israel's withdrawal from all Arab territories occupied in 1967, including Arab Al-Qods (Jerusalem).
2. The dismantling of Israeli settlements on Arab territories.
3. Guarantee of freedom of worship and practice of religious rites for all religions in the holy shrines.
4. The reaffirmation of the Palestinian people's right to self-determination and the exercise of its imprescriptible and inalienable national rights under the leadership of the Palestinian Liberation Organisation, its sole and legitimate representative, and the indemnification of all those who do not want to return.
5. Placing the West Bank and Gaza Strip under the control of the United Nations for a transitory period not exceeding a few months.
6. The establishment of an independent Palestinian state with Al Qods as its capital.
7. The Security Council guarantees peace among all states in the region including the independent Palestinian state.
8. The Security Council guarantees the respect of these principles.

The Fahd Plan was certainly comprehensive, if perhaps a trifle ambitious. It was nevertheless a marked advance on the Three No's of the Khartoum Summit held in 1967. However, it differed considerably from the Reagan Plan, which Hussein believed was worth following up, particularly since Reagan had recognised that it was the Palestinians who were the root cause of the troubles in the Middle East. The trouble was that both the Reagan and Fahd Plans had been announced at a time when the PLO were at their lowest ebb; Hussein was convinced that Israel would take advantage of this to declare that the PLO were too weak and too divided to participate in any peace negotiations. He therefore decided to thwart any such move by publicly reaffirming his own support for the PLO. He did this by sending two of his ministers to meet Arafat in Athens, in order to acquaint Arafat personally with Jordan's support.

Hussein felt the time had come for the reopening of a dialogue between himself and Arafat; but this was not helped by an open split in the PLO between those who supported and those who rejected the Reagan Plan. At a meeting in Algiers in February 1983, a majority in the Palestinian National Congress favoured letting Arafat see what could be done in co-operation with Hussein. However, the left wing called for rejection, which Arafat, anxious to avoid a split, regarded as decisive. There was at the time a danger that Fatah might split, encouraged by President Hafez Assad, who warned the PLO that he would close the Syrian border to them if they accepted the Reagan Plan; at the same time he was organising a PLO more amenable to his wishes. Moreover, the PLO executive committee meeting in Kuweit rejected an agreement worked out between Hussein and Arafat which defined their joint political moves within an Arab framework. This was a great disappointment to Hussein, and presumably also to Arafat; but in any case for him the struggle to retain the cohesion of Fatah took precedence over everything else.

In an official communiqué issued in Amman after the collapse of the Hussein–Arafat talks, it was made plain that Jordan recognised the PLO as 'the sole legitimate representative of the Palestinian people'. Accordingly, Jordan left it to the PLO and the Palestinians to 'choose the ways and means for salvaging themselves and their land . . .'. For its part, Jordan refused to negotiate on behalf of the Palestinians. It was an end to what had at one time seemed to offer a chance of bringing about hopeful negotiations. It had been wrecked by Syria. Hafez Assad's feud with Arafat was largely responsible for this. It culminated towards the end of 1983 in an armed clash at Tripoli in northern Lebanon that resulted in the expulsion of Arafat and his followers. This further emphasised the rift within the PLO. Meanwhile, the Israelis, in flagrant disregard of the Reagan Plan, continued with their settlement plan on the West Bank, which cast even more doubt on the American will to see it through. It was the President's credibility test, according to Khalad Hassan of the PLO, and the President failed it. If the USA, with all its power, was unable to put pressure on Israel to desist from action which the President had already condemned, then his plan for resolving the Arab–Israeli dispute was not worth the paper it was written on. Many Americans felt the same way, with the inevitable consequence that the Reagan Plan was allowed quietly to wither on the bough, while attention in Washington was switched to Central America and the Contras.

Hussein had scarcely concluded the latest of his long-continuing but frustrating dialogues with Arafat than he was plunged into preparations for the state visit to Jordan in March 1984 of Queen Elizabeth and the Duke of Edinburgh. This had been on the tapis for almost twenty years, ever since King Hussein's and Princess Muna's highly successful state visit to Britain; but the political situation in Jordan had never permitted it until now. As it was, it led to controversy in Britain, the London *Times* writing on 26 March 1984, 'no one, and certainly not a head of state, can touch any point in the Arab–Israel conflict without getting involved in some degree of controversy.' This is undoubtedly true, and it has to be remembered that Queen Elizabeth numbers many loyal Jews among her subjects. There was also concern for the Queen's personal safety, not helped by an explosion in the Amman Inter-Continental Hotel car park only two days before the Queen was due to arrive. There were clamours for the visit's cancellation, but the Queen would not hear of it, and as it happened the visit passed off successfully. It was unfortunate that a super-sensitive BBC directional microphone picked up the comments made by the two queens when an Israeli fighter boomed overhead while they were visiting the Jordan Valley. Queen Noor said it was 'appalling', and Queen Elizabeth said 'frightening', which needless to say was made much of in the Israeli newspapers.

Nineteen-eighty-four was also the year when Hussein recalled parliament, which had not met for ten years. This resulted in some ribald comment in the world press, some of the deputies attending having perceptibly aged in the interval. There was, however, a legal requirement to recall parliament before the legal quorum of forty deputies had disappeared for ever. Thirteen members attended from the West Bank, among them Edward Khamis from Bethlehem, who, at fifty-one, was one of the youngest to attend. 'I have as much right to speak for the West Bank as the Palestine Liberation Organisation,' he said, 'because I have lived there for nearly seventeen years of Israeli occupation. I feel there must be negotiations with Israel very soon. That is what most of us on the West Bank feel now, although we know that Israel is not prepared to give anything away.'[3]

Hussein of course shared the feelings of most of the rest of the Arab world over Egypt's peace treaty with Israel, but as a dedicated supporter of Arab unity he felt it was a mistake for Egypt, the most powerful Arab state, to be excluded indefinitely from Arab counsels. He also considered, with the Great Arab Revolt in mind, that it was wrong nearly seventy years after that great event that the Arabs should continue to quarrel among themselves. He thought it had been courageous of President Hosni Mubarak to receive Arafat in Cairo in December 1983 after the Tripoli débâcle, as indeed it had been for Arafat to accept. Quietly, therefore, and with the minimum of publicity, Hussein set about mending his fences with Egypt. This culminated in September 1984 when, in a speech from the throne, Hussein announced his intention of flying to Cairo to meet Mubarak and re-establish relations between Jordan and Egypt. It took all but his closest counsellors by surprise.

In November 1984, thirteen years after Hussein had driven the PLO out of Jordan, the Palestine National Congress (PNC) met in Amman at Arafat's request. Hussein opened its seventeenth session with a speech in which he urged the need to get away from the 'no peace, no war' status quo of the past years. 'The international position at large is one that perceives the possibility of restoring the Occupied Territories through a Jordanian–Palestinian formula,' he told them. 'This requires commitments from both parties which the world deems necessary for the achievement of a just, balanced and peaceful settlement.' If the PLO wanted to pursue a joint initiative, then Jordan would marshal support for it. If on the other hand they believed the PLO were capable of going it alone, then, said the King: 'Godspeed, you have our support. In the final analysis, the decision is yours.'

Hussein made plain the importance of Resolution 242 in providing a framework within which negotiations would be carried out. He hoped an international conference would be convened under the auspices of the United Nations, attended by all the interested parties, including the five permanent members of the Security Council, and also the PLO on an equal footing with the rest. Delegates from the West Bank who attended were hopeful that a working relationship between Jordan and the PLO could be achieved. 'For once our hopes were high,' said one of them. The PNC meeting was considered to be a success, despite a boycott by the more extreme elements, and hopes continued to be high in January 1985 when Hussein was told that the Executive Council of the PLO would work together with Jordan for joint political action. After so many years of accusation and counter-accusation, it seemed at last that the Jordan–PLO quarrel would be ended.

Arafat came to Amman in February 1985 for talks which ended in the signing of what has since come to be known as the 11 February Accord. It set out the principles that would govern a joint Jordanian–PLO negotiation with Israel, declaring that the peace negotiations would be carried out under the auspices of an international conference. All the other principles were there; total withdrawal from the Occupied Territories in return for peace; right of self-determination for the Palestinian people; resolution of the refugee problem in accordance with UN resolutions; and finally, and perhaps rather ambitiously, 'Resolution of the Palestinian question in all its aspects'. One Jordanian has commented that the feeling after the signing of the Accord was euphoric, adding, 'We had of course heard it all before; it all depended on whether Arafat could deliver or not, which I personally thought unlikely.'[4]

The euphoria notwithstanding, Hussein knew well enough that there would be difficulty in obtaining international agreement for the PLO to attend the conference in their own right. It was not only the Israelis who regarded the PLO as a gang of terrorists. One British comment was that 'they are just the same as the IRA'. People forgot the wretchedness of the refugee camps and remembered only the bombings and the hijackings; or that both Begin and Yitzhak Shamir had been terrorists long before they became transformed into respectable politicians. The PLO had created a reputation for itself that was to prove to be a major hurdle, but Hussein was undaunted. He embarked on an intensive campaign to explain his Accord with the PLO, and to win acceptance for the PLO's attendance at the international conference, which he was convinced must take place.

He found a valuable ally in Prime Minister Margaret Thatcher, who visited Jordan in September 1985. She met a great many people and visited the Baqa'a refugee camp outside Amman, where she saw for herself the conditions under which people were living. She admired the King for his courage and moderation, as indeed he admired her for her courage and determination.[5] It was while she was in Aqaba that Mrs Thatcher took the brave decision to invite a joint Jordanian–PLO delegation to London for discussions under the aegis of the British Foreign Secretary, Sir Geoffrey Howe. There was inevitably a storm of protest from British Jewry, as there would be from Ulster Unionists were Mrs Thatcher to invite a joint delegation of the Republic of Ireland and Sinn Fein to discussions in London. The speculation was that Mrs Thatcher had been persuaded by King Hussein that the time had come to take 'a risk for peace'. The formalities were left to be worked out between Geoffrey Howe and Jordan's Prime Minister, Zeid Rifai.

It all went lamentably wrong, as so often happens when the problem of the Palestinians comes up for discussion. A series of terrorist incidents, whether deliberately planned or not, highlighted the PLO's adoption of terror as a policy. Three Israelis, reputed to be members of Mossad (the Israeli security service) were murdered in Cyprus. This was followed by the hijacking of the Italian cruise liner *Achille Lauro*, in the course of which an elderly American tourist confined to a wheelchair was murdered. In between, the IAF had bombed the PLO headquarters in Tunis in reprisal for the murders in Cyprus. Finally, the Americans intercepted the Egyptian plane carrying the *Achille Lauro* hijackers to Tunis and forced it to land in Sicily. As a final twist, the two PLO delegates, Muhammad Milhem, who stood high in the PLO's counsels, and Bishop Elias Khouri, found it impossible to endorse a statement which included the words, 'as well as the right to secure existence of all the states within the area, including Israel within its 1967 borders'.

It had been assumed that this announcement had been drawn up with PLO agreement by Prime Minister Zeid Rifai, whose deputy, Abdul Wahab al-Majali, and Jordan's Foreign Minister, Taher al-Masri, formed the Jordanian half of the joint delegation; London was therefore outraged. It was thought at the time that Milhem, who is no extremist, had been concerned by the series of terrorist actions which had taken place so recently, but he insisted that he had not seen the proposed announcement until after his arrival in London; he had been in New York when the document was drafted in Amman. He said that as a Palestinian he was perfectly willing to accept the right of all states to live in peace behind secure borders, but that it would be different for him to recognise Israel's pre-1967 borders, since this implied a recognition of Israel's 'right to exist'. The meeting was cancelled at twenty-four hours' notice and there was uproar in British political circles. The Labour Party shadow Foreign Secretary, Denis Healey, described it as 'an appalling diplomatic shambles'. Mrs Thatcher was equally annoyed. 'We came so close to what might have been a really fruitful meeting,'[6] she said later. But she deserves full credit for agreeing to the meeting in the first place. It is one of the few instances when a really honest attempt has been made to shift the logjam.

This was not the only setback. The Jordanian–PLO Accord had run into trouble with the superpowers. The Soviet Union insisted that only the superpowers should attend the international conference, not the permanent members of the Security Council. It also objected to the proposed Palestinian representation. The US was similarly cool. It did not favour the proposal of an international conference, and was even less keen on PLO representation. Discussions with the Americans were additionally complicated by the fact that Hussein was also negotiating for a substantial arms deal, although he made it plain that the discussions were in no way linked. Nevertheless, anyone less determined than he is would probably have abandoned the attempt to sell the Accord as a non-starter in the face of Soviet and American opposition. In the interests of Arab unity, and of peace, Hussein however pressed on.

Intensive talks followed between Jordan and the PLO to agree the approach to be made to the Americans in order to soften their attitude. They agreed that Jordan should ask the US to receive a joint Jordanian–Palestinian delegation. After this meeting had taken place, the PLO would declare its acceptance of Security Council Resolutions 242 and 338. This would allow the US to recognise the PLO, having previously stated this would not be done until the PLO had accepted the Resolutions. Having removed this major obstacle, joint talks could then take place with the US for the convening of an international conference to discuss peace in the Middle East.

Formal proposals to this effect were made by Jordan to the US in March 1985, the American reply being received in April. The proposal was accepted in principle, provided the Palestinian members of the joint delegation were not leading members of the PLO or of any guerrilla organisation. After consultation, the names of three Palestinians were sent to Washington. They were turned down because they did not meet the American criteria. When this was discussed with Secretary of State George Shultz in Aqaba in May, he said he did not exclude members of the PNC but was adamant on the subject of the PLO. The Americans had no faith in the good intentions of the PLO. They thought it at least possible, if not probable, that the PLO, having succeeded in persuading the US government to receive a joint Jordanian–Palestinian delegation, would then renege on their part of the bargain to accept Resolutions 242 and 338. They would have secured thereby a considerable political gain at the expense of the US, subjecting the Reagan administration to domestic criticism and political difficulties. This is only another example of the extent of the distrust the PLO has managed to create.

Shultz's comments were conveyed to Arafat by Zeid Rifai on 19 May. It was then agreed that Hussein, who was due to visit Washington shortly, should make a statement already agreed between Jordan and the PLO. Accordingly on 29 May, in the White House Rose Garden, Hussein told the assembled newsmen: 'I have also assured the President that on the basis of the Jordan–PLO Accord of 11 February, and in view of our genuine desire for peace, we are willing to negotiate, within the context of an international conference, a peaceful settlement on the basis of the pertinent United Nations Resolutions, including Security Council Resolutions 242 and 338.'

The American view on the composition of the joint delegation was made clear to Hussein during his stay in Washington. The Palestinians were to be limited to four, two from the Occupied Territories and two from outside. The names were to be forwarded as soon as possible. This was communicated to the PLO on Hussein's return to Amman in June. The PLO accepted the American conditions. However, no list of names was received from the PLO until 11 July, when seven names which had been discussed and agreed by the PLO and Fatah were received in Amman. These were sent to Washington on 12 July and were presumably fed into the CIA computer. Hussein had originally agreed in Washington that there would be no public announcement at this stage but the names were public knowledge within a few days. There was an instant political reaction in the US, for the most part hostile to the administration. The end result was agreement on only two of the seven names, one from the West Bank and the other from the Gaza Strip. The Americans at the same time reiterated their suspicion that the PLO would not announce publicly their acceptance of Resolutions 242 and 338.

Zeid Rifai held a meeting in the Prime Minister's residence in Amman on 15 August 1985. He was accompanied by the Chief of the Royal Court (Marwan Kasim), the Minister of Court (Adnan abu Odeh), and the Foreign Minister (Taher al-Masri). The Palestinian delegation consisted of Yasser Arafat, Khalil al-Wazir, Abdul Razzaq al-Yahya and Muhammad Milhem. Zeid Rifai again made plain the agreement reached under the Jordanian–Palestinian Accord and asked Arafat whether he was ready to proceed with the acceptance of Resolutions 242 and 338. Arafat at once indicated his willingness. The Americans were then informed and were formally asked for a date for the joint meeting between American and Jordanian–Palestinian officials. The US reply received on 7 September was to the effect that it would *not* be possible to hold the meeting.

This came as a great disappointment. Hussein, who was due to visit the US to attend the celebrations to mark the fortieth anniversary of the UN, decided to keep the dialogue going by concentrating this time on the issue of an international peace conference. The Americans had turned this proposal down flat when it had been raised in May; they had proposed instead that, after the PLO had been brought into the peace talks, there should be a meeting held in an American city which would be attended by both Israel and a joint Jordanian–Palestinian delegation, under the auspices of the US government. On receiving this proposal, Hussein had promptly cancelled his visit and said he would return home. He was having nothing to do with bilateral negotiations with Israel and it was ridiculous of the Americans to imagine that he would.

The Americans then changed their tune and suggested that the talks should be held under UN auspices in Geneva. Hussein repeated his objection to bilateral negotiations and said he was unconcerned where the talks were held. What mattered to him was that there should be a comprehensive international conference attended by all parties to the conflict, together with the five permanent members of the Security Council, which included the Soviet Union and the US. The Americans had promised to reconsider. The matter came up again in October 1985 with an American proposal which Hussein at once rejected since it seemed to suggest a conference in name only. Hussein insisted that the conference should have clear powers. He also rejected the American suggestion that the Soviet Union should be invited only after it had resumed diplomatic relations with Israel; this was an Israeli condition, faithfully rubber-stamped by the US.

Hussein pointed out that an international conference held without Soviet participation must be flawed. If the reason for the Soviet Union's exclusion was because it had no diplomatic relations with Israel, the same argument should apply to the US, which did not recognise the PLO. He felt he hardly needed to point out to the State Department the absurdity of holding an international conference that excluded both the superpowers. It would be equally absurd to plan an international conference if any party had the right to place conditions on who should attend. It was essential that all parties to the conflict should receive invitations, which included Syria and the PLO, and also the five permanent members of the Security Council.

Three days of discussions followed, as a result of which the US accepted that an international conference should be held under UN auspices. Invitations should be issued as Hussein had proposed, and Security Council

Resolutions 242 and 338 should form the basis for the discussion. Attendance by the PLO was contingent on their acceptance of the two Security Council Resolutions. These conditions were agreed by Hussein on behalf of the PLO, Arafat having already signified his acceptance of them. All seemed to be set fair when the succession of terrorist incidents took place in the Middle East and made further discussion inappropriate for the time being.

The PLO had been kept fully informed of the talks in Washington. In particular it had been made abundantly clear that written acceptance of 242 and 338 would be required from them before an invitation to the proposed conference could be issued. Hussein required such evidence in order to convince the Americans that it would be worth their while to issue invitations to the conference, but it would not be made public until agreed by the PLO. The PLO were also told that Jordan would not attend the conference unless the PLO, Syria and other parties to the conflict had also been invited. Meanwhile Arafat visited President Mubarak in Cairo on 7 November and issued a denunciation of terrorism in all its forms, irrespective of their source. This was a very hopeful step forward.

Hussein visited London early in January 1986 for medical reasons. The pace he set himself had inevitably taken its toll of his never very robust health. However, he managed to find time for two rounds of talks with the American Assistant Secretary of State for Near Eastern Affairs. The purpose was to discuss the mandate for the international conference, but the key issue became the participation of the PLO. The Americans repeated their condition that the PLO must first accept 242 before they would enter into any kind of dialogue with the PLO. Even then they would not commit themselves to inviting the PLO to the conference. Hussein asked for a clear statement in writing of the US position which he could then pass on to the PLO. This written commitment was received in Amman on 25 January 1986 and read as follows: 'When it is clearly on the public record that the PLO has accepted Resolutions 242 and 338, is prepared to negotiate peace with Israel, and has renounced terrorism, the United States accepts the fact that an invitation will be issued to the PLO to attend an international conference. . . .'

After so many months of patient negotiation this must have seemed to Hussein and his advisers a moment of triumph. All seemed to be set for the convening of the conference which Hussein regarded as essential if there was ever to be any chance of real peace between the Arabs and Israel. All the possible obstacles had been cleared and the way to the negotiating table now appeared to be open. But as always in the tangled history of the Arabs and the Jews, there was to be an unforeseen snag.

Arafat, accompanied by many of the Palestinian top leadership, had arrived in Amman simultaneously with Hussein's receipt of the American message. Hussein had automatically assumed that the PLO would be as happy with the US statement as he was; the ground had after all been covered time after time between Jordan and the PLO. It was therefore both a surprise and a shock when the PLO refused to accept Resolution 242 within the context of the American message, although Arafat politely acknowledged Hussein's 'extraordinary effort' in bringing about the change in the American position.

In his Address to the Nation on 19 February 1986, Hussein said this 'extraordinary effort' could never have succeeded had it not been for 'the respect, credibility and trust' in which Jordan was held. He was being understandably modest. There was only one Arab leader whose credibility was such that Washington was prepared to put faith in his word, the ruler of one of the smallest and least powerful of all the Arab states. Only a statesman of world stature could have persuaded the world's two most powerful nations to change their minds, as Hussein had done. But he could not persuade the PLO.

It was a tragedy that it should have ended up a blind alley. The PLO insisted on a change in the wording of Resolution 242 to include a statement concerning the legitimate rights of the Palestinian people, including their right to self-determination within the context of a confederation between Jordan and Palestine. Patiently Hussein went over the old ground again. Self-determination within the context of a Jordanian–Palestinian confederation, he reminded Arafat and his colleagues, was a matter solely to be decided between the Jordanians and Palestinians. There was no reason for any other party to be involved. He said he had made this perfectly clear in his opening address to the PNC in Amman in November 1984, and had repeated it many times since. But the PLO could not be moved. Hussein then agreed to reopen the matter with the Americans, although his heart sank at the prospect. It had been a bitter blow, coming as it did when it seemed that all the difficulties had by some miracle been overcome.

The American response to Hussein's reopening of the dialogue was firm and uncompromising. They said the Jordanian–PLO Accord did not involve the US, although the US government did support the legitimate rights of the Palestinian people, as had already been made clear. The PLO, like any other party attending the conference, would be free to propose anything they wished, including the Palestinian right to self-determination. However, unless the PLO publicly affirmed their support of Resolutions 242 and 338, it could not expect to be invited to the conference.

Arafat was told of the American reply on 28 January. He asked Hussein to try again, which the King did, but without effecting any change in the US attitude. Arafat then said that he needed to consult the PLO leadership, to which the King agreed, stipulating that he should know their answer before Arafat left Amman. By then, however, the news had leaked out that the PLO had decided at a meeting held in Baghdad on 24 November 1985 to reject acceptance of 242. The Americans told Hussein on 29 January 1986 that they were ready to wait for the PLO's acceptance of 242; in the meantime they suggested that Palestinian participation could be secured by a delegation from the Occupied Territories. In reply Hussein made plain that there could be no settlement without the PLO, who alone had been empowered by the Arab League to act on behalf of the Palestinian people. It is a fact which neither the Americans nor the Israelis seem willing to recognise.

Yet another US proposal arrived on 5 February. This approved the convening of an international conference on the basis of 242 and 338; it would include consideration of the legitimate rights of the Palestinians. Hussein saw Arafat that same evening and Arafat promised to study the new proposals. At the same time he gave Hussein three differently worded texts, all of which amounted to the same thing, i.e. a reaffirmation of the PLO's position as had been stated at the outset of the negotiations.

Arafat, accompanied by Abdul Razzaq al-Yahya and Hani al-Hassan, met Prime Minister Zeid Rifai and Marwan Kasim, Chief of the Royal Hashemite Court, on 6 February. The Prime Minister was himself a Palestinian by origin, as was Adnan abu Odeh, Head of the Royal Diwan. Arafat acknowledged that there had been some positive developments on the Americans' part, but they still did not include recognition of the right of the Palestinian people to self-determination. Therefore, until this was done, the PLO could not accept Resolution 242. 'Thus came to an end another chapter in the search for peace,' Hussein told his people in his Address to the Nation on 19 February. It was a sorry ending to what at the outset had looked like being a promising enterprise. It is probably true, however, that the US would have pulled out much earlier had it not been for Hussein; and the same is likely to be true of the PLO, although it has not been openly admitted.

It is understandable that neither Arafat nor his colleagues should have been popular with Hussein and his ministers after the failure of their efforts to convene an international conference that might have resolved the Palestinian problem once and for all. By no means every Jordanian was equally confident, however. Some of them felt that the United States was lukewarm from the beginning, being only too willing to blame the PLO for their intransigence. They believed that the American aim had all along been to persuade Hussein to enter into bilateral negotiations with Israel, for all the danger that this would mean to the Hashemite dynasty. There were others too who did not share Hussein's belief in Resolution 242 as providing a framework for peace. They thought it might provide for a recognition of Israel's existence, but no more than that.

Arafat would doubtless argue that although he might be prepared to recognise Israel's existence as part of a peace treaty, it would be a different matter to admit publicly Israel's *right to exist*. By so doing the whole basis of the Palestinian case would cease to apply. Israel would not only be respectable, but also *legitimate* in Palestinian eyes. The Zionist argument is much the same. It is claimed that Israel's right to exist was established by history centuries ago. The fact that this completely ignores any rights of the original Arab inhabitants, who have inhabited Palestine for as long as, if not longer than, the Jews, is conveniently overlooked.

The King was both disappointed and angry, as he had reason to be after working so hard to secure for the PLO a place at the international conference. He concluded that Arafat's twisting and turning in order to achieve a consensus among his colleagues meant that no reliance could be placed on his pledged word. Moreover, Hussein's and Arafat's characters were diametrically different, which did not help to create mutual trust. Also there were Jordanians who believed that it was Arafat's ambition to head any Palestinian state which might emerge from the negotiations; this inevitably affected his willingness to compromise in order to secure the withdrawal of the Israelis from the Occupied Territories. They recognised his success in keeping alive the cause of the Palestinians, but were critical of his tactics. Nor did they believe that Arafat and his closest colleagues wholeheartedly supported Hussein's proposal of a confederation between the Palestinian state and Jordan.

By no means everyone agreed with them. Many would argue that Arafat represents the only real prospect of knocking any sense into the heads of the PLO. It is also true that Arafat is the popular hero of a great many Palestinians. Sir Brian Urquart, whose vast experience of the Palestine problem while serving as one of the Secretary-General's deputies at the UN gives him great authority, believes that Arafat is probably the only one among the PLO leadership who genuinely wants peace. He also considers him to be the only man who may be able to do a deal on behalf of the Palestinians. It should be added that Urquart is at the same time a great admirer of King Hussein, whose wisdom and moderation he has often praised.[7]

The most unfortunate result of the failure of the 11 February Jordan–PLO Accord was that it destroyed the Jordanians' faith in Arafat's ability, or even his intention, to deliver. He would say one thing today, the complete opposite tomorrow. He had already told Zeid Rifai that he was prepared to accept Resolutions 242 and 338. He went even further when he discussed the possible internationalisation of Jerusalem, a matter which had not been raised by the Jordanians. But sooner or later he reneged on everything. As Urquart has written, 'Leaders of liberation movements have to live to a large extent in a world of make-believe if they are to survive and keep their supporters with them. . . . They are allergic to compromise or pragmatic accommodations. They live in an unending series of Inter-Continental Hotels.'[8]

Although the King and his Prime Minister are convinced that the PLO must continue to exist as the focus for Palestinian nationhood, this does not necessarily mean that Arafat will continue indefinitely as the PLO's chairman. The scene in the Middle East constantly changes, like the sands of the desert. One recent example of this has been the rapprochement between Jordan and Syria after decades of enmity. On 21 October 1985 Jordan and Syria signed a three-point agreement in Riyadh under the approving gaze of the Saudis. It was explained at the time that this formed part of the attempt to convene an international conference to discuss the problem of the Occupied Territories, but no mention was made of the 11 February Jordan–PLO Accord in the communiqué. Zeid Rifai was supposed to be the Jordanian architect of this agreement. Like his father before him, he thought it was nonsense for these two Arab neighbours to remain at loggerheads. Both parties rejected the making of separate agreements with Israel; adhered to the Arab peace plan as agreed at the Fez Summit; and committed themselves to the acceptance of decisions reached at previous Arab summits.

Almost a year was to pass before Hussein finally decided to break with the PLO. He announced this in a broadcast to his people on 19 February 1986. 'After two long attempts,' he told them, 'I and the government of the Hashemite Kingdom of Jordan hereby announce that we are unable to co-ordinate politically with the PLO leadership until such time as their word becomes their bond, characterised by commitment, credibility and constancy.' It could not have been an easy decision and the announcement sent shockwaves round the Arab world. In Jordan itself there were many who doubted the wisdom of this move, although they recognised the King's exasperation with Arafat's backslidings. They nevertheless believed that the King should keep his bridges open with the PLO. There was inevitably an outcry on the West Bank and in Gaza, and the Jordanian flag was publicly burned. Professor Musa Mazzawi, a Palestinian himself although domiciled in England, published an article in *The Times* that was headed, 'If Arafat goes, everyone loses', and there can be little doubt that the majority of his compatriots agreed with him. He argued that Arafat was a moderate, and should he be replaced by a radical, 'there will be turmoil in the Middle East'.

The King's decision was furiously debated in Jordan, some people arguing that the only gainer was Israel, where Arafat was regarded as little more than the leader of a gang of bandits. Even those who agreed with the King's action doubted whether it would have much effect in the PLO, and pointed to the support for Arafat that it had generated inside the Occupied Territories. There was, however, no immediate crackdown on the PLO inside Jordan, where the organisation had been successful in establishing a large number of offices, much to the concern of those who still remembered 1970–1. Nor was any restriction placed on the movements of Khalil al-Wazir, Arafat's deputy in Jordan. Hussein has described him as being 'one of the best of them'.* There was also a PLA brigade camped near Zerqa, accepted by the King after the PLO's expulsion from Lebanon. Equipped only with small arms and vintage transport, they represented no threat to the Jordanians, who nevertheless kept a close eye on them. In June 1986, however, Fatah was ordered to close its offices in Jordan, and Khalil al-Wazir was given forty-eight hours to leave the country. Twenty-five out of thirty-seven PLO offices were summarily closed and placed under guard. The reason given for this action was an ill-judged statement issued on 19 June by Fatah's Revolutionary Council accusing Jordan of being involved in a plot with the United States to destroy the PLO. It is more likely that the government was concerned by the PLO's infiltration back into Jordan, largely through the network of offices it was establishing. As everyone knew, Lebanon contained thousands of Palestinians who were desperate to find somewhere else to live, Jordan presenting the obvious alternative. But neither Hussein nor his people would have anything of it. It had been tried before, and it had failed; enough was enough.

The failure of Hussein's hopes for the convening of an international conference to discuss the Palestine problem happened to coincide with the refusal of the American Congress to endorse an arms deal with Jordan. It concerned the provision of air defence weapons. Hussein, who is acutely air-conscious, knew that Jordan's rapid defeat in the June 1967 war was largely owing to superior Israeli air power. Although Jordan could not expect to match Israel's strength in the air, it should at least possess defences likely to deter attack from the air.

The King had been negotiating with the United States since 1979 in order to obtain the American Stinger shoulder-launched anti-aircraft missile system. There was certainly no intention to link these negotiations with those relating to the international conference. The two negotiations were entirely separate, as the King emphasised on more than one occasion. Unfortunately the Congress chose to block the arms deal, to the humiliation of the President and the anger of its staunch ally. Although President

* Khalil al-Wazir was assassinated in Tunis on 16 April 1988, reputedly by Mossad agents.

Reagan had assured Hussein that the deal was proceeding normally, an assurance that was repeated by Vice-President George Bush on a visit to Jordan, Reagan had to write on 31 January 1986 to explain his inability to proceed owing to Congress. This was of course due to Zionist pressure, as Hussein well knew, but it was nonetheless annoying. Hussein gave vent to this annoyance shortly afterwards in a speech which he delivered in New York. As one of the few Arab moderates, he might reasonably have expected to be treated differently. However, he made it plain that if he could not get the air defence weapons he required from America, he was prepared to go elsewhere, to the Soviet Union if necessary.

The British hoped he would choose their Javelin system, but Hussein went instead to the Russians. He arranged a $3 million package. The evidence was clear that if the US was not prepared to sell such weapons to Jordan, the Soviet Union suffered under no such inhibitions, provided the money was right. President Nixon was certainly correct when he commén-ted: 'For the Congress not to approve President Reagan's request for arms for Jordan because the King does not make a separate peace with Israel is both unrealistic and ill advised. The King is a powerful force for moderation in the Israeli/Arab conflict. It is in the interest of the United States to strengthen him rather than weaken him.'[9]

Glubb Pasha died in his sleep on 17 March 1986, a month before his eighty-ninth birthday. There was a memorial service for him in Westminster Abbey on 17 April which the King insisted on attending. This was brave of him since the Arab world was at the time united in its condemnation of the US for bombing Libya and of Britain for permitting the US planes to use British airfields. But Hussein would not be deterred. He was determined to honour the man who had served Jordan and the Hashemite House so well. He paid an eloquent tribute to Glubb Pasha in his address in the Abbey.

Although the PLO were temporarily out of the picture, the problem of the Occupied Territories grew worse with time. Israel continued with its settlement policy and tightened its economic squeeze on the West Bank. This caused increasing concern in Amman where the King was convinced that there had to be a relaxation in Israel's oppressive policy if there was not to be a popular uprising sooner or later.[10] Israel's leaders frequently complain that they can never find Palestinian leaders willing to negotiate with them, but this is because they refuse to have any dealings with the PLO. The British in Cyprus had the same feelings about Archbishop Makarios, whom they even deported at one stage, but in the end they had to negotiate with him. Unless there is a change in attitudes, it is hard to see how there can ever be peace. No one has more cause to suspect the PLO than King Hussein, who had to take up arms against the Palestinian commandos and militia in 1970–1. And yet the King has made it perfectly clear that the PLO have to be represented in any talks that may be held in the search for peace.

'Over almost twenty years of occupation,' Crown Prince Hassan told the Council of Europe,

> the West Bank has been converted from an Arab economic entity into a virtual Israeli dependency. . . . As a result, not only is the economic well-being of Arabs on the West Bank threatened but so is their distinct cultural identity. It is in no one's interest for the present state of affairs to continue and for the West Bank to remain a dividing line. Jordan seeks to transform the whole region into a terra media – a middle ground – for peace and development in which the traditional pluralist approach of our social and political life, with its roots deep in this cradle of civilisation, can flourish. The West Bank and Gaza development programme is a peaceful offensive to explore the frontiers of what is possible. Its main focus is to promote jobs and services so that the Palestine Arabs may sustain their presence in the land of their forebears. We welcome multilateral European support for the protection of the Arab identity of the Occupied Territories.[11]

The intention behind the development plan for the West Bank was to demonstrate Jordan's continuing concern for the welfare of its Arab population; as such it was entirely in line with King Hussein's support of Arabism. It would, however, require a great deal more money than Jordan could provide on its own and, although American support had been promised, most of the initial investment came from Jordan. The detailed plan was worked out by Crown Prince Hassan and his team of experts in collaboration with the mayors of the principal West Bank towns. Inevitably there had to be discussions with the Israeli authorities as well. There were those in Jordan who felt that the money would be better expended within Jordan itself, as well as some Palestinians who argued that the development plan was intended to undermine their support for the PLO. It is hard to see, however, in what other way King Hussein could lend support to the Arab population who were suffering under Israeli military occupation. Words of encouragement were just not enough.

CHAPTER NINETEEN

The American Dimension

'It is widely believed in Jordan that America has been working throughout to isolate Jordan by persuading King Hussein to sign a bilateral peace treaty with Israel. This is something His Majesty will never do.'[1]

American support for Israel, right or wrong, is taken for granted in Jordan. Certainly no Arab would expect to receive even-handed justice from the United States where Israel is involved. Zionist influence is so strong that no American administration can be expected to adopt a line that is in any way antagonistic to Israel, particularly if it happens to be an election year. On the other hand the average American citizen, who is more than likely to be descended from a refugee from foreign tyranny, finds it hard to understand why the Arabs, with so much territory at their disposal, have found it so difficult to resettle the few million Arabs who have been dispossessed as a result of the creation of the State of Israel. They seldom equate the longing of the Palestinians to return to the land of their fathers with the same longing cherished by the Jews throughout their long Diaspora. The two cases are presumably considered to be quite different. But they are not.

The adoption of terror as a policy by the PLO has done nothing to improve this situation. In far too many American minds Palestinians and terrorists are one and the same thing; and the same is of course true of many Israeli minds. This is the more unfortunate in the wake of the decision taken by the Arab states at Rabat in 1974, when it was agreed that the PLO was 'the sole legitimate representative of the Palestinian people'. It follows therefore that any agreement reached concerning the future of the Palestinians will not be legitimate in Arab eyes unless the PLO has participated in the discussions. At the moment Israel is adamantly opposed to this; and so is the United States, unless the PLO publicly subscribes to Resolutions 242 and 338.

When President Reagan came into office, King Hussein had high hopes of a fresh American initiative to tackle the Arab–Israeli problem. This was particularly the case after the President's speech on 1 September 1982. It was therefore all the more disappointing when the US administration appeared to lose interest and consigned the problem to the back burner.

Some of the blame for this was attributed to Secretary of State George Shultz, who had scorched his fingers badly in Lebanon. Not surprisingly, Shultz seemed unwilling to repeat that performance by getting involved in the intractable quarrel between the Arabs and Israel. This was compounded when 'Irangate' burst upon an astonished world, and when the subsequent Congressional enquiry revealed that Shultz had been by-passed in the negotiations to exchange hostages for weapons. Hussein was to criticise the deal as more a crime than a blunder, and it undoubtedly diminished American prestige in Arab eyes.

In an address delivered in London on 6 December 1984, King Hussein gave a critical appraisal of American policy in the Middle East. 'From about the mid-1970s,' he said,

> the United States assumed the role of peace broker between the Arab states and Israel, to the exclusion of all others. The abandonment of the joint approach with the Soviet Union, which characterised the first phase of peace-making at the Geneva Middle East Peace Conference after the war of 1973, marked a turning point for American power and influence in the region. Rather than consolidating that position however, successive setbacks in Lebanon, Iran, and with regard to the peace negotiations, have eroded the United States' position. The outcome has been detrimental to the peace process and to the long-term prospects for stability, since the net result has been greater polarisation on a global scale and interminable deadlock in national and regional conflicts.

He went on to say that 'fluctuation in American policy has been aggravated by domestic manipulation of the American political system. This has been particularly so in an election year. Pressure groups have been able to exploit the dynamics of American presidential elections so successfully that they have rendered the peace process in the Middle East an expendable item of foreign policy.'[2]

This disillusionment with America's strength of purpose in dealing with the Middle East, coupled with the conviction that the US would always take Israel's side when it came to the crunch, made the European Community's, and even more Mrs Thatcher's, intervention so welcome to Hussein. 'Peace cannot come', said Mrs Thatcher in September 1985, 'if large numbers of people in the Occupied Territories are denied the possibility of living under a system of government in which they have confidence.' She believes, however, that the PLO's espousal of terrorism has done the Palestinian cause great harm; nothing could help that cause more than an open rejection of terrorism and a formal acceptance of Resolutions 242 and 338. Should an international conference be convened, Mrs Thatcher seems to think that Palestinian representation in the absence of the PLO could be secured by means of a joint Jordanian–Palestinian delegation, but the Palestinians would need to have abjured violence and have accepted the UN Resolutions. This could be wishful thinking since it has become increasingly evident that the PLO have the support of the *majority* of Palestinians in the Occupied Territories. This is perfectly well recognised by King Hussein, and by Prime Minister Zeid Rifai, who said in an interview on 12 February 1988, 'We really have no differences with the PLO. Our only problem is that *we* are talking about what is possible. They are talking about what they would like to do. We support them in what they would like – but is it possible?'[3] However, it would seem that to hold an international conference without the participation of the PLO would be like playing *Hamlet* without the Prince of Denmark.

In an address to the Council of Europe on 29 January 1987, Crown Prince Hassan told his audience: 'The current differences between Jordan and the Palestine Liberation Organisation are over strategies on how to achieve peace. We differ in our perceptions of basic realities of the political situation.' Quite so – but how to reconcile these differing views? And how to persuade both the United States and Israel that the PLO cannot be by-passed in any peace negotiations? It never has been easy to make concessions in order to achieve peace with those with whom a bitter struggle has been waged over many years. The British discovered this often enough during the decline of empire, and so did the French. Even the mighty United States was compelled in the end to talk with the Viet Minh to bring to an end the contest in Viet Nam. There will not be peace without compromise, both on the part of the Arabs and on the part of Israel. As Sir Anthony Parsons has recently urged, there has to be compromise on both procedural and substantive issues in order 'to provide the prospect of a decent future for the suffering Palestinians and rid the region of the festering situation which inhibits normal social and economic development and poses a constant danger to regional and world peace'.[4]

In view of his reputation as a moderate in a violent region, it is natural that King Hussein should be regarded by the United States as a key figure in any negotiations for peace in the Middle East. The trouble has been all along that the American aim has been to persuade Jordan to enter into bilateral negotiations with Israel, as Israel itself would prefer. Quite apart from his own feelings in the matter, Hussein knows perfectly well that ever since the Rabat Summit in 1974 his power to negotiate on behalf of the Palestinians no longer exists. This is why he has never budged from his belief that the PLO must be included in any negotiations of this kind, however often he has been disappointed, and on occasions angered, by PLO intransigence.

This in large measure accounts for the King's conviction that the best, perhaps the only, way to negotiate for peace in the Middle East is by means of an international conference at which all the contending parties, including the PLO, would be represented, together with the five permanent members of the Security Council. Israel has blown hot and cold. When Shimon Peres headed its government there was good reason to expect Israeli participation, but when Yitzhak Shamir succeeded him the Israeli position was completely reversed.

When Hussein sent Prime Minister Zeid Rifai to Washington at the end of April 1987 to discuss the possibilities of a conference with the Secretary of State, George Shultz made it plain that the proposal was unwelcome. He began by insisting that all the modalities of such a conference must be agreed beforehand – as good a delaying tactic as any. When weaned away from this, he proposed a bilateral meeting between Jordan and Israel at Williamsburg under American guidance. This was rejected out of hand. Shultz then offered to hire conference space at UN headquarters in Geneva for Israel and Jordan to conduct negotiations. After an exasperated Zeid Rifai had said bluntly that Jordan was perfectly capable of hiring conference space wherever it chose to do so, the talks ended in deadlock. In view of what was to happen at the end of the year, it is possible that Shultz was to regret later that he had not been more positive.

Although Jordan's Foreign Minister, Taher al-Masri, told a press conference held in Amman on 1 September 1987 that the efforts to convene an international conference had not reached a dead end, few of his compatriots would have agreed with him. The general feeling was that with the prospect of a presidential election absorbing the attention of most Americans for the following twelve months, coupled with the absorption of the outgoing President and his administration in arms-control talks with the Russians, it would be virtually impossible to generate any American interest in the perennial problem of the Middle East. Many intelligent Jordanians felt that the United States had once again failed to grasp the nettle. The result has been a definite anti-American feeling in Jordan.

Hussein could be forgiven if his patience with Washington had run out. No one had worked harder to get peace talks started. There was however one American who did not regard the situation as lost. 'I believe the international peace conference will take place, with adequate encouragement from Washington,' wrote President Jimmy Carter. 'Most other leaders are showing support. There will be some progress, with maybe major agreements, if the conference is well planned and executed.' He went on to say that if the PLO should show 'a genuine willingness to participate (probably through intermediaries) in a peace conference and adopt a non-violent pledge during the negotiations, the image of Palestinians could improve greatly.'[5]

Attention in the Arab world was now switched to the Summit Conference due to take place in Amman early in November. Hussein, as always seeking to promote the cause of Arab unity, had worked hard to bring about the Summit in order to arrive at some kind of consensus over the Iraq–Iran war. He had begun by bringing together Hafez Assad of Syria and Saddam Hussein of Iraq for talks, at Al-Jifr in the Jordan southern desert, in April 1987. This was a considerable achievement since the two men were sworn enemies from opposite wings of the Ba'ath Party; moreover Syria supports Iran for its own reasons. The first meeting between the two had lasted for thirteen hours non-stop on the first day, followed by seven hours on the next. Both wanted to bury the hatchet, but only on their own terms. Hafez Assad wanted a treaty, its terms unspecified; Saddam Hussein wanted full recognition of his regime. Although nothing concrete emerged from the meeting, the fact that it had taken place at all was a remarkable tribute to Hussein's quiet diplomacy and powers of persuasion. If nothing else, the ice had been broken, as was evidenced by both Hafez Assad's and Saddam Hussein's attendance at the Amman Summit eight months later.

Jordan had supported Iraq in its war with Iran from the beginning, and as hostilities have continued so have most of the other Arab countries, with the exception of Syria and Libya, sided with Iraq. However, as the war continued, apparently indefinitely, and as the situation in the Gulf deteriorated dramatically, involving both the superpowers, the Security Council passed Resolution 598. This called for a ceasefire, agreed by Iraq but neither rejected nor accepted by Iran. Libya, under its maverick Colonel Gadaffi, took this as the opportunity to switch sides and support Iraq, but Syria kept its own counsel. It was Hussein's aim to persuade the Arab states to speak with one voice. This was the principal aim of the Amman Summit.

Although King Fahd of Saudi Arabia said he was unable to attend, he sent the Crown Prince in his place; and although Gadaffi too did not turn up, the Summit turned out to be a resounding success. Even Hafez Assad succumbed to the call for Arab unity and joined the rest in announcing the Summit's 'solidarity with Iraq'. Saudi Arabia received support for any action it might take to avoid a repetition of the unseemly scenes which had marred the *Hajj* in 1987, when Iranian pilgrims attempted to demonstrate within the sacred precincts of the Great Mosque; and it was also agreed to call for an international peace conference at which the PLO would be represented as 'the sole legitimate representative of the Palestinian people', and on 'an equal footing' with the other parties attending the peace conference. It had all been a great success and was described as 'a victory for Arab public opinion and also for King Hussein'.[6]

By their very nature Arab summits usually tend to be more productive of talk than of anything more concrete, but the Amman Summit proved to be an exception. This was very largely due to the careful preparations made beforehand, and to King Hussein's chairmanship. The PLO came out of it particularly well. Hussein has found it hard to forgive the PLO's sabotage of his patient efforts to persuade the Americans to invite a PLO delegation to the international conference he was advocating. There was therefore some general coolness at the start, but by the end it was all smiles. Egypt had been welcomed back into the Arab fold, something else which the King had worked for patiently over many months; Jordan and the PLO agreed to reopen their dialogue; and on 29 November relations between the PLO and Egypt were formally restored. It had truly been an achievement on Hussein's part.

Arafat's arrival in Amman was preceded by demonstrations in the Occupied Territories. The focus of these demonstrations was concentrated round the refugee camps, particularly in the Gaza Strip. The Israeli authorities responded with their usual toughness but the rioting continued with what were to be astonishing results. For many years Jordanian critics of Arafat and the PLO had been complaining that the basic error in PLO tactics was that their efforts to strike against the Israeli occupation had been mounted from outside, rather than from inside, the Occupied Territories. In this regard the PLO were operating rather like a government-in-exile, although the PLO had always repudiated any such suggestion. Their critics, however, made the point that all successful resistance movements, such as the FLN in Algeria, owed their success to the support generated from within the country. They lamented that there was little sign of this happening in the Occupied Territories, where the Israeli military presence effectively cowed the Palestinian population.

Nevertheless there were signs, according to King Hussein, of the traditional Palestinian leadership beginning to come forward – 'standing up to be counted', as the King described it,[7] although there was nothing to suggest a resistance movement of the kind the British had found so difficult to deal with between 1936 and 1938. Were anything of that kind to occur, the Israelis were supremely confident of their ability to deal with it, and most people would have believed them. They were to be proved wrong within a matter of weeks.

On 7 December, a month after the meeting of the Amman Summit, there were demonstrations in Gaza. Some Israeli settlers passing by a school fired a number of shots, killing a seventeen-year-old Palestinian schoolgirl who happened to be walking across the school yard. Her name was Intisar Atar. Although the settlers were at first arrested, they were later released. The girl's family were given her body at night and she had to be buried without a proper funeral, presumably to avoid the demonstrations that would have accompanied it. There followed on 9 December what can only be described as a spontaneous uprising (*intifada*) against the occupying forces, spreading rapidly from Gaza to the West Bank. As day followed day unarmed civilians, mostly youths but sometimes women as well, stoned Israeli military patrols, who seemed to have little idea of how best to handle the situation. All too often they resorted to firing their weapons or throwing tear-gas grenades. As the rioting continued and the world's television camera teams converged on the Occupied Territories, it quickly became apparent to those witnessing the scenes portrayed on their televisions that the much vaunted Israeli army was completely at a loss. This was accurately foreseen long before the present uprising by the experienced American reporter, David K. Shipler, when he wrote: 'Strict guidelines on opening fire have been promulgated, but little or no training has been given in crowd control, leaving every inexperienced soldier at the mercy of his fears with only a deadly rifle as his protection from angry stone-throwers.'[8]

World opinion, including many American Jews, was revolted by the sight of women and youths being mercilessly beaten as they were chased and caught after throwing stones. This treatment made not the slightest difference to the Palestinians, who continued with their acts of defiance with increasing loss of life, and the tougher the Israelis' counter-measures, the more support they were losing abroad. They were now being forced to learn the hard way the lessons the French had had to learn in Algeria, this time reinforced many times over by the presence of the media. Indeed, if they do eventually succeed in suppressing the uprising, Israel's image can never be quite the same again.

Arafat and the PLO were quick to benefit from the uprising although they had done little to direct it in the first place. It was people's power, they said. It had triumphed in India under Mahatma Gandhi against the British, and in the Philippines under Aquino against Marcos. Why not in the Occupied Territories? It certainly galvanised the American administration into resurrecting previous peace plans, sending Secretary of State George Shultz off on the equivalent of Kissinger's 'shuttle diplomacy' and producing an astonishing change of mind over the convening of an international peace conference.

The Americans proposed that there should be an international 'meeting' in April 1988, the object being to initiate direct talks between Israel and Jordan/Palestinians, to establish some kind of Palestinian autonomy in the Occupied Territories. There would then be municipal elections in the Occupied Territories, the object being to produce a new Palestinian leadership. This would be followed before the end of 1988 by negotiations on a final settlement of the Arab–Israeli conflict under an international umbrella, the Palestinians presumably being represented by their newly elected leaders, who would almost certainly be either pro-PLO or linked with the PLO.

When Shultz discussed this plan with Hussein in London early in February 1988, the King made it plain that Jordan rejected any 'partial, interim or unilateral settlement'. He also reiterated Jordan's adherence to the convening of an international peace conference, attended by the five permanent members of the Security Council and all other parties to the conflict, *including the Palestine Liberation Organisation*. This stymied the American attempt to exclude the PLO, now on the crest of the wave in the Occupied Territories. This also spelt the rejection of the American proposals by Jordan, which was soon to be followed by Israel's rejection when Prime Minister Shamir visited Washington in March. Once again in the Middle East the wheel has come round full circle, with the rioting and the shootings still going on, and the conscience of the world still being stirred by the portrayal of the incidents they see almost nightly in their living rooms.

There is always the danger of an Israeli backlash, particularly from those who have settled in the Occupied Territories. It is sobering to learn that a recent poll conducted in the newspaper *Ma'ariv* disclosed that nearly one-third of Israelis would support the forcible removal of the Palestinians from the West Bank and Gaza. This compares with the 40 per cent who would be opposed to such a step. An expulsion of this kind has of course been advocated for many years by the more extreme right-wing organisations in Israel, but were it to happen it would be disastrous for both Jordan and Israel. Jordan certainly could not digest such an addition to its population without suffering great economic hardship and subsequent unrest. Nor would it help Israel, which must in the long run reach some kind of *modus vivendi* with its Arab neighbours. It cannot continue indefinitely as an island in a sea of enemies, without its entire national character having to suffer. Moreover, in this age of the surface-to-surface missile with ranges of hundreds and hundreds of miles, Israel's strategic situation has been altered. The seizure of more and more territory can never provide the security it seeks.

When Queen Noor addressed the Kennedy School of Government at Harvard on 25 April 1985, she told her audience: 'If the Middle East is ever to enjoy genuine and lasting peace, all the countries must move closer to, and be mutually fortified by, a middle ground that sees equal political rights as the only foundation for a lasting peace.' She warned of the dangers inherent in the existing situation, out of which a local conflict might easily escalate into global war. 'I need only remind you', she said, 'that during the October 1973 Arab–Israeli war the United States put its armed forces on a worldwide nuclear alert.' The prospect was frightening then. It remains so today. The solution can only be compromise on the part of *all* the contending parties, backed up if at all possible by both the superpowers, and if not, by the United States alone. It is entirely wrong to assume that any one individual, such as Hussein, can act as the catalyst, as would appear to be the assumption in certain circles in the US and in Israel.

Although King Hussein has many admirers and supporters in the United States and Britain, neither country seems to understand the constraints that limit his freedom of action. An article in *The Times* (London) on 1 March 1988 went so far as to claim that 'Virtually every path to peace leads to, or passes close by, King Husain. It is on his word that progress heavily depends.' The implication is that if a specific course of action is supported by the King, the PLO and the rest of the Arab world will follow suit. This is far from being the case. Jordan is a very small country, nowhere near as powerful as Egypt, Syria or Iraq, nor as rich as Saudi Arabia, not to mention the Arab countries of North Africa. Its continued existence depends very largely on their goodwill. Moreover, with the exception of Syria and Lebanon, it is the Arab country lying closest to the menace of Israeli military action, which it could not possibly defeat on its own. There are also more than one million Palestinians living in Jordan, by no means all of them loyal to Hussein's regime, although the time must surely have come for them to make up their minds whether to be loyal Jordanians or find some other nationality; they cannot have it both ways.

Hussein's statesmanship, influence and wisdom give him a very important voice in the dialogue for peace, but certainly not for peace at any price. His belief in Arab unity and solidarity, and his conviction that the Hashemites have a vitally important part to play in bringing about this unity, makes it impossible for him to go out on a limb as Anwar Sadat did. Sadat in the end succeeded in splitting the Arabs, rather than in uniting them. Moreover, although it may appear to many Americans and others, including Israelis, that as the ruler of Jordan King Hussein can do more or less as he pleases or thinks fit, the reality is entirely different. The King is as much influenced in his actions and decision-making by public opinion as are leaders in the Western democracies, with this significant difference. When President Jimmy Carter's policies failed to commend him to the American people, they refused to elect him for a second term. In Hussein's case the result would almost certainly be the loss of the throne and the plunging of his kingdom into turmoil, with the near certainty of Israeli intervention. If he is to abide by the principles to which he has dedicated his life, King Hussein has every reason to be cautious.

CHAPTER TWENTY

Storm in the East

'We shall export our revolution to the whole world. Until the cry "There is no God but God" resounds over the whole world, there will be struggle.' Ayatollah Khomeini[1]

A remarkable upsurge in religious fundamentalism has been one of the features of the past twenty years. Most of the world's principal religions have been touched by it, more particularly Islam, which has throughout its history been affected by cyclical movements of this kind. Islamic fundamentalism has become the more prominent, some might claim menacing, as a result of the overthrow of the late Shah of Iran and his replacement by a theocracy headed by the Ayatollah Khomeini. It is too early as yet to determine whether the Iranian Revolution in 1979 will prove to have been one of those cataclysmic events that change the course of history, like the French and Russian revolutions. One thing is certain, however: it has greatly widened the gulf which has long existed in Islam between the two principal sects of Sunnis and Shias. Islamic fundamentalism has moreover become a matter for increasing concern to most of the established regimes in the Muslim world.

In his book, *Search for Peace*, Crown Prince Hassan of Jordan has commented on Islamic fundamentalism. He attributes its rise to 'the triumph of extremist politics, whether in Israel or the Arab and Muslim worlds. In Jewish and Muslim societies, politics have become infused by religious extremism and the precepts of religion have been used to produce political fanaticism; the activities of such groups as the Phalange of Lebanon, Gush Emunim of Israel and the Pasdarans of Iran have brought about a violence in the name of religion rarely known in the Middle East.'[2]

There is nothing new in theocracy, which has been defined as rule by priests in the name of God. The popes were temporal as well as spiritual rulers at one stage in the papacy's history. Islam also has seen many theocracies come and go, that of the Mahdi in the Sudan in the latter years of the nineteenth century being one of the most recent examples. The danger of theocracies however is that the leaders thereof, priests or mullahs, conceive of themselves as having a divinely inspired proselytising mission that can only be served by the overthrow of existing regimes and their replacement by their own. Throughout the ages religious fanaticism has been marked by violence and bloodshed, as we have seen so recently in Iran. Unspeakable crimes have been committed in the name of God by those who claim to be serving Him.

It has been said of Islam that it is not a religion but a complete way of life. It covers every aspect of human activity from men's attitude towards women to health, hygiene, politics and a host of other matters. The Holy Koran, the Hadith (traditions), and Sharia (laws) cover all that human beings need to know in order to conduct themselves properly and in a seemly fashion. Islam is moreover a way of life that good Muslims are happy to proclaim publicly, by praying openly the five prescribed times each day wherever they happen to be – in the street, a shop, the market place or while on a journey.

Like most religions, Islam has experienced many schisms. The most far-reaching of these has been the split between those we now know as Sunnis, and those we know as Shias, or Shi'ites. Shi'ites are followers of Ali, who was the fourth Caliph and the Prophet's cousin. He was also the Prophet's son-in-law through his marriage to Fatima, the Prophet's daughter. When Ali was murdered in AD 661, there was a dispute over the succession. The Sunnis were those who went outside the Prophet's 'family' for their choice of leader. Those who disagreed with them became known as 'Shi'at Ali', or 'Followers of Ali', now abbreviated to Shia. Sunnis and Shias have been in bitter dispute ever since.

Shi'ites believe that authority should descend through Ali, who became the first of their twelve imams, or religious leaders, all of them descendants of the Prophet through Ali and Fatima. They also believe that their priesthood, or mullahs, are empowered to interpret the application of divine ordinance. Sunnis believe the link to be a more personal one, directly from man to Allah and not through the medium of a priest. Sunnis form the majority in Islam but Shi'ites are stricter and more fanatical in the observance of their religion. Shi'ism has been described as being 'all about protest against authority, passion and constant rebellion'.[3] They are more militant than Sunnis, who disapprove of the public manifestation of grief every year during the month of Muharram when Shias commemorate the martyrdom of Ali's second son, Hussein, by bloody self-flagellation and the most extravagant demonstrations of sorrow. Hussein was the Prophet's grandson, killed in the battle of Karbala in AD 680; he is the Supreme Martyr of the Shias, and Karbala, which is in Iraq, is their holiest city.

Sunnis predominate in the Arab world, but there are significant numbers of Shias in Lebanon, Saudi Arabia and the Gulf states. Shias form the majority in Iraq although Sunnis hold the reins of power. This Sunni predominance has turned the Shias almost into a depressed class, as in

Lebanon, but it would now seem that they are beginning to make their voices heard and are demanding their place in the sun. The rise to power in Iran of a Shi'ite theocracy has lent impetus to this Shi'ite renaissance, and has made the Shias a force to be reckoned with throughout Islam. The upsurge of Islamic fundamentalism, although by no means confined to Shi'ism, has increased the dangers of religious fanaticism.

The Saudis have always insisted that they have no cause to fear Islamic fundamentalism since it was the Wahhabis who were the original Islamic fundamentalists; and it was the Wahhabis who played the leading part in helping Abdul Aziz bin Saud to establish the Kingdom of Saudi Arabia. They had to change their tune however when the Great Mosque in Mecca was seized by a body of religious fanatics in November 1979; and again more recently, on 31 July 1987, when the sacred precincts of the Great Mosque were desecrated by the conduct of Iranian pilgrims attending the *Hajj*. They had to be forcibly dispersed by police at considerable loss of life. The Saudis are now fully aware that no Muslim country can consider itself immune from the virus which is beginning to infect increasing numbers of Muslims, both Sunnis and Shias. Egypt, a predominantly Sunni state, has long been plagued by the Muslim Brethren, who are Sunnis; and Tunisia is another Muslim country which has recently had to grapple with the problem.

Fuel has been added to these religious flames by the progressive disintegration of Lebanon, evidence should such be needed of the ghastly consequences of religious conflict. There the presence of the Palestinian commandos helped to bring about the clash between the opposing factions. Iran has been sedulously stoking the Lebanese fires ever since. Even more ominous has been the Eight Years' War between Iraq and Iran, which Ayatollah Khomeini and his mullahs managed successfully to transform into a holy war, or *Jihad*, on the part of the Iranians. The war began on 22 September 1980 when Iraqi troops invaded Iran's southern province of Khuzestan; and it was only terminated when Iran followed Iraq in accepting Security Council Resolution 598, which called for a ceasefire. This ceasefire came into effect on 19 August 1988, but each country doubts the other's motives for agreeing to it.

When President Saddam Hussein launched his troops into battle in September 1980, there can be little doubt that he counted on an easy victory in the wake of the late Shah's overthrow. Iran was in the grip of revolution, its armed forces emasculated as a consequence of revolutionary fervour, its government in a constant state of flux. The immediate cause of the war need not concern us here but Saddam Hussein certainly did not achieve his easy victory. Indeed, after some early successes, the Iraqis were forced back on the defensive for several years, only regaining the initiative towards the end of 1987. Neither side has hesitated in taking the war to the civilian population, bombardment of cities having been a commonplace, and the use of chemical warfare by both sides, but most frequently by Iraq, has led to universal condemnation. The Arabs have been at loggerheads with the Persians for thousands of years, even to the extent of Iraq's Shia soldiers fighting bravely against their Iranian co-religionists, although doubtless this has been in some measure due to the draconian methods employed by President Saddam Hussein in ensuring loyalty to his regime.

Saddam Hussein also provided the Iranian mullahs with the opportunity to divert the revolutionary fervour of their followers into the less menacing activity of fighting and dying for their country. Here there is an interesting parallel with the wars for survival fought by revolutionary France in the aftermath of the French Revolution. Hundreds of thousands of Iranians have lost their lives, or their sight or their limbs, in the 'human wave' attacks launched time and again against the Iraqis. The economy of both countries is in ruins; the great port of Basra and the Shatt al-Arab waterway has been closed for eight years; Iran's oil refineries have been bombed again and again; and the cost in human misery has been incalculable. The war also led to a rift in the cause of Arab unity, to which King Hussein attaches such importance. For much of the war both Syria and Libya supported Iran, only changing sides during 1987 – and half-heartedly at that in Syria's case.

Although it was the Iraqis who murdered his cousin King Feisal and massacred the Iraqi branch of the Hashemites, Hussein has never forgotten that Iraq was the only Arab country to come to his aid during the dark days of June 1967. He was therefore quick to announce his support for Iraq when the war began. He worked tirelessly thereafter to bring about united Arab support for Iraq, finally achieving his aim at the Amman Summit in November 1987 when *all* the Arab states pledged their support for Iraq. From the outset of the war, however, Hussein foresaw the dangers that lay ahead in the Gulf. He urged the construction of an oil pipeline across Saudi Arabia from the Gulf states to Aqaba, thereby by-passing the Strait of Hormuz, and likewise tried to persuade the Iraqis to run a pipeline to the Jordanian oil refinery at Zerqa, from where Jordan would build a pipeline to Aqaba. His exhortations unfortunately fell on deaf ears, but had they been followed up the dangerous situation that has since arisen in the Gulf would probably have been avoided.

Hussein initially offered to send troops to fight alongside the Iraqis. This never got very far, provoking a violent reaction by Syria and very nearly leading to war between the two countries. There was an Arab summit due to be held in Amman but Syria refused to attend, accusing Jordan of widening the war. Syria's Foreign Minister declared that large-scale troop movements were taking place along the desert road between Jordan and Iraq.

This was not the case, the cause of the confusion being the phenomenal increase in civilian truck traffic between Aqaba and Baghdad as a result of the closure of the Shatt al-Arab and the port of Basra. The Syrians failed to check their facts, but hurriedly mobilised two divisions and sent them to the frontier with Jordan. Damascus and Amman Radios vied with each other in threats and counter-threats which resulted in a kind of war-fever in Jordan. For the first time this brought people together as Jordanians, rather than as East and West Bankers.[4]

The Jordanian reaction to the menacing Syrian troop concentrations was both swift and efficient. A division was moved to the frontier with great speed, arriving in its deployment area without the Syrians being aware of it. The Jordanian general then took his senior commanders across the frontier to reconnoitre the ground; during this reconnaissance they happened to bump into the Syrians engaged on a similar mission. After exchanging compliments in a civilised fashion, the Jordanian officers warned the Syrians that they were playing with fire. They would receive a bloody nose if they crossed the frontier, as had happened before in September 1970. The Syrians hastily disclaimed having any such intent. They had no wish to fight the Jordanians but were merely obeying orders. There were handshakes all round, after which both sides parted amicably. Not long afterwards the Syrians returned to their barracks, the radio war died down and the Jordanian troops returned to their peace garrisons.

Notwithstanding the war's dangerous overtones, Jordan has profited considerably from it. Iraq's use of Aqaba has resulted in a great expansion of its facilities. The wharves now stretch for miles along the eastern shore of the Gulf of Aqaba, while out in the stream cargo vessels and oil tankers lie at anchor waiting their turn to come alongside. This transformation is a remarkable sight for those who knew Aqaba when there was only a beach and a handful of wharves. Equally remarkable is the stream of trucks driving bumper to bumper along the Desert Road on the long haul to Iraq and back. They cross a wilderness which not all that long since saw only the flocks and herds of the bedouin tribes. There was not a yard of tarmac thirty-five years ago. The progress made in improving and extending Jordan's road system is one of the most notable features of the past decade.

If the ceasefire between Iraq and Iran holds successfully, it is to be hoped that the two countries will eventually agree to a peace settlement, devoting their energies thereafter to repairing the ravages of eight years of war. This will not however remove the threat posed to existing Arab regimes by the spread of Islamic fundamentalism, although perhaps Ayatollah Khomeini's death will see the emergence of a less fanatical regime in Iran, more concerned with improving the lot of the ordinary Iranian citizen than with exporting religious revolution throughout the world. But Islamic fundamentalism will continue to represent a threat to stability, not only in the Middle East but throughout the Muslim world. Crown Prince Hassan has said that Islamic fundamentalism is just as important, and as dangerous, for the future of Jordan as the problem of the Palestinians. It holds out a particular appeal for the young and for the deprived. Its increasing growth in the Gaza Strip is particularly significant, since it is there that the Israelis' shortsighted and repressive policies have provided just the kind of seedbed Islamic fundamentalism needs in order to flourish. More obvious perhaps is the strength of the movement in Lebanon, where the fanatical followers of Hizbollah are holding the world's most powerful nations to ransom.

Since Islamic fundamentalism means in essence the replacement of existing Muslim regimes by the rule of priests, conducted strictly in accordance with the teachings of the Holy Koran, it strikes yet another blow at the stability of the Middle East. Anwar Sadat has been only one of its many victims so far. The attraction it appears to have for youth may lie in a revulsion against the materialism of the West, or it may owe its origins to the ever increasing gap between living conditions in the West and those in the Third World. But whatever the reason for the attraction of Islamic fundamentalism for Muslim youth, the Sunni–Shia split would seem as much as anything to be developing into a struggle between the haves and the have-nots.

Jordan is a young country, a large proportion of its population being below the age of twenty. It is also in that delicate stage of a country's development when the old ways are passing, and new ways are replacing them. This does not by any means suit everyone. Many of the older generation of Jordanians complain of the disappearance of customs and traditions that have governed human relationships for centuries past. The emancipation of women, for example, which is such a feature of modern Jordan, does not meet with universal approval. The technological advances of the past fifty years have however had the most profound effects both on the way of life and on ways of thought. This cannot be avoided or ignored. A return to the age of the camel is certainly no answer to the problems of the present.

Well within living memory the only difference between a shaykh and his fellow tribesmen was that he owned a bigger tent and possessed more camels. Everyone slept on the ground and went thirsty when the rains failed. It is different today when the shaykh probably owns a handsome town house, sends his sons and daughters to schools abroad, drives around in a Mercedes, and would be completely flummoxed if required to deal with a sick camel. He should not be blamed for this. Times have changed since his grandfather's day. But no more should he be surprised if his all too evident affluence has made him an object of envy.

The difficulties involved in trying to bridge this gap causes King Hussein much concern. Crown Prince Hassan has embarked on a far-reaching reform of Jordan's educational system, the object being to make it more relevant to modern requirements. But as always there is the problem of money, as well as the need to provide appropriate employment for the young men and women coming out of Jordan's universities and technical colleges in steadily increasing numbers. The opportunities that once offered in the expanding economies of the Gulf states are no longer there, the places filled by the citizens of the countries concerned. Moreover, those who had previously found employment overseas are now returning home. How will they be provided with jobs that will enable them to maintain the standard of living to which they have grown accustomed? It is generally admitted in Jordan today that Jordanians on the whole are reluctant to accept menial jobs any more. They are too well educated.

Islamic fundamentalism holds out an undoubted attraction for those left behind in the struggle for existence. It has provided a new dimension for acts of political terrorism and has greatly widened the pool of recruitment for 'martyrs to the faith'. Its astonishing spread has led to a feeling of insecurity, particularly for non-Muslims, in a part of the world where there was once a remarkable tolerance between the faiths. It was not unusual, for example, to find Christians, and also Jews, holding high offices of state under the Ottomans. Not everyone, however, is pessimistic about the prospects. At the height of the Iraq–Iran war, when an Iranian victory seemed likely, and when the prophets of doom and gloom were prophesying a Shi'ite revolution all over the Arab world, Professor Eli Kedourie did not agree with them. He did not believe that an Iranian victory would automatically mean that the Shi'ites would 'surge irresistibly throughout the Middle East'. Instead he pointed out that the regimes under threat were almost all Sunni ones, which have had ample warning to take effectual counter-measures. He said that the Sunnis also have their fundamentalist movements, the Wahhabis being one, the Muslim Brethren another. He doubted whether there is, in any of the countries concerned, a figure 'who can play the role Khomeini played in Iran during 1978–79'.[5]

However, some may feel that the Professor is underrating the dangers, despite his distinction and high academic authority. The Shah's supposedly efficient security service (Savak) failed to save him in his hour of trial. And how can we be certain that there is not somewhere, in one of the numerous religious institutions in the Arab world, a militant cleric with the necessary personality and fanaticism who, given the opportunity, can galvanise his followers into revolutionary activity as Khomeini has done? In the early 1970s, when the Shah was riding high and lecturing the British on the frequency of their strikes and the power of the trade unions, who would ever have thought that a militant cleric then in exile would topple him from his throne, emasculate his armed forces and turn his country upside down?

Hussein is remarkably relaxed over his own security, but it remains a constant headache for those responsible for protecting him. The Jordanian Mukhabarat is reputedly efficient but the Middle East abounds in people ready to embrace martyrdom. Hussein is certainly less accessible nowadays than when first he came to the throne; but then the organisation around him is far more efficient than it used to be. There are inevitably opponents to his rule in Jordan but he does within the limits of prudence move freely among his people. By and large he has the support of the great majority. Open criticism of the regime is not very wise, however distinguished the critic. In October 1986 the publication of an open letter to President Hosni Mubarak of Egypt from a former Jordanian Prime Minister, Ahmed Obeidat, who was protesting against the expenditure involved in developing the West Bank, created a storm and resulted in the writer being stripped of his membership of the Senate. But many of those who read the letter agreed with Obeidat. It should also be remembered by those of Hussein's critics who accuse him of running a police state that after the King's expulsion of the PLO in 1971, the majority of the *fedayeen* took off their combat jackets and returned to the refugee camps, where they remain to this day. Some of them have become loyal subjects of the King, while others undoubtedly have not and remain under surveillance.

Hussein has survived so many attempts on his life that he must have become inured to the risks with which he has to live. He is of course a fatalist, like his grandfather before him, believing that his life is in God's hands. Among the many attempts on his life, that engineered by Colonel Gadaffi must surely be the most bizarre, surpassing even the attempt by the Syrians to force down his plane in November 1958. Aziz Shenib was the Libyan Ambassador in Amman in 1982 when Gadaffi summoned him back to Tripoli. 'King Hussein should be liquidated,' Gadaffi told the astonished Ambassador. 'He is a nuisance. He is pro-Western and not the right leader for Jordan, or for the region. The attempt should be made with the co-operation of another Arab country – Syria.'

It was planned to shoot down Hussein's plane or helicopter on one of his frequent trips to Aqaba. Shenib was provided with several million dollars and told to contact the Syrian Foreign Minister, Abdul Halim Khaddam, who is now Vice-President of Syria. Khaddam was to arrange to provide surface-to-air missiles (SAMs). It would also be necessary to raise two commando units, who must be Syrians, not Palestinians. 'You must not strike when the plane is low,' Gadaffi told Shenib, 'because there is then a chance that the King might escape. You must fire the missile when the plane is just beginning its descent, when the landing gear first comes down. Arrange the men and the weapons.'

Shenib was horrified but did not dare to say so to Gadaffi. Instead he told Hussein. Then he went to Damascus, where he was cordially received by Khaddam. 'If we had only shot down Sadat's plane before he went to Jerusalem,' said Khaddam, 'none of the problems now happening in the region would have happened.' President Hafez Assad, however, thought otherwise. He called the plan 'childish and stupid', pointing out that if it proved to be successful every ruler in the Middle East would be at risk the moment he took to the air. A very relieved Shenib returned to Amman, from where he defected to Cairo a few days later.[6]

The stability of Jordan depends to a very large extent on the loyalty of its armed forces. The King and his Commander-in-Chief are in almost daily contact, Field Marshal Zeid bin Shakir accompanying the King on most of his trips out of the country. As a front-line state in the struggle with Israel, Jordan can never afford to drop its guard, although the requirement to maintain under arms a force of more than 70,000 officers and soldiers places a great strain on the country's finances, particularly since the members of the armed forces enjoy many privileges. They are highly respected both within the country and among the other Arab states. There is conscription for two years, which cannot be said to be popular with everyone. There is also a People's Army of 200,000 men and women, charged with defending vulnerable points in time of war in order to release regular troops for the field. The People's Army is compulsory for all males between sixteen and sixty-five, but voluntary for women between sixteen and forty-five. Although these figures pale into insignificance when compared with those of many other Arab countries, it has to be remembered that Jordan's population is less than three million.

Hussein has been remarkably successful in transforming the chiefly pastoral and agricultural country to which he succeeded into the increasingly urban one of today. He has never tried to force the pace but has always promoted modernisation. His encouragement of education has had a profound effect on men and women of all classes of the population. He has also been instrumental in bringing women into the mainstream of the country's life, something his grandfather King Abdullah could never have contemplated. It is not in Hussein's character to play the tyrant, as his record plainly shows, but many bitter experiences during his life have taught him to hasten slowly.

Despite the many changes which have occurred during his reign, Jordan still values its old traditions. For example, Crown Prince Hassan was surprised recently to discover how few Jordanian children have slept away from home before adulthood. Conscription has inevitably widened these horizons but the old traditions still retain their hold, as Prime Minister Zeid Rifai was to find when endeavouring to obtain parliamentary agreement for the recruitment of women into the People's Army. It required all his eloquence and powers of persuasion.

Jordan is of course part of the Arab world. The developments taking place in that world profoundly affect it. There are those in the West for whom the Arab is still a dignified figure, wearing robes and riding a camel across the vastness of the desert; he lives in a tent and his language is Arabic. But far more Arabs speak English than Westerners speak Arabic. Very few of them live in tents. Fewer still ride camels. Certainly among the younger generation more of them wear jeans, T-shirts and trainers than wear traditional Arab costume. Although profoundly conscious of their ancient culture and superb literature, they are as much part of the modern world as most of their Western contemporaries. A great many of them are also returning to Islam, a manifestation of their recognition that Arabia is the home of one of the world's great religions. Every Arab government either recognises these changes or ignores them at its peril.

Nationalism, too, has altered. The dream of a united Arab nation still stirs the heart strings, but it is a different kind of nationalism. Syrians are Syrians, Jordanians are Jordanians. The frontiers which divide them may be wholly artificial but they have become sanctified by time. Every Arab country wants to stand on its own feet, proud to be beneath the umbrella of a universal language, culture and religion. Arab unity today is somehow different from that which was conceived by Sharif Hussein when he fired the first shot in the Arab Awakening (Al-Nahda), seventy-two years ago. It is perhaps more parochial, less universal. Each Arab state feels that it has its own interests and must be free to pursue them. But Islam, the language and the culture still remain a powerfully unifying factor. And there is one other matter which unifies the Arabs from the Pillars of Hercules to the Straits of Bab el-Mandab: the problem of Palestine and the fate of the Palestinians. On that at least they are united.

CHAPTER TWENTY-ONE

Statesman–King

'I have always admired Hussein's guts. But today I think I
admire him most for his statesmanship.' Earl of Stockton[1]

Jordan is a small country with a population of not much more than two and a
quarter million, roughly half of whom are of Palestinian origin. It has no oil.
Phosphate is its main natural resource, which is being exploited skilfully. In
order to carry out the series of development plans that have done so much to
improve standards of living, as well as the country's infrastructure, Jordan
has been largely dependent on aid from friendly countries, such as Saudi
Arabia, the Gulf states and the USA. Foreign aid has also been essential for
the modernisation and maintenance of her armed forces. With Israel still in
possession of the Occupied Territories, which includes of course the Old
City of Jerusalem, Jordan cannot afford to drop its guard.

It is remarkable that, despite these limitations, Jordan's voice in the
search for peace with Israel is much more important than either its size or
its economy would suggest possible. This is almost entirely due to the
reputation of King Hussein in the world's counsels. The fact that he has
been there in the centre of Middle Eastern affairs for close on forty years,
having outlasted all of the Arab and Israeli leaders who were prominent
when first he came to the throne, and that he has acquired both wisdom and
understanding in the process, has made him a key figure in the dialogue
between the Arabs and Israel. If anyone has put Jordan on the map, it is its
King.

However, it has not always been so. During Hussein's early years on the
throne, it was Nasser who dominated the Arab world. His and Hussein's
relations varied from the close to the distant. Nasser's philosophy of
government did not include monarchies, although in the end he came to
work with them. Hussein, with his dedication to Arab unity, felt that
Nasser too often missed the wood for the trees in his determination to make
Egypt the leader of the Arabs. When it came to the point he would always
put Egypt's interests first, at the expense of the solidarity which was
essential if the Arabs were ever to be unified. His policy sometimes created
more disunity than the reverse, according to Hussein. Nor was it easy to
forget the way in which Nasser deceived Hussein during the days of

Jordan's trial early in June 1967. Only a man with unusual magnanimity of character could have brought himself to speak to Nasser again.

Like Queen Victoria, Hussein has hardly ever known a time when he has been free of responsibility, and from the demands of protocol and personal security. This has undoubtedly influenced him in trying to bring up his children as normally as possible, an example which has been followed by his brothers and sister. Although Jordan has had to survive crisis after crisis, the country has nevertheless made the most remarkable progress, which is there to be seen at every hand. It is virtually unrecognisable to those who knew it only in King Abdullah's time. He is sometimes called the 'Founder' of the nation, and Hussein the 'Builder'. But a better description for him must surely be the 'Unifier', since it has been during his reign that the many different tribes and peoples of Jordan have come to look on themselves as a nation. Whereas thirty-five years ago a man might say that he was a Circassian, or a Palestinian, or a bedouin of a certain tribe, as like as not today he will say he is an Urdani (Jordanian). Although the influence of the tribe, and for that matter of the family, remains strong in Jordan, there is today a real feeling of nationhood that was certainly not evident when Hussein first came to the throne.

Hussein has his critics of course, and there is still a distinct opposition to the government, which is sometimes accused of being corrupt. Every Arab is a politician at heart, and in a small country like Jordan what goes on in the Palace is a favourite subject for speculation and discussion in the *sukh*. There are Ba'athists (of both persuasions); Communists; republicans; Palestinians who support the PLO, and those who don't; Islamic fundamentalists who wish to replace kings and presidents by the rule of priests; Syrians who still covet what was once part of Syria; traditionalists who would like to turn the clock back; and others who claim that the pace of reform has not been fast enough.

Muammar Gadaffi has described King Hussein as pro-Western. This is only partially true, however. Hussein is of course anti-Communist; what ruling monarch would not be? But this does not mean that he has always approved of Western policies. He did not agree with France over Algeria, nor has he approved of Western policies with regard to the Palestinians and the Occupied Territories. But it would be true to describe him as pro-Arab, his eyes always set on the prospect of Arab unity, however distant the goal and however difficult the road. Hussein is probably the only Arab leader who will carry conviction in capitals as diverse as Washington and Moscow, Baghdad and Damascus, owing largely to respect for his moderation and statesmanship. Even fervent supporters of the PLO, apart from the extremists, concede that he is essential for the resolution of the Palestinian problem.

Hussein has made mistakes of course, as he would be the first to admit. The retirement of General Glubb, for example, could certainly have been secured at far less cost to Hussein's own reputation and to Anglo-Jordanian relations. That he acted as he did was due to the impulsivenesss of youth, and for fear of a reaction in support of the Pasha from the Arab Legion's bedouin regiments. Glubb himself always recognised this, despite the hurt he felt. Hussein was genuinely surprised by the strength of the British reaction, although in the changed circumstances of the times, Glubb had become an anachronism, as he was himself beginning to realise.

It is easy to blame Hussein for throwing in Jordan's lot with Egypt early in June 1967, but in truth many of his closest advisers at that time say he had little other option. It was a matter of honour. But quite apart from this, Hussein was convinced that should Jordan stand aside and leave it to Egypt to bear the brunt of the Israeli onslaught, Jordan must inevitably be the next in the queue when it came to Israeli aggression. Sooner or later Israel would seize the opportunity to take the West Bank; and better by far when that moment came that Jordan should be fighting alongside its Egyptian ally rather than bearing the brunt of the Israeli onslaught entirely on its own. It was entirely consistent with Hussein's commitment to Arabism, and his belief in Arab solidarity, that he should have decided that if war came, Jordan should fight alongside Egypt. It should however be recorded that by no means all of Hussein's advisers approved of this decision. Sharif Nasser was one of those who disagreed; and another was Wasfi Tell, who begged the King to remain on the sidelines until the Egyptians had won the battle of the air – which of course they never did.

One of the most controversial of Hussein's decisions has been his breaking off of relations with Arafat and the PLO early in 1986. Even those who sympathised with the King for having been led up the garden path by Arafat and his colleagues profoundly doubted the wisdom of severing connections with the Palestinian leadership. They blamed the decision to do this more on Hussein's close advisers than on Hussein himself. They felt it could only emphasise still further the divisions which existed among the Arabs over the Palestinian problem. Many of those who felt this way were loyal subjects of Hussein who realised the strength of feeling that existed in the Occupied Territories for the PLO. It seemed to them that without the PLO any agreement reached with the Israelis would be valueless. They are probably right. However, in the curious way in which the Arabs seem to manage these matters, Hussein's relations with Arafat were once again restored at the Amman Arab Summit in November 1987 (and likewise restored thereafter were the PLO's relations with most of the other Arab states).

In Jordan, as elsewhere in the Arab world, the stability of the country rests largely on the loyalty of the army. Hussein in this respect is fortunate in having such a genuine affinity with his soldiers. At heart a soldier himself, he is never happier nor more relaxed than when with his troops, to whose welfare he devotes a good deal of his time. Jordan is still a country where the profession of arms counts for a great deal. The country is proud of its armed forces, which may be small in size but are strong in morale. There have been occasions during his reign when Hussein's very survival depended on the loyalty of his soldiers, most of all perhaps in 1970, when he was compelled to send the army into Amman to clear out the PLO commandos and reassert the authority of his government.

When it came to sending in the army, there will always be argument whether the King jumped or was pushed. It has been asserted by some writers that the generals faced him with what was virtually an ultimatum; but none of the generals consulted have endorsed this. They say the King had no other choice. He had either to bring the *fedayeen* to heel, or he risked being overthrown by them. Certainly Hussein agonised long enough before taking the plunge. One of his closest advisers has said that it was his fear of civilian casualties that made him hesitate for so long: 'He did not want Jordanian blood on his hands.' Hussein may even have wondered whether he could rely on the soldiers' loyalty. The army had more than doubled in size since the bedouin regiments had rallied to Hussein's side in Zerqa thirteen years previously. There was a considerable Palestinian element, officers as well as soldiers. Arafat had counted on many desertions but in the event it was less than 15 per cent, many of whom stayed quietly at home.

Hussein's relations with the PLO have seldom run smoothly. He deplored the adoption of terror as a means of publicising the Palestinian cause, and it is an open secret that he shares President Assad's feelings about Arafat himself. There can also be no doubt that for some time after the June 1967 war the PLO were an obstacle to the King's objective of recovering the West Bank from Israel. Moreover, after his expulsion of the PLO from Jordan in 1971, Hussein became the PLO's main target for vilification; the PLO even declared their intention to work for his overthrow. But nothing is permanent in the Middle Eastern scene. In 1985 came the Accord with the PLO, and since then relations have been easier, although suspicions remain on both sides.

The King, the Crown Prince and the Prime Minister have publicly emphasised the importance of the PLO in the search for peace. Any doubts on this score should therefore have been removed. Most recently, at the extraordinary Summit meeting held in Algiers in June 1988, Hussein supported the concept of an independent Palestinian state, if that is what the Palestinians want; whether such a state could ever be viable without some kind of link with Jordan is another matter. Hussein's attempts to obtain support for the inclusion of the PLO at any international conference held to resolve the Arab–Israeli problem have already been recorded above. Israel has long refused to have any dealings with the PLO, and America has followed suit, without the PLO's prior acceptance of Resolutions 242 and 338. It has been alleged that Kissinger, when drawing up the Egypt–Israel disengagement agreement in September 1975, guaranteed to consult Israel before making any change of policy with regard to the PLO. This was intended to allay Israeli fears that the US might support the rights of the Palestinians in order to obtain a peace settlement.

The uprising in the Occupied Territories has given Arafat a new lease of life, causing even Hafez Assad to invite him to Damascus. Although the uprising was as much a surprise to the PLO as to everyone else, the PLO have been quick to take advantage of it. Crown Prince Hassan made Jordan's position with regard to the Territories perfectly clear when he addressed the Council of Europe on 29 January 1987. 'Over almost twenty years of occupation,' he said, 'the West Bank has been converted from an Arab economic entity into a virtual Israeli dependency.' This was unacceptable to the Palestinian population, to Jordan and to the other Arab countries. The inevitable outcome must be rebellion, as has indeed occurred. Indeed, the current *intifada* in Gaza and the West Bank represents a far greater threat to Israel's future than the sum total of the *fedayeen* raids made into Israel during the past thirty years.

Visiting Canada recently, Prince Hassan was questioned about the result of a poll on the West Bank that indicated a large majority in the Occupied Territories in favour of the PLO and against a return to Hashemite rule. 'We are not in the popularity stakes,' said the Crown Prince. 'If it were only 3 per cent, I couldn't care less. The main thing is to maintain Arab identity in the Occupied Territories – to liberate those territories and to give the Palestinians the right of free choice.'[2] As a statement of King Hussein's policy, it could not have been put more clearly.

Some of Hussein's critics complain that he has no real policy. 'We call him the Day-to-Day King,' said Nassir Nashishibi, 'because he changes his mind so often.'[3] President Jimmy Carter also appears to have his doubts. After describing Hussein as 'enlightened, personally courageous, wise in his political decisions', he goes on to criticise him for 'so far not [being] daring enough when the crunch comes in not making the final move'. But then he adds, 'However, I can't say that his caution is not justified.'[4] The late Sir Charles Johnston, British Ambassador in Amman during the critical early years on the throne, thought Hussein's principal policy was to survive. 'He was like a man adrift in a small boat in stormy seas,' Johnston said, 'whose only concern was to remain afloat.'[5]

Crown Prince Hassan would deny this.[6] He makes it plain that Hussein has throughout been faithful to the principles taught him by his grand-father, King Abdullah, as set out in the Preface to this book. But Jordan's vulnerability to outside pressures, together with the lessons Hussein has learned in the course of his stormy reign, impose a caution that may not always satisfy his critics. Certainly no one can criticise Hussein for lack of personal courage; but this is not quite the same as political courage. A man may be entitled to risk his life in some great endeavour, but this would not justify him in risking his country or his dynasty.

In his search for peace Hussein has rested his case on Resolutions 242 and 338, which call for Israel's withdrawal from the Occupied Territories. There are however some authorities who believe that with the passage of time these resolutions have become out of date; they believe that only some kind of compromise on the part of both sides will result in the agreement which is so badly needed. Compromise does not come easily to Arabs, highly individualistic as they are. Nor will it come easily to the extremists on the other side; nor perhaps to other Israelis whose views are less entrenched. Shimon Peres, for example, has been reported as saying that there can be no present negotiations with the PLO; no return to Israel's pre-June 1967 boundaries; and no third state between Israel and Jordan. Secretary of State Shultz is reported as having endorsed these conditions.[7] There is not much evidence of compromise here.

Hussein has other problems with which to contend, besides the perennial problem of Israel. Land prices have risen phenomenally as Jordan's cities and towns have expanded and agriculture has boomed. Many people have prospered as a result and the evidence is there to be seen at every hand. There is however a gulf today between the rich and poor that was not so evident thirty years ago. In the opinion of one influential Jordanian, the country overstretched itself during the years of the oil boom when aid flowed in and imaginative efforts were made to improve Jordan's infrastruc-ture. Now it is proving necessary to cut back. There are not sufficient jobs at the moment and this greatly worries Hussein.

Crown Prince Hassan is working on a plan that envisages the creation of 200,000 more jobs. This is intended not only to revitalise the economy and cope with the natural increase in the population, but also to provide employment and maintain the living standards of those Jordanians who are being displaced elsewhere in the Arab world. At the same time Jordan embarked on an ambitious plan to improve the economy and raise living standards on the West Bank, as an encouragement to the Palestinian population to remain there. This was essential if Arab sovereignty is ever to be restored.

The long-term aim is to make Jordan an 'advanced technological and maintenance base serving the whole region', according to Prince Hassan.

He believes that in time Jordan can be transformed into the economic centre of the Arab Middle East, as once Lebanon was. He envisages a kind of Middle Eastern Benelux that would 'facilitate the free movement of people, goods and capital among the member states'. The concept is an exciting one but if it is ever to become anything more than a vision Jordan will require a great deal of help, both financial and otherwise. Such help will also be necessary to maintain Jordan's present internal stability, which makes it attractive for foreign investment. Few will quarrel with Prince Hassan's belief that bilateral negotiations are no substitute for regional co-operation and collaboration, but it remains to be seen if the Arabs' inherent tendency to quarrel among themselves will prevent this dream from being translated into reality.

Hussein has deputed the responsibility for the economic and scientific advancement of Jordan to Crown Prince Hassan, whose forte this happens to be. But, as *de facto* ruler of his country, the King has to take the big decisions himself. In the meantime he concentrates his attention on international relations and defence, travelling the world in order to do so. There is no other Arab leader who is as universally well known as King Hussein. Jordan is not of course a Western-style democracy; nor are any of the other Arab countries for that matter. This does lead to criticism in the West, as well as in certain circles in Jordan itself. The state's security apparatus is efficient, and dissent, although not actively discouraged, has to be voiced with discretion. Having survived many attempts on his life, and also an active rebellion against his authority in 1970–1, Hussein can be relied on to act firmly when he judges this to be necessary. He is, however, at heart a kindly man and his magnanimity is proverbial. It is not in his character to play the tyrant.

Jordan's remarkable economic leap forward has been largely the result of successive three- and five-year plans overseen by Crown Prince Hassan. Hassan's intellectual interests, particularly in the realm of economics and science, fit him well for this task. He has also been an articulate spokesman for his country at many international forums. Prince Hassan considers that the European Community, or the United Nations, should play a more prominent role in the Occupied Territories. He thinks some kind of mandated authority might be established to replace the Israeli occupation, until some more permanent solution can be agreed; the mandate would be exercised either by the European Community or by the UN. It is an interesting proposal but is unlikely to commend itself to Britain, with unhappy memories of its former Palestine mandate to look back on; nor for that matter to the French, with memories of Lebanon and Syria.

In Jordan, where the King is not only the ruler but also the symbol of national unity, the question of the succession is frequently discussed.

People know only too well the many attempts which have been made on Hussein's life. The general expectation would seem to be that Crown Prince Hassan would act as regent until Prince Ali, Hussein's son by the late Queen Alia, comes of age. There can be no doubt that Hassan would be a strong and enlightened ruler. Hussein has, however, two elder sons by Princess Muna, Princes Abdullah and Feisal, both of whom are serving in the Jordanian armed forces. They are both popular and efficient officers. The eldest, Abdullah, is in many ways remarkably like his father in character.

The three Hashemite brothers – Hussein, Muhammad and Hassan – present an interesting contrast in personality, character and style. All three are short in stature and slender in build, with aristocratic features and delicate hands and feet. Hussein is obviously the dominant personality, with a distinct aura about him. One cannot be in his presence without feeling that here is a most remarkable man. His massive head and deep deliberate voice make him seem to be a bigger man than he is. He holds himself erect, as a soldier should, and there can be no doubt about his charisma. There is at the same time a kind of humility which is unusual in those who have become long accustomed to the wielding of power. There is no stuffiness or pomposity about him. He seems always to be relaxed and friendly, although those who have experienced his displeasure say he is not a man to be lightly crossed. His courtesy is proverbial; so is his magnanimity, as many of those who have plotted against him have cause to testify. He has his grandfather's ability to evoke great loyalty and affection in those who serve him; and one young Jordanian, who found himself dining with the King, was astonished by Hussein's easy manner and interest in matters 'which could hardly concern a King'. His ability to put his interlocutors at their ease is one of his most marked characteristics.

Prince Muhammad is an entirely different personality. During his earlier years he was criticised for his impulsiveness and inattention to business. Since then, however, he has settled down to become a kind of elder statesman, a wholehearted admirer of his elder brother. During the years when he was responsible for tribal affairs, he acquired great influence among the bedouin tribes, and remains to this day their ear to the throne. He has in some ways an uncanny resemblance to his grandfather, in his fondness for chess, his interest in books and his love for Hashemite tradition. He has become an elder statesman of a kind peculiarly Arab, with a remarkably wide circle of acquaintances. He too has the Hashemite charm, invariably courteous and never condescending, his main concern to put his visitor at ease.

Crown Prince Hassan is different again. A man of great energy and many intellectual interests, he talks with almost machine-gun-like rapidity. His interests are wide and he is proud of his academic background. A man born to lead is the feeling one gets when meeting him, but a man who, at the same time, is impatient of bureaucratic resistance. There is nothing relaxed about Hassan who, like Cecil Rhodes before him, believes there is much to be done, and not all that much time in which to do it. He has a dynamism and an intellectual energy that make him a formidable personality. A great deal of Jordan's economic advancement has been due to his energetic direction. He has been responsible for the creation of Jordan's Royal Scientific Society; and Jordan's successive development plans owe a very great deal to his determination to push them through. In contrast to his two elder brothers, his manner is rather abrupt, conveying the impression of a man always in a hurry. Some of his critics complain that he undertakes too much. It is perhaps not surprising that his favourite pastime is polo, a game in which he has been successful in gaining for Jordan a place in the international polo circuit. His wife, Princess Sarvath, is equally dynamic and intelligent.

When Hussein came to the throne in 1953, Jordan was a poor and remote Arab country. It counted for little in the counsels of the nations, and was regarded by its Arab brethren as little more than a British satrapy. The Arab Legion was its main employer, and the Legion depended for its existence on a British subsidy. Amman was no more than a modest-sized town; and the country had been crippled by the influx of refugees from Palestine, for whom worthwhile employment hardly existed. There was a continual border war in progress against Israel on the West Bank; relations with Egypt, Syria and Saudi Arabia were at best cool; there was hardly any money in the Treasury; and there were those who did not believe that the monarchy would long survive the plots against it. Compare that situation with today, when Jordan's stability has led many firms, both Arab and international, to make Amman their headquarters in the Middle East; when Amman has become one of the most bustling and enterprising cities in the Arab world; and when, wherever one looks, there are signs of development and investment.

Jordanians, being Arabs, are always ready to criticise their government, but most of them would agree that the country's progress has been largely due to the King. One may hear criticisms of other members of the Royal Family, but seldom of Hussein himself. It is almost as if he is above the battle. It is said in Jordan that 'nothing can happen here without the Palace.' This places a great burden on the ruler who may be praised when things go right, but who will certainly be blamed when things go wrong. Jordanians are not a subservient people, nor are they slow to make their voices heard when they believe they have a genuine grievance. Although it is probably true to say that King Hussein has the support of the majority of his subjects, this does not mean that he can afford to take anything for granted. The

Middle East is a volatile region where conditions can change almost overnight.

In his commitment to the cause of Arab unity, Hussein has been successful in healing Jordan's long-standing feud with Syria; bringing together Syria and Iraq, although without as yet a real closing of the breach; establishing excellent relations with Saudi Arabia; and bringing back Egypt into the Arab world. Even the PLO has been accepted back, albeit under strict surveillance. In the world beyond, Hussein is widely respected. This is not on account of the size of his army, nor the depth of his Treasury, but because of his character and personality. He is indeed a man for all seasons, one of the shrewdest political leaders in the world today, and one who has never lost the common touch.

All this is a far cry from the Years of Survival, when few people would have cared to bet on the King's chances of retaining his throne. Those were times when Jordan seemed to be ringed round by enemies without, with more than a few enemies within. The King's own life seemed to be in constant danger. It has required a great deal of courage, a deep faith in God and in his Hashemite mission, and more than a little luck, to have won through it all. The shy and uncertain young Prince has grown up to be the father of his country and a world statesman – and Jordan has grown up with him.

Epilogue

'We have no designs, ambitions or goals other than the liberation of the Palestinian territories and enabling the Palestinian people to determine their own destiny on their national soil and regain their legitimate national rights.' King Hussein

It was the Uprising (*Intifada*) on the West Bank and in Gaza that led to the holding of an Extraordinary Arab Summit in Algiers from 7 to 9 June 1988. It was necessary to devise measures for the support of the Uprising by the other Arab countries. Despite Hussein's frequently repeated warnings that an uprising was inevitable sooner or later, when it came it took everyone by surprise. It became apparent immediately that the Israelis had no idea how to deal with it, other than by methods reminiscent of every other military occupation in history: by shooting, arbitrary arrest and internment, imposition of curfews, exile of prominent citizens and the virtual promulgation of martial law – all the actions in fact for which the Jews had blamed the British administration in Palestine during their struggle for statehood in the aftermath of the Second World War. The Israelis have even used British laws framed against them to legalise their suppression of the Uprising. What is more, as the British found with the Jews, these repressive measures merely serve to fan the flames and have led to widespread world condemnation, even in the United States.

In a long address delivered at the Algiers Summit, Hussein described the Uprising as a 'revolution' against Israeli rule. It was a most momentous event. He said it had 'entirely demolished the myth entertained by Israel that the Palestinian Arab people have resigned themselves to coexisting with it'; and he called for support from all the Arab countries to help sustain what had so clearly been a spontaneous revolt against 'colonial oppression'. He reminded his audience that Jordan had been closely associated with Palestine since his country's establishment as a state in 1921, a link that was inextricably strengthened by the union between Jordan and the West Bank in 1950. He was at pains to deny that this union was in any sense an 'annexation', emphasising that 'it was an elected parliament equally representing the East and West Banks which decided to unite the two Banks in April 1950.'

After defending Jordan's record concerning the Palestine problem, the King gave a detailed account of events since the June war in 1967. He was bitterly critical of the failure to convene an international conference at which the problem of Palestine and the Palestinians could be considered in every aspect, placing much of the blame for the failure on Israeli intransigence and on the reluctance of the United States to bring pressure to bear on Israel. He said the United States does not support the establishment of an independent Palestinian state, nor is it prepared to deal with the Palestine Liberation Organisation, although since the Arab Summit at Rabat in 1974 the Arab League had agreed that the PLO was the sole legitimate representative of the Palestinian people. 'Here I would like to place before my brethren the outcome of Jordan's experience with the United States over the past twenty-one years,' said the King. 'In sum, it is that the United States has no Middle East policy other than the support of Israel. The United States approach to the problem of the Arab–Israeli conflict is, unfortunately, based on a policy of crisis-management. The United States takes no political steps or initiatives unless there has been a recent eruption in the region taking on the aspect of war.'

Hussein made it clear that there could be no international conference without the participation of the PLO, either independently or as part of a joint Arab delegation. He gave unequivocal support for the establishment of an independent Palestinian state, were that a precondition for the convening of an international conference, and affirmed in the strongest possible terms that Jordan has 'no designs, ambitions or goals other than the liberation of the Palestinian territories and enabling the Palestinian people to determine their own destiny on their national soil and regain their legitimate national rights'. He could not have put it more clearly.

The King ended his speech by pointing out that ever since the Israeli military occupation in 1967, Jordan has been deeply involved in maintaining the Arab character of the Occupied Territories. Eighteen thousand public servants were being paid by Jordan, together with a further 6,000 in Gaza. Jordan was the West Bank's principal market. Pensions are paid, passports provided, and the fees of West Bank students at Jordanian universities and colleges are met by the Jordanian Treasury. Jordanian law still applies on the West Bank, the currency is still mainly Jordanian. All this has placed a severe financial burden on Jordan, which is still not receiving the full financial assistance agreed at the Baghdad Summit ten years ago. Hussein gave his audience a gentle reminder of the obligations they had entered into, warning them that Jordan might not be able to continue this financial support indefinitely.

The implicit warnings contained in Hussein's speech seem to have been missed, or ignored, by almost everyone. He objected strongly to the view

sometimes expressed in certain Arab circles, as well as elsewhere, that
Jordan had annexed the West Bank in 1950, since such an argument
provided an excuse for Israel to do the same, and was in any case untrue.
Nor could he see any reason why Jordan should be required to share the
blame for American failure to put pressure on Israel. He had no intention of
continuing the so-called 'Jordanian Option', whereby Israel refused to
negotiate over the West Bank with anyone other than Jordan. If PLO
refusal to agree Security Council Resolutions 242 and 338 should anger the
State Department, why should Jordan have to untie the knot? Year in, year
out, Jordan was a prime mover in trying to rectify the injury inflicted on
the wretched Palestinians. All it had received in reply to its efforts were
contumely, criticism and sometimes downright hostility from the very
people it was trying to help. Hussein himself, with his passionate belief in
Arab unity, had never spared himself. Yet he found himself being casti-
gated as a 'tyrant', intent only on liberating the West Bank in order to
restore it to his Kingdom. That might have been true in the earlier years but
certainly was not after the decision taken at Rabat fifteen years ago. There
were, too, a great many people in Jordan with memories of 1970–1, when
their King was compelled to fight for his life against the *fedayeen*. What is
more, there was no indication at Algiers that the other Arab states
recognised the enormous efforts Jordan had made on behalf of the West
Bank. Hardly a word of thanks was heard, but there were effusive welcomes
instead for the PLO, too much of whose 'freedom fighting' had been
conducted between themselves, with other Arabs, or against innocent
tourists gathered together in airport lounges.

Hussein could be forgiven if he felt bitter, not only with the Americans
but with his Arab colleagues as well. It was hardly surprising that he had
tired of being the fall-guy for America's lack of a policy, or for the PLO's
failure to honour its agreements. It was galling too, for a man of Hussein's
pro-Western orientation, to be denied by the US Congress the air-defence
weapons Jordan so badly needed, forcing him instead to turn to the Soviet
Union. But the announcement which the King made in a speech to his
people on 31 July 1988 could have been foreseen by very few. The have
claimed that they were neither warned nor consulted, but this may only be
an excuse in order to cover themselves lest they fail to deliver when it comes
to administering the West Bank in Jordan's place. On the other hand there
must presumably have been some prior consultation, however limited,
since it has been reported in *The Times* that Mrs Thatcher advised *against*
the course the King was proposing to adopt.

What Hussein told his people was that in order to help 'liberate the
occupied Palestinian land', he had dismantled Jordan's legal and
administrative links with the West Bank. He also explained why he had

decided to terminate the $1·3 billion Development Plan for the West Bank which had barely got under way. He had followed this by dissolving the House of Deputies, which contained thirty West Bank members. 'Since there is a general conviction that the struggle to liberate the occupied Palestinian land could be enhanced by dismantling the legal and administrative links between the two banks, we have to fulfil our duty and do what is required of us,' he said. 'To support the steadfastness of our brothers there today, we respond to the wish of the Palestine Liberation Organisation, the sole legitimate representative of the Palestinian people, and to the Arab orientation to affirm the Palestinian identity.' Hussein might have added, but of course did not, that this is what the Palestinians had been clamouring for throughout their revolt, and that now it was time for the PLO to stop the bickering and get down to business. They had spent years on the touchline abusing the referee; now the time had come for them to shoot their own goals. It remains to be seen whether they are capable of doing so, although at a subsequent press conference the King made it plain that he was perfectly willing to recognise a Palestinian government-in-exile.

There are many Jordanians who have for many years past been advocating the course of action taken by the King. They object to the kind of dual nationality so many Palestinians choose to adopt, Jordanians when it suits them, Palestinians at other times. They also remember the *fedayeen*. They resent the criticism to which the King has been subjected, despite all his attempts to find a solution to the Palestinian problem. They know perfectly well that some of the PLO's most vociferous supporters overseas, and *ipso facto* some of Hussein's most bitter critics, will never give up their comfortable living conditions to return to a liberated Palestine.

Others, however, are less enthusiastic. They are worried about the constitutional aspect of the King's declaration. Article I of the Jordanian constitution states: 'The Hashemite Kingdom of Jordan is an independent Arab state. It is indivisible and no part of it may be ceded. . . .' This Article is part of the amended constitution of 1 January 1952, which came into effect after the constitutional unity of the two Banks was promulgated. The West Bank therefore remains part of the Hashemite Kingdom. The only legal and constitutional way whereby the West Bank can be ceded is by legislation passed by the National Assembly – which in this case means the Senate and the House of Deputies – and the King. However, the King has dissolved the House of Deputies, so sessions of the Senate are also suspended. Severing the constitutional link, if this is intended, will therefore be much more difficult than the severing of legal and administrative links. Those who worry about this aspect of the King's decision feel that the steps now being taken may alienate the people of the West Bank, who will blame Jordan if the PLO fail to carry out their new obligations; and if the

PLO succeed in doing so, then Jordan's struggle to support the West Bank for the past forty years will be forgotten. They also consider it most unlikely that Israel will allow the PLO to take Jordan's place in administering the West Bank. This will drive an even deeper wedge between the West Bank and Jordan, never forgetting that more than half of Jordan's population is of Palestinian origin. If they raise their voices on behalf of their brethren on the far bank of the River Jordan, it is virtually certain that the other Arab countries will support them, and will criticise the King for having created such an unfortunate situation.

Hussein's critics may turn out to be right. Radical action in politics always requires courage, and a good deal of luck, if it is to succeed. Cutting a Gordian knot is never easy. Sooner or later, however, all those involved in the Palestinian problem had to be brought face to face with reality – the Arabs just as much as the Israelis and the Americans. It is a problem that will never go away but merely intensify with the years. There will never be peace in the Middle East without some kind of a Palestinian state; and to talk of one east of the River Jordan, as some Israelis do, does not resolve the problem. Such a state would in fact aggravate matters since the Arabs will continue to multiply and their yearning to return will grow ever stronger. It is just possible that Hussein's action will act as a catalyst in a situation in which emotions, on both sides, so often obscure the practicalities. One can only hope – *and pray*. Both Jews and Palestinians have suffered so many torments, endured so many humiliations, and have undergone so many privations that surely it is not beyond the wit of man to find them some remedy. In November 1988 the Palestine National Congress met in Algiers to consider the new responsibilities which have been thrust upon it; and in the same month Israel elected a new government and the United States a new president. The ground has been cleared for a fresh start. This book can therefore end on a note of hope.

APPENDIX

1

United Nations Security Council Resolution 242
22 November 1967

The Security Council,

Expressing its continuing concern with the grave situation in the Middle East,

Emphasising the inadmissibility of the acquisition of territory by war and the need to work for a just and lasting peace in which every State in the area can live in security,

Emphasising further that all Member States in their acceptance of the Charter of the United Nations have undertaken a commitment to act in accordance with Article 2 of the Charter,

1. Affirms that the fulfilment of Charter principles requires the establishment of a just and lasting peace in the Middle East which should include the application of both the following principles:

(i) Withdrawal of Israeli armed forces from territories occupied in the recent conflict:

(ii) Termination of all claims or states of belligerency and respect for and acknowledgement of the sovereignty, territorial integrity and political independence of every State in the area and their right to live in peace within secure and recognised boundaries free from threats or acts of force;

2. Affirms further the necessity

(a) For guaranteeing freedom of navigation through international waterways in the area;

(b) For achieving a just settlement of the refugee problem;

(c) For guaranteeing the territorial inviolability and political independence of every State in the area, through measures including the establishment of demilitarised zones;

3. Requests the Secretary-General to designate a Special Representative to proceed to the Middle East to establish and maintain contacts with the States concerned in order to promote agreement and assist efforts to achieve a peaceful and accepted settlement in accordance with the principles of this resolution;

4. Requests the Secretary-General to report to the Security Council on the progress of the efforts of the Special Representative as soon as possible.

2

United Nations Security Council Resolution 338
21–22 October 1973

The Security Council

1. Calls upon all parties to the present fighting to cease all firing and terminate all military activity immediately, no later than 12 hours after the moment of the adoption of this decision, in the positions they now occupy;

2. Calls upon the parties concerned to start immediately after the ceasefire the implementation of Security Council Resolution 242 (1967) in all of its parts;

3. Decides that, immediately and concurrently with the ceasefire, negotiations start between the parties concerned under appropriate auspices aimed at establishing a just and durable peace in the Middle East.

GLOSSARY OF ARABIC WORDS

Abu	Father. Traditionally fathers are known by the names of their eldest sons. Thus King Hussein may be known familiarly as Abu Abdullah.
Aib	Shame or shameful.
Al	Can mean either the definite article or 'the family of . . .'
Assifa	Codename for Fatah's first operation against Israel.
Bey	A Turkish title ranking below Pasha.
Bedu	Anglicised as bedouins.
Bedu (sing: *beduï*)	
Bin (or *Ibn*)	Son of . . .
Bint	Daughter of . . .
Burqa	Garment worn by Muslim women to conceal the outline of the body.
Emir	Prince.
Fedayeen	Name usually given to Palestinian commandos or guerrillas.
Fellah	Peasant (plur. *Fellahin*).
Hadhari	Those who live in stone houses. Term used in Jordan to differentiate between the settled and the nomadic inhabitants.
Hajj	The pilgrimage to Mecca and Medina.
Haram as Sharif	The Noble Enclosure (in Jerusalem).
Ikhwan	The Brotherhood: name adopted by the Wahhabis of Nejd who terrorised Central Arabia between 1919 and 1930.
Intifada	Uprising.
Irada	A royal edict.
Jebel	Hill or mountain.
Mukhabarat	Secret Security Service.
Mukhtar	Headman.
Qaimaqamiyyeh	District.
Qyada	Army headquarters.
Shamagh	Red and white headcloth worn in the Jordanian armed forces.
Sharaf	Personal honour.
Sharif	Noble (i.e. a descendant of the Prophet Muhammad).

Shurta	Foot police (the mounted branch are called *Darak*).
Sidara	Blue and red sidehat worn in Jordanian armed forces (usually by the police).
Sukh	Market.
Wadi	Watercourse (usually dry).

ABBREVIATIONS

APC	Armoured personnel carrier
CCPR	Central Committee of Palestinian Resistance
CGS	Chief of the General Staff
C-in-C	Commander-in-Chief
GHQ	General Headquarters
GOC	General Officer Commanding
IAF	Israeli Air Force
IDF	Israeli Defence Force
OC	Officer Commanding
PDF	Popular Democratic Front (Hawatmeh)
PFLP	Popular Front for the Liberation of Palestine (Habash)
PFLP–GC	Popular Front for the Liberation of Palestine – General Command (Ahmed Jabril)
PLA	Palestine Liberation Army
PLF	Palestine Liberation Front (Ahmed Jabril)
PLO	Palestine Liberation Organisation
PNC	Palestine National Congress
PRM	Palestine Resistance Movement
RJAF	Royal Jordanian Air Force
SAM	Surface-to-Air Missile
TJFF	Trans-Jordan Frontier Force
UAC	Unified Arab Command
UAR	United Arab Republic
UNEF	United Nations Emergency Force

NOTES

Author's Foreword

1. Francis King, *Sunday Telegraph*, 29 October 1985

Introduction: The House of Hashim

1. This play on the word Sharif (noble) was made by Lord Lloyd, who was British High Commissioner in Cairo at the time, at a banquet in Jerusalem given in honour of Emir Abdullah. Lloyd had himself served as one of the British army advisers with Emir Feisal during the Great Arab Revolt.
2. J.B. Glubb, 'The Bedouin of Northern Iraq', *Journal of the Royal Central Asian Society*, XXII (1), 1935.
3. Wilfred Thesiger, *Arabian Sands* (Longman, London, 1959), p. 186.
4. The Papers of Emir Zeid (as translated by Suleiman Mousa), in possession of HRH Prince Ra'ad bin Zeid.
5. Letter quoted in Suleiman Mousa, 'A Matter of Principle: King Hussein of the Hijaz and the Arabs of Palestine', *International Journal of Middle East Studies*, 9, 1978, pp. 183–94.
6. Brigadier J.B. Glubb, *The Story of the Arab Legion* (Hodder & Stoughton, London, 1952), and Lieutenant-General Sir J.B. Glubb, *A Soldier with the Arabs* (Hodder & Stoughton, London, 1957).
7. Sir Alec Kirkbride, *A Crackle of Thorns* (John Murray, London, 1956), p. 29.
8. Ibrahim Hashim to the author in 1954.
9. King Hussein, *Uneasy Lies the Head* (Heinemann, London, 1962), pp. 13–14.

Chapter One: The Succession

1. *King Lear*, Act IV, sc. vi.
2. Ahmed Effendi al-Khalidi was Emir Naif's tutor.
3. Suleiman Mousa, 'King Abdullah', *Jordan*, vol. 7 (3), Winter 1982/3.
4. *Haram es Sharif* (the Noble Enclosure) contains both the Mosque of Omar and the Mosque of al-Aqsa. It also contains the tomb of King Hussein bin Ali of the Hejaz and the Wailing Wall, sacred to the Jews as the last remnant of the Temple.

5. Nassir Nashashibi to author, 11 February 1986.
6. This account of King Abdullah's assassination has been taken from King Hussein's autobiography, *Uneasy Lies the Head*.
7. Glubb Pasha always insisted that he was not involved in the Talal–Naif controversy. He tried to steer clear of political issues and he was in any case out of the country on leave at the time. His preference for Talal was, however, perfectly plain.

Chapter Two: Crown Prince

1. Comment made to author by William Orchard, who sat next door to Hussein in form at Harrow, June 1988.
2. Glubb Pasha to author, 1981.
3. The late Sir John Colville to author, 24 June 1986.
4. Husssein, *Uneasy Lies the Head*, p. 23.
5. Letter to author, 22 January 1985.
6. Sharif Nasser bin Jameel, the King's uncle, to author, 1952.
7. Glubb Pasha declared to the author in 1982 that he had nothing whatsoever to do with King Talal's abdication. He greatly admired the King and was in any case out of the country at the time, reading about the abdication in the newspapers.

Chapter Three: The Profession of Arms

1. Francis Markham, *Five Decades of Epistles of War* (1565–1627).
2. Hussein, *Uneasy Lies the Head*, p. 36.
3. Interview, 10 December 1985.
4. Major-General Michael Hobbs to author, 21 July 1987.
5. Ba'ath means 'resurrection' or 'renaissance'. It was the name given to a nationalist party founded in Syria in 1943 by Michael Aflaq, an Arab Christian, and several others. It looked forward to a united Arab *socialist* nation. After taking root in Syria, it spread to Iraq, but unfortunately the Iraqi Ba'athists soon fell out with their Syrian comrades. The Ba'athists are, however, still strongly entrenched in both Syria and Iraq, and have their followers elsewhere in the Arab world too, although in Syria President Hafez Assad has brought them firmly under his control.
6. The Pact has since been renamed the Central Treaty Organisation (CENTO).
7. Interview, 4 April 1987.
8. Unpublished diaries of Colonel J.B. Slade-Baker of the *Sunday Times*

(London), in the Middle East Centre, St Antony's College, Oxford, vol. VII, March 1956.

9. Review by J.B. Glubb of Riad el-Rayyes and Dunia Nahas, *Politics in Uniform: A Study of the Military in the Arab World and Israel*, in *Survival*, XV, May–June 1973).

10. Sharif Nasser to author, October 1952.

11. Wing Commander J. Dalgliesh to author, 14 April 1987.

12. PRO FO 371/115686.

13. PRO FO 371/115683.

14. General Cooke to author, May 1955.

15. Humphrey Trevelyan, *The Middle East in Revolution* (Macmillan, London, 1970), p. 65.

Chapter Four: Dropping the Pilot

1. King Hussein to author, 10 January 1982.

2. Wing Commander J. Dalgliesh to author, 14 April 1987.

3. Baron Wrangel to author, 18 May 1987.

4. N. Aruri, *Jordan: A Study in Political Development 1921–1965* (Martin Nijhoff, The Hague, 1972).

5. Earl of Stockton to author, 5 June 1985.

6. Hussein, *Uneasy Lies the Head*, p. 118.

7. Major-General W.M. Hutton to author, 30 August 1987.

8. Sir Charles Johnston to author, 25 March 1985.

9. To the author (in London), January 1957.

Chapter Five: A Coup that Failed

1. Rectoral address to St Andrew's University by Sir James Barrie on 3 May 1922.

2. Baron Wrangel to author, 18 May 1987.

3. Ibid.

4. Charles Johnston, *The Brink of Jordan* (Hamish Hamilton, London, 1972), p. 155.

Chapter Six: A Coup that Succeeded

1. General Glubb to author, 1981.
2. Johnston, *The Brink of Jordan*, p. 91.
3. Nassir Nashashibi to author, 11 February 1986.
4. Lord Stockton to author, 5 June 1985.
5. Ibid.
6. Sir Charles Johnston to author, 25 March 1986.
7. Johnston, *The Brink of Jordan*, p. 106.
8. Ibid., p. 117.

Chapter Seven: Ringed Round by Enemies

1. Sir Charles Johnston to author, 25 March 1986.
2. Ibid.
3. Hussein, *Uneasy Lies the Head*, p. 185.
4. Letter from Wing Commander J. Dalgliesh, 27 October 1987.
5. Ibid.
6. Sir Charles Johnston to author, 25 March 1986.
7. Johnston, *The Brink of Jordan*, p. 140.
8. Hussein, *Uneasy Lies the Head*, p. 191.
9. Ibid., pp. 200–7.

Chapter Eight: Palestine, the Palestinians and the PLO

1. David K. Shipler, *Arab and Jew* (Bloomsbury, London, 1987), p. 65, quoting Ibrahim Kareen.
2. Comment made to author by Sultan Fadhl bin Ali, Sultan of Lahej and Minister of Defence of the short-lived Federation of South Arabia.
3. Told the author by one of King Hussein's former ministers.
4. Samir A. Mutawi, *Jordan in the 1967 War* (Cambridge University Press, Cambridge, 1987), p. 57.

Chapter Nine: The Unnecessary War

1. De Gaulle to Abba Eban in May 1967.
2. See Miles Copeland's *The Game of Nations: The Amorality of Power Politics* (Weidenfeld & Nicolson, London, 1969).
3. Alan Hart, *Arafat* (Sidgwick & Jackson, London, 1984), pp. 224–5.

4. Mahmoud Fawzi, *Suez 1956: An Egyptian Perspective* (Shorouk International, London, 1987).
5. Hussein of Jordan, Vance and Laqueur, *My 'War' with Israel* (Peter Owen, London, 1969).
6. Brian Urquart, *A Life in Peace and War* (Weidenfeld & Nicolson, London, 1987).
7. David Hirst, *The Gun and the Olive Branch* (Faber, London, 1977), p. 216.

Chapter Ten: June 1967

1. King Hussein's broadcast to the nation, 8 June 1961.
2. Anwar Sadat, *In Search of Identity* (Collins, London, 1978), p. 172.
3. General Amer Khammash to author, 1986.
4. Sir Philip Adams to author, 19 May 1986.
5. Sadat, *In Search of Identity*, p. 175. Sadat's account is however contradicted by Mohammed Heikal, editor of *Al-Ahram* and Nasser's confidant. On Channel 4 on 16 November 1986 Heikal said that when Nasser arrived at Egyptian GHQ around 10 a.m. on 5 June, Hakim Amer was afraid to tell Nasser the true story. He says the truth only came out later in the day, and that Hakim Amer tried to shoot himself in a lavatory in GHQ.
6. Chaim Herzog, *The Arab–Israel Wars* (Arms & Armour Press, London, 1982), p. 171.
7. Hussein, Vance and Laqueur, *My 'War' with Israel*, p. 111.
8. General Riad may not have been quite so convinced of the wisdom in sending 60th Armoured Brigade to Hebron as his Jordanian advisers thought was the case. Whereas all his other Operation Orders were authenticated 'General Abdul Munim Riad, Commander of the Advanced Post in Amman', in the case of Operation Order No. 7 (the one ordering the moves of 60th and 40th Armoured Brigades) the authentication was 'General Muhammad Fawzi, C-in-C of the Joint Arab Command, under delegation by General Abdul Munim Riad'.
9. Stephen Green, *Taking Sides* (Faber, London, 1984), pp. 204–11.
10. Sadat, *In Search of Identity*, pp. 179–80.
11. Ibid., p. 172.
12. Told the author by the doctor concerned.

Chapter Eleven: The Trojan Horse

1. Brigadier S.A. El-Edroos, *The Hashemite Arab Army 1908–1979* (Amman, 1980), p. 442.
2. Mary C. Wilson, *King Abdullah of Jordan: A Political Biography* (St Antony's College, Oxford, 1985), p. 356.
3. Hart, *Arafat*, p. 240.
4. Ibid., p. 235.
5. Nassir Nashashibi to author, 11 February 1986.
6. General Amer Khammash to author, 1986.
7. Letter from Prime Minister Begin to President Jimmy Carter on 17 September 1978, William B. Quandt, *Camp David* (Brookings Institution, Washington DC, 1986), p. 386.
8. Comment to author by an Indian diplomat in New Delhi in 1967.
9. Hirst, *The Gun and the Olive Branch*, p. 221.
10. Mohammed Heikal, *The Road to Ramadan* (Collins, London, 1975), p. 54.
11. Hart, *Arafat*, p. 260.

Chapter Twelve: The *Fedayeen* Insurrection

1. King Hussein to author, 27 August 1986.
2. Comment made in Amman in August 1986.
3. Hart, *Arafat*, p. 304.
4. Brigadier S.A. El-Edroos, *The Hashemite Arab Army 1908–1979* (Amman, 1980), p. 442.
5. Hirst, *The Gun and the Olive Branch*, p. 304.
6. Interview in January 1982.
7. Hirst, *The Gun and the Olive Branch*, p. 304.
8. Hart, *Arafat*, p. 275.
9. Interview January 1982.
10. Interview 1985.
11. Abu Da'oud was later captured, tried and sentenced to death. Although the death sentence was confirmed, the King commuted it to life imprisonment on condition that the PLO should cease all activities against his government. The PLO described this as blackmail, a crime they knew all about, having practised it often enough themselves.
12. John Newhouse, 'King Hussein', *New Yorker*, September 1983, p. 83.
13. Field Marshal Sharif Zeid bin Shakir to author, 31 August 1986.

Chapter Thirteen: Black September 1970

1. Malcolm H. Kerr, *The Arab Cold War* (Oxford University Press, Oxford, 1971), p. 140.
2. HRH Prince Muhammad to author, 1987.
3. El-Edroos, *The Hashemite Arab Army*, p. 459.
4. Interview, April 1986.
5. Interview, January 1982.
6. John Bulloch, *The Making of a War* (Longman, London, 1974), p. 66.
7. Hart, *Arafat*, p. 322.

Chapter Fourteen: Expelling the PLO

1. A bedouin officer to author, January 1982.
2. Kerr, *The Arab Cold War*, p. 153.
3. Hart, *Arafat*, p. 332.
4. Ibid., p. 330.
5. Interview, 1986.

Chapter Fifteen: An Uneven Road

1. Henry Kissinger, *Years of Upheaval* (Weidenfeld & Nicolson and Michael Joseph, London, 1982), p. 1036.
2. Hart, *Arafat*, p. 336.
3. Ibid., p. 322.
4. Peter Snow, *Hussein* (Barrie & Jenkins, London, 1972), p. 252.
5. Lecture given by Walid Jumblatt at St Antony's College, Oxford, on 12 May 1988.
6. M. Hudson, *Arab Politics: The Search for Legitimacy* (Yale University Press, 1977), p. 19.
7. *25 Years of History: The Complete Collection of H.M. King Hussein ben Talal's Speeches 1952–1977*, vol. 2 (Samir Mutawi & Associates Publishing, London, 1979), p. 314 (in Arabic).
8. Sir Philip Adams, British Ambassador in Amman 1966–70, to author, 19 May 1986. The author is much indebted to Samir A. Mutawi's detailed description of the way Jordan is governed, to be found in his *Jordan in the 1967 War*.

Chapter Sixteen: The October War – 1973

1. Sun Tzu, *The Art of War* (Oxford University Press, Oxford, 1963), p. 66.
2. King Hussein to author, 27 August 1986.
3. James Callaghan, *Time and Chance* (Collins, London, 1987), p. 291.
4. President Nixon in letter to author, 21 January 1987.
5. Henry Kissinger, *The White House Years* (Weidenfeld & Nicolson and Michael Joseph, London, 1979).
6. Badr was the victory gained by the Prophet Muhammad and the Muslims over the Meccans in AD 624.
7. El-Edroos, *The Hashemite Arab Army*, p. 488.
8. Crown Prince Hassan to author, 2 May 1988.
9. Henry Kissinger to author, 14 October 1986.
10. Bulloch, *The Making of a War*, p. xv.
11. Urquart, *A Life in Peace and War*, pp. 270–1.

Chapter Seventeen: The Search for Peace

1. King Hussein's address to the European Parliament on 15 December 1983.
2. Jimmy Carter, *The Blood of Abraham* (Sidgwick & Jackson, London, 1985), p. 135.
3. Comment to author, August 1986.
4. Quandt, *Camp David*, p. 320.
5. Ibid., p. 83n.
6. Ibid., p. 316.
7. Carter, *The Blood of Abraham*, p. 169.
8. Ibid., p. 140.
9. Comment to author in Amman, August 1986.
10. Audience with Queen Noor, 2 September 1987.

Chapter Eighteen: Journey Up a Blind Alley

1. Letter from President Jimmy Carter to author, 2 October 1987.
2. Marwan Kasim, Chief of the Royal Hashemite Court, to author, 27 August 1986.
3. *The Times* (London), 11 January 1984.
4. Jordanian comment to author, April 1987.
5. Mrs Thatcher to author, 30 July 1987.

6. Ibid.
7. Urquart, *A Life in Peace and War*, p. 337.
8. Ibid., p. 271.
9. Letter from President Nixon to author, 21 January 1987.
10. King Hussein to author, 27 August 1986.
11. Crown Prince Hassan's address to the Council of Europe, 29 January 1987.

Chapter Nineteen: The American Dimension

1. Mrwede Tell to author, April 1987.
2. *RUSI Journal*, March 1985.
3. *The Times* (London), 12 February 1988.
4. *Middle East International*, no. 307, 29 August 1988.
5. Letter from President Jimmy Carter to author, 2 October 1987.
6. *Middle East International*, no. 313, 21 November 1987.
7. King Hussein to author, 13 July 1987.
8. Shipler, *Arab and Jew*, p. 415.

Chapter Twenty: Storm in the East

1. Quoted in Robin Wright, *Sacred Rage* (André Deutsch, London, 1986), p. 27.
2. Hassan bin Talal, Crown Prince of Jordan, *Search for Peace* (Macmillan, London, 1984), pp. 106–7.
3. Wright, *Sacred Rage*, p. 63.
4. Ambassador Dean Brown to author in Washington DC on 23 October 1986.
5. *Sunday Telegraph* (London), 16 August 1987.
6. *Sunday Times* (London), 15 December 1985.

Chapter Twenty-One: Statesman–King

1. The late Earl of Stockton to author, 5 June 1985.
2. *Maclean's* magazine (Canada), 22 June 1987.
3. Nassir Nashashibidi to author 11 February 1985.

4. Letter from President Jimmy Carter to author, 2 October 1987.
5. The late Sir Charles Johnston to author, 25 March 1985.
6. Crown Prince Hassan to author, 2 May 1988.
7. *The Times* (London), 5 April 1988.

ACKNOWLEDGEMENTS

I have consulted a great many people in the course of writing this book and I am most grateful for the help and consideration afforded me. Some of them have requested anonymity and I have of course respected their wishes; nonetheless, I am most grateful to them, as I am to those whose names are listed below. If by some mischance I have omitted anyone whose name should be included, I trust my apology for the omission will be accepted.

First and foremost I have to thank His Majesty King Hussein for the trust and confidence he has shown in me. Without the King's agreement in the first place, this book could never have been written. I am deeply grateful to His Majesty.

I have also to thank Her Majesty Queen Noor for the interest she has shown in the book, and for her kindness in receiving me. King Hussein's two brothers, His Royal Highness Prince Muhammad and His Royal Highness Crown Prince Hassan, have also been extremely kind. Prime Minister Zei al-Rifai found time in his busy day to talk with me, as did Field Marshal Sharif Zeid bin Shakir.

Other Jordanians who have been both helpful and encouraging are Marwan S. Kasim, Chief of the Royal Hashemite Court, and Adnan abu Odeh, Court Minister and Head of the Royal Diwan. Fawaz abu Tayeh, Chief of Royal Protocol, has been a tower of strength; I do not know how I would have managed without him. I am deeply grateful for his support.

I owe a special debt of thanks to two old friends and comrades of Arab Legion days – Generals Shafiq Jumean and Ma'an abu Nowar. Their interest and support has meant a great deal to me.

I have also to thank: former President Richard M. Nixon; former President Jimmy Carter; Vice-President George Bush; the Rt Hon. Margaret Thatcher MP; the late Earl of Stockton; Lord Home of the Hirsel; the Rt Hon. Denis Healey MP; the Rt Hon. Julian Amery MP; the late Sir Charles Johnston; Glen Balfour-Paul; Sir Anthony Parsons; Sir John Moberly; Sir Philip Adams; A.J. Coles; Dr Henry Kissinger; General Sir Tom Pearson; Andrew Faulds MP; Dr Albert Hourani; Air Vice-Marshal Erik Bennett; Wing Commander Jock Dalgliesh; Dr Abba Eban; Dr Rafe Eban; Michael Adams; Sir Donald Logan; Archie Roosevelt; Jack O'Connell; Miles Copeland; Ambassador Dean Brown; John Newhouse; Sir James Craig; Mrs Helen Thompson; the late John Fistere; Professor Musa Mazzawi; Baron Alexis Wrangel; Raouf Sa'd Abujaber; Ayman Majali; Shehab A. Madi; General Ammer Khammash; Dr Adnan Halasa; Joseph Khoury; Mrwede Tell; the late Jerome Camanida; Colonel David Sutherland; Faris Glubb; Lieutenant-Colonel George Coles; Dr Wilfred Knapp; Mrs N. Alford; Sir John Colville; Michael Wall; Colonel and Mrs J.B. Chaplin; Nabih al-Nimr; Professor Gregory and Mrs Macnamara of Reading University; Nasser Nashashibi; Philip Robins; Theodore Larsson; F.F. Steele; Captain Sidney Overall, USN (retd); Major-General David Horsfield; Abdullah Saraj; Nassir Judah; Dr Fuad Ayyoub; Colonel D.C. Whitton; Marjorie Panning; Patricia Story; Elizabeth Corke; Celia Walls; Linda Jackman; Margaret Matthews; Caroline Grantham; Robert Wilkins; Sir Evelyn Shuckburgh.

The Middle East Centre, St Antony's College, Oxford, has been as always both welcoming and helpful. I owe my thanks to its Director, Dr Derrick Hopwood, and to Gilian Grant (Archivist) and Diane Rigg (Librarian).

I am grateful for the help I have received from the staff of the Public Record Office.

Hermione Byrt has drawn the maps. I am most grateful to her.

For permission to reproduce the illustrations I have to thank my old friend Robert Young, who was the Arab Legion's official photographer; and the talented Zohrab Markarian, official photographer to the Royal Hashemite Court.

Suleiman Mousa, a distinguished Jordanian historian, has not only helped me with most useful advice but has also drawn the Hashemite family tree. I owe him my thanks; as I do Dr Abbas Kelidar, who has been very helpful.

Charles Irwin, a friend for forty years, has read the manuscript, improving it by his trenchant criticism and correcting some of my more grievous errors. He will know how grateful I am.

Bruce Hunter of David Higham Associates, my literary agents, has been a great support, particularly at times when I felt I was making little headway. I owe him my thanks; as I do my publishers, Adam Sisman of Macmillan and Bruce Lee of William Morrow, who have left me to get on with the job without harrying me. I have also to thank Peter Shepherd of Harold Ober Associates in New York for his encouragement.

Finally, but in no way least, I have to thank my wife who has borne so patiently my frequent absences in the course of my research. Her support has never wavered. I only hope she will find the book to be worthy of its subject.

James Lunt

SELECT BIBLIOGRAPHY

Abdallah (King Abdallah of Jordan), *My Memoirs Completed (Al-Takmilah)* (Longman, London, 1978).

Antonius, George, *The Arab Awakening* (Hamish Hamilton, London, 1939).

Brown, L. Carl, *International Politics and the Middle East* (Tauris, London, 1984).

Brzezinski, Zbigniew, *Power and Principle* (Farrar, Strauss, Giroux, New York, 1983).

Bulloch, John, *The Making of a War* (Longman, London, 1974).

Bush, Captain Eric, *Salute the Soldier* (George Allen & Unwin, London, 1966).

Callaghan, James, *Time and Chance* (Collins, London, 1987).

Carr, Winifred, *Hussein's Kingdom* (Leslie Frewin, London, 1966).

Carter, Jimmy, *Keeping Faith: Memoirs of a President* (Bantam Books, New York, 1982).

Carter, Jimmy, *The Blood of Abraham* (Sidgwick & Jackson, London, 1985).

Collins, Larry, and Dominique Lapierre, *O Jerusalem* (Weidenfeld & Nicolson, London, 1972).

Dayan, Moshe, *Breakthrough* (Weidenfeld & Nicolson, London, 1981).

Eban, Abba, *An Autobiography* (Random House, New York, 1977).

El-Edroos, S.A., *The Hashemite Arab Army 1908–1979* (Amman, 1980).

Elon, Amos and Hassan, *Between Enemies* (André Deutsch, London, 1974).

Fawzi, Mahmoud, *Suez 1956: An Egyptian Perspective* (Shorouk International, 1987).

Gabriel, Richard A., *Operation Peace for Galilee* (Hill & Wang, New York, 1984).

Glubb, Brigadier J.B., *The Story of the Arab Legion* (Hodder & Stoughton, London, 1948).

Glubb, Lieutenant-General Sir John, *A Soldier with the Arabs* (Hodder & Stoughton, London, 1957).

Glubb, Lieutenant-General Sir John, *Peace in the Holy Land: An Historical Analysis of the Palestine Problem* (Hodder & Stoughton, London, 1971).

Glubb, Sir John, *The Changing Scenes of Life* (Quartet, London, 1983).

Green, Stephen, *Taking Sides* (Faber, London, 1984).

Hamid, Dina Abdel, *Duet for Freedom* (Quartet, London, 1988).

Hart, Alan, *Arafat* (Sidgwick & Jackson, London, 1984).

Hassan bin Talal, Crown Prince of Jordan, *Search for Peace* (Macmillan, London, 1984).

Heikal, Mohammed, *The Road to Ramadan* (Collins, London, 1975).

Heikal, Mohammed, *Autumn of Fury* (André Deutsch, London, 1983).

Herzog, Chaim, *The Arab–Israeli Wars* (Arms & Armour Press, London, 1982).

Hirst, David, *The Gun and the Olive Branch* (Faber, London, 1977).

Hirst, David, and Irene Beeson, *Sadat* (Faber, London, 1981).

Hussein, King, *Uneasy Lies the Head* (Heinemann, London, 1962).

Hussein of Jordan, Vick Vance and Pierre Laqueur, *My 'War' with Israel* (Peter Owen, London, 1969).

Jaber, Kamal abu, *The Jordanians and the People of Jordan* (Amman, 1980).

Jarvis, C.S. *Desert and Delta* (John Murray, London, 1947).

Johnston, Charles, *The Brink of Jordan* (Hamish Hamilton, London, 1972).

Kazziha, Walid, *Revolutionary Transformation in the Arab World* (Charles Knight, London, 1975).

Kerr, Malcolm H., *The Arab Cold War* (Oxford University Press, Oxford, 1971).

Kirkbride, Sir Alec, *A Crackle of Thorns* (John Murray, London, 1956).

Kissinger, Henry, *The White House Years* (Weidenfeld & Nicolson and Michael Joseph, London, 1979).

Kissinger, Henry, *Years of Upheaval* (Weidenfeld & Nicolson and Michael Joseph, London, 1982).

Lacey, Robert, *The Kingdom* (Hutchinson, London, 1981).

Laffin, John, *The Arab Mind* (Cassell, London, 1975).

Laqueur, Walter, *The Road to War* (Weidenfeld & Nicolson, London, 1968).

Lewis, William Roger, *The British Empire in the Middle East 1945–51* (Oxford University Press, Oxford, 1984).

Lunt, James, *Glubb Pasha* (Collins, London, 1984).

Meinertzhagen, Richard, *Middle East Diary* (Cresset Press, London, 1959).

Meir, Golda, *My Life* (Putnam, New York, 1975).

Morris, James, *The Hashemite Kings* (Pantheon, New York, 1959).

Mutawi, Samir Abdallah, *Jordan in the 1967 War* (Cambridge University Press, Cambridge, 1987).

Nixon, Richard, *The Memoirs of Richard Nixon* (Grosset & Dunlap, New York, 1978).

Parsons, Anthony, *They Say the Lion* (Jonathan Cape, London, 1986).

Quandt, William B., *Camp David* (Brookings Institution, Washington DC, 1986).

Rabin, Yitzhak, *The Rabin Memoirs* (Little, Brown, Boston, 1979).

Radji, Parviz C., *In the Service of the Peacock Throne* (Hamish Hamilton, London, 1983).

Sadat, Anwar, *In Search of Identity* (Collins, London, 1978).

Shipler, David K., *Arab and Jew* (Bloomsbury, London, 1987).

Snow, Peter, *Hussein* (Barrie & Jenkins, London, 1972).

Sparrow, Gerald, *Hussein of Jordan* (Harrap, London, 1960).

Thesiger, Wilfred, *Arabian Sands* (Longman, London, 1959).

Trevelyan, Humphrey, *The Middle East in Revolution* (Macmillan, London, 1970).

Tzu, Sun, *The Art of War* (Oxford University Press, Oxford, 1963).

Urquart, Brian, *A Life in Peace and War* (Weidenfeld & Nicolson, London, 1987).

Vatikiotis, P.J., *Politics and the Military in Jordan* (Cass, London, 1967).

Wilson, Mary C., *King Abdullah of Jordan: A Political Biography* (St Antony's College, Oxford, 1985).

Wright, Robin, *Sacred Rage* (André Deutsch, London, 1986).

INDEX